·ba

Most

·VE

Barbarians in Our Midst

A History of Chicago Crime and Politics

Barbarians in Our Midst

A History of Chicago Crime and Politics

By VIRGIL W. PETERSON

FOREWORD BY ESTES KEFAUVER

An Atlantic Monthly Press Book

Little, Brown and Company · Boston

ATLANTIC–LITTLE, BROWN BOOKS
ARE PUBLISHED BY
LITTLE, BROWN AND COMPANY
IN ASSOCIATION WITH
THE ATLANTIC MONTHLY PRESS

Published simultaneously
in Canada by McClelland and Stewart Limited

PRINTED IN THE UNITED STATES OF AMERICA

To
TOMMIE
and my parents

Preface

FROM the 1951 fall election returns, it was evident that everywhere in America the people were revolting against criminal-political alliances. The usually complaisant Philadelphia voters put an end to a Republican rule that had existed since 1884. Little Rock, Arkansas, for the first time in sixty years, elected a Republican mayor. In Boston, the perennial candidate, James Michael Curley, was defeated by the largest plurality in the city's history. In New York City, Rudolph Halley, who had distinguished himself as counsel for the special United States Senate Committee to Investigate Organized Crime, defeated machine candidates and was elected president of the city council.

Only a few months before the elections, the people throughout the country had followed with amazement the findings of the Senatorial investigation of organized crime. Millions had watched the proceedings over television. Other millions had followed daily accounts of the hearings in the press or over the radio. To the housewife, the businessman, the laborer, the white collar office worker, the farmer and the college student just reaching the voting age, it was apparent that political organizations in virtually every section of the land were either controlled or greatly influenced by the racketeers and gangsters. The temper of the American people was aroused as seldom before. The uprising at the polls in November 1951 was sufficient proof that the voters were angry and eager for the chance to "throw the rascals out."

Generally overlooked, however, was the fact that these conditions are not of recent development. The expensive and corrupt governments which have characterized most large cities have stemmed in substantial measure from the political power which has been wielded by racketeering and underworld elements. The purpose of this book, most of which was completed long before the Senate Crime Committee was formed, is to trace the history of Chicago, showing in particular the origin and development of organized crime and its influence on city government. A history of Chicago's underworld unfolds an important part of its political history. The same is true of many other large municipalities — only the dates, the names and the places are different.

VIRGIL W. PETERSON

Foreword

IN the midst of a world-wide struggle against a ruthless external enemy, law-abiding Americans must devote some of their time and energy to a struggle against a ruthless internal enemy. He is often difficult to deal with. For, as Mr. Virgil W. Peterson shows, he is ingenious, untiring, rich, and gifted with the evil genius of corrupting law officers on many levels. His weapons are bribery, beatings, murder, banishment of rivals from the local scene, attempted intimidation of all those who would stand in his way from the honest citizen at the ballot box to the juror in the juror's box.

Nor is this all. Long tolerated in some of our great communities, he has acquired by toleration what is a seemingly prescriptive right to crime. The stranger coming into such a community rubs his eyes in amazement at the sights he sees, and is the more bewildered when he notes that citizens accept organized crime as a commonplace of their daily life. Can this be the Orient, he asks himself, where by centuries-old usage, the giving and taking of bribes is the custom of the country? And if we have come into this state, he wonders, does this mean that we are prepared to accept gang rule for democratic rule, and let our democratic system go by default?

The great danger in all this was long ago stated by Governor Joseph W. Folk of Missouri, whom I am proud to claim as a kinsman. He said that the evil of political corruption is that it tends to convert representative government, responsive to the interests of all citizens, into an oligarchy responsive only to the interests of a few.

Mr. Peterson's book is an illuminating study of the manner in which a great American community has been sorely afflicted by gangsters; how, in many respects, it is ruled, not legally, but extra-legally by Stone Age criminals who are often themselves untouchable by law. If this were a study, say, of the old Mafia in Sicily that for decades ruled the island by assassination, bribery, and terror, we might give ourselves the dubious comfort of saying that this could not happen here. But Mr. Peterson is writing about a great *American* city; a city of your country in your time. And, mind you, while he is writing about Chicago, do not grow smug if you live elsewhere. For, as many investigations reveal, gang rule and political corruption are evil phenomena manifesting themselves in many American communities.

We Americans have long believed in the inevitability of progress; another way of saying that we believe ourselves capable of solving the problems that confront us. Thus, for example, we are convinced of our ability to meet the threat of communism as that threat arises in our midst. If we had been as apathetic toward it as we are toward organized crime, it would soon become our master and we its slaves. But we meet the communist threat with energy and resolution and so we keep in control, if we cannot stifle, this conspiratorial underground movement.

The threat of organized crime to our democratic system of government, while of a different nature from the threat of communism, is real. It is admittedly complex and difficult to deal with. But we do not — we must not — say that we are incapable of dealing with it, for this would be to abandon our democratic system by default. There are no problems of man's making that cannot be solved by man; including the problem of organized crime. Crime commissions, such as the Chicago Crime Commission, of which the author of the book is the Operating Director, have shown how people, working together, can combat crime.

If facts be needed, here they are in startling array in Mr. Peterson's book. Reading it, one is ashamed that the conditions depicted by the author are permitted to exist among us, while at the same time one is grateful to him for bringing them to our attention.

I, for one, believe with Woodrow Wilson that when the American people know the facts, they will find a way to cope with the problem.

ESTES KEFAUVER

Contents

Contents

Barbarians in Our Midst

A History of Chicago Crime and Politics

CHAPTER I

Early Character Traits

CHICAGO is a city of beautiful homes and apartment buildings as well as ugly tenements; a city with a reputation for friendliness, hospitality and charity — but also known for its surly taxi drivers, its intense hatreds, its violence, its high murder rate; a city of religion and churches — but widely condemned for its vice centers and corruption; a city of unsurpassed national and international transportation facilities — yet a city of disgruntled straphangers who struggle daily with a snarled and congested traffic problem; a city of neighborliness — and a center of world isolationism; a city which has spent millions to provide free entertainment and instruction for its citizens and visitors — yet a city abounding in night spots specializing in vulgarity and lewdness at exorbitant prices.

As a motorist enters Chicago across its southern boundary, he may pass through portions of spacious Jackson Park. If he wanders from the beaten path a trifle he may find himself in the midst of the vine-covered buildings of the University of Chicago or near the popular Museum of Science and Industry. Passing the museum and proceeding north on the Outer Drive, he will observe the impressive skyline of the business district in the distance. The traffic moves fast, but even as he speeds along he is impressed with the city's beauty and cleanliness — an impression which is strengthened as he glances to the east toward Lake Michigan, the most beautiful of the Great Lakes. As far as he can see there is nothing but an immensity of blue water and space. If he should happen to leave the Outer Drive at Pershing Road, however, and proceed west, he would find himself within a few minutes in the heart of one of the nation's most disgraceful slum areas, a district of filthy streets and alleys, of crowded tenements, of crime and corruption.

In downtown Chicago many of the nation's greatest artists appear each year in the impressive Civic Opera Building that stands at Wacker Drive and Madison Street. Thousands of Chicagoans find cultural entertainment there. But if one leaves the Opera Building and walks slowly west on Madison Street, in less than five minutes he finds himself in the midst of America's worst skid row, a veritable jungle of forgotten men. In the hot summer, dirty drunken human beings, covered with flies, sprawl on the sidewalks oblivious of the constant clanging of speedy Madison streetcars passing by. In abandoned lumberyards, in alleys, hundreds of social outcasts and misfits sleep off drunken stupors while those less intoxicated steal their shoes, pants, or the few pennies in their pockets. Then they scurry away to exchange the stolen articles for enough cheap wine to enable them to join their fallen comrades in a sleep that resembles death. Taverns catering to this clientele are unbelievably dirty and for many years have violated every regulation of health and decency.

Few cities have a more magnificent thoroughfare than Chicago's Michigan Boulevard. At night the dazzling lights and the well-kept store fronts offer an enchanting sight. Walking north on Michigan Boulevard from downtown Chicago, the sightseer soon comes to the bridge which spans the Chicago River. Just beyond rises the stately Tribune Tower, and in the immediate distance the Palmolive Building with its powerful beacon that guides the airplane pilots to safety. But within a stone's throw to the west of these buildings are garish neon lights on the night spots and dives of Rush and Clark Streets that were never intended to guide anyone to safety. Here organized vice rings do a flourishing business. Profits are high and so are the crime rates.

Chicago has been a city of extremes and contrast from the very beginning of its history, which dates back to the seventeenth century. Then the Jesuit missionary, Jacques Marquette, spent some time within the present city limits. While Marquette was preaching the gospel, Chicago's first bootlegger, Pierre Moreau, also known as "the Mole," was selling firewater to the Indians. Almost two hundred and fifty years later, as priests were ministering to the souls of men in the Holy Name Cathedral on Chicago's near North Side, armed bootleggers were killing one another across the street, and stray bullets from their guns pierced the walls of the cathedral. Crooks and men of the cloth have both played major roles in the city's social development. Politically, however, blacklegs and bootleggers have usually been far more influential than churchmen.

In the 1820's the area which later became Chicago was nothing more than a frontier post that afforded protection from the Indians who had ceded this territory to the United States in August 1795. Neither the location nor the inhabitants of this settlement gave any indication that the place was destined to become one of the greatest cities of the world. A few filthy huts occupied by men who were hardly the equal of the neighboring Indians presented a most uninviting picture to the national government, which was considering the location of a harbor there. In fact, had it not been for the efforts of a young army engineer, Jefferson Davis, the harbor might have been established in Milwaukee, Wisconsin, or Michigan City, Indiana. Congress followed the advice of the future Confederate President, however, and a thousand-foot pier was erected at the outlet of the Chicago River.[1]

When Chicago was incorporated as a town on August 10, 1833, fewer than two hundred persons inhabited the place. If the people of this hamlet entertained hopes that Chicago would grow into an important metropolis, the frequent rains which fell dampened their enthusiasm. When it rained there was mud everywhere — black, sticky mud in which horse-drawn vehicles became so deeply mired that they had to be abandoned. In order to develop the new town, financial assistance was imperative, and an appeal for a loan went out to bankers of Shawneetown, Illinois. Representatives of the bank, mounting their horses, and accompanied by their dogs, started on a weary journey of over three hundred miles to inspect the new village. The glorified mudhole called Chicago was not impressive to the critical eye of the Shawneetown bankers. They summarily disapproved the loan with the observation that only fools would attempt to build a town on such marshy land. And they concluded that only bigger fools would invest money in the future of this unpromising place. But long before Chicago had celebrated its hundredth anniversary, Shawneetown had lapsed into obscurity. Now it is only when the Ohio River overflows its banks and compels the Shawneetown inhabitants to abandon their homes, that this southern Illinois town is ever prominently in the public eye. From Chicago's impossible swamps, meantime, there emerged a city of skyscrapers and magnificent boulevards. The mudhole became one of the greatest centers of commerce, industry and finance of the entire nation.

Among the "first sons" of Chicago were many who gave the town its tradition of lawlessness. Professional gamblers, panders, blacklegs, grog sellers, horse thieves and political parasites hastened to take advantage of the utter confusion and instability which prevailed in this boom town. No group thrived more than the professional gamblers. Gambling was everywhere. Men wagered on horse races, dice, cards and land. This was a period of insane land speculation, and the general gambling spirit which it generated brought overflowing crowds to Chicago's numerous gambling dens. Fast profits, greatly augmented by expert swindling, attracted blacklegs from other parts of the country. When public uprisings drove the gamblers from Natchez, Vicksburg and other Mississippi River towns, many of them drifted to Chicago. By 1840 only New Orleans and some of the large eastern cities could count more gambling places than Chicago.[2]

The pattern for Chicago justice was established at the town's first murder trial, in the fall of 1834, at which an Irishman was charged with killing his wife. He was brought to trial in an unfinished store building on Dearborn Street just north of Lake Street. The evidence seemed conclusive to support a verdict of manslaughter. But the jurors were misled by the instructions of the court and the wiles of the lawyer, and the defendant was acquitted.[3] This procedure was to be repeated thousands of times during the following century.

In this frontier town firearms were in constant evidence and the men who carried them did not hesitate to use them to settle their differences. This was the era of the rugged individualist. The man who was quick on the trigger depended on neither laws nor policemen to uphold his rights, actual or pretended. During the first two years of the town's existence there were no duly constituted law-enforcement officers to curb the activities of the criminal. It was not until August 5, 1835, that the first "police constable," one O. Morrison, took office. While this embryo police department was not particularly effective, the appointment of Constable Morrison did give evidence of a recognition of the need for some semblance of law and order in the growing town. The new Board of Trustees, in

August 1835, also enacted a code of municipal laws designed to strike at some of the principal sources of crime and disorder. The chief provisions of the new code prohibited gaming houses and the firing of guns and pistols in the streets.[4]

Only three years after Chicago was incorporated as a town the settlers began demanding a city status. On January 23, 1837, the project was discussed at a town meeting held in the Saloon Building Hall on the southeast corner of Lake and Clark Streets, and on March 4, 1837, an act incorporating the city was passed. On May 2, 1837, came the first city election. Seven hundred and nine votes were cast for the candidates. William B. Ogden, a Democrat, was elected mayor. The first mayor was only thirty-two years of age; two years earlier he had migrated to Chicago from New York, where he had served one session in the legislature. Arriving in Chicago he had plunged into extensive real estate operations, a common pursuit of the day.[5]

When Mayor Ogden took office in 1837, there were 4170 persons living in Chicago. Within a period of four years the population had increased twentyfold. But the panic year 1837 marked a temporary end to the rapid growth of the future metropolis. "It was during this year," wrote a contemporary historian, "that the consequences of speculation . . . were experienced to a most ruinous extent." Everyone had been gambling in real estate:

Very few were found able to resist the temptation; all classes of people, ultimately abandoning the usual avocations of society, devoted themselves exclusively to speculation, and hazarded their all upon this sea of chance. This wild spirit found its way ultimately into the halls of legislation, and controlled the conduct and policy of states, as it had done that of individuals.[6]

Many of the ablest businessmen had caught the gambling fever and were now insolvent. The orgy of gambling into which the people had plunged brought scandal, disgrace, poverty and ruin to the entire community. The crisis was general across the nation, but Chicago, in particular, received a crushing blow. "It was," recorded the historian of that period, "a season of mourning and desolation." [7] For the next three years the growth of the city was retarded. Its population of 4470 in 1840 represented an increase of only three hundred persons over the 1837 figures.

During the early years of Chicago's existence, Jacksonian democracy was at its height. The spoils system had fastened itself on government everywhere. And the numerous opportunities for graft present in the new town naturally attracted political parasites and crooked contractors in large numbers. Politics offered rich prizes for which men were willing to shoot and kill. As early as 1840 a tradition of violence at the polls was being established. The Presidential "hard cider log cabin" campaign of 1840 was hard fought in many sections of the nation, but on election day in Chicago, there was vicious fighting and bloodshed on both the North and South Sides. Disorder on the South Side reached such proportions that Sheriff Ashbel Steele found it necessary to arrest one of the ringleaders of the disturbance. Immediately a mob, headed by a supreme court judge, marched to the lockup and ordered the sheriff to release the prisoner. The sheriff gained courage when a number of his political followers came to his aid. He stood his ground, unholstered his gun and threatened to kill any man who attempted to storm the jail.[8] The violence that manifested itself at this early Chicago election was merely a preview of many future political campaigns.

By 1840, the effects of the financial crash had worn off. There was new hope, and renewed activity. In 1839, ships left the port of Chicago with cargoes valued at $33,843. In 1840 the value of such exports had jumped to $228,635, almost seven times greater than during the preceding year. People began pouring into the city again. By 1843 the population totaled 7580, of which 2256 were of foreign birth. Of those originating from other countries, the Irish, Germans and Norwegians predominated. Negroes had not yet started to migrate to Chicago in any great numbers; only sixty-five lived there in 1843.

By 1844 Chicago's future appeared bright and secure. The glamour and romance surrounding the mushroom growth of the city again centered on the plungers — those willing to risk all to win a fortune quickly. These were the men who were largely responsible for the chaos growing out of the panic of 1837. But in the background, without fanfare, were men and women of substance quietly building the solid foundations that were to assure Chicago a place among the foremost cities of the world.

Rush Medical College, the first of its kind in Illinois, was founded

by an act of the state legislature on March 2, 1837. The Rush Medical
College building was completed in 1844, and on December thirteenth
of that year it was formally dedicated with an address by Daniel
Brainard, president of the faculty. The *Weekly Democrat* reported
that the citizens "may well be proud of the intelligence and enterprise, which in so short a time have erected a beautiful and costly
edifice dedicated to science. . . ." The brick building with stone
facings accommodated the forty students then attending the school
and was constructed at a cost of $3500.[9] The school was named after
Dr. Benjamin Rush, one of the most distinguished men of his time.
He had been one of the original signers of the Declaration of Independence, a member of the Constitutional Ratification Convention
in 1787, treasurer of the United States Mint in Philadelphia, a professor of medicine at the University of Pennsylvania, an attending
physician in the Philadelphia Hospital and a writer of distinction.

In 1785, Dr. Rush published an essay entitled "Inquiry Into the
Effects of Ardent Spirits on the Human Body and Mind" which
served to initiate a great nationwide temperance movement. Although Chicago was a "wide-open" town with almost every second
shop a groggery, nevertheless it felt the impact of the temperance
movement. By 1844, the Washington Temperance Society claimed a
membership of 1100. The Catholic Total Abstinence Society had
500 members, the Mariner's Temperance Society, 271 and the Junior
Washington Temperance Society, 118. Assuming that membership of
these societies was composed only of Chicago residents, almost one
out of every four persons in the city took the pledge. During this
time it is also reported that the "groggeries were the favorite resorts
of two-thirds of the population." [10] That accounted for almost everybody.

Even a number of hotels advertised as temperance houses. This was
true of Washington Hall, on North Water Street near the Clark
Street bridge, the Chicago Temperance House on LaSalle Street,
and the American Temperance House at the corner of Lake and
Wabash Streets near the steamboat landing. A temperance house was
supposed to be a hotel in which no intoxicants were served. However, the city's first directory, published in 1844, records the occupation of George Cook as a "barkeeper at American Temperance
House."

The young men streaming into Chicago found that the jobs available were extremely diversified. This same 1844 directory records the employment of men as wigmakers, teamsters, blacksmiths, coopers, soap and candlemakers, tinsmiths, coppersmiths, saddlers, harness makers, pawnbrokers, tanners, peddlers, watchmakers, gunsmiths, lard oil makers, curriers, brewers and clerks in lottery offices.

With Chicago's damp and changing climate, with poor housing facilities and the constant influx of strangers, there was naturally much illness. But Dr. Egan's "Sarsaparilla Panacea" offered "astonishing cures from the use of this Article." In Dr. Egan's advertisement he proudly published a testimonial which assured prospective customers that "We take him to be above quackery, and are confident he would not, if he could, palm a useless nostrum upon the public, for the sake of paltry gain." For those suffering from mental disorders and shattered nerves growing out of the strain and strife of living in this fast moving city, one Dr. Tew offered his services as a "Phrenological & Magnetic Examiner." In a half-page advertisement in the city directory, Dr. Tew proclaimed that "The application of his Remedies will . . . relieve, or cure, any case of Monomania, Insanity, or recent Madness. . . ."

Although Chicago's growing reputation for wickedness was well deserved, many churches had been established to look after the moral and religious life of the people. Among the faiths represented were Presbyterian, Unitarian, Catholic, Universalist, Baptist, Episcopal and Lutheran.

Cultural values also received some attention. The Chicago Female Seminary, on the corner of Clark and Washington Streets, offered courses of education to "mould the character" and "cultivate the manners" of young ladies. Books were available through library societies and the Chicago Lyceum. The Young Men's Association, organized in 1841, had a membership of 206 in 1844. It maintained a reading room and during the winter months sponsored public lectures. The Association was originally formed as an answer to newspaper complaints that "There is no place of general resort where a leisure hour can be passed in quiet and rational amusement." [11]

Apparently, however, quiet and rational amusement did not attract the vast majority of the city's male population. Men did not rush to early Chicago primarily to read good books or to develop manners and culture. Their goal was money. They had projected themselves willingly into the rough and tough setting of a frontier town. They worked hard and they played hard. Recreation they found at the gaming tables or in the saloons. And Chicago had more than its share of both. Gambling profits were greatly increased through cheating and fraud. The authorities were co-operative and the victims uncomplaining.

Some of the more prominent gamesters of the period were accepted as a part of the social and economic structure of the town. This was true of the richly attired and handsome John Sears, of George C. Rhodes, "King Cole" Conant, Walt Winchester, George "One Lung" Smith and his two brothers Charles and Montague.[12] The gamblers maintained close and cordial relations with the saloonkeepers and the drivers of public hacks. Hackmen could be depended upon to direct strangers to the gaming tables of friends where they were quickly relieved of their money. Even at private clubs of professional and commercial men, gambling was a favorite diversion. Dr. Egan of the famous "Panacea" and a number of judges were members of a club which purported to improve the mind. But frequently the development of the intellect took a back seat while the club members indulged in games of chance for very high stakes.

Chicago's underworld was not organized, but this fact is not surprising, for Chicago society in general was not well organized. In the space of a few years Chicago had advanced from an impossible mudhole to a city that was attracting wide attention throughout the Midwest. Its population had increased fortyfold since it was incorporated as a town eleven years earlier. It could — and did — boast of a thriving commerce, a medical college, churches, newspapers, some semblance of law-enforcement machinery, schools and even its underworld.

The new town had a great thirst for news — a thirst satisfied in some measure through the columns of six newspapers which were in publication at the beginning of 1844. The oldest was the *Chicago Democrat*, a weekly, that had been published since November 26, 1833. The sole daily newspaper was the *Chicago Express*, which also published a weekly edition. On May 20, 1844, the first issue of the *Gem of the Prairie* was printed. About three years later this paper was to merge with the *Chicago Tribune*, which had then started on its long and prosperous journalistic career.

But there were serious handicaps to Chicago's growth and development. Transportation and communication facilities were inadequate and unbelievably slow. When war was declared on Mexico, May 11, 1846, the news "spread like wild fire," but it was nine days before word of this momentous event reached Chicago. At the beginning of 1848, there were almost 20,000 inhabitants in a city which had neither a railroad nor a canal. Local captains of industry and finance had to await the arrival of horse-drawn vehicles or slow-moving boats on Lake Michigan for important messages. When the roads were bad, the city was without mail for a week at a time. A quick trip from New York to Chicago by combined rail and boat required seven days.

On January 11, 1848, Chicago received its first telegram, which was dispatched from Milwaukee, about eighty miles to the north. On April 6, 1848, the first telegram was received from the East. With the establishment of telegraphic communication with the financial centers of the East, time was no longer a factor which worked to the disadvantage of Chicago's commerce and industry. The year 1848 also marked the completion of the Illinois and Michigan Canal, which was to prove highly significant in the future rapid growth of the city.

For several years there had been agitation for a railroad to Chicago. As early as the 1835–1836 session of the state legislature a charter was approved for a railroad between Galena, Illinois, and Chicago. Galena was then considered by far the more important of the two towns. There was considerable opposition to the proposed railroad and with the financial crash in 1837 the project failed. In 1847 the charter was amended and the railway company was reorganized with Chicago's first mayor, William B. Ogden, as president. Ogden had long been interested in railroads. In 1834, the year before he moved to Chicago, he had been a member of the New York State Legislature for the sole purpose of advocating a measure in favor of the construction of the Erie Railroad. In 1848, Ogden again plunged wholeheartedly into the promotion of the Galena and Chicago Union Railroad. The task was not easy. Stubborn opposition to the idea of a railroad operating within the city limits had to be overcome. Merchants feared that a railroad would take more business away from Chicago than it would bring. Only a portion of the stock was subscribed and money had to be borrowed in the East. Ogden, as a member of the city council, introduced an ordinance designed to give the railroad the necessary right of way from the West into the city. The council voted against the ordinance, but permission was finally granted to build a temporary track — rail transportation was probably only a passing fad anyway. How could such a monstrosity as a locomotive possibly compete with the trustworthy horse or the lake and river boats? The new railroad nevertheless purchased in New York a secondhand locomotive called the *Pioneer* and shipped it by boat to Chicago. There was considerable excitement as it was unloaded on a Sunday in October 1848. When some old freight cars arrived, the railroad became a reality. In November 1848, a few editors of Chicago newspapers and a number of skeptical stock-holders were given a ride on Chicago's railway system, which extended ten miles west to the Des Plaines River.[13] A circular distributed that year for the purpose of attracting eastern capital boasted that within fifteen years four Chicago railroads would be completed. Of course nobody believed such fantastic claims. But within ten years Chicago had twelve important trunk lines of about 3000 miles in length, in addition to numerous branches. Railroad earnings had soared from nothing in 1847 to over $18,000,000 by 1858, and Chicago was considered the greatest railroad center of the world.[14]

By the end of 1848, grain was arriving by rail daily from outlying western shipping points. Time and distance were no longer barriers to the city's development. But this was true only with respect to Chicago's intercourse with the outside world. Within the city limits, the number one problem was mud, as it had been fifteen years earlier. In bad weather the streets were impassable, and business was virtually at a standstill. In the heart of the business district scores of wagons and drays were frequently abandoned for days at a time. Over some of the deeper mudholes, town wits placed signboards with the warning: NO BOTTOM HERE; THE SHORTEST ROAD TO CHINA. When efforts were made to fill bad holes, the boards or stones would merely sink deeper and deeper into the mud until they completely disappeared. Sidewalks were practically nonexistent. Only a few planks here and there aided the man on foot to walk along the streets. The city had no sewers. Water was hauled in carts and carried into houses by the bucketful.[15] Health and sanitation conditions were deplorable. Smallpox and cholera epidemics swept over the population at frequent intervals. One of the most severe cholera epidemics started late in 1848. Within a period of less than one month during the following summer one thousand residents were stricken with cholera and three hundred and fourteen of them died.[16] Many of the victims were dead and buried in a matter of hours after the first sign of illness. Terror gripped the survivors.

An adequate sewerage system, a purified water supply and hospitals were essential to protect the health of the city residents. There were leaders who were not unmindful of these needs, but laying steel tracks aroused more interest than laying sewers. And early in 1849 when news reached Chicago that gold had been found in California, scores of the earliest settlers hurried for the west coast, never to return. The gold fever spread through the city like an epidemic. For several months wagon makers made nothing but emigrant wagons. They doubled the number of their workmen and still could not meet the demand. Revolvers, salt provisions and mackinaw blankets were purchased in such large quantities that the merchants' entire supply was exhausted. Prices for this type of merchandise soared. From the time the first two parties left Chicago for the gold fields, on March 29, 1849, there was an exodus that extended throughout the balance of the year.[17] New settlers were still streaming into Chicago in sufficient numbers, however, so that the population increased from 20,023 in 1848 to 23,047 in 1849.

The character traits of an individual and a city usually develop within the first few years of life. The life span of a city is many times that of an individual and its problems are infinitely more complex, but the early years of Chicago determined its character right down to the present. Its earliest traditions forecast both its glory and its shame.

CHAPTER 11
Law but Little Order

CHICAGOANS have always taken a secret pride in the wickedness of their city — but a pride which is strangely offended when outsiders make any reference to its bad reputation. As early as 1850, visiting farm boys, traveling salesmen, and businessmen were returning home with tales of the scarlet women, gambling dens, wild dancing halls and countless saloons which they had observed — and patronized — in the city. Any visitor who was sufficiently clever to save a portion of his bankroll from the clutches of the blacklegs who operated crooked roulette wheels, chuck-a-luck cages and faro games, still had to run the gauntlet of pickpockets and holdup men. Local businessmen suffered frequent losses from the depredation of the numerous yeggmen and robbers who made Chicago their headquarters. Chicago was well on its way toward earning its reputation as the most wicked city in the nation.[1]

Its bad name, however, had not prevented men of substance from settling there and exerting leadership which oftentimes approached genius. When thoroughfares to the city became bogged down in mud, hindering traffic, plank roads were constructed. The first in the entire state to be completed was the sixteen-mile-long Southwestern Plank Road, extending from Chicago to Brush Hill, which was finished in 1850. An addition to this, built a short time later, was known as the Naperville and Oswego. Others quickly followed. By the end of 1850, a total of fifty miles of plank roads leading out of Chicago had been constructed at a cost of $150,000. Thousands of wagonloads of produce streamed into the city over these roads, the building of which had been viewed with unusual confidence. Why build costly and impractical railroads, it was argued, when plank roads are better and less expensive? This was the tenor of a typical letter appearing in the *Chicago Democrat* in 1848. After setting forth facts to establish the superiority of plank roads over rail transportation, the writer remarked with finality, "One of the reasons most argued with those in favor of the proposed railroad . . . is that if we don't build one, Milwaukee will. The people of that city are not able to build a railroad of any length; if they were, they are not so simple." [2] But with customary daring and energy, Chicagoans plunged into large-scale projects of building both rail and plank roads. Such boundless enthusiasm got results. From a town of some 200 inhabitants in 1833, Chicago had grown to a city of 29,963 in 1850. Already it ranked eighteenth in size among the cities of the nation. It is true that Chicago was smaller than its principal rivals: Cincinnati with a population of 115,435, or St. Louis with 77,860.[3] But even its most bitter rivals began to respect the bombastic claims that emanated from the Windy City. By 1852, there were 38,734 persons living in Chicago and only one year later, 1853, its population had soared to 60,662.[4]

Chicago had become a hustling, bustling metropolis in which speed appeared to be the essence of all activities. Even its trains were running with reckless abandon. On April 25, 1853, a wreck of first magnitude occurred when Michigan Central and Michigan Southern trains collided at Grand Junction. Eighteen people were killed outright while forty others were seriously injured. Indignant citizens met and passed resolutions condemning the wanton carelessness which had resulted in the tragedy, but the pressure for speed went on.

The working man also felt the increased tempo of the period. There was much unrest and dissatisfaction with working conditions. In August 1853, this discontent broke out into the open. Laborers, for the first time in Chicago, staged a strike which lasted two weeks. Work in general stopped. Although the strike ended in failure, the laboring man had demonstrated that he possessed a weapon to be reckoned with in the future.[5]

Among the thousands of people who had been streaming into Chicago were many foreigners who had lived in America but a short time. In Chicago, as in most large cities, the votes of such immigrants were frequently controlled by crooked politicians who obtained fraudulent naturalization of the new arrival in return for his vote at the polls. These abuses reached scandalous proportions in several cities. Foreigners of the same nationality naturally had a tendency to live together in one section of a city. They were regarded as clannish and their frequent outspoken criticism of American institutions resulted in a growing hostility toward them. Out of this resentment grew a new political movement called the Know-Nothing or American party, which had for its aim the elimination of naturalized citizens and Roman Catholics from political life in this country. The large number of Irish immigrants, who were preponderantly Catholic and extremely able and successful in politics, had caused the Catholic church to be singled out as a symbol of foreign political influence. By 1854, the Know-Nothing party had become influential in city and state elections in several sections of the country and was gaining in national politics as well. In Chicago it had grown to considerable strength. On July 4, 1854, Stephen A. Douglas, the popular United States Senator from Illinois and a resident of Chicago, delivered a speech in Philadelphia in which he vigorously denounced the Know-Nothing political movement and the bigotry and intolerance on which it was based. He also spoke in favor of the Kansas-Nebraska bill which he had introduced into Congress that year. The popular sovereignty provision in the bill made slavery legally possible in a vast new area and was to hasten the outbreak of the Civil War. The Philadelphia speech of the "Little Giant" had at one stroke aroused the bitter enmity of the strong Know-Nothing party and the antislavery voters as well.

After Congress adjourned in August, Douglas headed for Chicago, where he was scheduled to speak in North Market Hall on the night of September 1, 1854. He was confident that the magnetism of his voice and the charm of his personality would easily appease the wrath of his constituents. However, he had failed to appraise accurately the extent of their anger. The Know-Nothing party and the Free Soil elements joined forces to prevent the scheduled address, labeling Douglas a "public enemy" — a term that Chicago has always used freely. The *Democratic Press*, once a supporter of the Senator, now attacked him with a vengeance. Some of the Protestant clergy admonished their flocks to prevent this disciple of anti-Christ from uttering his blasphemy from a public platform. Rumors circulated that when Douglas spoke he would be surrounded by a guard of 500 armed Irishmen. On the night of his speech, North Market Hall was filled to capacity. Streets surrounding the building were swarming with angry, surging crowds. About eight o'clock the Senator mounted the platform and attempted to speak. In a moment, pandemonium broke loose among the "howling, raging mob" that comprised his audience. Douglas, surrounded by a few friends, vainly sought to make himself heard. For two hours the crowd roared, hissed and booed. Finally, in despair, the "Little Giant" gave up and made his way slowly from the hall. And as he departed, rowdies showered him with rotten apples. Chicagoans took their politics seriously.[6]

The Douglas meeting was a disgraceful exhibition of ill manners, intolerance and mob psychology in action. It was also a show of strength on the part of the Know-Nothing party, which was riding on the crest of its popularity in Chicago. Men were deserting their old party affiliations and joining the ranks of the Native American group. At the municipal election on March 8, 1855, the city government passed completely into the hands of the Know-Nothing party. Dr. Levi D. Boone, a former Democrat and a grand nephew of the famous frontiersman, Daniel Boone, was elected mayor.

Immediately upon taking the oath of office, Dr. Boone initiated action to rid the city of its numerous disreputable saloons, which served as hangouts for the lawless elements. Mayor Boone recommended to the city council that the saloon license fee be raised from $50.00 to $300.00 a year. He contended that only the higher type of saloonkeeper would pay the increased fee, thus automatically eliminating the disreputable dives.

Mayor Boone and his Know-Nothing council, which approved the measure, had unrealistically ignored the strong organization existing among the liquor interests. As soon as the ordinance was passed, the saloonkeepers started a vigorous program of agitation against it. Meetings of brewers and proprietors of saloons, held frequently at North Market Hall, pledged money to resist the enforcement of the new ordinance. In righteous indignation, the liquor interests pleaded with the people to rebel against this infringement of personal liberty and freedom. An added grievance was Dr. Boone's announcement that he would enforce the Sunday closing law, which had been completely ignored in the past. The Germans who operated beer gardens were particularly incensed. Sunday was their most profitable day. The proprietors of saloons and beer gardens began openly defying the mayor and the city council. Within a few weeks almost 200 saloonkeepers were arrested and charged with selling liquor without a license or violating the Sunday closing law.

One attorney was retained to represent all the violators. The saloon proprietors, however, had no intention of relying entirely on the abilities of high-priced legal talent, the justice of Chicago courts or public opinion to win their cases. On the morning of April 21, 1855, when the first court appearance was scheduled, the liquor interests formed a mob which marched en masse to the courthouse. Accompanied by fife and drum, the group entered the courtroom, swearing and shouting threats. Not content with intimidating the judge, the mob then gathered at the intersection of Clark and Randolph Streets, completely obstructing traffic, and contemptuously defied the forces of law and order of the entire city government. Mayor Boone ordered the mob dispersed and the streets cleared. Taken by surprise when police officers appeared, the lawless group retreated to the near North Side. But this was merely a strategic maneuver. The liquor interests were marshaling their forces for a second attack. The mayor, sensing further trouble, hurriedly deputized an additional 150 men to the police force. Military units were called out and cannon were mounted at two corners of the courthouse. About three o'clock on the afternoon of April 21, the mob started to march south on Clark Street toward the heart of the city. Upon reaching the drawbridge which spanned the river, one detachment of rioters was permitted to pass over unmolested. When the second group arrived, the bridge tender swung the draw, leaving one segment of the infuriated mob stranded on the north bank of the river.

The mayor gathered his police on the south bank and gave orders to return the bridge to its normal position. The mob, armed with guns, clubs, knives and brickbats, surged over the bridge screaming, "Shoot the police!" A double-barreled shotgun, leveled at officer George Hunt, blew off his left arm. The police returned the fire, killing Peter Martin, one of the rioters. Numerous persons were wounded, including bystanders. Approximately eighty rioters were arrested and lodged in jail before the mob was finally dispersed and

order restored. Although hundreds of rioters participated in the disorder, only fourteen men were indicted. After a trial lasting fifteen
days, all but two of the defendants were acquitted. Eleven days later
the court granted the two convicted rioters a new trial, which was
tantamount to an acquittal. The proceedings were then dropped entirely.[7] After all, an armed rebellion, murder and mayhem were
considered justifiable in Chicago to preserve the sacred right to dispense intoxicating beverages on Sunday and to maintain a low
liquor-license fee.

The riotous conduct of the Douglas audience the preceding September and the mob violence on April 21, 1855, were merely symbols
of the general lawlessness prevailing. Street brawls were commonplace among the criminals infesting the city. There was no law enforcement worthy of the name. The police force was composed of an
elected city marshal and nine police constables, with one constable
elected from each of the nine wards in the city. This force was
completely political in character, insufficiently manned and poorly
organized. To provide more adequate police protection, ordinances
were passed by the city council in April and June 1855, creating Chicago's first police department and providing for three precinct stations. The mayor promptly appointed a chief of police, eight commanding officers with the ranks of lieutenant and sergeant and
fifty-eight patrolmen. All of these men had been born on American
soil and were in the good graces of the Know-Nothing party.[8]
The political complexion of Chicago's first police department was
to become a permanent tradition — a tradition which has habitually
rendered law enforcement in the city relatively ineffective.

The city had continued to be derelict in protecting the health of
the residents. Recurring epidemics were taking heavy death tolls.
Constant open streams of refuse and filth from distilleries, packing
houses, hotels, business places and dwellings poured into the river.
The stench from this body of water was nauseating, and its im-
purities endangered public health. Still nothing was done to correct
the evil.

Early in April 1854, there were reports of a few scattered cases
of cholera. The Board of Health promptly denied the presence of
the dreaded disease. The fair name of the city must be preserved!
Chicago officials early developed the practice of solving both crime

and health problems by the simple expedient of denying their existence. By July, however, the cholera epidemic had spread through the city like the sixteenth-century plagues of London. No longer was it possible to dismiss reports of cholera with the explanation that they were being circulated by enemies trying to besmirch the reputation of the city. The death cart rolled along the streets continually. Citizens became frantic, leaving Chicago in droves. Mortuary records revealed that 1424 persons died from cholera in 1854. Only two years earlier another cholera epidemic had taken a toll of 630 lives. It was apparent that no city could long endure such frequent visitations of wholesale death and suffering.

On February 14, 1855, the Board of Sewerage Commissioners was incorporated by legislative enactment. It conducted surveys to determine the best methods to give the city an adequate system of drainage and sewage disposal. The low position of the streets made the problem a most difficult one. In many places they were just barely above the river level. Filthy water stood on the streets and seeped into the cellars of homes and business houses. The plan formulated to solve this problem was characteristic of the ingenuity and daring that had been responsible for the city's unusual growth and development: Chicago's streets must be raised to a height several feet above the existing level. A storm of indignation greeted this "impractical and preposterous" suggestion. The first floors of costly buildings would suddenly become basements. The expense would be prohibitive. Millions of cubic yards of earth would be required.

Despite these protests, the work of raising the streets and constructing sewers began in 1856 and lasted for a number of years. The river was dredged and the mud and sand obtained from its bottom were dumped on the streets. As the streets were thus elevated, entire blocks of business houses had the appearance of sinking out of sight in the mud. Angry property owners sought the intervention of the courts but judicial decisions upheld the right of the city to complete the project. Businessmen then turned to a young contractor, George M. Pullman, who agreed to raise the buildings even with the new street level. He had met with success in raising houses along the Erie Canal in New York. Now in Chicago entire blocks of brick and stone buildings were raised without causing any interruption of business. The famous Tremont House was elevated several feet while fully occupied. The amazing feat of virtually lifting an entire city out of mud in which it had been hopelessly mired for over twenty years attracted attention throughout America and Europe.[9]

By 1856, Chicago had a population of 86,000. Within two decades it had grown from an insignificant Indian trading post to a city which was exporting twenty million bushels of grain each year. Instead of the lonely howl of prairie wolves at night, Chicagoans were now disturbed by the shrill whistles of locomotives and the banging of freight cars. The first suburban trains were placed in operation between Chicago and Hyde Park in June 1856. For a number of years real estate promoters, with tongue in cheek, had been making exorbitant claims regarding the city's future development. Neither they nor anyone else believed these bombastic predictions. Yet the actual growth of Chicago and the expansion of its business and industry had far exceeded the wildest boasts of the promoters.

Over the years, in spite of sporadic attempts at reform, such patriarchs of gambling in the city as John Sears, Bill McGraw, Dan Oaks, "Little Dan" Brown, "Dutch" House and others had become bolder and richer. The influx of professional gamblers continued, and in their wake followed the prostitutes, panders, burglars, holdup men and thieves. Although the underworld still had not become efficiently organized it was already exhibiting an interest in city elections and contributing to the frequent disorder and lawlessness at the polls. On March 3, 1857, Chicago witnessed another bloody election. There was furious fighting at the polls in the old Seventh Ward on the North Side where one man was killed. Riots broke out at the polling places in the Tenth Ward and before order was restored some of the voters were badly wounded.[10]

There was much crime, immorality and disorder in Chicago when the reform administration of Mayor "Long John" Wentworth came into power in 1857. Wentworth, according to a legend that may or may not be reliable, had walked into town barefoot in October 1836. The new mayor was born in Sandwich, New Hampshire, on March 5, 1815, and was graduated from Dartmouth College in 1836. As editor and publisher of the *Chicago Democrat*, Wentworth had taken an active interest in the political life of Chicago. He was known as a man of direct action. He possessed a towering physique, standing six feet six inches in height and weighing three hundred pounds.

A district known as the Sands was probably the worst of many disreputable spots in Chicago. Located just north of the river and extending to Lake Michigan, the Sands was filled with gambling dens, houses of prostitution, and lodging houses of the most unsavory character. Men were lured into this area and robbed. Murders were frequent. Mayor Long John Wentworth decided on drastic action. On April 20, 1857, he personally descended on the Sands with a raiding party of thirty police officers. They demolished nine buildings. A fire which broke out that same afternoon destroyed six other structures. Nationwide attention focused on Chicago's mayor and his unique methods of dealing with vice resorts.

The professional gamblers also found the mayor's hands firm and unrelenting. Through the columns of the *Chicago Democrat*, he warned them to close their places or suffer the consequences of vigorous action by the police. His threats received little attention — the gamblers had enjoyed immunity for so long that they were confident the mayor would not have the temerity to interfere with their activities. But the swaggering blacklegs were part of a thriving underworld that was rapidly getting out of hand. They were closely allied with the proprietors of brothels and the keepers of disorderly saloons. They were parasites who contributed nothing to the city's welfare and helped give Chicago its bad reputation. Long John went after them.

On a hot summer afternoon in 1857, the mayor dispatched two police officers to a gambling den on Randolph Street known as Burrough's Place. Gaining entrance through a rear window on the second floor, the officers took the gamblers by complete surprise. In confusion they rushed headlong down the stairway. Their blind flight led them directly into the hands of the massive mayor and his officers who were waiting below. Wentworth had left nothing to chance. He personally supervised the booking of prisoners and made certain they were actually jailed. He warned city license holders that if they furnished bail for the arrested gamblers, he would revoke their licenses. This threat was directed in particular at saloonkeepers and hackmen who long had been working in collusion with the blacklegs. A gambler's attorney, Charley Cameron, appeared at the jail demanding the right to confer with his client. His request was denied. When he attempted to talk with the gambler through the bars of an open window, the mayor himself seized the lawyer and locked him up.[11] The mayor's methods, while sometimes extralegal, were effective. For the first time in the city's history, the professional gamblers beat a retreat. Throughout the remainder of Wentworth's first term the gambling business was at a low ebb.

The Chicago gambling industry was not the only one passing through a period of depression, however. The entire nation was in the midst of one of its periodic panics. Financial disaster struck over 200,000 business concerns in America before the Panic of 1857 had run its course. In Chicago the private banking house of E. R. Hinckly and Company closed its doors on July 3, 1857. A month later there was a disastrous run on Hoffman's Bank. On September twenty-ninth the banking house of R. K. Swift, Brother and Company closed. On November seventh the large Cherokee Banking and Insurance Company suspended business. Nine days later Walker, Bronson and Company, one of the largest produce firms in the city, failed. For six months the sales of this company had averaged $100,000 a day. Yet it could not withstand the onslaught of the panic which had completely demoralized business. A total of 117 Chicago business firms with liabilities amounting to six million dollars were ruined. And when the numerous financial reverses had the business life of the city reeling, disaster struck. On October 19, 1857 a fire broke out in a large store on South Water Street. Property valued at $500,000 was destroyed and thirteen persons died in the conflagration.[12]

The optimism which had become a part of Chicago's character was rapidly disappearing. Construction work stopped on half-finished buildings. Their ghostlike appearance served as tombstones to remind passers-by that business in the community was dead. Even the effervescent real estate promoters had to temper somewhat the enthusiasm which usually characterized their advertisements. Several months after the peak of the crash had passed a circular of one promoter stated: "The panic of 1857 came at last. . . . I confess it has brought a result which I did not anticipate. Never could I have believed that by any influences prices would again be depressed here as they now are." Quickly regaining his composure, the promoter urged his clients to take advantage of the low prices then prevailing and assured them of Chicago's bright future even though the whole nation failed. "No earthly power," his circular proclaimed, "not even the dissolution of the Union, can divert from Chicago the business and traffic of the great Northwest." [13]

With the collapse of business, thousands of men were thrown out of work. Many of them, roaming the streets idle and penniless, turned to crime. Desperadoes, petty criminals and just plain riffraff deserted their usual haunts throughout the Midwest and boarded trains which dumped them into Chicago. This was too much for even Long John's hard-fisted law-enforcement policies, and almost every issue of the newspapers carried lurid accounts of holdups, burglaries and assaults. People became frightened and when it appeared that the administration was unable to protect them, their fear turned into indignation. They armed themselves to protect their families from the depredations of the criminals. Respectable citizens returning to their homes after dark were in danger of being mistaken for felons and shot by well-meaning neighbors. The underworld was completely out of hand. "The city," said the *Chicago Tribune*, "is at the mercy of the criminal classes" — a complaint that was to be registered countless times during the following century. [14]

Angered by the hard times and prevailing lawlessness, Chicago citizens blamed the administration of Long John Wentworth for their ills. On March 2, 1858, the voters went to the polls and elected John C. Haines mayor. During his two successive terms in office, there was a substantial economic recovery. And among the first to feel the end of the depression were the professional gamblers. The new administration looked upon the swindling fraternity with a benevolent eye. Before long the streets of Chicago again swarmed with blacklegs. Chicago once more resumed its place among the foremost gambling centers of the nation.

CHAPTER III

A Heyday for the Underworld

AS the year 1860 opened, the public mind of Chicago was tuned to politics. Excitement had never been at a higher pitch than during the municipal election held March 6, 1860. With their eyes fixed on the coming national elections, both major parties selected their strongest available candidate. The Democrats pitted Walter S. Gurnee, who had served two terms as mayor in 1851 and 1852, against the colorful and massive Republican candidate, Long John Wentworth. (Mayors were still elected for just one year. It was not until 1863 that the term was extended to two years and the four-year terms did not start until 1907.) Long John's previous administration was still fresh in the voters' minds. In the troublesome Seventh and Tenth Wards, partisan voters took their lunches and camped out all night around the polling places in order to make certain that the rights of their favored candidate should be protected. When the votes were counted, Wentworth was declared the victor by a majority of 1200. Immediately Republican papers all over the country headlined the Chicago election as "the first gun for 1860," and predicted that the Republican party would likewise sweep to victory in the coming presidential contest.

The national attention which centered on the Chicago election was indicative of the growing importance of this midwestern city. With a population of 109,420 in 1860, Chicago was now the ninth largest city of the land. Only New York City, Philadelphia, Brooklyn, Baltimore, Boston, New Orleans, St. Louis, and Cincinnati had larger populations. As further proof of the significance of Chicago in the American political scheme, it was chosen as the site of the 1860 Republican National Convention. With the municipal contest out of the way, city leaders launched into elaborate preparations for this grand affair.[1]

By the night of May 15, 1860, the hotels and streets of Chicago were teeming with over twenty-five thousand strangers from all parts of the nation. Almost fifteen hundred stayed in the Tremont House. They were packed in so tightly that it was barely possible for the guests to go from one room to another without shoving and pushing or stepping on toes. Among the notables stopping at the Tremont House was the New York publisher, Horace Greeley, who was surrounded by gaping crowds wherever he went. Thousands walked over to the corner of Market and Lake Streets to obtain a preview of the curious "Wigwam" where the delegates would meet the following day. Others spent their time gazing at a huge bowie knife, seven feet long and weighing forty pounds, which was on display.

On May sixteenth the Republican convention was officially in session. Two days were spent in the adoption of the platform and attending to other routine matters, but on Friday morning, May eighteenth, the "Wigwam" was a bedlam. New York's favorite son, William H. Seward, was considered the strongest candidate. One thousand of his backers had marched to the convention in military style. Dressed in brilliant uniforms and caps with waving white and scarlet feathers, they made an impressive sight. On the first ballot Seward led the field of candidates with 173½ votes. On the second ballot he gained a few votes but not enough for victory. It became clear that he could not marshal sufficient strength for the nomination. On the third ballot, consequently, the required number of votes switched to the second-place candidate to give him the nomination. Abraham Lincoln, the rail splitter from Illinois, was nominated by the Republican convention for the Presidency of the United States. The delegates did not know it; the nation did not know it, but in Chicago there had just been nominated for President the greatest of all American statesmen.[2]

Chicago's reputation by 1860 was world-wide. But Chicago's renown was not confined to its meteoric rise from a small hamlet to a city of major importance or to its commercial achievements. Throughout the land it was known as a place abounding in filth,

where crime flourished and life was cheap. The pretentious underworld in Chicago had little to fear from the authorities. As usual the
underworld was dominated by the gamblers, many of whom had
served their apprenticeship on the lower Mississippi River. (This
element in particular, with Southern traditions deeply imbedded,
generated a considerable amount of sympathy for the South in Chicago during the Civil War. It is worthy of note, however, that the
pro-Southern sentiments of the blacklegs were not sufficiently deep
to make them suffer the rigors of war in the ranks of the Confederate Army.)

When Long John Wentworth had relinquished the mayor's chair
in March 1858, the city was again overrun with criminals and
swindlers of every description. Conditions were the same when
Wentworth became the chief executive for a second time in March
1860. During Long John's first administration he had struck boldly
at the heart of the underworld — the brothels and gambling dens.
He knew that public opinion was not always solidly behind him —
the traditions of the wide-open town were already too deeply imbedded. The people were in favor of catching burglars and robbers
after they had committed unlawful acts, but they were not too much
interested in destroying their breeding places. The mayor also
confronted other pressing problems. He found that the city had
contracted a large floating debt. Adopting the slogan "Liberty and
Economy," Wentworth decided upon the police department as an
expedient place to launch his economy drive. Soon large areas were
left without any semblance of police protection. Criminals by the
hundreds were arriving in the city, while the police department became steadily weaker.

Aggravating this situation, was Wentworth's penchant for inter-
fering with the most trivial of police details. During his first term as
mayor, Long John had proudly invented a leather badge which
patrolmen wore on their caps to distinguish them from other citizens.
They carried heavy canes in the daytime and batons at night. Although the geographical area of the city was growing larger, the
means of transportation were still slow. Occasionally after an officer
had overpowered a culprit, he would have to load him in a borrowed
wheelbarrow and push his cargo to the police station. Patrolmen
assigned to a beat were unable to communicate with headquarters.

There were no patrol boxes. Patrolmen were furnished with noise-making devices called "creakers" which were merely distress signals that had been used three centuries earlier by the watchmen of London to call for help. During the administration of John C. Haines the policemen were outfitted in short blue frock coats, blue caps with gold braid and brass stars. Long John's economy drive would not tolerate such a display of extravagance. The uniforms were promptly discarded and the leather badge replaced the brass star.

Toward the end of Wentworth's term of office, with the police department reduced to a captain, six lieutenants and fifty patrolmen, criminals were having a field day. The public clamored for protection, and when aid was not forthcoming from the city the people turned to the state legislature in Springfield. A law was passed on February 16, 1861, which virtually stripped the mayor of control over the Chicago police department. Approved on February 21, 1861, the new act established a board of three police commissioners in which authority over the Chicago police force was vested. The law also provided for a general superintendent of police, a deputy superintendent and as many patrolmen as the common council authorized.

The new law was a direct slap in the mayor's face. Every man in the department was his personal appointee. In effect it was his personal police force. And now his authority over it had been removed. Long John was determined to avenge the insult. On the night of March 21, 1861, the Board of Police Commissioners held its first official meeting. As soon as the police board adjourned, Long John Wentworth summoned every man in the police force to his office. Lashing at the new police board, the mayor said its purpose was to humiliate and degrade his police officers. He had no intention, he said, of permitting his political enemies to accomplish these evil designs. Apparently Long John decided that if there was to be any humiliating he would do it himself. At two o'clock in the morning the mayor discharged every man in the police department. Chicago, ninth largest city of the nation, overrun with criminals, was left with no police protection at all.

At 10 A.M. on the same morning, March 22, the three members of the Board of Police Commissioners hurriedly met to deal with this unexpected emergency. They appointed new officers to the police department, and a number of Wentworth's men also returned to the police rolls. Before long officers were again patrolling the streets of Chicago. On April 16, 1861, Julian S. Rumsey, a Republican, was elected mayor. A week later, April 23, Cyrus P. Bradley became the first superintendent of police under the new law; his first official act was to name Captain John "Jack" Nelson as his deputy.[3]

While Long John was waging his battle with the police board, relations between the North and South were becoming more and more strained. Martial fervor was mounting everywhere. In Chicago a plea went out for the formation of an Irish volunteer regiment to fight for the Union cause. A rally of Irishmen at the North Market Hall on April 20, 1861, dedicated itself to the honor of the old land and the defense of the new. Among those who signed the notice of this meeting was one M. C. McDonald, a notorious gambler.[4] History fails to record that Michael Cassius McDonald ever played any part worthy of mention in the eventual Northern victory, but this king of gamblers was to have a dominant role in the political history of Chicago during the years ahead.

During the Civil War period the city was infested with outlaws and swindlers who were incessantly creating disturbances. Typical of this group and one of its leaders was a character known as "Captain" Hyman, a professional gambler and blackleg. When he was drunk, which was often, he delighted in whipping out a six-shooter, threatening death to anyone who might cross him. This Captain Hyman took more than a passing interest in politics. One evening in 1862, in the midst of an exciting political campaign, the captain, revolver in hand, took possession of the Tremont House. The guests fled and the management sent for the police. They arrived in full force but Hyman remained unperturbed. Flourishing his gun as usual, he defied the officers to arrest him. None accepted the challenge. For over an hour he kept the policemen at bay. Captain Hyman's siege was finally broken by the appearance of his friend, the Deputy Superintendent of Police, Jack Nelson, to whom the gunman obligingly agreed to surrender.[5] It is doubtful if the gambler was even locked up. At any rate, it is clear that the beautiful friendship between Hyman and the deputy superintendent of police was not marred in any respect.

The proprietors of the gambling establishments were frequently rugged gunmen. One of the most prosperous places, located at the northeast corner of Clark and Madison, was operated by Theodore Cameron, who was known as a "Bad man from Texas and handy with a gun." His reputation was not based on idle gossip. One night an ex-convict lost his entire bank roll at Cameron's gaming tables in such short order that he knew he had been swindled. Leaving the place he quickly recruited the aid of four of his cronies. Returning, three of the gunmen entered while two were stationed beside the door outside. With drawn gun, the ex-convict demanded the return of his money. Cameron's blazing revolver was his answer. Patrons ran for cover during the furious exchange of shots that followed. When quiet was once more restored the ex-convict lay dead beside the gaming tables. Cameron was uninjured. Life was cheap in Cameron's place but the profits were high. Before long he opened an expensively furnished establishment at 68 Randolph Street, where luxurious rooms, choice liquors and fancy cigars tried to give an air of respectability to offset the systematic cheating at the gaming tables.[6]

In 1863, one of the most unscrupulous gangs of swindling gamblers ever to infest any community settled in the city. Steerers for the gang roamed the streets looking for prospective victims with large bank rolls. Frequently the steerer would even hang around the hallways leading to a rival gambling house. Turning out the gaslights, he would wait in darkness for the patrons of the place to enter. Upon their arrival they were informed that the establishment was closed. The steerer would then obligingly lead the victims to a den where they were virtually robbed of their money. In one instance, the operator of a gambling hell cultivated the friendship of the treasurer of a well-known corporation. Through the guidance of the blackleg, this official embezzled $31,000 which he promptly lost at the gaming tables. But the gambling house proprietor still was not satisfied. He persuaded the corporation official to burglarize his company's safe. Late at night, the gambler held the lamp while the treasurer opened the safe and removed $20,000. Promptly taking possession of all of the stolen money, the gambler issued an ultimatum to his accomplice that he must flee to California. Arriving on the west coast, broken in health and destitute, the defaulting treasurer sent frantic appeals to the gambler for assistance. When these entreaties were ignored, the embezzler returned to Chicago and confessed. The gambler was lodged in jail until he returned the $20,000 to the corporation.[7] But this was one of the few instances when a member of the swindling, gambling fraternity saw the inside of a jail. It is small wonder that many of the most notorious blacklegs of the period decided to make Chicago their permanent residence.

The most popular gambling resort was the elegantly furnished establishment operated by George Trussell. He was a man of sufficient political influence to control gambling privileges in the city. Gamesters who failed to make satisfactory arrangements with Trussell found their places visited by destructive raiding parties from the police department. Trussell was a fierce rival of Captain Hyman. Frequently when these two gamblers met on Randolph Street they drew their guns and fired at one another while bystanders scurried for cover. Evidently both men were poor shots, since it appears that neither ever wounded the other.

The rivalry between Hyman and Trussell was not based on gambling spoils alone. There were other prizes to be won. The gamblers were liberal patrons of the numerous houses of prostitution that comprised an important segment of Chicago's commerce and industry. Madames of swanky parlor houses were commonly the mistresses of the gambling chiefs. Not infrequently the gamesters furnished the funds to establish gaudy brothels. This was true of the famous place operated by Carrie Watson at 441 Clark Street. She started in business with money supplied by one Al Smith who ran a prosperous gambling house at 91 Clark Street. And George Trussell, the most powerful of all gamblers of the time, had as his consort a madame called Mollie, who operated a parlor house on Fourth Avenue. Mollie, whose real name was Mary Cossgriff, had been an inmate in a brothel before she decided to go into business for herself. Money was plentiful during the war period. Liquor flowed freely and with women readily accessible, fights broke out constantly among the gamblers. In fact, because of their numerous shootings the area on Randolph Street between Clark and State Streets became known as "Hair Trigger Block."[8] So predominant were the gamblers on Randolph Street that it was also commonly referred to as "Gambler's Row."

Throughout the Civil War years bad men from the West and South, thugs, pickpockets, gunmen, yeggs, confidence men drifted to Chicago where they prospered with little interference from the authorities. The gambling houses naturally served as their headquarters. While the gambling lords had not yet achieved the status of powerful ward or city bosses, as they would in the years ahead, their business was closely allied with politics. Politicians were indebted to the gamesters who were consequently able to obtain protection for themselves and to intercede on behalf of others. The gamblers were the overlords of a thriving underworld. One of the most profitable schemes of the time related to organized bounty jumping. Under the regulations then existing, a person selected for military duty could have a substitute serve in his place if he paid a designated sum of money to the government. The substitute, after enlisting and receiving the bounty, would desert as quickly as possible. He was then ready to repeat the procedure. The ring of bounty jumpers which flourished in Chicago was under the domination of a group of Southern gamblers. While they themselves profited handsomely they also had the satisfaction of assisting the Confederate cause.[9]

Bounty jumpers as well as other desperadoes found refuge in scores of dens and boarding houses located on the east side of Market Street from Van Buren to Madison. These places were the scenes of frequent brawls and murders. Trouble was forever brewing in Roger Plant's resort called "Under the Willow," on the southeast corner of Wells and Monroe Streets, in Ben Sabin's saloon on Wells Street and in saloons kept by Tim Reagan and Andy Routzong near Clark and Van Buren Streets. On River Street, from South Water Street to the bridge and on North Water Street from Wolf's Point to Clark Street were many dives which served as the headquarters for some of the most dangerous criminals in the Middle West. The outlaws and bounty jumpers became bolder and bolder. The police being, as usual, helpless, respectable citizens were obliged to form vigilante committees to deal with the situation.[10]

The spirit of Chicago even penetrated Camp Douglas, where Southern prisoners of war were confined on a sixty-acre tract of land located in the vicinity of 34th Street and Cottage Grove Avenue. A former New Orleans gambler improvised a faro "layout" in the camp and proceeded systematically and ruthlessly to swindle his fellow prisoners. The morale of the entire camp was broken. An investigation conducted by the commanding officer uncovered the location of the gambling operations. The place was raided by the military authorities and $150,000 confiscated.[11]

As the Civil War came to a close, no city had a more formidable underworld than Chicago. Crime news filled the newspapers, and desperate men stalked the thoroughfares. Approximately two thousand prostitutes solicited business on the streets. Some of them opened establishments in office buildings in the heart of the business district. The gambling game of keno had become such a rage that spacious, first-floor establishments that had mushroomed on Randolph Street between State and Clark could not accommodate the crowds. Frequently at night people who were clamoring to gain entrance into the keno rooms blocked the sidewalks and overflowed into the streets. These conditions were accompanied by police and official corruption that reached scandalous proportions.[12] And as the Union soldiers were being discharged from the army in 1865, Chicago's array of gamblers, swindlers, harlots, and other underworld characters welcomed them with open arms. The ex-soldiers were relieved of their mustering-out pay in very short order. The situation became so critical that General John Cook detailed two extra companies in Chicago to act as a provost guard to prevent the indiscriminate robbery of discharged military men.[13]

As the war spirit gradually faded, the gambling gentry turned its attention to horse racing. George Trussell, the gambling czar, became the managing owner of Dexter, a record trotting horse. On September 3, 1866, Dexter was entered in a trotting race which offered a purse of five-thousand dollars. Trussell had promised his mistress, Mollie, that he would return home early after the race. As a madame of a well-known parlor house, Mollie was constantly dealing in faithlessness on the part of her customers, but Mollie would brook no faithlessness from her lover. When Trussell failed to return at the appointed hour, she immediately had visions of a rival. When the prosperous, fastidiously-dressed gambler finally made his appearance at the entrance of Price's Livery Stable, Mollie opened fire. Trussell dropped dead. The murder was headline news from the east coast to the west, but Mollie never spent one day in prison and was soon running her brothel again.[14]

A few days later, on September 22, 1866, during the deciding heat of a trotting race, an unknown person knocked the driver of one of the horses from his sulky. The victim's body was found on the track, his head crushed. The murderer had vanished into the darkness which engulfed the track before the final heat began. The plot availed the gamblers nothing, however, since all bets were declared nullified.[15]

With George Trussell, Chicago's most powerful gambler, removed from the scene, Captain Hyman's star ascended. Shortly after the murder of his rival, Captain Hyman was married to a madame, known as gentle Annie Stafford, who had been one of Mollie's chief competitors. The wedding was an elaborate affair. The captain and his wife announced the purchase of a fancy roadhouse called Sunnyside at North Clark Street and Montrose Boulevard. The opening was a gala affair and the large number of city officials who attended gave evidence of the political significance that was attached to gambling, as well as to the oldest profession. The guest of honor was Jack Nelson, Chicago's deputy superintendent of police. In the early part of the evening decorum prevailed, but following the elaborate banquet at midnight, with champagne flowing freely, the demimonde, gamblers and distinguished guests could restrain themselves no longer. The party ended in a glorious brawl and for several days officials were busy issuing warrants for assault and battery.[16]

But neither the absence of civic virtue nor the ravages of civil war could retard Chicago's rapid growth. In fact, war had merely served to accelerate its material progress. As the supply center for the great army of the West, men and money had poured into Chicago to furnish the needs of the armed forces. Its population of 109,420 in 1860 had almost doubled by 1866 and had jumped to 298,977 by 1870. The city's thoroughfares were more congested than ever. Bridges which spanned the winding river that separated the downtown section from the West and North Sides were always overcrowded. Something had to be done to speed up traffic. Men of action decided to construct tunnels under the river. The first one, running east and west, was built on Washington Street at a cost of $517,000 and was ready for use on January 1, 1869. A similar project was started on LaSalle Street on November 3, 1869 to relieve the congestion of traffic moving north and south. The LaSalle Street tunnel, 1890 feet in length and costing $566,000, was opened for public use on July 4,

1871. Even the city hall was no longer adequate to handle the affairs of the rapidly growing municipality. In 1869 and 1870 two wings as well as another story had been added to the County Building. The city purchased the west half of this structure and remodeled it at a cost of $467,000. Locating the City Hall in the County Building was a handy arrangement for the taxpayers, who frequently had business with both city and county officials. Political bosses were also happy. Almost all of the leading politicians of both city and county were now at their beck and call under one roof.

Commerce and industry had expanded enormously during the war years. In 1860, the 469 manufacturers then located in Chicago employed 5593 men. By 1870, there were 1176 manufacturing establishments in the city, which had a payroll of 27,076 employees and turned out products valued at $83,000,000. Produce and material exported from Chicago in 1860 amounted to $33,737,489. By 1870, these exports had increased to $182,743,578. As early as 1867, only three other cities, New York, Philadelphia and Boston, outranked Chicago in the magnitude of gross returns from the sale of goods. Gross earnings of Chicago's railroads soared from $17,690,314 in 1860, to $48,886,348 in 1869.[17]

Chicagoans as always were proud of their city. And they were given to loud and incessant boasting — which was as much responsible for the nickname "the Windy City" as the steady breeze which blew off Lake Michigan. A friendly article which appeared in the *Jacksonville* [Illinois] *Journal* during this period observed that the average Chicagoan talked of his city "as the greatest place on the Western continent — the center around which all creation revolves — the great hub, in comparison with which all such hubs as Boston are too insignificant to be mentioned."

Residents of Chicago's principal rivals, St. Louis and Cincinnati, bitterly resented the exaggerated claims. Part of this resentment was based on natural jealousy. Chicago had already supplanted Cincinnati as the largest hog-butchering center of the nation. It was outstripping St. Louis in the field of commerce and industry. The feeling between St. Louis and Chicago was particularly acrid, and much of the public discussion of the relative merits of the two cities was juvenile and unworthy of the true greatness of both municipalities. However, the ill will toward Chicago was not limited to citizens of its natural rivals. It was not based entirely on civic jealousy or the boasting of the city's self-appointed emissaries. Said the *Jacksonville Journal:*

What are the causes of all the ill-feeling which exists against Chicago, we do not propose to discuss; probably the many scamps and rascals who hail from there, and go through the country cheating people, have given to Chicago, in the minds of some persons, an unenviable reputation. . . .[18]

If Chicago's reputation was bad, its business was good. Its rapid growth had captured the imagination of America and the world. Its leaders possessed foresight, daring and a touch of genius. The majority of its people were substantial, hard-working citizens. Regardless of its crime, its filth and its deficiencies in civic virtue, Chicago had established itself among the great cities of the land.

CHAPTER IV

An Era of Violence, Destruction and Machine Politics

AS the sun rose over Lake Michigan on October 8, 1871, everything was peaceful and quiet in Chicago. It was Sunday, and before long the city's 175 churches of various denominations would be providing places of worship for almost half of Chicago's 300,000 residents. Among those who would be sitting in church pews that morning were a few who had been a part of Chicago since its beginning less than four decades earlier. Walking or riding to their churches they could see around them everywhere physical evidence of a great city — the Chamber of Commerce Building, spacious hotels, theaters, railroad terminals, fine residences, and the city's 27 bridges which had been built over the river to handle the traffic to and from the business center. Chicago was truly a great city. On October 8, 1871, its possibilities for future development appeared unlimited. Then within the space of a few hours this great municipality — the pride of American industry, imagination and ambitious free enterprise — lay in a shambles of ashes and smoldering embers.

A small fire broke out in the two-story barn of Patrick O'Leary in the rear of 137 De Koven Street about 9:05 P.M. on that Sunday, October eighth. Under ordinary circumstances the fire would not have been particularly serious. But during the preceding summer very little rain had fallen. The frame buildings of the city were as dry as tinder. A strong wind was blowing and the flames whipped from building to building. Within a short time a three-pronged inferno was rushing onward destroying everything in its path. Fire-fighting equipment was totally inadequate to cope with the rapidly spreading conflagration. Many of the fire engines were enveloped in the flames and destroyed. The torrent of fire soon overtook the Chamber of Commerce Building, the Sherman House, Hooley's Theater, and the County Courthouse. The main telegraph office was located in the Merchants Insurance Building. Operators were frantically sending messages throughout the nation describing the progress of the fire and pleading for help. Many of the messages were unfinished. The building caught on fire and the operators dashed from the structure barely in time to save their lives. A second prong of the fire engulfed the Michigan Southern depot, the Grand Pacific Hotel, the post office and the New Bigelow House. A third path of destruction wiped out residences and churches on Wabash and Michigan Avenues. Both the *Tribune* and the *Times* buildings were destroyed. Masses of glowing timbers were crashing every-where. About three o'clock in the morning the waterworks caught and soon lay in ruins, making the fire fighting even more difficult.

When the jail caught fire, thieves and robbers were turned loose; many of them began looting or became drunk and riotous, adding to the general turmoil. All night Sunday and all day Monday the fire raged. About three o'clock in the morning on Tuesday, October tenth, rain began to fall and the fire was at last extinguished. By that time much of the city was in ruins: an area covering 2024 acres of land was leveled by the fire, which had extended over 73 miles of city streets. At least 18,000 buildings were destroyed, including the homes of 100,000 people. Three hundred persons were believed to have lost their lives. Property losses totaled $200,000,000.

During and following the fire, Chicago's huge criminal population had a field day. Business houses were robbed. Everything in sight was stolen. Hoodlums from other localities poured in to take ad-vantage of the disorganization. Mayor Roswell B. Mason sought aid from the United States Government and the city was placed under martial law by General P. H. Sheridan.[1]

For a few hours only, the spirit of the people appeared broken, then as relief began pouring into Chicago from all over the world, the prostrate city began to give evidence of renewed life. The resolute character of its citizens reasserted itself, and they demanded, first of all, a strong and efficient government.

On November 7, 1871, less than a month after the disaster, a city election was held. Joseph Medill, a distinguished citizen with an excellent record, running on a "Union Fire-Proof" ticket, was elected mayor. Never had a chief executive of a major city confronted a more formidable task. The entire city was in need of rebuilding. Schoolhouses, police stations, bridges, miles of sidewalk, a city hall and fire fighting equipment — all destroyed by the fire — had to be replaced. And the city treasury was depleted.[2] The public also demanded protection from the thieves, confidence men, gamblers and gunmen who had made Chicago their headquarters. In keeping with his campaign promises, Mayor Medill's first official act was to close the gaming houses, which comprised the backbone of the underworld.[3]

Sincere efforts to suppress gambling and to enforce the laws generally continued throughout Medill's administration. Conditions were most unfavorable, however, for any program of rigid law enforcement. With an entire city in need of rebuilding, work was plentiful and wages high. For several months during the spring and summer of 1872, mechanics, carpenters, bricklayers and day laborers swarmed into Chicago at the rate of almost 5000 each week. And with each trainload of newcomers came more underworld characters. The instability that prevailed in the city gave them effective cover. The police department, consisting now of 450 men, faced an almost impossible task. Following the fire many of the streets were impassable for several months. Old landmarks were obliterated. The charred ruins of thousands of buildings served as hideouts for burglars, holdup men and murderers.

Society itself was demoralized. Of the thousands of citizens who saw all of their worldly possessions go up in smoke, many lost all hope for the future. They often resorted to reckless and sometimes vulgar dissipation. Drunkenness became a major problem. Saloons, concert halls, brothels and gambling dens, like vultures, sought to exploit the misery and despair of the population. Conditions prompted a group of leading citizens and clergymen to form a Committee of Seventy to battle crime and the abuses of the liquor industry. Another group, the Committee of Twenty-five, was formed to improve the moral fabric of the city.[4]

Meantime Mayor Medill's warfare against the lawless element, in spite of tremendous obstacles, continued to meet with considerable success. Many of the notorious gambling houses were permanently closed.[5] The Medill administration thus incurred the bitter enmity of the entire professional gambling fraternity and of the liquor interests. When the mayor pressed his campaign against them the gamblers, saloonkeepers and criminal element united for political action. They held a mass meeting in Kingsbury Hall on September 27, 1873, and adopted a platform of principles favorable to the liquor interests in particular. At the polls on November 4 they managed the election of Harvey D. Colvin as mayor. The sporting element affectionately called the new mayor by his first name. The gambling chiefs and dive operators expected to reap the rewards of their victory, and they did not have long to wait. "Saloons were virtually freed from municipal surveillance . . . gambling hells and brothels flourished and vice held high carnival." [6] The city again became a happy hunting ground for criminals of every stripe. Even Colvin's superintendent of police caught the spirit of the time: He became involved in a whiskey fraud conspiracy against the government.[7]

The gambling and liquor interests, closely allied with the underworld, had demonstrated a political power of tremendous strength — a power which was to play an increasingly important role in the affairs of government in the years to come. One of the mayor's staunchest supporters was Michael Cassius McDonald, whom we met at the "Irish Rally" in 1861, and who was now, during the Colvin regime, king of Chicago gamblers. McDonald was the boss to whom tribute had to be paid by anyone wishing to engage in the gambling business. The underworld was at last getting organized in a big way.

As in 1861, the people again looked to the state government for help and the state legislature passed an act which was designed to reorganize the city government of Chicago. This act was submitted to the people at the city election on April 23, 1875, and adopted. Under its provisions the Board of Police Commissioners which had controlled the Chicago Police Department since 1861 was voted out of existence. The police board, which had come into being during the second administration of Long John Wentworth because of public alarm over widespread crime and police inefficiency, was now, fourteen years later, abolished because of more lawlessness and police ineptitude. Actually it was of small moment whether a board of police commissioners did or did not control the administration of the Chicago Police Department. The underworld had helped elect a mayor. Naturally, it was able to exert considerable influence over the police department and its policies. In reality, the police department had been demobilized for effective action against law violators. The numerous unsolved crimes which alarmed the public and discredited the Colvin administration were the inevitable products of a political system which closely allied political power with the underworld. It was a system which was to become a permanent fixture in Chicago and to give the city its reputation as the crime capital of the nation.

The new city charter of 1875 threw the political affairs of Chicago into a temporary state of confusion. One of the provisions in the charter changed the date of city elections from November to the third Tuesday in April. A dispute immediately arose as to when the next mayoralty election should be held. Some 25,000 voters attended a mass meeting at Exposition Hall and decided that the next election would be held in April 1876. At this April election, Thomas Hoyne was overwhelmingly elected mayor and out of thirty-six aldermen only eight Colvin partisans were successful. Colvin promptly challenged the legality of the election, and for over two months Chicago had two mayors, Harvey D. Colvin and Thomas Hoyne. An appeal to the courts resulted in a decision upholding Colvin's contention. Consequently a special election was held in July 1876, and the Republican candidate, Monroe Heath, a leading merchant and manufacturer, won out.

When Heath took office the affairs of the city were in a sad state. Uncollected taxes amounted to $5,469,576. Losses through defalcations on the part of two former officials, a city treasurer and a city collector, totaled over $400,000. The finances of the city were so shaky that an ordinance was passed by the city council to light only half of the street lamps. Fortunately the mayor vetoed this proposal. Salaries of all municipal officers were reduced from twenty-five to fifty per cent, while some offices were abolished. The prevailing hard times and the high costs of former misgovernment made the people economy minded.[8]

Unstable economic conditions were by no means confined to Chicago, however. The nation was again in the throes of a depression. During the Presidential campaign of 1876, the major issues concerned economic and financial matters. The Republican national platform emphasized programs intended to insure commercial prosperity and preserve the national credit. The Democrats charged the Republicans with financial imbecility and wasting the nation's resources. The Greenback party demanded the rescue of the country's industries from ruin and disaster.

At the regular city election in April 1877, Mayor Monroe Heath was returned to office by a majority of 11,432 votes, at a time when industrial unrest was rapidly spreading throughout the land. In July 1877, a general strike was called in Pittsburgh. Just grievances of workers were whipped into a white flame of anger by incendiary speeches of agitators. Mob action followed and hundreds of people were killed. Railroad shops were taken by storm and 125 first class locomotives destroyed. When the state militia was called out, the mob turned in a body on the armed forces of the state and forced them to flee in a rout. There was rioting in Allegheny City, Wilkes-Barre and Harrisburg. Trouble was also brewing in Cincinnati and St. Louis.

Chicagoans followed the developments in Pittsburgh with interest. During this period Chicago was politically the most radical city in the country. Its Socialist Labor party believed in extreme measures, even bloodshed, to attain an improvement in the workingman's lot. Radicals such as Albert R. Parsons furnished the leadership for the Socialist Labor party. These men were experienced agitators of no mean ability.[9] On Sunday, July 22, 1877, the *Chicago News*, which had started regular publication as a newspaper in January 1876, came out with an extra carrying the latest news from Pittsburgh. That night mass meetings held under the direction of the Socialist Labor party passed resolutions sympathizing with the Pittsburgh strikers. Alarmed at the inflammatory nature of the speeches, citizens implored Mayor Heath to suppress any further meetings. Heath refused on the ground that the agitators were merely exercising their constitutional right of free speech.

On Monday night, July 23, at a mass meeting attended by 5000 persons, the harangues of Albert R. Parsons and other radical leaders found an eager and sympathetic audience. Early Tuesday morning mobs began to form, while groups of men went from place to place demanding that laborers cease work immediately. Conditions grew more serious hour by hour. The city police force, consisting of 481 patrolmen and their commanding officers, were unable to restore order. As always, Chicago's huge criminal population took full advantage of the prevailing chaos. Of the mobs that angrily marched through the streets, hundreds were hardened criminals. Holdup men pillaged the gun store of H. J. Pribyl at 522 Halsted Street and stole hundreds of guns of every description. At another mass meeting on Wednesday, July 25, 1877, Carter H. Harrison, then a member of Congress, charged that while a few laboring men had started the strike it was "the idlers, thieves, and ruffians" who were carrying it on. At a special meeting of the city council on the same day, resolutions urgently asked all citizens to aid the police. The mayor appealed for help to the governor of the state and the United States government. Companies of militia and a battalion of United States Army regulars were dispatched to Chicago to help restore order. By July twenty-fifth there were at least 20,000 men under arms in the city and pitched battles were being fought between the rioters, the police and the soldiers. Four hundred men surrounded the Chicago, Burlington and Quincy Railroad roundhouse, smashing windows, wrecking locomotives and cars, even making efforts to burn entire buildings. Assaults were made on the McCormick reaper factory and on packing houses in the stockyards. Order was finally restored two days later. By that time hospitals were filled with injured and wounded men. From twenty-five to thirty-five persons had been killed and three hundred rioters had been arrested.[10]

The riots had thoroughly frightened the people. For almost a week the citizens of Chicago had been at the mercy of angry, howling mobs. It was evident that the police department was not equipped to cope with serious disorders, that its size had failed to keep pace with the tremendous growth of the city. Within the five-year period which elapsed between the great fire in 1871 and the inauguration of Mayor Heath in 1876, Chicago's population had grown to 407,661, an increase of over 100,000. After the riots the public demanded a larger police force, but no public funds were available to hire more policemen. The city council, however, passed an ordinance authorizing the mayor and the finance committee to borrow money to add 100 mounted police officers to the department.[11]

The troublesome times of 1877 and the fiscal difficulties which beset the city probably discouraged the political aspirations of Mayor Heath. When the parties began making preparations for the city election of 1879, Heath refused to be a candidate. Bloodshed, riots and city debts did not discourage such opportunists as Mike McDonald, however. With the election of Harvey D. Colvin as mayor in 1873, McDonald had demonstrated that under proper leadership, the gamblers, liquor interests and brothelkeepers could be welded into a formidable political power. Under the Colvin administration, these groups had enjoyed wild prosperity. Important municipal offices were filled with friends of McDonald's and his crowd. A temporary setback occurred with the election of Mayor Heath, but during Heath's administration McDonald had been active consolidating the gains he had made during Colvin's term of office. By 1879, he was ready to emerge as one of the most powerful figures in Chicago's turbulent political history.

Mike McDonald was only fifteen years old when he first came to Chicago about 1854. He gained business experience early in his career as a news butcher and candy vendor on railroad trains. This boy had an imagination which was not circumscribed by a troublesome conscience or any ethical standards. Half-filled boxes of candy, glass jewelry and fake prize packages the youthful Mike sold in large quantities. He developed a glib tongue and a philosophy of life which held that a sucker should never be given a break. This was to remain his philosophy throughout a career which raised him successively from a news butcher to a swindling blackleg; from a gambling house proprietor to the political boss of Chicago. By the time the Civil War started, McDonald had demonstrated qualities of leadership, particularly among the Irish immigrant group. Throughout the war years, he steadily grew in stature within the ranks of the city's gambling fraternity.

It was McDonald who was to create Chicago's first real political machine. His elaborate gambling establishment the "Store," at Clark and Monroe Streets, became the headquarters and meeting place for leading city officials. The political destinies of mayors, senators and congressmen as well as ward leaders were in the hands of Mike McDonald. Election campaigns were financed with the money that rolled in from his faro banks, roulette wheels, chuck-a-luck cages, dice and card games. The underworld rallied to the support of candidates endorsed by the party known as "Mike McDonald's Democrats." He purchased a newspaper, the *Chicago Globe*, which he used to help sell his candidates to the electorate. He became treasurer of the Lake Street Elevated Railroad Company, which was known among the gamblers as "Mike's Upstairs Railroad." [12] Mike McDonald had arrived at a position of great wealth and power, and his name was linked with some of Chicago's best-known official personages.

In the 1879 election, Carter H. Harrison was chosen as the standard bearer for Mike McDonald's Democrats for the first time. Harrison received 25,685 votes to 20,496 for his Republican opponent, Abner M. Wright. The Socialist party candidate, Dr. Ernest Schmidt, polled 11,829 votes. Harrison had moved to Chicago from Kentucky in 1858. He had attended Yale University and by training was a lawyer. However, it was as a real estate dealer that he gained wealth in Chicago. He had served as a member of the county commissioner's court and been elected to Congress in 1874, and re-elected in 1876. "Our Carter," as the new mayor was affectionately called by his admirers, was a colorful figure with tremendous vote appeal. The slouch hat which he generally wore stamped him as one of the common herd — a considerable virtue in American political life. The Chicago voters frequently watched their 225 pound mayor astride his favorite horse, riding furiously through the city streets. "Our Carter" knew how to endear himself to his people. But more important, the machine politicians loved him and his policies. Harrison was an ardent advocate of the "wide open town." Saloons, beer gardens and dives of every description were permitted to stay open day and night with little if any restrictions. Prostitution flourished, with two thousand places operating. Many of them were disorderly and gunplay was frequent. [13]

This was another era of rare prosperity for the professional gamesters. Carter Harrison served four consecutive terms as mayor, from 1879 to 1887. The alliance between the gambling interests and the professional politicians proved to be the backbone of a political organization that was unbeatable at the polls. Now gambling also became strongly organized. Mike McDonald formed a bookmaking syndicate with the Hankins brothers and Harry "Prince Hal" Varnell which controlled gambling at the Chicago and Indiana race tracks. The venture was highly profitable, the syndicate clearing as much as three fourths of a million dollars in one year. Prince Hal operated one of the most elaborately furnished gambling houses in Chicago at 119 North Clark Street.

Like his syndicate partner, Mike McDonald, Varnell was influential politically, and in 1880 served as warden of the Cook County Insane Asylum. He spent money lavishly transforming the institution into an asylum for worthy politicians, several of whom actually lived there. It became a favorite haunt for many of the prominent political figures of the time. But the misuse of public funds was so flagrant that even Mike McDonald's political influence could not save Varnell from the toils of the law, and he served a year in the Illinois State Penitentiary at Joliet.[14]

As the mayoralty campaigns began in the spring of 1883, public attention focused on the character of the political organization backing Carter Harrison. The newspapers charged that Mayor Harrison's campaigns were "conducted by the gamblers, under the leadership of McDonald and Joseph C. Mackin, who controlled the party machinery, and certain aldermen who had the worst elements of the population subject to their commands." [15] "Oyster Joe" Mackin had been influential in First Ward politics for quite some time. His saloon on Dearborn Street was a favorite hangout for politicians, and many questionable political deals were hatched there. (He got his nickname from his practice of giving away an oyster with each drink.)

The political power of Mike McDonald and his underworld cohorts was formidable, and his wealth by now was fabulous. But with all his power and riches, he could not buy respectability. Some of the more substantial citizens began to rebel against a political leadership which was dominated by gamblers and social parasites. They formed a committee representative of both major parties and held meetings in Fairbank Hall in the Central Music Hall Building. They became known as the "Fairbank Hall Silk Stockings." Before the election of April 1883, the Fairbank Hall group gave their support to Eugene Cary, the Republican candidate, to oppose Carter Harrison. "Our Carter" had been renominated by acclamation by Mike McDonald's Democrats. The election was fraught with excitement, but out of 72,189 votes cast, Carter Harrison received a majority of 10,263 and began serving his third consecutive term as mayor.[16]

Professional gamblers never gamble. They always insist on a sure thing. This is true whether they are operating roulette wheels, chuck-a-luck cages or dice games. It is equally true when they are active in politics. Vote frauds are always prevalent whenever the gambling interests become an integral part of a political organization. The outcome of doubtful wards or precincts can be made certain by the simple expedient of manipulating election returns. And during the two decades that Mike McDonald remained at the helm of gambling and politics in Chicago, fraudulent activities frequently impaired the integrity of the ballot box.[17]

In 1884 an election fraud trial in Federal court in Chicago attracted national attention. That year the state legislature was to elect a United States Senator and consequently the Federal government had an interest in this state election. After the ballot box of the Second Precinct of the Eighteenth Ward had been placed in the custody of the county clerk, the original ballots were removed and forged ballots substituted. A forged tally sheet corresponded with the changed results. Interest in the Federal trial that followed was intensified because one of Mike McDonald's close associates was a principal defendant. Joseph C. Mackin was accused of having conspired with others to perpetrate the election fraud. Only a year earlier "Oyster Joe" and McDonald had been in control of the party machinery which had elected Carter Harrison mayor for the third consecutive term. But neither Mackin's political prestige nor his association with McDonald could assure him immunity in the Federal court. He was convicted and sentenced to the penitentiary for two years. While this case was pending on appeal to the United States Supreme Court, the Cook County Grand Jury indicted Mackin for perjury. He was convicted and sentenced to the Illinois State Penitentiary in Joliet for a term of five years. Again he appealed, but his conviction was upheld.

In the municipal election of 1885 there was also evidence of intimidation of voters, fraud and theft of ballot boxes. One man who stole a ballot box was apprehended and sentenced to the state penitentiary for five years. But this was small consolation in view of the large number of equally serious offenders who went undetected and unpunished.[18] Because of the scandalous vote frauds in the 1885 election it was difficult to determine which of the candidates was actually the voters' choice. The official count of the balloting credited Carter Harrison with only a microscopic majority of 375 votes out of a total of 86,329 cast.

The public was sufficiently aroused over the vote frauds and thefts to force the passage of a new law which was intended to prevent such gross irregularities in the future. The official reaction, however, was typical of Chicago statesmen's response to charges of crime and corruption. On April 23, 1885, eighteen Democratic members of the city council passed a resolution which charged that excitement over the election results had been aroused by unfair statements of partisan newspapers and rash millionaires. The resolution deplored the fact that

. . . the fair name of the city has been traduced and vilified, and the impression has been spread around that Chicago is not only a sinkhole of iniquity and corruption, but infested with thieves, bummers and ballot-box stuffers and disreputable characters generally. . . . The tendency of all these misrepresentations has been, not only to injure the fair credit and standing of the city, but drive away trade that has its natural market here. . . .

It was therefore resolved that

. . . the city council hereby most vehemently denounces such utterances and characterizes them as malicious and unfounded. . . . We can most confidently and truthfully assure people in all parts of the country, that not only are the lives and property of our citizens perfectly secure and safe, but also that our city is less infested with crime and lawlessness than any city in the United States, in proportion to its population. . . .[19]

But throughout the next sixty-six years, at least, organized crime and corruption would continue to flourish in Chicago. Hundreds of gang murders would give the city nationwide notoriety. And city officials would continue to denounce bitterly any publicity relating to disgraceful conditions as an effort to besmirch the "fair name of the city."

With Carter Harrison's election to the post of mayor for a fourth term, he could properly take pride in the fact that no Chicagoan had been similarly honored before. He was also justly proud of the city over which he presided. In size, it now ranked fourth in the nation. By 1880, during Harrison's first term, Chicago's population had passed the half million mark with an official count of 503,185. Within the city boundaries were 23,040 acres of land, of which 789 were devoted to public parks. Even the great fire of 1871, which had virtually destroyed the entire city, had proved to be but a temporary obstacle in its surge toward greatness. Of criminals there were still too many; of prostitutes, panders, thugs and gamblers the city still had many more than its share. But the average citizen gave them little thought — the prevalence of vice, crime and official corruption was casually ascribed to the youthful virility of a swiftly expanding municipality.

Chicago's social and political ills had attracted undesirables other than members of the underworld. By 1886 more anarchists had settled in Chicago than in any other city in the nation. While the members of this group probably did not exceed three thousand, several of the leaders were skilled agitators who incited a considerable amount of discontent. Heading the list of anarchist leaders were Albert R. Parsons of the Socialist Labor party, a prominent figure in the riots of 1877; Michael Schwab of *Die Arbeiter Zeitung;* Samuel Fielden, an ex-Methodist minister; Oscar Neebe, the organizer of the Beer Wagon Drivers; Adolph Fischer, a printer; George Engel, a toymaker; Louis Lingg, a Carpenters' Union organizer; and August Spies. For some time previous to the election of 1885, the Socialist Labor party had representation in the city council, although it was weak and ineffective. In the 1885 election, all Socialist Labor candidates were badly defeated. The anarchist leaders immediately screamed that political action was futile. Votes, they said, would not bring relief to the laboring man. Instead of ballots, the workingman should henceforth use dynamite, firearms and arson to bring the capitalists to terms. They talked incessantly of the impending revolution which would wipe out the intolerable class barriers that separated employees from employers.

Their arguments were frequently incoherent, inconsistent and illogical, but they fell on sympathetic ears. Times were hard. The winter of 1885–1886 was a severe one. Hungry, jobless men wandered about the streets in an aimless manner. Mayor Harrison opened soup kitchens to feed them. On Christmas day in 1885, anarchists organized a parade which marched down fashionable Prairie Avenue as a protest against the workingman's lot. The Knights of Labor sang their war songs in saloons and in the city streets.

It was during this period that the eight-hour-day movement was gaining momentum throughout America. In Chicago, the agitation for acceptance of the eight-hour day was particularly intense and the leadership rested almost solely in the hands of the anarchists. Albert R. Parsons and Samuel Fielden spoke before huge labor rallies during the winter and early spring of 1886. Red flags, symbols of the people's revolutionary spirit, were prominently displayed at rallies on the lake front. The Board of Trade inopportunely opened a palatial new building at the foot of LaSalle Street on April 28, 1886, thereby immediately becoming the target of abuse from Parsons and Fielden, who dubbed it the "Board of Thieves."

Labor trouble had been brewing in the McCormick reaper works for some time. In February 1886, there was a lockout, and one of the labor groups affected was Louis Lingg's Carpenters' Union. Lingg was an outspoken anarchist and he fervently believed in the use of violence to advance the workingman's cause. On May 3, 1886, a crowd gathered near the reaper works. Feeling ran high. Inside the factory were nonunion men who had been hired to replace those locked out. August Spies was addressing the mob on the outside when the factory whistle blew and the nonunion workers poured out of the plant. A pitched battle immediately took place. The police hurried to the scene of disorder and opened fire on the crowd, killing several persons and wounding others.

August Spies rushed to the office of *Die Arbeiter Zeitung* and prepared a revenge circular. On the morning of May 4, the front page of *Die Arbeiter Zeitung* screamed for lead, powder and blood. Leaflets were circulated calling for a protest meeting that night in Haymarket Square. Mayor Harrison remembered the riots of 1877 and sincerely wanted to avoid the violence which had disgraced the city nine years earlier. About 3000 persons attended the meeting in Haymarket Square. The mayor counseled moderation and displayed a sympathetic understanding of the workingman's plight. As the anarchist leaders were delivering their harangues to the assem-

blage, rain began to fall. The crowd dwindled and by about ten
o'clock only 500 people remained. Mayor Harrison left the meeting and walked to the police station. He expressed the opinion that
nothing was likely to occur and departed. A few minutes later, 176
police officers were ordered by an inspector to march on Haymarket Square. Samuel Fielden was in the midst of a speech when
a police captain approached the speaker's stand and ordered him
to stop. The captain told the crowd to disperse. There was a moment
of silence, then a flash and a deafening explosion. A bomb had been
hurled from the alley near the speaker's stand. Bedlam broke loose.
The police officers opened fire upon the crowd. Workmen returned
the fire. Within two or three minutes sixty-seven policemen were
wounded, many seriously. Seven of them died. The exact number
of casualties among the workers was never determined.

For once the police of Chicago could not be described as "helpless," but their drastic action had far-reaching consequences. The
people of Chicago were stunned and outraged. From the press, the
pulpit and the man on the street came loud demands to hang the
anarchists. The Chicago Knights of Labor issued official statements
denouncing the anarchists and expressing the hope that this "gang
of outlaws" would be "blotted from the face of the earth." The entire police force of 924 officers was turned loose to raid anarchist
hangouts. Scores of bombs were located and seized. Chicago wheels
of justice moved swiftly. Indictments were returned against Albert
R. Parsons, Michael Schwab, Samuel Fielden, August Spies, Adolph
Fischer, George Engel, Louis Lingg, Oscar Neebe, William Seliger
and Rudolph Schnaubelt. (The charges against Seliger were later
dismissed and Schnaubelt fled to Europe.) On August 19, 1886, a
jury found Parsons, Spies, Lingg, Fielden, Schwab, Fischer and
Engel guilty, and Judge Joseph E. Cary sentenced them to death.
Oscar Neebe, also found guilty, was given a sentence of fifteen
years in the penitentiary. When Louis Lingg was asked to address
the court, he defiantly boasted of his hatred for the judge, the laws
and authority. Lingg screamed, "Hang me for it!" And as if to
carry his contempt of the courts and laws to a logical conclusion,
on the day he was scheduled to be hanged, Lingg exploded a per-
cussion cap in his mouth, blowing off his head. On the same day,
November 10, 1887, the Governor of Illinois commuted the sen-

tences of Schwab and Fielden to life imprisonment. On the following morning, Parsons, Engel, Spies and Fischer walked to the gallows and were hanged. The last words spoken by Engel were, "Hurrah for anarchy!"

The Haymarket Riot and the subsequent trials and executions attracted world-wide attention. In America there was a great revulsion against the labor movement. Within a month after the tragedy, the Knights of Labor lost 200,000 members. Strikes that were called ended in failure. Lockouts became commonplace. The labor movement was set back an entire generation.

During the twentieth century, however, gangsters were to take a leaf out of the book of the Haymarket Square anarchists. Dynamite and bombs were to become effective weapons in the hands of gangsters in their fight to dominate labor unions and trade associations and to control rackets of every nature. And in no American city were dynamite and bombs to be more commonly used by the criminal classes than in Chicago, the home of the Haymarket Riot.[20]

The carnage at Haymarket Square was still fresh in the public mind when it was time for the mayoralty campaign to begin in the spring of 1887. Nobody appreciated the possible effects of the Haymarket tragedy on the Chicago voter better than Carter Harrison, a masterful politician. Following the riots of 1877, Mayor Monroe Heath had refused to run for re-election. When Carter Harrison was again offered the Democratic nomination for mayor in 1887, he unexpectedly declined, leaving his party without a candidate. In these circumstances the Republican candidate, John A. Roche, had little difficulty in winning the election by an overwhelming majority.

The new mayor had been a successful businessman. He had promised the voters that if elected he would give them an economical administration, that public gambling would be suppressed and disreputable saloons closed.[21] Immediately upon taking the oath of office, Mayor Roche set out to fulfill his campaign pledges. His drive against the professional gamblers was effective. They left the city in hordes. With them fled thugs and disreputables of every variety. This was a severe blow to the operators of big gambling establishments. It meant a large reduction of income to Mike McDonald, in particular. And the failure of his Democratic party to

run a candidate in the 1887 mayoralty election left his immediate
political future uncertain. But Mike McDonald soon recovered from
this sudden turn of events. Many of the politicians who remained
in office were still under his control, and he continued to dominate
the machinery of the Democratic party, which was far from im-
potent in city and county affairs. With a typical gambler's attitude,
McDonald reasoned that his streak of bad luck must inevitably be
followed by good fortune. After having placed innumerable officeholders on the city payroll, he now had visions of giving himself the
prestige and honor that accompanies high office. And so Mike
McDonald began to lay plans to get elected to Congress.

But fate was again unkind. Before he could achieve his ambition,
a scandal broke which blasted his hopes of becoming a leading statesman in the nation's capital. A gang of political vultures, of which
McDonald was the ringleader, offered to paint the county building
with a secret fluid which was intended to preserve the bricks and
stones of the structure. Bribes were offered to the Board of Aldermen and the Board of County Commissioners as an inducement to
enter into the contract. The secret fluid came highly recommended,
since its inventor was Harry S. Holland, Mike McDonald's right-
hand man. When a bill was presented to the county for $128,250 the
public learned that a huge fraud had been perpetrated. The secret
fluid was largely colored water. Its preservative value was equal
to the precipitation frequently sprayed on the building gratuitously
from the skies. A few of the boodlers were sent to prison, but
McDonald was so powerful that he was not even prosecuted. However, the public clamor against the fraud made it inexpedient for
him to launch his campaign for a seat in Congress.

The election of Mayor Roche in 1887 had severely injured the
gamblers financially. Political scandals involving McDonald and his
associates had damaged their prestige. But Chicago gamblers headed
by McDonald still constituted a political influence with which any
realist had to reckon seriously. The successful efforts of Mayor
Roche in suppressing their activities called for concerted action.
And in the spring elections of 1889: "The gamblers were a unit
against him, and were prepared to assist in defeating him for re-
election not only by solid financial aid but by the employment of
every devious means known to the disreputable ward politician." [22]

Their organized efforts brought about the defeat of Roche and the election of his Democratic opponent, DeWitt C. Cregier.

With Cregier safely in the mayor's chair for two years, Chicago's gambling industry embarked upon a program of expansion. Gambling house proprietors entered into two-year leases, "in some cases giving the previous tenants a bonus to move out." Partitions were removed, entrances enlarged and new stairways built to accommodate the crowds of patrons. Having been instrumental in electing the chief executive of the city, the professional gamesters were assured of friendly law enforcement policies. Profits would again be high. One notorious establishment maintained an average of forty men on its payroll, and had twenty gaming tables in full operation at one time. This place catered almost exclusively to poor laboring men. In fact, the patrons of this den were commonly known as the "dinner pail brigade." Yet the annual net profits of this one gaming house amounted to a quarter of a million dollars.

The blacklegs were well organized. Mike McDonald headed what was commonly referred to as the "gamblers' trust." Each week the various gaming house proprietors paid into a pool either a fixed sum of money or a stipulated percentage of the profits. Individually, the gamblers were growing rich. Collectively, their power was reaching menacing proportions. As usual, however, the huge profits enjoyed by the gamesters only whetted their appetites for still greater riches. In July 1890, gamblers specializing in selling pools on horse races began fighting over control of this lucrative business, in which one of the biggest operators cleared $190,000 during the 1889 racing season. Not satisfied with this meager sum, in 1890 he decided to remove all competition. He hired private detectives to suppress the activities of his rivals. His competitors, in retaliation, enlisted the aid of the Chicago Police Department to put an end to his operations. Charges and counter-charges were filed in the courts, and the resulting scandal seriously impaired public confidence in the mayor and his administration.[23] The gamblers, however, were so powerful that scandals did not disrupt their operations. Over 2000 joints ran wide open. Play at the gaming tables was fast and stakes were high. Disputes were frequently settled with six-shooters.[24]

Throughout Cregier's term of office, there was much agitation among the civic leaders for action which would bring the world's fair to Chicago. For some time plans had been under discussion in Congress for a world's fair to commemorate the four-hundredth anniversary of Columbus's discovery of America. At the beginning it was generally conceded that the exposition would be held in New York City. There were many New Yorkers who wanted the fair but the interest in New York City as a whole was not great. St. Louis and Washington, D. C. were also contenders for the honor of acting as host to the World's Columbian Exposition. With its customary smug feeling of superiority — to the eyes of Chicagoans, at least — New York City unenthusiastically raised $5,000,000 to defray the cost of the fair and confidently awaited the grand opening there. However, youthful and brash Chicago saw in the world's fair a golden opportunity to advertise the city. On July 22, 1889, the city council passed a resolution urging the location of the fair in Chicago, and a Committee of One Hundred was promptly formed to induce Congress to award the Columbian Exposition to Chicago. With their usual zeal, Chicagoans threw themselves into the contest, which became particularly bitter after the formal introduction of the World's Fair Bill in the United States Senate in December 1889. Chicagoans referred contemptuously to the $5,000,000 raised by New York and promised to double that amount. Congress was impressed with Chicago's representations and on February 24, 1890, selected the midwestern metropolis as the place for the Exposition.

A tract of land covering an area of 645 acres, about seven miles south of the City Hall, was chosen as the Exposition site. Bounded on the east by Lake Michigan, the land was little more than a huge marsh, a veritable wilderness covered by tangled undergrowth and unsightly trees. This swamp had to be drained. Canals and lagoons had to be built; grass, flowers and shrubs, planted. Very few people could have envisioned the transformation of this ugly plot of land, located at Jackson Park and the Midway Plaisance, into a place of beauty within a period of a few months. There were improved parks in the city that could have served as the site for the fair. But Chicagoans' love of bigness probably was a deciding factor in making Jackson Park the choice. They boasted that the site of 645 acres in area covered "nearly three times the space of any previous exposition." They proudly pointed out that there would be 5,000,000 square feet under roof, "nearly twice as much as the greatest exposition of the past." The vast undertaking of constructing the numerous buildings commenced on July 2, 1891, with the Mines Building. In short order, Daniel H. Burnham, Director of Works, had construction started on scores of Exposition buildings. The coming fair became the talk of the town.[25]

With the thoughts of most people centered on the Exposition, politicians gazed with longing eyes on the mayor's chair. To be remembered as Chicago's world's fair mayor was an honor that any chief executive would covet. The municipal election of 1891 afforded an opportunity to gain political strength that would be extremely important in the mayoralty contest two years hence. Gambling scandals had marred the administration of DeWitt Cregier, but he had strong backing and sought re-election. Carter Harrison, four times mayor, also threw his hat in the ring. Both Cregier and Harrison claimed to be the "regular nominee" of the Democratic party. Hempstead Washburne, who had served as city attorney for two terms from 1885 to 1889, became the Republican candidate. At the election on April 7, 1891, a total of 136,476 votes were cast for the three highest candidates, Washburne, Cregier and Harrison. With the Democrats dividing their votes between Cregier and Harrison, Washburne won, defeating Cregier by only 369 votes and Harrison, who ran third, by 4026 votes.

The Washburne administration naturally concentrated on preparations for the Columbian Exposition. The city wanted to make a good impression on the visitors who would throng to Chicago from all parts of the world. Its dirty streets, which had long given the city an unkempt appearance, had to be cleaned. Hundreds of miles of sidewalk had to be repaired. During the year of 1891, the city paved 117 miles of streets and built 603 miles of sidewalk. Chicago was so busy preparing for the fair that it made no effort to obtain the national conventions scheduled for 1892. Nevertheless, even without overtures from Chicago, the Democratic party decided to hold its convention there. Grover Cleveland, who had served as President of the United States from 1885 to 1889, was chosen as the party's standard bearer. Adlai Stevenson of Bloomington, Illinois, whose grandson was to become governor of Illinois in 1948, was named for the vice-presidential candidate. The Democrats won a sweeping victory at the national election, and the state of Illinois, for the first time in forty years, elected a Democratic governor, John P. Altgeld of Chicago.

Mayor Washburne, however, was confronted by so many local problems that he could not become too much concerned with either state or national politics. The job of giving the city a clean physical appearance was a herculean one, but the mayor also felt the need to remove some of the underworld activities that gave the city its bad reputation. He waged vigorous warfare against the big gamblers, who were opulent, powerful and defiant. In particular, the Garfield Park race track crowd felt the mayor's wrath. Among those vitally interested in gambling operations at Garfield Park was Prince Hal Varnell, who had served his jail term and again taken his place as a member of Mike McDonald's syndicate. The Garfield Park gamblers had strong backing in the city council. With justification, they believed they could defy the mayor as well as the local residents who loudly protested the presence of the track in the neighborhood. When police attempted to raid the place, a tough gambler drew his gun and dared the officers to arrest him. They accepted the challenge. Before the battle ended, two policemen as well as the defiant gambler were killed.[26] The scandal resulted in the permanent closing of the track.

Carter Harrison, who had ranked only third in a field of five mayoralty aspirants in 1891, again announced his intention of becoming a candidate in the municipal election of 1893. The sixty-eight-year-old veteran of many political campaigns was determined that no stone should be left unturned in order to achieve his ambition. He named as the active manager of his campaign the politician and gambler, Alderman John Powers. Powers was well versed in the art of political intrigue and manipulation. But the mastermind of the campaign was Mike McDonald, who worked directly from the Harrison headquarters at 137 West Monroe Street. To this headquarters gamblers brazenly called to pay their respects — and money, summoned there by their boss, McDonald. Big time gamblers such as Prince Hal Varnell, Johnny "Fix-em" Condon, George Hankins and Billy Skakel, all members of McDonald's gambling syndicate, were active in raising huge contributions to assure Harrison's election and a wide-open town.

The underworld from other localities did not even wait for the election before rushing in. Confidence men, prostitutes, procurers, pickpockets, gamblers, madames, saloonkeepers — all headed for Chicago eager to pluck the big "sucker" crowd expected to attend the Columbian Exposition. Chicago had taken on the appearance of a Western frontier boom town. The press, noting the financial support and activity of McDonald and his gambling fraternity in behalf of the Democratic candidate, became alarmed. They predicted that the election of Harrison would be an open invitation to widespread gambling, crime, graft and corruption.[27] Although Harrison's tradition of invincibility at the polls had been broken in 1891, his "lost touch" returned in 1893, and at the end of a bitter campaign he was declared the victor in the mayoralty race.

On the evening of April 17, 1893, Carter Harrison took the oath of office as Chicago's mayor for the fifth time. A huge throng of loyal followers gathered for the impressive ceremony. Massive floral pieces, including one of red roses blazing forth affectionately "Our Carter," decorated the setting. In an impromptu inaugural address, Harrison leveled his fire at the "reckless press" which he complained had heaped "shameless abuse" upon him during the campaign. He complimented the people who had voted for him upon their ability to exercise intelligently the rights of a free government.[28] The gamblers, however, headed by Mike McDonald and Prince Hal Varnell, were little offended by the tirades of the press. They were even less interested in the intelligence of the electorate. To win the election they had invested heavily in time, effort and money. With them it had been a business proposition pure and simple, and they lost no time in reaping fat returns on their investment. Seldom has any American city witnessed unrestrained gambling on such a big scale.

But the official lid was not removed completely. Those who had neglected to fall in line behind Mike McDonald before election learned that the eyes of the law can be ever vigilant. On the very next morning after Harrison became mayor, police raiding parties descended in force on gambling establishments in the First Ward. The new alderman, "Bathhouse John" Coughlin, had committed the unpardonable sin of postponing his advocacy of Harrison's election until the last moment. All places under his protection were invaded by the police, while the elaborate gambling emporiums of Varnell, the Hankins brothers and Mike McDonald, located in the same ward, flourished as never before.[29]

Bathhouse John Coughlin was a voluble, uncouth person of few scruples, who operated a bathhouse at 145 West Madison Street. His patrons were largely gamblers and race-track men. Coughlin now found himself in the awkward position of an official protector who was unable to protect, although only a year earlier he had been placed in the city council through the efforts of Prince Hal Varnell. Hempstead Washburne, who had served as mayor during 1891 and 1892, had taken steps to close the Garfield Park race track in which Varnell was vitally interested. Nicholas A. Cremer, then alderman of the First Ward, had failed to protect the race track gambling interests to the extent demanded by Varnell and his associates. Prince Hal therefore wanted an alderman in the First Ward who could be relied upon to work tirelessly in behalf of the race-track gamblers. At that time he felt that in John Coughlin he had such a man. Coughlin was a fanatic on horse racing and as a member of the city council he could be depended upon to wage a relentless fight to keep the Garfield Park track open. Under these circumstances Varnell decided to replace Alderman "Nicky" Cremer of the First Ward with Bathhouse John. And in the aldermanic election of 1892 Coughlin became a member of the city council.[30] A few months later, however, the same interests which had placed him in the council were responsible for the harassing raids on his gambling constituents. His power and prestige were being destroyed. Bathhouse John was dejected; his political fortunes were at a low ebb.

Among the gambling parlors in the First Ward which had been subjected to destructive police raids was one operated by Michael "Hinky Dink" Kenna above his saloon. Hinky Dink was a quiet, soft-spoken man of few words. While Alderman Coughlin had been fuming and storming in every direction, Kenna had been carefully thinking out a plan which would preserve his business. He proposed to the alderman that they form an organization which would prove attractive to the gamblers and brothel keepers of the ward. All proprietors of houses of prostitution and gambling establishments were to make regular payments to Coughlin and Kenna in consideration for protection from the authorities. A certain percentage of this money was to be utilized for the defense of any gamesters or madames who might be arrested. Two lawyers were to be placed on a retainer fee basis. Immediately upon the arrest of any Coughlin-Kenna followers these barristers were to appear in court, armed with writs of habeas corpus and ready to institute any legal maneuvers which would assure the prompt release of the law violators.

The plan favorably impressed Bathhouse John. He envisioned a steady flow of money into the coffers of his ward organization. It meant wealth and power. The First Ward defense fund was soon established. Promising attorneys, such as John Caverly, who later became a judge, received large fees and political preferment from their association with the Coughlin-Kenna organization. The alliance between Hinky Dink Kenna and Bathhouse John Coughlin formed in 1893 proved to be highly lucrative for the underworld. Strongly organized, the gamblers, procurers, thugs and sharpers of the First Ward operated with complete freedom. The formation of the syndicate was also a stroke of genius for the political fortunes of the two politicians.[31] And the year 1893 marks the beginning of one of the most fabulous political regimes in America — a regime which was to place one of Chicago's most important wards under the domination of Coughlin and Kenna for a half century.

In addition to the cheap honky-tonks, flophouses, brothels and gambling houses of the near South and West Sides of Chicago, the First Ward includes the rich downtown shopping district — fine department stores, magnificent skyscrapers, theaters, first-class restaurants, the city's best-known hotels and the largest banks. Encircling this center of business activity of America's second largest city are the elevated railway tracks. From the north, the south and the west, crowded elevated trains bring the shoppers, workers and employers to the downtown area, make a loop around the business district and start back to the outlying sections from which they started. This entire downtown business area is known as the Loop; in its huge office buildings giants of industry, commerce and finance have guided the fates of million dollar corporations. Their brains and initiative have contributed materially to the economic welfare of the entire nation. But the political destiny of Chicago's First Ward was in the hands of the Coughlin-Kenna organization — a structure based on gambling and vice and perpetuated for half a century through the same interests.

The First Ward organization had selected a most propitious time
to start functioning. Chicago had been widely advertised as a
modern Sodom. Out-of-town visitors who came to view the scientific wonders displayed at the fair also flocked to the dives of the
First Ward to get firsthand glimpses of the city's wickedness. They
were not disappointed. And before the end of the summer of 1893,
Bathhouse John was back in the good graces of Mayor Carter
Harrison. Then it was rumored that the five-time mayor of Chicago
would seek election to the United States Senate. Coughlin and Kenna
hurriedly sought an audience with Harrison and assured him of the
support of the First Ward organization. Whatever faults may have
been attributed to Harrison, he was never accused of lacking political acumen. He saw the potentialities of the First Ward organization
and readily made peace with Bathhouse John whom he publicly
honored with a place on a world's fair reception committee.[32] Coughlin, in the space of a few months, had risen to a position of power
and influence in the political affairs of the city. Mike Kenna's quiet
scheming and maneuvering in the background had paid big political
dividends to the blustering bathhouse keeper. And Coughlin rewarded him by naming Hinky Dink the Committeeman of the First
Ward.[33]

Alderman Coughlin was pleased with his appointment to the reception committee. He had little appreciation of the cultural aspects
of the fair but even he understood its importance. The World's
Columbian Exposition had never been equalled by any similar fair
in either magnitude or beauty. Impressive ceremonies attended its
opening on May 1, 1893. President Grover Cleveland was there for
the dedication. On the following day, Thomas W. Palmer, the president of the Exposition, gave a banquet in honor of the Duke of
Veragua, who came as the direct representative of the ruler of
Spain. There were concerts by the Boston and New York Symphony
Orchestras, the Kneisel Quartet, Apollo Club, Arion Society, Max
Bendix String Quartet, Western Choral Societies and a Russian
choir. There were congresses dealing with education, industry,
literature and art. Other congresses related to moral and social reform, philanthropy and charity, architecture, health and insurance.
Still others dealt with Sunday rest, youth and missions. There were
angling tournaments, homing pigeon contests, poultry shows, sheep

and swine exhibitions and athletic events. Just outside the fair grounds William F. Cody, better known as Buffalo Bill, operated his spectacular Wild West Show. All summer long railroad trains, steamboats and cable cars left downtown Chicago with capacity crowds for the Exposition. There were few who were not impressed with its beauty and its buildings with their notable exhibits relating to science, art and industry.

But it was not the displays that made the Exposition so remarkable. These had previously been equalled in the world's fair in Paris in 1889 and were later surpassed by those in St. Louis. No world's fair, however, had surpassed the Columbian Exposition in sheer beauty. Art and nature had a new meaning for the millions of Americans who visited it. Many easterners and Europeans who had previously thought of Chicago only as a rough and tough frontier town viewed the city in a different light after their visit to the fair. The official census figures of 1890 placed Chicago's population at 1,099,850, revealing that it had doubled within a period of ten years. The tall buildings, railroad terminals and large hotels stamped Chicago as a truly great metropolis. One historian remarked that the Columbian Exposition "must remain one of the enduring civic glories of the city of Chicago; and because of it, Chicago became known all over the civilized world as the most vitally American, if not the greatest, city of the Western Hemisphere." [34]

As the closing days of the great world's fair were approaching, Carter Harrison delivered a masterful speech before a meeting of mayors on October 28, 1893. He praised the audacity of the wild and woolly West. Chicago's greatness, suggested Harrison, lay in its fearless spirit, in its firm conviction that it could accomplish anything it attempted. A few hours later, a man suffering from a deluded notion that he should have been named corporation counsel called at the Harrison residence. He demanded an audience with the mayor, who met him at the dining room door. The disgruntled office seeker fired three shots at close range and within fifteen minutes "Our Carter" was dead. [35] The entire city went into mourning. Thousands of friends who sincerely loved him, political enemies who had bitterly fought him and those to whom Carter Harrison was largely a name — all regretted the colorful mayor's passing. He had long been an important part of the city, typical of its traditions, its strength and its weaknesses. In one sense it was fitting that Mayor Harrison's end came almost simultaneously with the closing of Chicago's crowning glory, the World's Columbian Exposition.

Chicago had sought the world's fair as a means of "selling" the city. It wanted to impress visitors with its greatness. And most of those who came for the Exposition were favorably impressed with the city. There were a number of visitors, however, who were not overawed by the city's bigness, its indomitable will power, its scientific achievements, or its flourishing commerce and industry. They were disturbed by the suffering and distress that prevailed among thousands of poor families. They were shocked at a city that was indifferent to entire blocks of streets occupied by houses of prostitution and managed by pompous, gaudy madames who paid large sums of money each week for protection. They were perplexed at a city that professed greatness and yet would permit the heads of gambling syndicates to become political rulers. They were amazed at the extent of the boodling, graft and corruption that prevailed in many departments of city government. And they noted that these great social and political ills were condoned and accepted by many of the residents.

Chicagoans were not easily shocked. But when a noted British editor, William T. Stead, spoke before an overflowing audience in Central Music Hall and gave his frank impressions of the city's shortcomings, many came away with a feeling of guilt. Their sense of civic consciousness awakened with a jolt and they responded by forming the Civic Federation. Stead told Chicagoans, "You are gigantic in your virtues and gigantic in your vices. I don't know in which you glory the most." Later the British editor put his impressions in print. His book carried the bold title *If Christ Came to Chicago!* It was sensational. It besmirched the "fair name of the city." But it was filled with many facts concerning Chicago's indifference to vice, gambling and corruption — facts that could not easily be laughed off. Chicago was a proud city riding for a fall and, said Stead, in need of every known device of sociology or religion to save it.[36]

It required no soothsayer to foretell the coming of trouble in Chicago and other large cities. Again America was in the grip of a serious depression. Unemployed rolls were swelling. Misery and suffering visited thousands of homes. There was evidence of unrest in many parts of the country. In the fall of 1893, Jacob Selcher Coxey was launching his ill-fated movement to march on the nation's capital and force Congress to relieve social distress. He urged the organization of the unemployed into peaceable armies that would march to Washington, D. C., without food or supplies, begging as they went. In Illinois, California, Massachusetts, New Jersey and Oklahoma, local leaders of Coxey's movement issued manifestoes. "On to Washington!" was the battle cry. Early in the spring of 1894, there were 20,000 persons marching to Washington by different routes. Most of them lost heart before they arrived there. But on May 1, 1894, General Coxey led 600 of his men through the streets of the nation's capital. Mounted police obstructed their path. Coxey and two of his aides broke ranks and ran through the shrubbery toward the Capitol steps. They were arrested and jailed for short terms. Coxey's army had been a failure. Newspapers treated it as a joke. But there were many thoughtful persons who understood that Coxey's army was merely an outward manifestation of a social illness requiring sympathy and expert attention, not ridicule.

Coxey's army was still in the headlines when trouble of a much more serious nature broke out near Chicago. In the spring of 1894, the Pullman Company, because of poor business, reduced the number of its employees by one third. Wages were cut thirty or forty per cent, but rent for company-owned houses, in which almost all employees lived, was not reduced. In May 1894, Pullman Company employees went on a strike. The strike was about a month old when the American Railway Union convention met in Chicago, on June 12. Eugene V. Debs, a tall and lean labor zealot, had started this union in 1893, and within one year its membership had grown to 150,000. Debs attempted to enter into negotiations with the Pullman Company to arbitrate the strike, but his overtures were coldly ignored. Debs then ordered a boycott on June 26, 1894, against the Pullman Company on all western railroads. When the railroads discharged the boycotters, all unions affiliated with the American Railway Union struck. The railroads attempted to run their trains in defiance of the unions. Mobs hurled bricks at the locomotives. Entire trains of freight cars were overturned. Scores of freight cars were burned. Men assigned to switch towers were assaulted and forcibly removed from their posts of duty. Men were shot and killed in Chicago railroad yards. An explosion which occurred on Grand Boulevard killed three persons. Pieces of shattered metal, blown into nearby houses, endangered many. Groups of men roamed through the city streets wrecking property. Even mail trains were blocked by locomotives wrecked in their path. Rail transportation was at a standstill and the city's supply of foodstuffs dwindled. President Grover Cleveland ordered troops to Chicago, and martial law was declared. Rioters obstructing trains and destroying property were ordered to return peacefully to their homes before noon on July 9, 1894. At last the strike was broken and another chapter of violence in Chicago ended.[37]

An epoch of Chicago's political history was also drawing to a close. For the greater part of two decades, Mike McDonald, king of the gamblers, had been the political boss of the city. He had founded its first real political machine, which had remained intact for almost twenty years. Now, however, McDonald's star was setting. Although gambling interests were to remain a dominant factor in the city's political affairs, they were to exercise their influence under a new leadership. At a special election following the assassination of Carter Harrison, John P. Hopkins, a merchant, was chosen mayor to fill out the unexpired term. With the election of Hopkins, Roger C. Sullivan, a clerk of the Probate Court, became the most powerful figure in the Democratic party in the state of Illinois. As a result of deals engineered during the new mayor's short term of office, Hopkins did not seek re-election in 1895. Both Hopkins and Sullivan, however, remained very influential in local, state and national Democratic politics. In Chicago's important First Ward, the leadership of Hinky Dink Kenna and Bathhouse John Coughlin was still in the ascendency.

New faces in the political arena had not changed the complexion of the gambling business. Under the protective hands of new political bosses, gambling establishments operated twenty-four hours a day within the shadow of the City Hall. Prince Hal Varnell regularly employed twenty-four faro dealers, twelve croupiers and sixty other employees in his lavishly furnished emporium. The well-known places of Curt Gunn, Ed Wagner and the Hankins brothers, George,

Jeff and Al, were continuously filled with patrons. Fabulous sums were lost by gambling addicts in Billy Fagan's notorious "House of David," sensually decorated with gaudy paintings of nudes. Substantial citizens, including influential businessmen, became alarmed at the brazen operations of the professional blacklegs, particularly in view of the suffering that prevailed generally in the city.

The economic panic of 1893 had taken its toll in Chicago as elsewhere. Sixty thousand jobless, underfed and improperly clothed, walked the streets daily. Yet throughout all this distress and suffering the vice and gambling kings waxed fat from the licentiousness which flourished in the heart of the business district. It was useless to appeal to the authorities. The gambling lords were an integral part of the political machine which ruled the city. Intolerable conditions, however, finally aroused latent civic virtue. In September of 1894, members of the highly respectable Civic Federation, armed with crowbars and axes, descended upon the gambling establishments, virtually demolishing some of them. These drastic measures, applauded by many, were frowned upon by others. Gambling was a part of Chicago's tradition, they said. It should not be destroyed. After all, a wide-open town is good for business. And the wealth of the Mike McDonalds, Harry Varnells and the boodling politicians could testify to the truth of this proposition.[38]

CHAPTER V
A Touch of Reform

FOR sixty years, Chicago had accepted its lot as "the wickedest place in America" without much protest. Most efforts to improve its reputation were sporadic, unorganized and ineffective. Any criticism was regularly denounced by politicians as vicious slander, and ordinarily the devastating charges of William T. Stead, an outsider and a foreigner besides, could have been dismissed with a shrug of the shoulders. After all, what right had a total stranger from England to condemn Chicago's failings?

But to the amazement of local politicians, the furor created by Stead did not die when he left. The gamblers and their political counterparts had overplayed their hands. Everyone knew that Stead's charges were substantially true. Men who had a genuine interest in Chicago's welfare and development were determined to take a hand in removing some of the conditions that gave the city its bad reputation — men who could not be ridiculed as impractical idealists or long-haired reformers. Clear-thinking and hard-headed businessmen, such as the prominent banker, Lyman J. Gage, furnished the leadership for the newly-created Civic Federation. And it was soon evident that the Civic Federation meant business. Following its exposé in September 1894, of gambling dens operating openly with official consent, it attacked crooked elections. After the ballots of the November 1894 election had been counted, the Civic Federation forced the local authorities to prosecute vote thieves and manipulators. There were twenty-one convictions. One man was actually sentenced to the penitentiary. Public attention then focused on the gray wolves of the city council. The Civic Federation boldly charged that fifty-seven of the sixty-eight aldermen were grafters.[1]

The opportunities for graft were never greater than in 1895. A group headed by Charles T. Yerkes was promoting a trolley system to replace the old horse-cars. Another group had started to build the elevated railway around the Loop. Although the city badly needed improved transportation facilities, there was intense opposition to the new trolley system. The exposed wires would endanger lives, it was said. And the excessive speed of the new trolleys would constitute a further menace. Yerkes was not too much concerned over the protests registered against his trolley system, because his relations with the city council were most cordial. When he needed a right of way he called the aldermen to the back room of some saloon and held a private meeting. He always got what he wanted. And, incidentally, so did the aldermen. They suddenly became the owners of new race horses, new homes and new bank deposits. In the meantime, Yerkes was growing fabulously wealthy. Through generous watering, securities in his companies that had a maximum actual value of $46,000,000 were priced on the market at $118,-000,000. Everything he touched seemed to turn to gold.[2]

Although money was flowing into the pockets of Yerkes and his subservient aldermen, times were hard with the average taxpayer. The nation was still suffering from a severe depression. As the presidential campaign of 1896 gained momentum, there were many panaceas advanced to end the country's economic woes. The theories of Henry George, who advocated the "single tax," as well as those of the machine politicians such as "Pitchfork" Ben Tillman of South Carolina, had a large following. But by far the most ardent partisans were those who looked to the "free silver movement" as a means of ending all industrial and agrarian evils. "Free silver" became the rallying cry as the Democratic party held its national convention in the old Coliseum on Chicago's South Side.

Among those in town for the convention was William Jennings Bryan, then only thirty-six years old. When he registered in the old run-down Windsor-Clifton Hotel at Monroe Street and Wabash Avenue, his principal assets were ten dollars in cash and a gifted tongue.[3]

And before long his oratory was to raise the emotions of the convention delegates to a high pitch as he cried, "You shall not press down upon the brow of labor this crown of thorn. You shall not crucify mankind upon a cross of gold." And, said Bryan in his famous convention speech, "The humblest citizen of all the land, when clad in the armor of a righteous cause is stronger than all the hosts of Error." Bryan's oratory won him the Democratic nomination for President.

In the same year that Bryan became the unsuccessful candidate for President, Chicago found its humble citizen "clad in the armor of a righteous cause" in the person of George E. Cole, the head of a company of stationers and printers. Under the guidance of the banker, Lyman Gage, another reform agency, the Municipal Voters' League, was started on February 13, 1896. Fifty-year-old George E. Cole, short, thick-set and baldish, was chosen president. This man with the piercing eyes, firm jaw and a strong face adorned with a mustache and goatee, was truly a humble citizen. Few people had heard of him before he became head of the League. Within a few months, Cole was to be known as a human buzz saw as he made savage reports on the city's politicians. The traction king he scornfully referred to as "Yerkes the Boodler." When Hinky Dink Kenna sought a seat in the city council, the Municipal Voters' League pointed out acidly that this proprietor of a saloon at 120 East Van Buren Street was an intimate associate of the gambling element and utterly unfit for office. Alderman John Coughlin, the Municipal Voters' League charged, had voted for all questionable ordinances. In addition to his bathhouse at 145 East Madison Street, which was patronized principally by gamblers and racing men, the report added that the Silver Dollar Saloon which he operated at 169 East Madison Street served as a resort for prostitutes, gamblers and thieves. (Incidentally, Coughlin had christened his saloon the "Silver Dollar" in honor of Bryan's free silver movement during the 1896 presidential campaign.) Bathhouse John was described as uneducated and coarse in conduct, an associate of thugs and a disgrace to his ward and city.

After the press had given wide publicity to this report, Hinky Dink and Bathhouse John indignantly walked into the stationery and printing establishment of George Cole and demanded an audience with the head of the Municipal Voters' League. They informed Cole that a grave injustice had been inflicted upon Coughlin in the report and demanded a public correction of its inaccuracies. Cole replied that the Municipal Voters' League was prepared to prove Coughlin was an associate of gamblers, thugs and thieves and it was a matter of record that he had voted for questionable ordinances. Bathhouse John was unimpressed. He said, "That is not the point, Mr. Cole. In this record you say I was born in Waukegan. Now, Mr. Cole, I was born right here in Chicago, and I am proud of it." [4] Public charges of his association with the underworld were not damaging. He received both money and votes from that source. But in the matter of his birthplace accuracy was important — his enemies might make political capital of his "foreign" origin in Waukegan, Illinois, a town some forty miles north of Chicago. This conceivably could cost him votes. It was important to have the record corrected.

Kenna and Coughlin well understood the source of their political power. The Municipal Voters' League was no match for the First Ward organization when an election was at stake. And in 1897 Hinky Dink was elected alderman for the first time. There were then thirty-five wards in the city of Chicago with two aldermen elected from each ward. Bathhouse John and Hinky Dink now monopolized the rich First Ward's representation in the city council.[5]

The year 1897 was notable for other political events. On January eighth, the Illinois Democrats staged a big Jackson Day dinner at the old Tremont House with William Jennings Bryan as the featured speaker. Heading the reception committee was Michael Cassius McDonald. Assisting McDonald as a member of this important committee was another well-known gambler, Matt A. Hogan.

Several years earlier Hogan had been a prominent figure in the night life of New Orleans where he lived chiefly by his wits. He was arrested so frequently for gambling and fighting that he once ordered a load of furniture delivered at the police station there, explaining to the chief of police that since he spent so much time in jail he wanted a cell adequately furnished. Later he opened a restaurant in Chicago which catered principally to gamblers. His prices for food depended entirely on what the traffic would bear. Hogan became influential in Chicago politics and was particularly close to John P. Hopkins, the former mayor and powerful Democratic party leader. After Hogan had squandered his money playing faro, Hopkins provided him with an income for the balance of his life.[6]

The Jackson Day dinner on January 8, 1897, lasted until three o'clock the following morning. At least half of those present became thoroughly intoxicated. The atmosphere was hardly fitting for the principal speaker, William Jennings Bryan, who later was to devote many years of his life to the cause of prohibition. During the course of the speaking and drinking, the politician Robert E. "Bobby" Burke was busy perfecting some carefully laid plans. Burke had planted several of his followers in strategic places throughout the audience. During a flowery speech by Carter H. Harrison, Jr. in which he lauded Bryan and his principles, a gusty roar emanated from Bobby Burke's thick-tongued "plants." Harrison for mayor, was the cry. "He's a regular chip off the old block," they yelled. A Harrison for mayor boom had been launched.

Carter H. Harrison, Jr. was then thirty-six years of age. His father had been elected chief executive of the city five times. The name Carter H. Harrison would be magic with the voters. The boom was launched under most favorable circumstances. Young Harrison's future was quite largely in the experienced and able hands of Bobby Burke and Joseph S. Martin, a close friend and associate of Mike McDonald.[7]

For many years Martin owned and operated one of the most profitable gambling establishments in Chicago, which was ideally located on Madison near State Street in the heart of the Loop. And like his friend McDonald, he had gradually become a powerful figure in municipal politics. In state politics Martin had espoused the cause of John P. Altgeld, who served as governor from 1893 to 1897. Martin followed Altgeld with a blind devotion and Altgeld in turn honored his disciple with an appointment to a state office. As the proprietor of a gambling house, Martin naturally became very friendly with many underworld characters, among them Eddie Guerin and his brother, Paddy, who were the leaders of a tough gang on the West Side and a constant source of trouble to the police. Eddie Guerin was to achieve the status of an international criminal when he was convicted for shooting a man in a Paris railway station and was sentenced to Devil's Island for life. Joseph Martin, who was in the habit of fixing such matters in Chicago, did not forsake his friend just because his crime was committed in a foreign country. In 1900, he went to Paris where he gained an audience with the President of France. After some fast talking, Martin received permission to visit Guerin in prison. His real mission soon became apparent. Martin arranged for a boat which enabled Guerin to escape from Devil's Island. The loyalty of Martin to his friends was legendary, matched only by his intense hatred for those he considered his enemies. Martin bitterly detested Johnny Dowling, a well-known gambler. The two gamblers met one day on Dearborn Street. They instantly drew their guns and began shooting wildly at one another. Nobody got hurt, and the feud went on. Martin hated policemen, too. The world, he contended, would be a much better place without them.[8]

With practical-minded politicians of the talents of Martin and Burke pulling the strings, Harrison's candidacy steadily gained momentum. On February 21, 1897, Martin and Burke engineered a coup that threw the opposition forces into confusion. The Populist party held its convention and through the maneuvering of Martin and Burke it named Carter H. Harrison, Jr. as its candidate for mayor. The Populist party had polled a heavy vote in Chicago only two years earlier. But during the presidential campaign of 1896 the Democratic party had adopted the Populist principle of free silver as a part of its platform. Consequently most of the Populist party's membership had been absorbed into the ranks of the Democratic party. The Chicago Democrats were thus faced with the alternative of nominating Harrison for mayor or running the risk of losing the substantial free silver vote. With the backing of the Populists it was also possible that William Jennings Bryan, the national leader of the Democratic party, might come to Chicago and actively campaign for Harrison. Harrison's opposition capitulated. No other name was presented for consideration. The strategy of Martin and Burke had worked to perfection.

Following his nomination, young Harrison engaged in a vigorous campaign to win the election. His platform advocated an eight-hour day with universal employment of union labor, an extension of the city's electric street lighting system and lower telephone rates. These were the usual campaign promises without too much vote appeal. Harrison's real emphasis was on his family name. In the numerous foreign neighborhoods Harrison dwelled at length on that part of the platform which promised "the fullest measure of personal liberty consistent with the maintenance of public order." Harrison's interpretation of this plank was couched in plain language. It meant open saloons on Sunday.

George E. Cole and his Municipal Voters' League actively opposed young Harrison. But when the votes were counted following the election on April 6, 1897, Harrison was declared victor by a large majority. For the first time in its history Chicago had elected a native-born citizen as mayor. And Joseph S. Martin, the one-time powerful gambling house proprietor became the city collector.[9]

At the time that the Democrats of Chicago were celebrating their victory, Richard Croker, the corrupt boss of Tammany Hall, was laying the groundwork to regain control of New York City. The revelations of police graft by the famous Lexow Committee in 1894 had resulted in a political upheaval in New York. William L. Strong, a reform candidate, had been elected mayor and his police commissioner, Theodore Roosevelt, had struck hard at the Tammany organization. The vice, gambling and liquor laws were effectively enforced, thus cutting off an important source of money, votes and power to Tammany Hall. This was a crippling blow to Boss Croker and his henchmen, Timothy D. "Big Tim" Sullivan, the millionaire gambling house proprietor, to Albert J. "Al" Adams, the policy racket king, and to Charles Francis Murphy, heir apparent to the Tammany throne. Boss Croker was determined to regain control of the mayor's chair for Tammany Hall. After much deliberation, Croker selected as his candidate an obscure judge, Robert A. Van Wyck. The judge had been a loyal Tammany man for many years. He was descended from an old Knickerbocker family, which would please the Dutch and German voters, and his judicial career had been so inconspicuous that he was untouched by public scandal.[10]

Early in the fall of 1897, Boss Croker visited Mayor Harrison in Chicago and requested his aid in the coming New York City election. The organization known as the Cook County Democracy was invited to come to New York and march down Broadway in full regalia. Chicago politicians have always bitterly resented any interference in local affairs by outsiders, but apparently they saw no inconsistency in their meddling in a strictly local New York City election. Perhaps the ideals and motives of Tammany Hall were so similar to those of the Cook County Democracy that they believed they were fighting for a common cause. Whatever the reason, they chartered a special train and headed for New York. The official mission of the trip was to help Boss Croker elect Robert A. Van Wyck, of whom most of the delegation had never heard. Many of the New Yorkers who turned out to see the Chicagoans march down Broadway were particularly eager to get a glimpse of the inimitable pair, Hinky Dink Kenna and Bathhouse John Coughlin. They were not disappointed. In their official marching uniform of long frock coats, dark trousers, silk hats, white gloves and neatly folded umbrellas, these two cut quite a figure. The motley crew that marched down Broadway consisted of many prize representatives of Chicago statesmanship. There was Alderman Johnny Powers, president of the Cook County Democracy and recognized leader of the boodlers in the city council. There was the vice-president of the organization, whose wife operated a Chicago hotel as a house of assignation. There was a former deputy coroner whose zeal in arriving on a death scene had given him the nickname of "First-Search." These men were good copy for the New York papers, which made the most of their opportunities.[11]

The New York trip certainly did not enhance the reputation of Chicago. But it did attract wide attention and resulted in reams of publicity — bad publicity. It undoubtedly prompted nationally read magazines and newspapers to send their representatives to Chicago to observe at first hand the crime and corruption that existed there. In December 1897, Franklin Matthews of *Harper's Weekly* investigated conditions in Chicago with the co-operation of local police officers and reporters. He found that the lowest grades of vice and wide-open gambling were tolerated because of the demands of politicians who wanted to levy tribute. A system of police blackmail existed which matched "in its unscrupulous nature and extent the worst phases of the police blackmail that was levied in New York under the palmy days of Tammany rule" wrote Matthews in *Harper's Weekly* on January 22, 1898. Gambling houses paid a minimum of fifty dollars a month for protection, "panel" houses thirty-five and fifty dollars a month, and houses of prostitution from fifty to two hundred dollars. Saloon licenses were under the direct supervision of the

alderman of each ward. For a saloon license the alderman demanded
one hundred dollars. A payment of five hundred dollars to the alderman would restore a revoked license. Most of the gambling dens
visited by Matthews were owned and operated by politicians. Several of these places were managed by aldermen. The gambling establishment of Alderman W. J. O'Brien and Alderman John Powers,
located over their saloon, flourished with the patronage of thieves
and thugs of the basest variety. Aldermen O'Brien and Powers were
powerful leaders in Chicago Democratic politics. Powers, together
with Mike McDonald, had managed the senior Harrison's successful
mayoralty campaign in 1893. His talents in the field of political
manipulation and corruption approached genius.

When Matthews confronted Mayor Harrison with the irrefutable
facts which his investigation had uncovered, the mayor indignantly
denied the existence of wide-open gambling. Chicago, alleged Harrison, was better morally than New York. And Harrison's Superintendent of Police, Joseph Kipley, while admitting that gambling
places were operating, weakly complained of his inability to get
around much. He had too much work to do in his office. After all,
said Kipley, "It isn't right to expect me to know everything that is
going on in town." [12] But this ability to close his eyes to flagrant
violations of the law was the very quality that recommended him for
the position of superintendent of police. In the First Ward alone,
some two thousand professional gamblers were plying their trade
with impunity. Houses of prostitution were expanding their operations under the careful direction of Ike Bloom, "King of the
Brothels." Andy Craig, from his saloon on Customs House Place,
served as the broker for thieves in disposing of stolen goods. Murderers, burglars and stick-up men could use Craig's place as a headquarters with the assurance that no police officer would have the
temerity to search for them there. [13] It is small wonder that the celebrated author, H. G. Wells, after visiting some political saloons in
Chicago with Alderman Hinky Dink Kenna, remarked that he ". . .
would as soon go to live in a pen in a stockyard as into American
politics."

Alderman Kenna and Alderman Coughlin of the First Ward were
among the more powerful supporters of young Mayor Harrison.
Hinky Dink was a masterful organizer. He molded the tramps, pan-

handlers, cardsharps, ten-cent flophouse inmates, saloon and gambling house patrons of the ward into a well-disciplined army of voters completely subservient to his will on election day. The going rate was fifty cents a vote.[14] The voters were satisfied, particularly when filled up with beer and free lunches at Kenna's saloon. Several thousand votes could be purchased without making much of a dent in the protection fund which flowed in from the gamblers and vice mongers of the district.

"A rare conglomeration of city fathers ruled Chicago in the 'nineties,' " wrote Carter H. Harrison, Jr. many years later, when he had grown old and full of civic virtue. From Harrison's own pen we learn that Chicago's citizens "permitted the control of public affairs to be the exclusive appanage of a low-browed, dull-witted, base-minded gang of plug-uglies, with no outstanding characteristic beyond an unquenchable lust for money." [15] Each of Chicago's wards, he explained, was largely under the domination of a single man or of a small group and with few exceptions these men were gamblers or saloonkeepers. Yet their word "as far as the choice of delegates was concerned was supreme." [16] These various observations of Harrison's in retrospect were more accurate than his denials, when mayor, of prevalent gambling and vice. Moreover his appraisal of the political ruling class could apply to almost every period of Chicago's history, before and after, as well as during, his tenure of office.

The prevalence of gambling, vice and debauchery which received the encouragement and protection of venal politicians undoubtedly contributed to a serious juvenile delinquency problem. During a six months' period in 1898 there were three hundred and thirty-two boys ranging from nine to sixteen years of age who were committed to the House of Correction known as the Bridewell. In this filthy institution the children were placed in cells with habitual drunkards, thieves and other dregs of society. In 1899, as Carter H. Harrison, Jr. began his second term as mayor, the Illinois General Assembly enacted legislation which created the Juvenile Court in Chicago.[17] This was an enlightened and constructive act. It is generally conceded that the Juvenile Court established in Chicago was the first court of that nature in the entire world, and political leaders were not backward in taking full credit for their progressive social thinking. It could be argued that more juveniles would have been saved by

removing some of the conditions which contributed to their downfall, but the same harsh observations are equally true a half century
later. Today corrupt ward leaders still rise to personal wealth and
political power through the protection of gambling dens, houses of
prostitution and the taverns that illegally sell liquor to minors. Yet
for public consumption these same leaders are in the front ranks
fighting juvenile delinquency. From the proceeds of illegal establishments that aggravate the juvenile crime problem these politicians
sometimes dole out a few dollars to help support boys' clubs and
playgrounds. In the eyes of their constituents, including some social
workers of the area, they pose as public benefactors for rebuilding
the characters of juveniles they helped to destroy in the first place.
Human nature has changed little in the past fifty years.

As the new century opened on January 1, 1900, Chicago faced
many difficulties. Its population had grown to 1,698,575, which represented an increase of approximately 600,000 within a ten-year
period. Home building had failed to keep pace with the needs of the
rapidly growing metropolis. Housing had become a major problem.
In official quarters there was total indifference to the city's inadequate living facilities. (This was not true of Jane Addams, who with
Ellen Gates Starr had established the social settlement known as Hull
House in 1889. A Hull House report spoke plainly of Chicago's
"filthy and rotten tenements," dingy courts and tumble-down sheds,
broken sewer pipes and piles of disease-breeding garbage. It told
of people living over dirty stables and of basements used as sweat-
shops.)
With the return of more prosperous times early in 1900, there was
much building activity. It appeared that substantial relief was on the
way for the severe housing shortage that existed among the poor
working classes. Then, almost without warning, all construction
work was at a standstill. A real or imaginary grievance based on
inconsequential restrictions over the amount of labor that could be
used on machinery resulted in a strike. By February 1900, seven
thousand workers were idle. Before the end of the year the number
reached 50,000. Chicago was in the midst of the longest and most
bitter struggle between contractors and unions in the city's history.
The entire business life of the city suffered. Sales and collections

of stores dropped to the danger point. There was much suffering among the poor people.

Behind the trouble lurked the figure of M. B. "Skinny" Madden, Chicago's first big labor grafter. He was surrounded by a coterie of sluggers who enforced his demands with brass knuckles and strong-arm methods. Madden's formula was simple. It formed the basis for many fortunes amassed by labor racketeers in later years. Madden would call a strike. Then for a sum ranging from $1000 on small construction jobs to $20,000 on large buildings he would call off the strike. As conditions grew more serious in 1900, Mayor Harrison and civic leaders attempted unsuccessfully to arbitrate the differences between the unions and the contractors. Finally, after many months, the strike ended without either side having won a clear-cut victory.[18]

Although civic leaders were unable to make much headway in dealing with the building strike or solving the housing shortage they were eminently successful on other fronts. The Municipal Voters' League, started only four years earlier, had awakened the civic conscience to a degree never before attained. The vigorous onslaught of its president, George Cole, against boodling aldermen and the traction king, Charles Yerkes, had at last borne results. Mayor Harrison had allied himself with the forces of decency in the fight against the corrupt traction interests. His leadership and courage in this battle won for him the wholehearted praise of Cole, who had vigorously opposed his first candidacy for mayor. The caliber of the city council began to improve.

Through the efforts of the Municipal Voters' League a number of outstanding men were brought into public life, among them William E. Dever, many years later a mayor of Chicago. In the spring of 1900 the Municipal Voters' League was searching for a Republican in the Second Ward who could defeat an undesirable candidate for the city council. A young man, about thirty years of age, was finally chosen as the League's candidate. He was wealthy, came from a good family, and was a capable football player and yachtsman. The League was told by his sponsors that he could do no harm; "The worst you can say of him is that he's stupid." This young man who launched his political career in the name of reform and under the sponsorship of the Municipal Voters' League was William Hale Thompson. A few years later he was to become the mayor of Chi-

cago and was never again charged with anything that even remotely
hinted at reform.[19]

During the closing months of 1902 and the early part of 1903 Chicago suffered from one of its periodic crime waves. Armed holdups,
burglaries and shootings were again becoming commonplace. As
usual, police efforts were weak and ineffective; the underworld with
its political affiliations was powerful. As the fears of the citizenry
mounted they turned to anger. They attended mass meetings and demanded official action. They raised funds to bring Captain Alexander
Piper of New York to Chicago to investigate the inefficient police.
He placed officers suspected of corruption under surveillance, a practice regarded by the police department as unethical snooping. It
became known as "piperizing," a name which still retains its same
ignominious connotation to police officers.

A city council committee heard evidence of police corruption.
The state's attorney presented facts to the grand jury. Patrolmen
were indicted for levying tribute on slot machine owners and prostitutes, for bribery, for operating confidence games and for obstructing justice. The Civil Service Commission heard testimony which
resulted in the dismissal of officers from the force. From the evidence
presented to the various official bodies, it became clear that the real
head of law enforcement in Chicago was neither Chief of Police
Francis O'Neil nor Mayor Harrison. Orders that required unwaver-
ing obedience issued from persons who controlled gambling and
prostitution in various sections of the city. On the North Side, Mont
Tennes, with the assistance of "Hot Stove" Jimmy Quinn, was
coming to the fore as a powerful gambling boss. (Later Tennes was
to become the czar of horse race handbook betting throughout the
United States.) Gambling in the stockyards district on the South
Side was dominated by Jim O'Leary, a scion of the family which
became legendary when the starting point of the great fire of 1871
was traced to their cow barn. Tom McGinnis controlled gambling
on the near South Side. Patsy King ruled over the policy racket. In
the hands of these men rested the political fortunes of aldermen and
ward leaders. They were in a position to dictate the law enforcement policies to chiefs of police and mayors as well. Public indignation, at the power of the gambling and vice lords, mounted to a
high pitch in 1903. Only the Iroquois Theatre fire on December 30,

1903, which resulted in the loss of five hundred seventy-five lives, caused a temporary abatement of the investigation started by an angry populace. By 1905 wide-open gambling was being suppressed in Chicago and in the surrounding county. The investigation established that the police department could enforce the laws "if protected from the vice ring and its agents in political office." [20]

Carter Harrison, Jr. completed his fourth consecutive term as mayor in 1905. He had been the successful candidate in the municipal elections in 1897, 1899, 1901 and 1903. In each of the four contests, it is doubtful if any other factor contributed as much to Harrison's success as the support he received from the First Ward organization headed by Hinky Dink Kenna and Bathhouse John Coughlin. Harrison referred to them as, "The Two Rocks of Gibraltar." [21] Through four city elections their organization had produced the necessary votes, much in the same manner that Mike McDonald and his underworld organization had assured the election of Harrison's father five times. Twenty-six years had elapsed since the elder Harrison was first elected mayor in 1879. That period included thirteen mayoralty elections, and either Carter H. Harrison, Sr. or his son had been the successful candidate nine times — a remarkably long period for one family to retain control of the helm of a city as large as Chicago.

In many respects the Harrison dynasty served the city well, with the administration of the younger Harrison somewhat of an improvement over that of his father.[22] Despite sporadic attempts at reform, the political machinery remained largely under the control of aldermen and ward leaders who were gamblers or saloonkeepers, and throughout the years the wide-open town policy became more and more firmly imbedded in the city's tradition.

The militant citizens' revolt against lawlessness between 1903 and 1905 made Harrison's fourth term as mayor a trying experience. He grew weary battling the problems of city government. In addition, his son, Carter H. Harrison III, was seriously ill. Consequently he decided against becoming a candidate in the spring election of 1905. He relinquished his place as head of the Democratic ticket to Judge Edward F. Dunne, a man closely allied with social reformers and a strong advocate of municipal ownership. But Dunne, with all his idealism, found it politically expedient to endorse publicly the candidacy of Hinky Dink Kenna, who was seeking re-election as alderman. Kenna and his underworld connections became an issue in the campaign. Public denunciation of Hinky Dink, however, could not injure him with his powerful First Ward organization which also assisted in the election of Dunne by a plurality of almost 25,000 votes.

A violent strike of teamsters' unions in the summer of 1905 greeted the new mayor. Murders were committed; police officers were assaulted as they attempted to restore order, and terror walked the streets until the strikers went back to work. Also, throughout Dunne's term as mayor there was a vigorous battle between the so-called radicals and conservatives. They fought over gas prices, education policies and transportation. Dunne's enemies labeled him a radical. The truth was that many of his department heads were weak, his administration failed to grow in popular appeal, and dissatisfaction was in evidence among the professional politicians.[23] As the 1907 municipal elections were approaching, these unofficial rulers decided to put a "good fellow" in the mayor's chair. In line with these plans, Fred Busse received the Republican nomination and was elected with the full support and assistance of the Democratic organization controlled by boss Roger C. Sullivan.[24] The gray wolves who have so frequently dominated Chicago's politics have never considered party labels of any great significance when their selfish interests were involved. Bipartisan deals have always featured the city's political history.

Fred Busse, the new mayor, was the first to serve a four-year term under an Act passed two years earlier. He was a product of the near North Side, a spawning place of many tough hoodlums, and had grown up in an atmosphere of practical politics. Charles T. Yerkes, who looked upon politicians as commodities to be bought and sold, maintained his headquarters in offices located on the northwest corner of North Clark and Division Streets. The saloon on the opposite corner was the favorite hangout of Busse for many years. This was the establishment of Tom Burke, a political giant of the district. Over his saloon, Burke operated a big gambling establishment whose roulette wheels and crap tables were always well patronized. Burke's place served as a political headquarters in which ward leaders gathered, planned their strategy and directed their campaigns.

Before entering politics, Busse had become wealthy in the coal business. He was once a member of the state legislature and had served as postmaster of Chicago. He was affiliated with the Republican faction headed by the powerful William "Billy" Lorimer, onetime streetcar conductor, constable, congressman — and almost a United States Senator. After Lorimer was named United States Senator in 1909, one of the blackest political scandals in the annals of Illinois came to light. Charges were made that bribes totaling one hundred thousand dollars had been paid to assure Lorimer a place in the Senate. After a long and bitter fight the Senate finally unseated him in 1912.[25]

Of the various organizations and individuals responsible for the election of Fred Busse in 1907, none worked more diligently than the gangster Barney Bertche, a Busse acquaintance of long standing. (Bertche was to become a powerful figure in big-scale gambling activities during the 1920's.) When Busse became mayor he named Paddy Guerin, a friend of Bertche's, as his bodyguard. Busse also prevailed upon a friend to rent a vacant store building to Bertche for a period of five years in order that the gunman might become a saloonkeeper. Although a man of Bertche's bad reputation could not qualify under the Illinois law, the mayor issued a liquor license to him. But Barney had mapped out for himself a more important role than that of a saloonkeeper. He began selling protection to gambling houses, a practice that eventually caused the mayor embarrassment. Busse called Bertche to his office and instructed him to quit dealing in gambling privileges. Barney at once suspected that his friend Paddy Guerin, the mayor's bodyguard, had double-crossed him, and a short time later when Guerin and Bertche met in a basement restaurant at Adams and Wabash Avenue, they drew their guns and started firing at each other — unhappily, without effect. Not long afterwards another gun battle occurred in Barney Bertche's saloon. This time two police officers were shot. The smoke had barely faded away when Bertche became involved in another skirmish of even more serious proportions. Just east of the corner of Clark and Randolph Street, he engaged in a gun battle with three detectives, killing one and wounding the other two. Barney himself was badly wounded, but recovered and was able to resume his place in the political and gambling affairs of the city.[26]

Fred Busse had occupied the mayor's chair but a short time when it became evident that his administration intended to let the town run wide open. This pleased the professional politicians who had wanted a "good fellow" in office. It gratified their allies, the gamblers, who envisioned profits running into millions of dollars. But some of the gambling lords had no intention of submitting to an equitable distribution of the spoils. They were severally determined to control the rich prize. By 1907 Mont Tennes had become the most powerful gambling house operator in Chicago, but there were many other important figures in the gambling setup. In the Loop area the blacklegs were principally under the domination of Hinky Dink Kenna and Bathhouse John Coughlin. Also influential in the same district were Tom McGinnis, Pat O'Malley and John F. O'Malley. On Chicago's West Side, Alderman Johnnie Rogers was the gambling boss. In the stockyards district on the South Side, Jim O'Leary was the kingpin.

Horse race betting in establishments called handbooks or poolrooms had long been popular in the midwestern city. By the time Busse became mayor, Chicago was considered the largest handbook center in the United States. And Mont Tennes was determined that his control of handbook gambling should be absolute. He was ruthless in dealing with competitors. A successful handbook establishment requires prompt returns on horse races from the various tracks throughout the country, and one John Payne of Cincinnati, Ohio, had established a telegraph service which provided these. Tennes reasoned that if he could control this racing information service in Chicago, he could become the undisputed czar of all handbooks in the city. With that objective in mind, he entered into a contract with the Payne News Agency which gave him exclusive control over the wire service in Chicago. He paid three hundred dollars a day to Payne for this monopoly, with the result that no gambling establishment could secure returns on horse races by telephone or telegraph unless Tennes consented. For the privilege of obtaining the wire service the handbook operator was required to turn over fifty per cent of his net daily receipts to the Tennes syndicate. In addition to furnishing prompt racing returns, Tennes assured the gambling establishments of protection from the officials. Handbooks that attempted to operate without the wire service could not hope to compete with those subscribing to the Tennes service, and were soon forced out of business.

The exclusive control which Mont Tennes had established over the wire service was not accomplished without a struggle. In July 1907, a bomb shattered part of the home of John Condon, who was affiliated with the Tennes syndicate. A second bomb exploded in the basement of a saloon at Clark and Kinzie belonging to John F. O'Malley of the Loop ring. A third bomb was deposited at the door of the garage of Mont Tennes's own residence at 404 Belden Avenue.[27] It was a warfare of the jungle — a battle of extermination waged by Chicago's gambling chiefs for the control of a racket worth millions of dollars in profits and tremendous political influence and power. It was a bloody conflict which was to continue unceasingly for decades with a death toll running into several hundred lives.

To the tune of violence and exploding bombs, Mont Tennes was rising steadily to the gambling throne of Chicago, while the career of another gambling king was coming to an end. Mike McDonald, who for two decades had ruled Chicago's gamesters and politicians, was dying, broken in health and in spirit. In 1898 McDonald, then an elderly man, had married a second time. His first marriage to Mary Noonan had ended in failure. Once she ran away with a minstrel singer to San Francisco where McDonald found her and brought her back to Chicago. In 1889 she deserted the gambler again, this time eloping with a Belgian priest, and was gone for good. Nine years later McDonald met thirty-year-old Dora Feldman, the wife of Sam Barclay, a professional baseball star. He financed Dora's divorce from Barclay and married her in 1898.

This same year Dora had become acquainted with Webster Guerin, then a youth of sixteen. Their relationship continued until February 21, 1907, when tenants of the Omaha Building at 134 Van Buren Street heard a shot and crashing glass. They ran to Room 703. A bullet had fractured the glass in the door leading to this suite. Sprawled on the floor was the body of Webster Guerin, killed by a bullet, and over him stood Mrs. Mike McDonald, holding a small pearl-handled revolver. Mike McDonald was stunned. Retaining the experienced lawyer and politician, J. Hamilton Lewis, to defend his wife, he made known his intention of standing by her. But he never recovered from the shock. Before the trial he suffered a nervous breakdown and on August 9, 1907, Mike McDonald died. He left property valued at $2,500,000. Several months later, on January 20, 1908, his widow Dora was brought to trial and in typical Chicago fashion the jury acquitted her of the murder of Webster Guerin.[28]

The day before McDonald died, August 8, the *Chicago News* commented editorially:

. . . Mike McDonald is dying. When the city had a scant half million [people] this man ruled it from his saloon and gambling house by virtue of his political power. During many succeeding years he had a controlling influence in the public affairs of this community. . . . Bad government was accepted as a matter of course. Vice sat in the seats of power and patronized virtue with a large and kindly tolerance, asking only that it remain sufficiently humble and not too obtrusive. Gambling was a leading industry. Clark Street was thronged night and day with men going in and out of the wide open gambling resorts. The wretched conditions then prevailing were excused on the theory that vice "made the town lively." Gambling was necessary, it was said, to attract strangers. As for the "king of gamblers" he was a "good fellow." He "always stood by his friends." Boodle aldermen lorded it in the city council. Boodle county commissioners stole everything they could lay their hands on . . . contracts for public works that had thievery written between the lines were let and carried out to the large profit of the conspirators. Elections were controlled by the sweet and simple methods of chasing away voters and stuffing ballot boxes. . . .

But at last there was an awakening of the citizens, the editorial continued. And through the combined efforts of independent voters, alert civic organizations, an efficient state's attorney and the press, the yoke of Mike McDonald had been thrown off. His days, although quite recent, seemed almost those of a "mythical period." [29]

The *News's* editorial on McDonald's passing expressed the hope that good morals and good government would accompany the city's growth in the future. This was wishful thinking. Only a few years were to elapse before the city would again be in the grip of gangster rule — a rule that was to last for decades. In fact, even at the time the editorial was written, Chicago was in the midst of a reign of terror while bomb throwing gamblers engaged in a bitter fight for power. Five days after McDonald's death, the gambling resort of James O'Leary at 4183 South Halsted Street was bombed.

A few days later, on August 19, a second attempt was made to bomb the Mont Tennes residence. His wife and four children were going to bed about ten o'clock at night, when a dynamite bomb exploded in the yard. Windows were shattered in the Tennes's home, and other houses in the vicinity were damaged. Frightened neighbors pleaded with Tennes to hire special police to prevent further violence. On September 24, 1907, the distributing office for the Mont Tennes racing wire service, located in Forest Park, a Chicago suburb, was bombed. Another bomb damaged the house of the Sheriff of Cook County, James Pease. On September 26, a bomb exploded in the rear of the Western Cash Register Company store at 123 North Clark Street, in the heart of the Loop. This place was a front for a large gambling establishment operated by Tennes. The gamblers' bombing war terrified Chicagoans. No section of the city appeared immune from attack. The inaction of the police indicated that the law enforcement bodies had capitulated to the underworld.

An aroused public once more demanded official action and a grand jury investigation started on September 28, 1907. Evidence in the possession of the state's attorney showed that Mont Tennes had established a dictatorship over hundreds of Chicago bookmakers and that he operated with the full knowledge of Mayor Fred Busse and Chief of Police George M. Shippy. With friendly official backing the Tennes syndicate had grown powerful and defiant. It even showed its contempt for the grand jury in session. When Alderman John Rogers appeared before the grand jury in response to a subpoena, his gambling house at 345 West Madison Street was promptly bombed. This was intended as a warning to possible witnesses that even an appearance before the grand jury might place their lives in jeopardy. Mont Tennes and his syndicate were no longer amenable to the law; they were above it. The gambling war continued. By January 1909, Tennes was in absolute control of handbook gambling in Chicago. But even then the violence did not end.[30] Government had completely broken down.

The gambling war focused public attention on that phase of underworld activity. Equally brazen were the vice operators in Chicago's world-famed red-light district. To many Chicagoans the segregated district was not an object of shame; it was a source of secret pride — a gaudy example of the wickedness that made the city famous. A pamphlet describing the wonders of Chicago highlighted two famous institutions which visitors "must not miss" — the stockyards and the Everleigh Club. The Everleigh Club was a notorious bawdyhouse, probably the most elaborately furnished place of its kind in the world. Located in a twin stone building at 2131–33 South Dearborn Street, it had been opened originally to cater to the pleasure seekers of the Columbian Exposition in 1893. It was not until seven years later, however, that two sisters, Minna and Ada Lester who had started in the brothel business in Omaha in 1898, came to Chicago and purchased the business for $50,000. Adopting the name of Everleigh, the sisters spared no expense in getting the place in readiness for the grand opening on February 1, 1900. From the very beginning it was a huge success and its profits were enormous. During the 1907 financial panic, the Everleigh sisters had cash in three Chicago banks totaling a quarter of a million dollars.

On January 31, 1910, a meeting of the Church Federation representing the clergy of six hundred congregations convened in the central Y.M.C.A. building to discuss vice in Chicago. It passed a resolution urging the mayor to appoint a vice commission which would thoroughly investigate conditions and "map out such a course as in its judgment will bring about some relief from the frightful conditions which surround us." [31] On March 5, 1910, Mayor Busse appointed such a vice commission with Dean Walter T. Sumner as chairman. Dean Sumner was in charge of an Episcopal cathedral near the Des Plaines Street police station, secretary of the Episcopal city missions and influential in the federation of churches. The commission included Protestant, Catholic and Jewish religious leaders, the presidents of educational institutions such as Northwestern University and Armour Institute, members of the judiciary, hospital and medical society officers, businessmen, and civic leaders, including the philanthropist, Julius Rosenwald.

Mayor Busse emphasized that the commission should not publicly expose the details of Chicago's vice problem, which he said was "exactly like that of any American city." Many believed the mayor had received some assurance that the commission would recommend a continuation of the segregated district. By inference he criticized the laws against prostitution which he said had developed from "temporary outbursts of sentiment," and were not the result of careful thought. No Chicagoan would have disputed his observation that the laws prohibiting commercialized vice were generally ignored. The mayor asked the commission to inquire, "Should vice be segregated? If so, what would be the method of maintaining control of segregation districts?" [32]

If the mayor hoped for a continuation of the segregated district with the Vice Commission's blessing, it was even more apparent that some of the aldermen did too. The political strength of the First Ward Aldermen Kenna and Coughlin depended on their revenue from the red-light district as well as from gambling. Yet on June 27, 1910, when the city council officially created the Vice Commission and appropriated money for its work, Aldermen Kenna and Coughlin voted in favor of the ordinance, which passed without a dissenting vote. The Vice Commission secured offices and began active work on July 5. [33] Before it completed its investigation, however, Busse's four-year term had ended and he no longer occupied the mayor's chair when the commission submitted its official report.

In April 1911, Carter H. Harrison, Jr., was elected mayor for the fifth and last time. The balance of power in this election rested largely with the gamblers. Rumor had it that Mont Tennes spent twenty thousand dollars in this mayoralty contest. With the revenue derived from the gamblers and vice operators of the First Ward it was possible for Aldermen Coughlin and Kenna to buy flophouse votes in large quantities. The plurality for Harrison in this one ward was 3647. Harrison himself attributed his victory "beyond a shadow of a doubt" to the foreign element support and the flophouse votes of the First and Eighteenth Wards. Said Harrison: "On election day, as previously on primary day, my old-time friends of the First Ward, Hinky Dink and Bathhouse John, came through with flying colors." [34] With the election of Harrison it was commonly understood that gambling would be permitted to flourish without interference from the police. Immediately gamblers from all parts of the United States rushed to Chicago. In June 1911, there were twenty-five wide-open gambling establishments in the Loop area, operating seven days a week. By August the number of such places in downtown Chicago had increased to fifty. Even hotels started the operation of games and employed "cappers" and "ropers" to entice customers to their tables. A gaming establishment of one kind or another could be found in almost every block in the Loop. And few places remained in business unless they subscribed to the protection service furnished by the Tennes syndicate. Protection was dispensed on a strictly businesslike basis. To assure immunity from police interference, Tennes demanded sixty per cent of the net profits from crap game operators. Horse race, poolroom and faro establishments divided the profits equally with Tennes, while roulette wheels were required to pay him only forty per cent of the net profits.

Tennes was growing opulent, but he still was not satisfied. His wire service, which he called the General News Bureau, had engaged in an expansion program. The Payne News Agency resisted the encroachment of the General News Bureau in territory outside of Illinois. The dispute between the wire services became so bitter that official investigations were initiated in three states and the Interstate Commerce Commission conducted a national inquiry. Internal troubles also beset Tennes. His partner, Timothy Murphy, filed a civil suit on August 27, 1911, in which he charged Tennes with wrongfully withholding thirty-five thousand dollars from him. But Tennes was a fierce competitor. With the aid of dynamite and arson he overcame all sales resistance in over twenty American cities and drove the Payne system out of business. Annual profits amounting to a half million dollars were pouring into the General News Bureau from all parts of the country. Mont Tennes had become the most powerful horse race gambling figure in the nation.[35]

In spite of state and national investigations, civil litigation between Tennes and rival gamesters and front-page publicity, gambling establishments continued to operate openly. It was obvious that their proprietors were receiving the co-operation of friendly officials. In September 1911, the Civil Service Commission conducted an investigation into alleged police bribery, with the result that several police officials were eventually discharged. The gamblers became jittery at this unexpected turn. They raised a slush fund which they hoped to use in buying off the prosecutors, and just before the first police trials started, the homes of witnesses were bombed. Every possible method of bribery and intimidation was resorted to in an effort to thwart the official investigation. Even the prosecutor received a warning on September 23, 1911. Testimony before the commission revealed the huge conspiracy between gamblers, politicians and the police to drive nonsyndicate gamblers out of business. Named in the plot were Mont Tennes and his friends, the First Ward aldermen Kenna and Coughlin, Tom Carey, the South Side politician and gambler, Tom McGinnis, Mike "de Pike" Heitler, Ben R. Hyman and important police officials. The gambler Ben Hyman testified that police raids were made only on instructions of the syndicate. The places raided were those of gamblers who attempted to operate in competition with the Tennes organization. They had the alternative of going out of business or joining the syndicate and paying tribute to it.[36]

The first year of Mayor Harrison's fifth term was an eventful one. The gambling war in Chicago and the interstate fight between the General News Bureau and the Payne News Agency had focused national attention on the city. Shortly before the Civil Service Commission began its hearings the Vice Commission appointed the preceding year submitted its official report. The sordid facts related in this document had been developed by a staff of competent investigators and carefully verified. The report was a record of civic failure — a report of a business dealing in prostitution, degeneracy and debauchery which netted its operators annual profits of $15,690,449.[37]

Over five thousand commercial prostitutes operated on a full-time basis in Chicago.[38] The policy of segregation with police supervision had been an abject failure. There were more houses of prostitution in residential localities lying outside the red-light district than in the restricted area itself. New bawdyhouses were being established in residential sections at an alarming rate.[39] The so-called medical examination of prostitutes required by the policy of segregation was absolutely worthless and a source of much graft. Inmates were frequently allowed to ply their trade even though they were infected with venereal disease, with the full knowledge of the attending physician and the brothel keepers.[40]

Likewise the police supervision of houses of prostitution in the red-light district was a farce. Only a portion of the bawdyhouses was recorded on the official police list. Even the most famous and luxuriously furnished house of prostitution in the nation, the Everleigh Club, was not among those mentioned on the original list submitted to the Vice Commission by the police department.[41] The

segregated district served as the chief medium through which prostitution was advertised, and the very presence of the red-light area
encouraged and spread the patronage of brothels.[42] Many of the
gamblers in Chicago were attached to houses of prostitution or lived
off the proceeds of the women. The same was true of robbers and
other crooks.[43]

Working in conjunction with the brothel was the saloon. To all
intents and purposes many saloons were actually in the prostitution
business. In 1911, there were 7152 licensed saloons in the city or one
saloon to every three hundred inhabitants. An ordinance enacted on
November 1, 1906, had provided that new saloon licenses were not
to be issued until a sufficient number had lapsed to reduce the ratio
of saloons to population to one for five hundred people. It was estimated that under the 1906 ordinance no new saloon licenses would
be issued during the following twenty-five years. After a period of
five years had passed it was obvious that the ordinance was a failure.
Saloons were as numerous as before. The only tangible result had
been to increase the value of the saloon license which originally cost
$1000 to $2500. The liquor interests were greedily buying up all
the licenses they could find which drove the price higher and
higher.[44]

The Vice Commission's report did not even spare aldermen
Coughlin and Kenna, although it did not mention them by name.
For many years they had promoted a First Ward Ball at the Chicago Coliseum attended almost exclusively by gamblers, pickpockets, safeblowers, thugs, drug addicts and the madames, inmates
and procurers attached to the bawdyhouses of the district. This
ball for the underworld finally became so turbulent that the aldermen had to abandon it. Describing the affair in ultraconservative
language, the Vice Commission report stated:

For several years it has been customary for a certain political club to
give an annual ball in the Coliseum for the purpose of raising money for a
campaign fund. This ball was notorious from the fact that those who
attended it were for the most part immoral women and men who are
engaged in the social evil business, the sale of liquor and gambling. The
giving of this ball has always been a disgrace to the city of Chicago. It is
the opinion of the Commission that this and any other similar affair
should never be allowed again.[45]

Hinky Dink and Bathhouse John were little impressed with this portion of the report. After all, their First Ward Ball had already been stopped because of the pressure of public opinion against this annual public display of unbridled license.

The Vice Commission report was a blow to the segregated vice idea but neither the brothel owners nor their political protectors had any intention of giving up without a struggle. As public opinion mounted against the red-light district, the powerful resort owners banded together for a fight to the finish. Leadership was furnished by "Big Jim" Colosimo, who, with his wife, operated a prosperous place at Twenty-first Street and Armour Avenue, and Ike Bloom, proprietor of the notorious Freiberg Dance Hall on Twenty-second Street between State Street and Wabash Avenue. Both Colosimo and Bloom were important figures in the First Ward political organization of Bathhouse John and Hinky Dink. Colosimo, in particular, through his relationship with the pair had become one of the most powerful politicians in the vice district. Ike Bloom and "Big Jim" Colosimo held many conferences with Minna and Ada Everleigh of the Everleigh Club. The Everleigh sisters, more intelligent than most of the madames, had noted a change in public sentiment. They expressed the opinion that even their friend, Bathhouse John, would not be able to save their business much longer. They were right. Moreover the Everleigh sisters committed a blunder which aroused the ire of the mayor and speeded up the demise of their fabulous institution. They issued a brochure advertising the luxurious furnishings of the Everleigh Club. There were pictures of various elaborate parlors, the spacious hallways and the front of the building. Newspapers featured the brochure. When the mayor attended a banquet in another city, a local resident showed him a copy of the Everleigh Club booklet. The Club was giving the city a bad reputation. For this unpardonable sin, the mayor decreed that the Everleigh Club must go.

About noon on October 24, 1911, Mayor Harrison handed official orders to the police department calling for the immediate closing of the Everleigh Club. For over twelve hours the order was mysteriously ignored. Until one o'clock the following morning, the Club was packed. The last night was a gala affair. When the police arrived, Minna and Ada Everleigh closed their shop quietly and the guests departed peacefully. The gold piano, valuable paintings, tapestries and furniture were carefully covered and the two sisters prepared to leave on a six-month trip to Europe. "Big Jim" Colosimo and Ike Bloom assured them that when they came back, Bathhouse John would have everything fixed and their establishment could reopen.

But on their return in the summer of 1912, the Everleigh sisters found that public opinion against the red-light district was still gathering momentum, forcing officials to take action. Based on evidence gathered by a civic group, five resort owners were indicted on September 25, 1912. Among those named in the indictment was A. E. Harris, a Democratic precinct captain and a righthand man of Hinky Dink Kenna. A few days later, October 4, State's Attorney John E. W. Wayman, under terrific pressure from the public, started a vice drive. Warrants were issued for 135 brothel proprietors and their lieutenants. "Big Jim" Colosimo, Harry Guzik, Roy Jones and the notorious madame, Vic Shaw, were among those named in the warrants. Still the prostitution interests refused to surrender. An organization of madames called the Friendly Friends attempted to raise a huge slush fund to bribe officials and a total of $30,000 was subscribed. Ike Bloom called on the Everleigh sisters and asked them to subscribe $40,000 as their share. Bloom insisted that he was acting on direct orders from the chief of police. But the Everleigh sisters had become millionaires in the vice business. They were not interested in fighting a losing battle and they refused to give Bloom the money.[46]

For the next several years the entrenched vice interests fought on. Closely allied with the brothel keepers in this battle were politicians and law enforcement officials who had no desire to aid in the elimination of a business that was highly profitable to them. Typical of prevalent official insincerity was the disposition of the case against Mike "de Pike" Heitler, the West Side vice king. Heitler admitted that he collected from $50.00 to $150.00 a month from each house of prostitution in his district for police protection. The judge fined him $50.00, which was the equivalent of a light slap on the wrist to one of the most vicious characters in Chicago. The drive by State's Attorney John E. W. Wayman, however, resulted in the conviction of Police Inspector Edward McCann for receiving bribes from resort owners. He was sentenced to the Illinois State Penitentiary in Joliet. Inspector John Wheeler and Lieutenant John R. Bonfield were suspended from the police department after a trial on graft charges. The Chief of Police, John McWeeny, was removed from office by the mayor on November 3, 1913, for failure to close notorious dives, and James Gleason was named in his place. In the meantime, Maclay Hoyne, a Democrat, had succeeded Wayman as state's attorney on December 1, 1912. He announced that vice conditions in Chicago were the responsibility of the chief of police and his office would not attempt to solve the problem.

But violence on the part of some of the brothel kings forced Hoyne to reverse his position. A murder was committed in a notorious saloon and vice resort operated by Roy Jones at 2037 South Wabash Avenue. A short time earlier, W. C. Dannenberg, who had been placed in charge of the morals squad by Major M. C. L. Funkhouser, a Deputy Commissioner of Police, revealed that he had been offered $2200 a month to protect the Twenty-second Street vice district. When Dannenberg's men went to Roy Jones's saloon to investigate the murder, they were attacked, and one of the officers was seriously knifed. On July 15, 1914 a gang of hoodlums connected with the vice trust shot and killed detective sergeant Stanley Birns of the morals squad and wounded another officer. The *Chicago Tribune* on July 18, 1914, realistically charged:

There are three reasons why the tragedy of the levee could not have been avoided. First, is Alderman "Hinky Dink" Kenna . . . who is the boss and absolute overlord of the First Ward. The levee exists because it is by the denizens of the levee that he rolls up the voting power which causes such men as Carter Harrison and Roger Sullivan to consult with him as a political peer . . . Second, is "Bath-house" John Coughlin, the junior partner of the "Hink" in representing the First Ward in the City Council . . . Third, is Captain Michael Ryan of the Twenty-second Street Police Station. He is the Chief of Police of the First Ward. The "Hink" put him there. The "Hink" and the "Bath" keep him there. He has been denounced as either notoriously corrupt or incompetent. But Funkhouser, Dannenberg, Gleason, and Hoyne, himself, cannot budge Ryan from that station. They have all tried and failed.

State's Attorney Maclay Hoyne could no longer ignore Chicago's vice problem. He launched a grand jury investigation which revealed that First Ward precinct captains and workers held jobs as bailiffs and clerks in the courts. In the jail they served as guards. They held important positions in the sheriff's office, the county jail, the House of Correction, the county treasurer's office and in any other position where they could assist law violators friendly with the First Ward organization. Hoyne's investigation disclosed the operation of three important vice syndicates in the South Side levee including the one headed by Big Jim Colosimo and John Torrio. Minna Everleigh testified that she had paid over $100,000 to the vice lords for protection. She admitted having contributed $3000 to the Kenna-Coughlin fund which was used to defeat a bill introduced in the legislature forbidding the sale of liquor in disorderly houses. She also related that a murder committed in a disorderly house had been hushed up by the officials. It was obvious that the political importance of the prostitution and gambling interests of the First Ward made it possible for these law violators to control the police and to dictate law enforcement policies. And symbolical of this power was the picture of Ike Bloom, the King of the Brothels, which proudly hung in the squad room of the Twenty-second Street police station.[47]

As Mayor Harrison's fifth term of office came to a close he noted that public sentiment had definitely turned against the policy of restricted districts under purported police supervision. There was some indication that the nation's second largest city was growing up. Its civic conscience, awakened two decades earlier by William T. Stead, had remained alive and active. Many evils had been eliminated while others were prevented from growing worse. A vigorous fight had checked traction graft and boodling aldermen. And Carter Harrison as mayor of Chicago, now a city of 2,185,283 inhabitants, could take pride in having exerted leadership in that fight. He was not able, however, to take effective action against the organized underworld — his political fortunes were too closely tied up with those of Hinky Dink and Bathhouse John, whose power stemmed from the very backbone of the underworld. During the preceding twenty years, Chicago had experienced a touch of reform, but its reputation would continue to grow blacker.

CHAPTER VI

Let's Play Cowboy—An Age of Foolishness

ON June 28, 1914 the Archduke Francis Ferdinand was assassinated at Sarajevo. His murderer was an agent of the Serbian society "Union or Death," a Black Hand terrorist organization. This society had been expressly founded to agitate against Austria in behalf of Serbian aspirations. One month later, July 28, Austria declared war on Serbia. Within a few days Germany had officially entered the conflict against Russia, France, Belgium, England and Serbia. The assassination of the Archduke Francis Ferdinand not only started the first World War, but it also had political repercussions in Chicago, a city with a large German population. Carter Harrison, again seeking the Democratic nomination for mayor, could not compete successfully with the German named Robert M. Sweitzer. From the passionate appeals made by Sweitzer's adherents to the German voters, it might reasonably have been expected that he personally intended to avenge the murder of the Archduke and lead an army that would defeat England, the bitter enemy of the fatherland. But the vicissitudes of politics are strange. The alleged pro-German sentiments of the Democratic candidate which won him the nomination backfired in the 1915 elections, and the way opened for a relatively unknown Republican candidate, William Hale Thompson, to become mayor.

Thompson was the creature of James A. Pugh and his Sportsman's Club. His campaign had been successfully handled by Pugh and Fred Lundin, the "poor Swede," a self-abasing man given to flattery but a political conniver without a peer. Thompson's campaign managers were direct personality opposites. Pugh was a bold promoter, yachtsman and playboy. He entered speed boats in national and international races. He bought aristocratic bulldogs, paying as high as $2000 for a single animal. In personality, he was quite similar to the new mayor. His colleague, Fred Lundin, until a few years before the election, had ridden through the remote streets of Chicago in a horse-drawn wagon, accompanied by two banjo-playing Negroes, selling a soft drink which he called Juniper Ade. Crowds gathered in the streets while the Negroes strummed their banjos and Lundin extolled the virtues of his concoction. But "the poor Swede" built up sufficient political strength to elect him to Congress in 1910. All of Lundin's actions were designed to emphasize his humility. He invariably wore a long black frock coat, a white shirt with a flowing black tie and a broad-brimmed hat. In crowds, his movements were of the slinking variety.

During the campaign, Big Bill Thompson had been to all men all things. To the gamblers he promised a wide-open town; to the respectable voters, a program of rigid law enforcement; to the Germans he was anti-British, and to the others he paraded his one hundred per cent Americanism.[1] With the aid of many Harrison Democrats who voted for the Republican candidate, Thompson's plurality over Robert M. Sweitzer mounted to 147,477 votes. Thompson retained Harrison's secretary, Charles C. Fitzmorris, and named Captain Charles C. Healey Chief of Police.

The new mayor, born in Boston, Massachusetts, in 1869, had been brought to Chicago as a mere infant. His father, a very wealthy man, had always provided for his son's every want. As a boy, young Bill detested school, so his parents sent him West. There he worked for a while as a brakeman for the Union Pacific Railroad. He later became an assistant cook on a ranch where he gained skill in roping and shooting. Before reaching his majority, Bill returned to Chicago but he never completely abandoned his cowboy ways. His real estate business occupied part of his time but he consumed more time in his capacity as a playboy. Several years before he became mayor, in 1915, Thompson had become affiliated with the discredited Billy Lorimer faction of the Republican party. Big Bill's background did not warrant particularly high expectations for his administration, and his record in office never exceeded those expectations.[2]

Almost as soon as Thompson was inaugurated he was beset with troubles. Economic conditions were bad. An army of unemployed demanded jobs and food. A building trades strike added almost 100,000 workers to the already swelled ranks of the jobless, and 15,000 others were thrown out of work when a strike was called on the Chicago streetcar and elevated railway lines. Transportation was paralyzed. On July 24, 1915, another major disaster visited Chicago. A large manufacturing company chartered an excursion boat called the *Eastland* to give its employees an outing on Lake Michigan. Hundreds of pleasure seekers boarded the boat which was moored near the Clark Street bridge. Loaded beyond its capacity, the *Eastland* began to sink lower and lower until its keel finally rested on the river bed. The upper structure of the steamship was top-heavy and when many of the excursionists crowded to one side the boat toppled over. Eight hundred and eleven persons were drowned.[3]

These were problems of first magnitude, but Big Bill, always unpredictable, proceeded to create a problem of his own. Although he was a firm advocate of the wide-open town with all of its implications, Thompson issued orders on October 4, 1915, closing the saloons on Sundays. Perhaps the orders were the result of pressure from a grand jury that was investigating lawlessness in the city. Perhaps the saloons were ordered closed on Sundays to force them in line politically. Whatever the motives, Thompson found himself in a head-on collision with Anton J. Cermak and his powerful United Societies. Organized in 1906 by Cermak and the saloonkeepers, brewers and distillers, the United Societies had grown into a formidable political power. Exploiting the liberal liquor philosophies of the foreign-born groups, the United Societies had coerced the city council into passing ordinances favorable to a wide-open town. It had exerted pressure on the Illinois State Legislature to enact laws pleasing to the saloon and liquor interests. And using the foreign-born groups as a front, the United Societies had prevented any decent regulations of saloons and vicious dance halls or the closing of gambling houses.[4] Following Thompson's edict of October 4, 1915, the United Societies organized huge parades in protest. Thompson was politically embarrassed and his program of closing saloons on the Sabbath soon fell by the wayside.

An underworld which for years had been growing stronger and bolder had few if any misgivings about the new mayor, however. Big Bill stood for the wide-open town, a happy omen for Chicago's criminal world, which had never been backward in taking advantage of its opportunities. Before long slot machines were operating with such reckless abandon in many sections of the city that in August 1916, the Civil Service Commission initiated an investigation. Charges were made that political interest in the slot machines started with their manufacture and extended all along the line to the operating level. The "one-armed bandits" which were clicking merrily throughout the city were manufactured by the Mills Novelty Company with politicians sharing in the profits. But of greater public interest was the Civil Service Commission's implication of the Sportsman's Club as a medium through which graft was paid by the rapidly expanding gambling industry. Mayor Thompson was closely identified with the Club. His name appeared on letterheads which were mailed to gamblers, saloonkeepers and vice resort operators soliciting one-hundred dollar life memberships. State's Attorney Maclay Hoyne charged that the membership fees were nothing more than protection money paid by law violators to the city administration. In support of this contention it was disclosed that prominent among the members of the Sportsman's Club was Mont Tennes, while the club's attorney was Henry Seligman, who was also the lawyer for Tennes's bookmakers. The membership list also included Raymond Tennes, a son of the gambler; James V. Mondi, who later became a dominant figure in Al Capone's gambling empire; John J. Lynch, powerful gambling house proprietor and one-time partner of Tennes in the General News Bureau; Herbert S. Mills, head of Mills Novelty Company and the largest slot machine manufacturer in the nation; O. D. Jennings, another large slot machine manufacturer; and Big Jim Colosimo, vice lord of the First Ward. And alongside these illustrious names were those of Mayor Thompson, Chief of Police Charles C. Healey, and Morgan Collins, a police captain.[5] Whatever part, if any, the Sportsman's Club may have played in the city's gambling setup, the membership lists did indicate that Chicago's mayor and his principal law-enforcement officers were maintaining a friendly relationship with those in control of gambling and vice.

And these facts constituted a scandal of major proportions.

The Civil Service investigation of 1916 was only the beginning of a series of official inquiries that rocked the Thompson administration. In fact, the Civil Service hearings were relegated to the background and almost forgotten as State's Attorney Hoyne launched an independent investigation of a huge political graft ring. On January 16, 1917, indictments charging bribery and graft were returned against eight men. Those named in the indictments were Chief of Police Healey; Tom Costello, a police captain who allegedly collected graft for Healey; Mike "de Pike" Heitler; William R. Skidmore, saloonkeeper, gambler and politician; Tom Newbold, proprietor of the Normandie Hotel; Willie Weinstein, a former partner of Newbold; Patrol Sergeant John Walsh, and Detective Sergeant Steve Barry. Newbold was one of several men who admitted having made graft payments to officials. At the trial, evidence indicated that three of the principal figures in a gigantic graft ring involving high public officials were Chief of Police Healey, Captain Tom Costello and William R. Skidmore. But prosecution of officials in Chicago for protection of gambling and vice has rarely been successful. This case was no exception and Healey was acquitted. However, the indictments resulted in his suspension and within a short time he retired.[6]

While public interest was running high as a result of the disclosures of the state's attorney and the Civil Service Commission, a third investigation was initiated in the United States District Court in Chicago. Federal Judge Kenesaw Mountain Landis directed this inquiry which arose out of straw bonds given in a blackmail case. The bondsmen were professional gamblers affiliated with the Mont Tennes syndicate and subscribers to the General News Bureau. It was brought out that before the alleged blackmailer, George Irwin, became a fugitive, a twenty-five thousand dollar fund had been raised by gamblers to defend him. A parade of prominent gamblers appeared before Judge Landis. Mont Tennes stood mute, but some of his underlings talked. Revealing testimony was given which reflected that gambling was big business in Chicago and that it operated with immunity. Mont Tennes had grown rich, but his profits, said Judge Landis, were covered with dirt and slime because young men were being made criminals as a result of his activ-

ities.[7] Only three years later the dirty and slimy money of professional gamblers fixed a World Series baseball game, nearly ruining
the national pastime. Judge Landis was then called upon to act as
the czar of organized baseball. He became a figure of national
prominence and throughout a colorful career waged incessant
warfare to keep gamblers and gambling out of baseball.

In the midst of these official investigations of gambling, vice and
graft, public attention was diverted from the local scene as America
became more deeply involved in the conflict across the Atlantic.
Germany had long shown an utter disregard for the rights of
Americans on the high seas. Protests to the government of Kaiser
Wilhelm II did nothing to ease the strained relations that had devel-
oped between the two nations, and on April 6, 1917, the United
States officially declared war on Germany.

There were approximately a half million people of German
descent living in Chicago and Mayor Thompson loudly opposed
America's entrance into the war. He also vigorously protested the
conscription of men into the army. Shortly after the United States
entered the war, a French Commission headed by the famous general
Joseph Joffre arrived in this country and announced a tour of several
large cities in behalf of the war effort. Reporters rushed to City Hall
and asked Mayor Thompson if he intended to invite the French
Commission to visit Chicago. The mayor hesitated for a moment
and then bluntly replied that he wanted first to know the purpose
of the Frenchmen's visit. He mentioned that while many Americans
were hungry, it was proposed that food be shipped abroad. "Are
these people here to add to the suffering of the people?" asked
Thompson. Although the French Commission later visited Chicago
on official invitation, Thompson's attitude and comments were given
wide attention in the press in the United States and abroad. His
political enemies dubbed him "Kaiser Bill," a name that was to be
used against him effectively in his unsuccessful campaign for the
United States Senate in 1918.[8]

Neither Big Bill's pronouncements on the war nor the preoccupa-
tion of the public with "making the world safe for democracy"
completely overshadowed the city's crime problem, however. Conditions were bad and the people knew it. Chicago's first daylight
payroll robbery occurred in 1917, when two messengers were shot

and killed as they delivered money to a plant engaged in the manufacture of shell casings for the Federal Government. Angry citizens
demanded action, and the Chicago Association of Commerce appointed a committee of ten outstanding residents to investigate and
report "upon the prevalence and prevention of crime in the city of
Chicago." On June 13, 1918, this committee recommended the formation of a commission of leading citizens which would secure the
proper administration of the criminal laws by the "officials charged
with such administration." The need was apparent for such a commission, which, unfettered by political ties, could force the officials
to perform their sworn duty.

Following the recommendation of the Association of Commerce
committee, a group of civic leaders formed the Chicago Crime
Commission which began to function on January 1, 1919. Its first
president was Edwin W. Sims, a former United States District
Attorney and secretary of the famous Vice Commission of Chicago
which was appointed in 1910. With the aid of a full-time staff, the
Chicago Crime Commission was to become known as the "Watchdog of Crime" and to serve as a model for similar citizens' organizations in other large municipalities.

In the 1919 city election, 349,057 Democratic votes were divided
between two candidates, Robert M. Sweitzer, the party standard
bearer, and Maclay Hoyne who ran as an independent. William Hale
Thompson was the beneficiary of the fight between two Democratic
candidates and was re-elected with a plurality of 21,522 votes over
Sweitzer in a bitter campaign. The composition of Chicago's population had changed appreciably since Thompson first took office
only four years earlier. During the war there was a great shortage
of workers in the stockyards, steel mills and factories, and Negroes
from the South migrated to Chicago in hordes to meet the labor
needs. When the war started there were approximately 44,000
Negroes in Chicago. By the time the armistice was signed on
November 11, 1918, the city's Negro population had grown to
100,000. Thompson fully appreciated the increasing political importance of the Negro and had met with considerable success in
corralling the colored vote. Originally, the Negro population was
largely concentrated in a relatively small area on the South Side
near the levee district. Naturally, the thousands of colored laborers

who poured into the city during the war could not be housed within this area. Expansion of the so-called black belt was necessary and inevitable, and Negroes moved into fine apartment buildings on Grand Boulevard. They found living quarters in the once exclusive Prairie Avenue section. They pushed as far south in some places as Sixty-third Street. But this expansion was not without racial tensions and bitterness. During 1918 several Negro homes were bombed by ruffians who believed that the black man had encroached on territory sacredly reserved for the white race.

On a hot summer Sunday, July 27, 1919, the Twenty-ninth Street beach on the South Side was filled with bathers. While both blacks and whites used the beach, custom had decreed that Negro bathers should not go beyond a fixed point. A seventeen-year-old Negro boy swam across this imaginary line and a group of white boys hurled stones and rocks at him. A bitter altercation arose between the black and white bathers and the seventeen-year-old Negro boy drowned. All the resentment and bitterness that had been smoldering within the breast of the Negro broke loose. Like a prairie fire the news spread that "white people have killed a Negro." Pitched battles were fought on the streets. Negro homes were invaded and set on fire. Youthful gangs of white hoodlums roamed the streets and engaged in acts of violence. There were stabbings and shootings. On Monday night, July 28, a strike on the surface cars and elevated railway added to the general confusion. The riots, the worst in Chicago's history, raged for five days. The police were helpless. At times they made no effort to protect Negroes who were being viciously assaulted in their presence. Finally, on the sixth day the state militia which was belatedly called out brought the riots to an end.

Governor Frank O. Lowden appointed a nonpartisan, interracial Chicago Commission on Race Relations to investigate the causes of the riots and to make recommendations. The report of this commission admonished the police, prosecutors and the courts for their inequitable and discriminatory handling of cases involving Negroes. It recommended better police protection at beaches and playgrounds. It requested the authorities to condemn and raze all houses unfit for human habitation. It criticized the city officials for their neglect in the disposal of garbage and rubbish in Negro communities. And the report asked that the authorities "promptly rid the Negro residence areas of vice resorts, whose present exceptional prevalence in such areas is due to official laxity." The Negroes were requested to protest "vigorously and continuously" against the presence of any vicious resort in their residence areas.[9] For the next three decades Negroes would protest "vigorously and continuously" against vice and other rackets — but without much effect. The political leaders have always been too deeply indebted to the vice and gambling lords, for money and power, to give much heed to the complaints of the common citizen. In this respect, conditions vary but little in white and Negro neighborhoods.

The race riots of 1919 will forever remain a blemish on Chicago's history, but few fair-minded persons would lay the blame for the riots on Mayor Thompson's doorstep. He had been a friend of the Negro and had fought discriminatory measures introduced in the city council. And although his police department was ineffective in handling the riots, the police departments under most of Chicago's mayors, both before and after Thompson, would have been just as ill equipped to handle any real emergency.

Early in Mayor Thompson's first term of office certain changes in the political vice setup should have served as a foreboding of evil times ahead — of the impending rise of gangster rule which was to give Chicago its well-deserved reputation as the crime capital of the world. In the first place, Thompson curtailed the power of the morals squad which had been assigned to enforce the vice and gambling laws. Throughout the police department he shuffled officers like a deck of cards, to make certain that ward committeemen received police personnel who would permit wide-open conditions. In the First Ward, Alderman Kenna designated his aide, Dennis Cooney commonly known as the "Duke," to take charge of the disorderly hotels of the area, using the Rex Hotel, 2138 South State Street, as a base of operations. Cooney met with the full approval of Big Jim Colosimo, who now became the overlord of vice in the district.

It would be a grave error to blame Thompson alone for the bizarre gangsterism which blossomed during his three terms in office. The roots of any great social or political evil run deep. Almost from the beginning of Chicago's history the underworld had been inextricably interwoven in the social and political structure of the city. And beginning with the reign of the gambling king Mike McDonald, about 1873, Chicago's criminal world had been organized for political action. For almost a half century the underworld, composed chiefly of gamblers, saloonkeepers and vice resort operators, had constituted the most powerful political force in the city. The balance of power rested in their hands. Under such conditions it was inevitable that sooner or later an Al Capone or some other gangster of imagination and audacity should decide to take full advantage of the opportunities presented by the city's criminal political system. But if Mayor Thompson was not responsible for the system, he did nothing to change it. He had neither the mental capacity nor the moral courage necessary to save the city from gangster rule. Chicago needed a major operation to remove the criminal-political system that had made it a happy hunting ground for the underworld. But a major operation requires a skilled surgeon, and the city got instead a blustering buffoon with a cowboy hat. Big Bill the Builder advocated a "wider" wide-open town — and he got it.

Big Jim Colosimo's elevation to vice lord of the First Ward was the genesis of the Capone gang. The story of Colosimo was a success story of the "rags to riches" type. Immigrating to the United States in the 1890's he soon got a job as water boy for a section gang. Through the good graces of Aldermen Kenna and Coughlin, he graduated to a white uniform and a broom, as a street-sweeper. He was made a precinct captain and delivered the vote for the First Ward aldermen. His rise was rapid. From a street-cleaner he advanced to poolroom operator and saloonkeeper. He became an entrepreneur in the First Ward's flourishing prostitution business. His first wife, Victoria Moresco, had been the madame of one of the most profitable brothels in the district. With her assistance and the protecting hands of Hinky Dink and Bathhouse John, Big Jim Colosimo prospered. He and his wife soon operated several houses of prostitution. He opened a restaurant at 2126 South Wabash Avenue. Colosimo's Café became known from coast to coast. Big Jim's power eventually exceeded that of Aldermen Kenna and Coughlin. His flashy clothes outshone even those of Bathhouse John.

He wore diamond rings, diamond stickpins, diamond studded garters and diamond bedecked watch fobs.[10]

Life had been good to Colosimo. He was wealthy. He was powerful. But still he did not have security. He received menacing threats and decided he needed a bodyguard. For this assignment he imported in 1910 a New York gunman, John Torrio. For about five years during the early 1900's Torrio had been leader of the James Street gang which operated along the waterfront of the East River area in New York City.[11] This experience was invaluable to him in dealing with Chicago gunmen. He had developed qualities of leadership, organizational ability and the art of intrigue. Under Big Jim's tutelage he rapidly acquired a knowledge of the city's politics and politicians — an indispensable requirement for anyone expecting to get ahead in Chicago's underworld. And Torrio got ahead. He knew which politicians could be bought and he bought them. He envisioned a monopoly over gambling and vice for the entire county with himself in control — and without Colosimo! Torrio was not a dreamer, he was a man of action; and he lost no time in laying the groundwork which would make him ruler of Chicago's underworld.

Torrio's rise to power was perhaps made easier by two events that occurred in 1919. The first was the re-election of William Hale Thompson as mayor. The second was the passage of the National Prohibition Act on October 28. Under the provisions of the act, national prohibition was to become effective on January 16, 1920. During Thompson's first four years as chief executive of the city, the underworld had reached unheard-of heights of prosperity. Gamblers and vice lords had entered into alliances with officials at almost every level of government. It was claimed that since the advent of the Thompson administration politicians were even sharing handsomely in the profits of Mont Tennes from the General News Bureau. With Thompson's re-election the gamblers and their political counterparts could look forward to another four years of unrestrained activity. National prohibition was to afford the criminal element a new field for illicit profits and the opportunity to organize on a vaster scale than ever before. The control of the new illegal liquor industry was to remain largely in the hands of the gambling and vice lords. But they would also draw into the swirl of criminal activity those who had previously remained on the fringe. The time was ripe for a man of the talents and ruthlessness of John Torrio to seize the throne of Chicago's criminal empire. Torrio was ready. He had been making increasing demands upon Colosimo, many of which were rejected. Bad blood was developing between Big Jim and his bodyguard.

In the early part of 1920 Colosimo divorced Victoria Moresco. He had become enamored of Dale Winters, a singer in his café. On April 20, 1920, Big Jim and Dale Winters were married. For several days most of Colosimo's thoughts centered on his new bride. Torrio on the other hand was concerned with more earthly things. He was making definite plans for his future — a future which would hold no place for the diamond-studded bridegroom. Calling on Jim O'Leary, gambling boss of the stockyards district, he arranged for two truckloads of whiskey to be delivered to Colosimo's Café at exactly 4 P.M. on May 11. At the appointed time Colosimo awaited the arrival of the contraband liquor. The liquor never came. Instead a gunman suddenly made his appearance, and within a matter of seconds vanished. Big Jim was dead at the hands of a paid killer, probably Frankie Yale, said to have been imported from New York by Torrio for the assassination.

Colosimo's funeral was a gaudy, maudlin extravaganza. It was open testimony of the alliance between crime and politics in Chicago — a public demonstration of how low official morals had been driven by the wide-open town policy which had prevailed for over half a century. The only claim to prominence which the deceased could make was the successful operation of a string of brothels. He was a glorified pimp, who had learned how to run a restaurant. Yet so important was Big Jim Colosimo to Chicago politicians that his honorary pallbearers included three judges, an assistant state's attorney, Congressmen John W. Rainey and Thomas Gallagher, State Representative Michael L. Igoe who later became a Federal judge, numerous aldermen including Hinky Dink Kenna, Dorsey Crowe, John Powers, James P. Bowler and John Toman. Other honorary pallbearers were Mike Merlo, the head of Unione Siciliana, Mike Potson and John Torrio. Mike Potson incidentally was to follow in the footsteps of Big Jim. He became the manager of Colosimo's Café, and through the operation of lucrative gambling games in the café and from bawdyhouses, he amassed a fortune. Although he was not a pallbearer, Alderman Bathhouse John Coughlin prominently displayed himself kneeling beside the casket.[12] The bold attendance of Chicago's officialdom as mourners and pallbearers at the funeral of an underworld chieftain was a sordid episode in Chicago's political history. It was a public announcement that the criminal world ruled the city, and political success depended upon the favor of those in control of gambling and vice. The voice of the general public which abhorred such criminal-official alliances was weak and politically insignificant. The city had capitulated to the underworld. And the explanation was not to be found in national prohibition! The blame could not be fixed solely on the corrupt Thompson administration. Rather the unholy surrender resulted from the natural evolution of a vicious political system dating back at least to Mike McDonald.

John Torrio spent little time in mourning before assuming supreme command of Chicago's underworld. This was by no means a sudden jump from obscure ranks to the position of ruler of the city's criminal empire. For several years Torrio had been a kingpin in the politically protected gambling racket. During Mayor Thompson's first term of office, Torrio's power had grown steadily. Before the advent of national prohibition, Chicago cigar stores had turned over their back rooms to Torrio-controlled gambling operations. His influence had even been extended to some of the suburban towns. In fact, in some respects Torrio's power exceeded that of his boss, although Colosimo had been reaping the lion's share of the profits.

Torrio's growth in stature among the criminal element was due in large measure to his ability as an organizer. He surrounded himself with gunmen who were able to maintain discipline within the ranks and who would eliminate any pretenders to his throne. His principal assistant and field general was young Al Capone, a veteran member of the Five Points Gang in New York City. Before Torrio brought him to Chicago as his lieutenant, Capone had already been questioned by New York City police concerning two murders. Capone was a "stand-up guy." He was ruthless. He had ambition. Torrio was a judge of gunmen and he made no mistake in his selection of Capone. As early as 1919, Capone as field general for Torrio lined up the gambling dens and made certain that they remained lined up.[13] Before the death of Colosimo, Torrio had established himself as the czar of gambling and vice in the suburban town of Burnham, Illinois, south of Chicago. This town was wide-open, the officials friendly, and Torrio made the most of his opportunities. Jack and Harry Guzik, Ike Bloom and other Torrio associates of the Twenty-second Street levee had opened vice and gambling resorts in southern and western Chicago suburbs as early as 1916.[14] The principal headquarters of the Torrio gang, however, was known as the Four Deuces, located at 2222 South Wabash Avenue in congenial Chicago.

The Four Deuces was a four-story building. Torrio's office and a saloon occupied the first floor. The second and third floors were used exclusively for gambling operations and the top floor was a brothel. The place was naturally frequented by some of the most dangerous criminals in America. Friendly politicians and political fixers also could be seen there almost any time. William R. Skidmore, who was to become one of the big gambling bosses of the city during the Kelly-Nash regime several years later, spent much of his time in the place. His usual companion was the notorious North Side gunman, Barney Bertche. It was claimed that twelve unsolved murders had been committed in the Four Deuces. But this number paled into insignificance when compared with the wholesale slaughter that followed in the wake of Torrio and Capone gang activities in the years ahead.[15]

The criminal organization headed by John Torrio was rapidly becoming more powerful than the city government. And while Chicago was being overrun by one of the most vicious gangs of hoodlums in American history its playboy mayor, cowboy hat in hand, was still preaching the blessings of the wide-open town. It was good for business, he said. It was good for business all right — the business of John Torrio and his ruthless well-organized band of gunmen. Chicago became the undisputed headquarters in America for crime and vice. A hearing of the United States Senate Judiciary Committee on May 10, 1920, disclosed evidence that Chicago was the center of handbook gambling for the nation. The wires from Mont Tennes's General News Bureau spread out from Chicago to every major city in the country. On May 12, 1920, charges were made that the Chicago handbook syndicate had profited to the extent of several hundred thousand dollars the previous Saturday when a "long shot" won the Kentucky Derby. Sinister implications accompanied the charge, but Chicago's handbooks enjoyed ironclad official protection.[16]

A new and lucrative field was the beer business, which was being organized on a city- and county-wide basis with Torrio and his gang occupying the predominant role. There were indications that the organization of the liquor industry had the consent of City Hall. At least the mayor was not unfriendly to the illegal liquor interests. And his police entered into the spirit of the times wholeheartedly. Mayor Thompson's chief of police in 1921, Charles C. Fitzmorris, candidly stated that a large percentage of the city's police officers were actually engaged in the illicit liquor business.[17] It was no mystery, then, why the police were helpless in dealing with the growing number of gang killings in the city. The forces of law and order were in league with the lawless elements.

Crime was on the rampage, and so was the Thompson-Lundin political machine. The machine was drunk with power. It considered itself unbeatable. In April 1920, Thompson candidates captured the prized position of ward committeeman in thirty-four of the city's thirty-five wards. Only in the old Nineteenth Ward was the Thompson candidate defeated. There the victor was "Diamond Joe" Esposito, a man with gangster affiliations and a ward leader in the Charles S. Deneen faction of the Republican party. Eight years later he was killed by gangster bullets as he walked on the street between two bodyguards. Esposito was credited with being the power behind the notorious Genna brothers, Angelo, Jim, Mike, Pete, Sam and Tony. "The terrible Genna's" became powerful bootleggers during the early 1920's when they hired hundreds of Italians and Sicilians to cook alcohol for them in West Side tenements and figured prominently in Chicago's vicious gang warfare.

The year 1920 was filled with events of political import for the city, state and nation. On April fourteenth, less than a month before the murder of Big Jim Colosimo, the powerful Democratic boss of Illinois, Roger C. Sullivan, died. He was succeeded by his loyal follower and lieutenant, George E. Brennan. The Sullivan-Brennan Democratic organization at times had given a helping hand to the

Thompson Republican machine, but such bipartisan deals had long featured political affairs in the city and county. In 1920, too, the Republican party again selected Chicago as the site of its national convention. By now Chicago had grown to a city of 2,701,705 people. Sixty years earlier, when Abraham Lincoln won the Republican nomination for the Presidency, the city's population was 109,420. The convention of 1920 featured the manipulations of political bigwigs in smoke-filled hotel rooms. General Leonard Wood and Illinois's favorite son, Governor Frank O. Lowden, were the two preconvention leaders for the Presidential nomination. Mayor Thompson, once a political supporter of Lowden, had broken with the Illinois governor and was determined to marshal all the forces at his command to prevent his nomination. More influential than any of the delegates attending the convention, however, was Senator Boies Penrose of Pennsylvania. From his sickbed in Pennsylvania Penrose made known his wishes by long distance telephone. On June 12, 1920, Warren G. Harding received the nomination. The way was paved for his election and the scandal of Teapot Dome.[18]

Mayor Thompson's hatred for Governor Lowden was bitter and intense. "Big Bill" considered the smashing of Lowden's presidential aspirations as a personal triumph. Now Thompson was determined to place a man friendly to himself in the governor's chair in Springfield. For this honor, Big Bill selected Len Small, a farmer and banker from Kankakee, Illinois. Small, a friend of Fred Lundin, was no novice in the game of politics. He had been a state senator and state treasurer. With the backing of the Thompson forces he became a formidable candidate.

Only a few days after the close of the Republican National Convention, Big Bill received an unpleasant reminder that the control of the judiciary and the office of State's Attorney of Cook County was of greater immediate importance to him than the governorship. Thompson's School Board had long been the center of heated controversy. Charges of graft and corruption had been leveled at it. A Democratic state's attorney initiated a lengthy investigation of the charges and several members of the Board were indicted. On June 22, 1920, Mayor Thompson appeared in the courtroom of Judge Kickham Scanlan to lend his support to members who were in legal difficulty. He was shocked when Judge Scanlan found nine members of the board, together with the board attorney, guilty of contempt of court and imposed both fines and jail sentences on several of the defendants.[19] Big Bill was impressed with the power of the courts and he solemnly swore he would do something about it. He also blamed an unfriendly state's attorney for the predicament of his School Board and promptly launched a campaign to place one of his loyal followers in this important office. The man selected by Thompson and Lundin was Robert E. Crowe, Chief Justice of the Criminal Court.

Thompson entered the political campaign of 1920 with a vengeance, hurling vicious charges against candidates opposing the Thompson-Lundin slate and singling out Governor Lowden for particularly bitter attacks. The *Chicago News* and the *Tribune* denounced the Thompson administration as corrupt and unworthy of confidence and support. Crowe and Thompson lashed back. Resorting to typical political chicanery, the Thompson forces charged the papers with injuring the fair name and reputation of the city. Thompson then introduced a new refrain in his tiresome tune. Said Big Bill, "I wouldn't sing 'God Save the King' in return for complimentary newspaper articles." Thompson had stumbled on a new issue — King George of England. In the future when political opponents talked of the prevalence of crime, gangsters and corruption, Big Bill would wave his arms and wage an all-out offensive against King George. There was no defense to frequent charges that gangsterism had swept the city during his administration. But among many of the electorate, his promise to "punch King George in the snoot" carried vote appeal. Of course such statements made Chicago ludicrous in the eyes of the rest of the world, but as long as they made votes for Thompson, he cared little about the city's reputation. In this respect, he was no different from most Chicago politicians, either before or since. Finally, under Thompson's influence, the English language was boycotted by the state of Illinois, and a law was passed by the Illinois Legislature which declared that "The official language of the State of Illinois shall be known hereafter as the American language." [20]

On November 2, 1920, the Thompson-Lundin slate was victorious. Robert E. Crowe was elected State's Attorney of Cook County and Len Small became the governor of Illinois. Only a few months later, July 20, 1921, the Sangamon County Grand Jury indicted Small on charges of embezzlement and other offenses allegedly committed while he was state treasurer. The case was fought on the front pages of the newspapers as well as in the courts. Small contended he could not obtain a fair trial in Sangamon County and the case was finally transferred to Waukegan, Illinois, the county seat of Lake County. After months of spectacular legal battling Small was acquitted in Waukegan on June 24, 1922.[21]

Few political organizations of Chicago have been more powerful than the one controlled by Thompson and Lundin in 1921. Offices of the mayor of the city, the governor of the state and the county prosecutor were in its hands. But just when it appeared unlikely that anyone could successfully challenge this power, Thompson, Lundin and Crowe overreached themselves in their greed to make their political domination absolute. Thompson had learned in the School Board cases that the judges were not always inclined to bow to his wishes. This was a weakness in his armor which must be corrected. As the June 1921, judicial election was approaching, Thompson, Crowe and Lundin were determined to place men on the Circuit and Superior Court benches who were subservient to them. They would accept no suggestions from any source as to their slate of judicial candidates. They considered themselves all-powerful and were prepared to defy the bar association, the press and the public. Immediately the cry was raised that the City Hall was conspiring to seize the judiciary. Big Bill and his cohorts had not anticipated that public opinion could be roused sufficiently to overcome the tremendous strength of their political organization. Only seven months earlier this organization had made a clean sweep at the polls. Now, all of its judicial candidates were overwhelmingly defeated, and public anger at the power-hungry Thompson machine spread to the legislative halls in the state capital. Thompson had an important transportation bill pending in the Illinois General Assembly. He expected little difficulty in pushing the bill through the legislature with the aid of the governor whom he had selected and helped elect. Mayor Thompson and Fred Lundin went to Springfield to plead with the state lawmakers to pass the transportation bill. Their pleas were ignored and a state senator, Otis F. Glenn, who led the attack against Big Bill, won such popular acclaim and attention that the way was paved for his elevation to the United States Senate some time later.[22]

Unfortunately, all of the political issues in 1921 were not being settled by votes at the polling places or in the state legislature. Many were decided by sawed-off shotguns and bombs. In the Nineteenth Ward, Democratic Alderman John Powers, once president of the Cook County Democracy, had ruled supreme since 1888. Originally this had been a predominantly Irish ward, but by 1916 the majority of the voters were Italian and efforts were made to wrest control from Powers. The leader of this movement was Anthony D'Andrea, an unfrocked priest who had been a powerful figure in the old red-light district. His name had been linked with a gang of Italian forgers and he had served thirteen months in the penitentiary on a counterfeiting charge. Anthony D'Andrea had become the head of the Hod Carriers' Union, after the former president, Joseph D'Andrea, who incidentally was not related to Anthony, was shot and killed in a labor dispute. He was also president of the Unione Siciliana.

In the aldermanic election which was held on February 21, 1921, Anthony D'Andrea, running as a nonpartisan candidate, opposed John Powers. On February 7, two weeks before the election, when three hundred people were attending a meeting in behalf of D'Andrea's candidacy in a hall located at 854 Blue Island Avenue, a bomb was hurled in the hall and five persons were seriously injured. D'Andrea charged that his political enemies were responsible for the bombing. On February 18, the home of Joseph Spica at 1028 Newberry Avenue was bombed. Spica's son-in-law who lived with him was one of D'Andrea's political lieutenants. Later a bomb was hurled at the political headquarters of D'Andrea himself. Several months earlier Alderman John Powers's home at 1284 McAllister Place had been bombed. James Bowler, the junior alderman of the ward and political ally of Powers, charged that imported gunmen were conducting a systematic campaign of terrorism throughout the Nineteenth Ward. Sinister voices warned him over the telephone that he was to be kidnapped and "bumped off." The home of Alderman Powers was under continual armed guard. In this atmosphere of fear and violence, Powers defeated D'Andrea by a margin of 435 votes. There were charges and countercharges of vote stealing and fraud. And the official tally of the votes did not end the bitter election campaign. On March 9, 1921, Paul Labriola, one of John Powers' loyal supporters and a Municipal Court bailiff for fifteen years, was shot and killed at West Congress and Halsted Streets, and a short time later another Powers adherent, Harry Raimondi, was assassinated.

In an effort to stem the rising tide of violence, Thompson's new Chief of Police, Charles Fitzmorris, issued a sweeping transfer order affecting 712 police officers. The entire police personnel of the Nineteenth Ward was changed but there was no improvement in conditions. The Nineteenth Ward was an armed camp. Gangs of hoodlums, armed with sawed-off shotguns, toured the streets in stolen automobiles and terrorized the entire district. A letter was received at the D'Andrea residence with the warning: "He killed others. We are going to do the same." It was signed "Revenge." Another letter threatened to blow up the building and kill the entire D'Andrea family. The letters were called to the attention of the police. They dismissed them as being the products of "practical jokers." D'Andrea, however, was thoroughly frightened. He announced that he had severed all connections with Nineteenth Ward politics. But his announcement came too late. On May 11, 1921, Anthony D'Andrea was ambushed and mowed down with slugs from a sawed-off shotgun. He was given a royal funeral attended by eight thousand people. The funeral procession was two and one half miles long, and among the honorary pallbearers were twenty judges. The active pallbearers included "Diamond Joe" Esposito, Pete Fosco of the Hod Carriers' Union and Carmen Vacco, the city sealer. But even the D'Andrea murder did not end the violence. Before the year 1921 came to an end three additional D'Andrea followers were assassinated.[23]

The bitter political feud in the Nineteenth Ward, with its bombings and shotgun slayings, was merely symbolical of the complete breakdown of government that had occurred in Chicago. The police department was helpless and equally ineffective was the office of state's attorney. And adding to the ineptness of the official crime-fighting forces was the internecine warfare that broke out between the city police and State's Attorney Robert E. Crowe. Crowe had resented the mayor's appointment of Charles C. Fitzmorris as chief of police. As a result, relations between Thompson and Crowe grew more and more strained until their quarrel became a matter of public knowledge. The state's attorney's police conducted raids on syndicated gambling and vice resorts, arousing the anger of the Thompson administration. Crowe charged that gambling and vice lords were paying huge tribute to the local police. But if Crowe had no confidence in the city police department, he also had little faith in his own police contingent of forty officers headed by his Chief Investigator, Ben Newmark. Newmark had been foisted on Crowe by important politicians whom he dared not defy. Crowe privately referred to Newmark and the forty policemen assigned to him as "Ali Baba and the forty thieves." [24] To many people, Newmark was regarded as a racketeer, and in 1928 he was killed in a typical gang murder. It is small wonder that law enforcement in the nation's second largest city was a farce and justice was reserved for the small-time thief without money or political connections.

With little to fear from either state's attorney or police, the criminal and racketeering elements felt free to wage open warfare on many fronts. The economic as well as the political life of the city fell under a rule of force. For many years Chicago had been plagued with an acute shortage of housing facilities. Rents had soared while the building industry remained stagnant, until in 1921 a bitter dispute arose between the builders and the unions. Federal Judge Kenesaw Mountain Landis was chosen to arbitrate the differences. "The building industry in Chicago," Judge Landis said, "had become rotten with manipulative combinations, uneconomic rules and graft, which caused the stagnation of building." With customary vigor, Landis struck at the exclusive combinations of employees. He decided in favor of a reduction in wages, the arbitration of disputes and outlawing sympathetic strikes. His findings became known as the Landis Award and a citizens' committee was formed to enforce them. Although the Landis Award was bitterly resented by many union members, the Building Trades Council officially ratified it on October 1, 1921.

The official ratification of the Award, however, only seemed to intensify the opposition to its provisions. Sluggings and bombings became commonplace. During 1922, at least fourteen buildings were bombed as a result of the Building Trades war. On May 9, 1922, a policeman, Thomas Clark, was shot as he was patrolling his beat in front of the Tyler-Hippach Company factory at 623 Orleans Street. This factory building was bombed the same day. A police lieutenant and squad leader, Terrence Lyons, observed three men in a car whom he suspected to be the murderers of police officer Clark. When he attempted to stop the car, he was shot and killed. Two vicious murders and a bombing had been committed within twenty-four hours. The state's attorney ordered wholesale arrests. He named "Big Tim" Murphy, Fred "Frenchy" Mader and Cornelius "Con" Shea as the "Big Three" responsible for the police murders. Associated with them in the Building Trades war were the infamous Torrio gangster, Dan McCarthy, known as "Dapper Dan," and many others of his stripe. The Big Three were arrested and released on bonds totaling $150,000. It was charged that these men were members of a conspiracy which had for its object "the establishment of a reign of terror in Chicago." Through trickery and intimidation, Frenchy Mader had been elected as head of the Building Trades Council. Whenever disputes arose between employers and unions which opposed the Landis Award, Mader and Big Tim Murphy offered to "iron out" the difficulties for fees ranging from $75,000 to $100,000. Mader personally led raids upon buildings that were being constructed under the Landis Award. Dapper Dan McCarthy furnished explosives to sluggers with instructions concerning their use. The state's attorney charged that the conspiracy of these men and others to terrorize the building industry in the city was responsible for the murder of the policemen. With typical Chicago justice, prosecution of the principal offenders met with utter failure. Only a minor underling, John Miller, who admitted having driven the murderers' car when Lieutenant Terrence Lyons was killed, was convicted. Miller denied knowing any of the other defendants. Upon conclusion of the trial, Frenchy Mader and Dapper Dan McCarthy gratefully shook hands with Miller, saying, "If you had told the police the labor unions hired you to bomb buildings you would be a free man and there would be a noose around our necks." In the eyes of Frenchy Mader and Dapper Dan, John Miller had proved himself a man. He accepted his fourteen-year prison sentence without squealing and, as usual, the principal racketeers went scot-free.[25]

The bombing war reached its height in April 1922. Two homes were bombed on April tenth. On April twelfth the Parise Restaurant at 11560 Front Avenue in the Kensington area was bombed for the second time in three weeks. There was no bombing on April 11, probably because the gangsters were too busy at the polls. A primary was held on that day which was of unusual importance to the future of Chicago and Cook County. Although the Democratic leadership of George E. Brennan was bitterly challenged, his entire slate of candidates was successful. Brennan had established himself as the new boss of the Democratic party — the rightful successor to Roger C. Sullivan. The defeated Democratic candidates screamed that frauds at the polls had robbed them of the nominations. County Judge Frank S. Righeimer ordered a recount which uncovered vote frauds on a wholesale basis in many sections of the city. The judge imposed jail sentences on many election officials but through swift legal action in another court the offenders were promptly released. Not a single guilty election official went to jail.

Among Brennan's successful candidates in the primary on April 11, was Anton J. Cermak, who won the Democratic nomination for president of the Cook County Board of Commissioners. Cermak had grown to political power as secretary of the United Societies which had been organized by the saloonkeepers, brewers and distillers. He had served as Chief Bailiff of the Municipal Court of Chicago. Now he was ready to run for his first major elective office. On November 7, 1922, he was elected president of the Cook County Board of Commissioners. This office was very influential in law enforcement matters in the county outside of Chicago. In effect, Cermak became the "mayor" of Cook County. A running mate of Cermak's on the Democratic ticket was Edmund K. Jarecki who was elected county judge for the first time. Jarecki would continue for three decades to hold this powerful office which controls the election machinery.

Having captured several key offices in the November 1922 election, the Democrats gazed with longing eyes on the mayoralty contest which would take place the following spring. For eight hectic years, Big Bill Thompson and his Republican administration had ruled the city. Whatever else might be said of the Thompson regime, it was never lacking in excitement. The underlying cause of Chicago's ills, said Chief Justice Michael L. McKinley of the Criminal Court, was "An alliance between predatory politics and professional crime that reaches into every quarter of community life." Gambling, said the chief justice, "has grown gigantically as a business which produces nothing but grafters, embezzlers, forgers, confidence men, pickpockets, burglars and bandits. . . ." The police department was at the mercy of ward bosses who were able to deliver the vote of the "vicious elements" in return for a promise of police protection. And as long as adequate protection was furnished, the criminal syndicates delivered a percentage of their profits to the ward bosses and exerted "all of their influence to the organization whose political partners they are so long as the *status quo* continues." [26] The system described by Chief Justice McKinley was not new. It had existed in Chicago for decades. But under the encouragement of the Thompson administration it had expanded until conditions were completely out of hand. To all intents and purposes organized gunmen were in control of the City Hall.

CHAPTER VII

King George Dethroned — King Al Takes Over

AS the two major political parties began making preparations for the 1923 city election, William Hale Thompson sadly realized that the fortunes of a politician can change very rapidly. Only two years earlier he had been virtually invincible. Among his political assets at that time he could list the governor of the state, the State's Attorney of Cook County, and thirty-four out of thirty-five ward committeemen in the city. A nod of approval from Big Bill assured success in the political affairs of city, county and state. As for himself, he was entertaining serious hopes that he would soon be occupying the White House. But following the zenith of his power in 1921, disaster had overtaken the cowboy mayor. He had come to a parting of the ways with State's Attorney Robert E. Crowe. His relations with Fred Lundin had cooled and were about to break into open hostility. It was obvious even to the optimistic mayor that his political machine had completely disintegrated.

At least part of the dissension between Thompson and his former allies, Crowe and Lundin, grew out of their efforts to control the police department. From time immemorial the Chicago Police Department had been one of the most political of all branches of city government. Few positions were considered of greater importance to politicians than the post of chief of police, and when Big Bill appointed Charles Fitzmorris to that office in November 1920, he aroused the ire of both Crowe and Lundin. A feud was started which grew in intensity until Thompson's political ambitions lay in a heap of ruins. And while the city's political leaders were fighting over the control of the police department, rival gangs rode through the streets waging open warfare against one another. The Thompson administration was completely discredited. The man who hoped to be President of the United States could not be re-elected mayor of Chicago, and he knew it. Big Bill decided against seeking a third term as mayor and the Republicans nominated Postmaster Arthur C. Lueder as their candidate in the spring election. Significantly, Lueder's principal backing came from forces hostile to Thompson. In effect, the two-term mayor had been repudiated by his own party.

The Democrats, having tasted defeat at the two preceding mayoralty elections, were in no mood to take chances. Boss Brennan had no interest in destroying alliances between criminals and politicians unless they were hostile to him, but for vote-getting purposes he wanted to capitalize on prevalent public disgust with the Thompson administration. Under proper circumstances, therefore, Brennan was willing to accept a candidate who had the respect of civic groups and their leaders. Judge William E. Dever was such a man. He had started his political career over two decades earlier with the blessing of the Municipal Voters' League. In public office he had conducted himself with dignity and had displayed unusual ability. His character was unassailable. On April 3, 1923, William E. Dever was elected mayor of Chicago.

The new mayor was a man of high integrity; he was capable and courageous. But he was no miracle man. And the conditions of city government had sunk to such a low that only a man endowed with supernatural powers could have coped with them successfully. Furthermore, the machine of McDonald, Sullivan and Brennan had certainly not selected Judge Dever because they actually wanted a civic house cleaning. Resorting to a typical Tammany Hall maneuver, the party leaders had chosen Dever solely for window dressing. Before honoring him with the nomination, they had exacted a promise that he would permit Boss Brennan to dispense the patronage of the mayor's office.[1] By this simple expedient the new mayor was left with the responsibility but without the power to eradicate the strong influence of the underworld on government. Brennan was assured of remaining in control of the party machinery and the possibility of Dever's building a rival organization was virtually eliminated. Since Boss Brennan, in doling out jobs, relied heavily on the counsel and advice of such party stalwarts as Hinky Dink Kenna and Anton Cermak, it could hardly be expected that the key positions of government would be filled with men who would fight the very system which gave them their power.

It is questionable whether the change in the city administration placed much fear in the heart of John Torrio. The members of his organization were too firmly fixed in the political structure of the city to become very much concerned over who occupied the mayor's chair. Almost simultaneously with the election of Mayor Dever, however, Torrio began giving more attention to the development of his illicit operations beyond the city limits. His gambling and vice resorts in Burnham, Illinois, were still flourishing. He was well established in Stickney, Illinois. He now conceived the plan of establishing the headquarters for his gambling and beer distribution activities in Cicero. The principal obstacle to this move was Eddie Tancl, a Bohemian prize fighter and café proprietor who was strongly rooted in Cicero. And Tancl had no intentions of moving aside for John Torrio or anyone else. In overcoming the opposition of Tancl, Torrio resorted to a carefully planned stratagem. Without seeking any official protection, he opened a bawdy-house in Cicero. Naturally the police raided it with dispatch. He moved it to a second location and again the Cicero police raided the brothel and forced it to close. Now Torrio was ready for his master stroke. At the gangster's instigation, Sheriff Peter Hoffman moved into Cicero with raiding parties and put its flourishing slot machines out of business. The blow was fatal. An immediate truce followed between Torrio and Tancl without a shot having been fired. Torrio and his first lieutenant, Al Capone, started gambling and beer operations in Cicero. The slot machines began clicking again.[2] Peace reigned temporarily, but Cicero still remained disputed territory.

John Torrio was rapidly becoming one of the most powerful gangsters in the nation. From gambling and illicit beer operations he had become tremendously wealthy. He owned the West Hammond and Manhattan breweries and was interested in others. With his family he toured Europe. In Italy he purchased a villa for his mother. He was held in high esteem by the William Hale Thompson Republican organization. His political power even extended to the state capital in Springfield. When Harry Guzik and his wife, Alma, were convicted as panders, Torrio had sufficient influence to secure their pardons from Governor Len Small before they had served any part of the sentences imposed on them.[3]

It is not surprising that as the Cicero elections approached in the spring of 1924 that the political support of the Torrio gang was sought by opportunistic politicians. For many years the organization headed by Joseph Z. Klenha, president of the village board, had controlled Cicero as a result of clever political deals. But in 1924 the Democrats decided to enter a separate list of candidates on the ballot. This maneuver presented a threat to the political fortunes of Klenha, who was running on the Republican ticket. To prevent a possible Democratic victory, Republican committeemen conceived a brilliant plan of action. Edward Vogel, a slot-machine boss, was designated as an emissary to approach the Torrio gang for support for the Republican candidate. Vogel consulted with Louis La Cava, a Torrio lieutenant, and an alliance between the Cicero Republicans and the Torrio criminal organization became a reality.

Election day in Cicero arrived on April 1, 1924. The Torrio stalwarts had no intention of permitting any element of chance to enter into the contest. They were professional gamblers — and gamblers never gamble! In one of the most disgraceful episodes in American municipal history, Torrio gangsters conducted an armed invasion of the thriving suburb of Cicero. Armed with machine guns, they manned the polls. Automobiles filled with gunmen patrolled the streets. Polling places were raided and ballots stolen at gunpoint. Voters were kidnapped and transported to Chicago where they were held captive until after the polls closed. Others were slugged and shot. A reign of terror prevailed. The county judge in charge of elections dispatched seventy patrolmen, five detective bureau squads and nine automobile squads from Chicago to Cicero to restore order. When Chicago police approached a polling place manned by Torrio gunmen a pitched battle took place. In the fusillade, Al Capone's brother, Frank, fell mortally wounded and another man was seriously injured. It is needless to mention that the Torrio-Capone candidate for village president was elected.[4] And Cicero became known throughout the nation as one of the toughest places in America, a reputation it was to retain for many years. Its main streets were filled with gambling establishments and houses of prostitution. It remained the Torrio headquarters for illicit beer distribution. The only law observed in the place was the law decreed by the Torrio-Capone gangsters. They owned Cicero — lock, stock and barrel.

Following the election day gun battle, Frank Capone was given an elaborate funeral. Floral pieces costing over twenty thousand dollars were supplied by Dion O'Banion's florist shop, which was across the street from the Holy Name Cathedral, only a few blocks north of Chicago's busy Loop.[5]

Dion O'Banion, incidentally, was a most unusual florist; he not only furnished flowers for funerals but also provided the corpses. Mayor Dever's chief of police, Morgan Collins, once attributed at least twenty-five murders to this tough gunman who had been reared on the city's "near North Side." While still a mere youth he had served sentences in the House of Correction for robbery and for carrying concealed weapons. During a fierce newspaper circulation war he was employed as a terrorist. He also tried his hand at safe-cracking. In the midst of blowing open the safe of a labor union in the Postal Telegraph Building he was caught red-handed by the police, but after the payment of bribes, the police became forgetful and it was decided the case against him was weak. On another occasion O'Banion shot two men in the entrance of the LaSalle Theatre. This time he was not even prosecuted. He had developed into a powerful underworld leader in his own right, and his prestige was further enhanced when he became aligned with John Torrio, who placed him in charge of gambling and bootlegging activities on the North Side. Although it was outside his territory, the Torrio gang also promised O'Banion a percentage of the profits of the Ship, one of the most notorious gambling houses in Cicero.

On November 3, 1924, O'Banion attended a conference held in the Ship for the purpose of dividing the previous week's profits. Also present at the meeting called by Al Capone in the absence of Torrio were Frank Nitti, Frank Maritote (alias Frank Diamond), Earl "Hymie" Weiss, Frankie Rio and Vince Drucci. Capone explained to his confederates that Angelo Genna had lost $30,000 at the Ship's gambling tables the week before and had left his I.O.U.'s covering that amount. Capone suggested that the debt be cancelled.

Dion O'Banion strenuously objected and issued an ultimatum to
Angelo Genna by telephone giving him one week to pay. Angelo
Genna was a powerful leader in the Unione Siciliana. He was a
vicious killer and was not easily intimidated. It so happened, therefore, that on November 10, 1924, three men entered O'Banion's
flower shop at 738 North State Street in Chicago. One of them
grasped the outstretched hand of O'Banion in a friendly greeting.
The other two emptied their revolvers into his head at close range.
A silver-bronze casket valued at $10,000 was brought from Pennsyl-
vania in a special car for O'Banion's corpse. His wake was attended
by prominent politicians including five judges of the Municipal
Court. Also present to pay his respects was Alderman Dorsey Crowe.
Only a short time before his death O'Banion had worked diligently
in behalf of Crowe's election. As the hearse carried the tough gangster to his last resting place, it was followed by a huge funeral procession made up in part of judges, legislators and aldermen.[6]

By 1924, John Torrio had reached the height of his power. Politicians vied with one another for his support. Rival gangsters feared
him. His allies included Louis Alterie, Frank McErlane, Hymie
Weiss, Dapper Dan McCarthy, Dan McFall, and scores of others.
Some of the nation's most vicious killers were at his beck and call.
Nevertheless Torrio's position was still far from impregnable. His
power stemmed from corrupt political alliances and was enforced
by the guns of gangsters, but it was a power that lacked stability.
Politicians could usually be kept in line. Gangsters, however, had
a habit of changing sides. The lines of battle were constantly shifting. Guns spitting forth bullets and death in behalf of Torrio and
his gang one day were frequently employed by the same killers the
next, in the interest of opposing forces. The murder of Dion
O'Banion touched off a series of gang slayings. Angelo Genna was
murdered on May 26, 1925, his brother Michael was killed on June
13, and a third brother, Anthony, was ambushed and slain on
July 8.[7]

Several months before the O'Banion murder an incident occurred
which was to serve as the beginning of Torrio's downfall. On
May 19, 1924, Chief of Police Morgan Collins directed a raid on
the Sieben Brewery where thirteen truckloads of beer were waiting
to be convoyed through the streets of Chicago by Torrio gunmen.

Among the numerous men arrested were John Torrio, Louis Alterie and Hymie Weiss. The defendants were turned over to the Federal government for prosecution. Rushing to the aid of the gunmen in custody, William Skidmore, professional bondsman and gambler-politician, secured the release of several on bail. A total of thirty-eight defendants were indicted by a Federal grand jury. John Torrio received a sentence of nine months in the Lake County Jail. The gang leader's ironclad immunity had been broken, and the Chicago police had given the Federal authorities a helping hand. This was not only perplexing — it was utterly humiliating.

On January 24, 1925, just before Torrio began serving his sentence, an attempt was made to assassinate him. Three men, believed to have been George "Bugs" Moran, Hymie Weiss and Vince Drucci, were the assailants. One witness positively identified Bugs Moran as the man who jumped from a car and fired upon Torrio, but Moran was not even indicted. Torrio was rushed to the Jackson Park Hospital where he was brought back to health, but not happiness. His escape from death had been only by the narrowest of margins. With one gangster after another meeting violent death, Torrio decided to abdicate his throne to Al Capone and leave the turmoil of Chicago gangland battles forever. After serving his nine-month jail sentence he therefore returned to New York City where he eventually became affiliated with an underworld group which included such well-known gangsters as Frank Costello, Charles "Lucky" Luciano, Meyer Lansky, Benjamin "Bugsy" Siegel and many others. About ten years later he was sentenced to two and one-half years in jail for evasion of the Federal income tax.

The illicit empire which Torrio was abandoning was worth millions. This fact was definitely established by records seized by the police on April 6, 1925, during a raid on lavishly furnished offices at 2146 South Michigan Avenue in Chicago. The South Michigan Avenue address had served as the gang headquarters since the syndicate had been ousted from the Four Deuces several months earlier. Arrested by police in the raid were John Patton, who had won fame as the "Boy Mayor of Burnham," Robert Larry McCullough, once convicted for burglary, Frank Nitti, Leo Clark, Joseph Piza, Joe Fusco, Anthony Arasso and Phillip Kimmle, a former partner of Mike "de Pike" Heitler. Torrio's field general Al Capone was not present when the police arrived; he was already in hiding for the slugging of a policeman and a newspaper editor in Cicero. Records seized by the raiding officers revealed that John Torrio, John Patton, Al Capone, Jack Guzik and others were reaping an annual revenue amounting to millions of dollars from bootlegging and disorderly house operations. Four large breweries were operated by the syndicate to produce beer for Chicago's thirsty customers. Liquor was brought to the Windy City from New York, Miami and New Orleans. Carefully recorded were the names of police officers and Federal prohibition agents who were on the gang's payoff list. Complete customers' records were maintained. Everything was handled with the efficiency of one of the country's largest corporations. Torrio was a master at organization. The criminal syndicate which he had created was one of the most powerful in America's history.[8]

Torrio had no reason to complain of the treatment he received while he was sojourning in the Lake County Jail in Waukegan. Gang chiefs were considered important people and were frequently the recipients of special privileges from officials. Eventually charges were brought against the Lake County sheriff in Federal Court for the overindulgent manner in which he had handled the Chicago gang chieftain. Although these charges were not substantiated, a major scandal involving Peter M. Hoffman, Republican Sheriff of Cook County, virtually wrecked his political career. In 1924, Federal Judge James H. Wilkerson enjoined the operation of an illegal brewery owned by Terry Druggan and Frankie Lake, two renowned gangsters who were kingpins of the Valley on the Southwest side. Druggan and Lake defied the Federal injunction and Judge Wilkerson sentenced them to one year jail terms for contempt of court. But Sheriff Hoffman firmly believed that the underworld stature of Druggan and Lake entitled them to unusual kindness and respect. Whenever Druggan grew tired of his jail surroundings, he was permitted to visit his luxurious Lake Shore apartment. During the year Druggan was supposed to be languishing in jail, he was granted the privilege of leaving the institution at least ninety times. Of course, he was glad to pay handsomely for these extraordinary privileges. It was claimed that Druggan gave officials an average of $1000 a month while he made the jail his official headquarters. Later Sheriff Hoffman was found guilty of contempt of court and sentenced to serve thirty days in the Dupage County Jail. A fine of $2500 was also imposed against this prominent Republican leader. Hoffman's subordinate, Captain Wesley E. Westbrook, who was directly in charge of the jail, was sentenced to jail for four months.

When Hoffman retired as sheriff in 1926, it was no longer expedient to parade him in the front ranks of Republican politics. His political influence, however, was far from ended. Perhaps his preferential treatment of Druggan and Lake assured him of the power to control many important underworld votes. At any rate, Cermak, the Democratic leader and president of the Cook County Board of Commissioners, rewarded Hoffman with the position of assistant forester of the Forest Preserves at a salary of $10,000 a year.[9] Choice sinecures of this nature are given only to faithful party workers who are expected to deliver handsomely at the polls.

Cermak's appointment of a former Republican sheriff to a $10,000 job was only one of a series of maneuvers designed to further the political ambitions of the one-time secretary of the United Societies. While Cermak presided over the Cook County Board of Commissioners, large tracts of land were purchased by the county and added to the forest preserves. Huge sums of money were spent for various public improvements — and also for the improvement of deserving politicians. On February 24, 1925, a bond issue of $4,500,000 was approved by the people for a new county jail. Through Cermak's influence the old jail site on Chicago's North Side was abandoned and the new building was situated on land purchased near Twenty-sixth Street and California Avenue, in the heart of his political domain on the Southwest Side. The new location was unhandy and inefficient but it was politically sound. And Cermak thought in terms of votes and power. The Citizens' Association and the Better Government Association investigated Cermak's county transactions and charged that about $4,000,000 of the taxpayers' money had been wasted in his various construction programs. It was claimed that part of this waste stemmed from dummy land purchases and political rings of contractors. Cermak promptly appointed an advisory committee of leading citizens to pass on future transactions and public indignation soon subsided. As president of the Cook County Board of Commissioners, Cermak had jurisdiction over such important suburbs as Cicero, already the stronghold of the criminal gang ruled by Torrio and Capone. The Cicero local government was in the hands of officials friendly to this underworld group, and with the liberal policies of Cermak prevailing in the county, lawlessness broke out in Cicero on a scale seldom observed in any American community.[10]

When John Torrio decided to leave Chicago, he had no intention of attempting to return to the city at some later date. However, William Hale Thompson's decision against running for mayor in 1923 carried with it no such finality. Almost as soon as William E. Dever took the oath of office as the new chief executive, Thompson began making plans for a sensational comeback in the mayoralty election four years away. This meant keeping himself in the public eye. And whatever else might be said about Big Bill, he knew how to capture headlines. With the usual fanfare and at a cost exceeding $25,000 Thompson built a "tide water cypress" sailing yawl equipped with a Diesel engine. The ship was appropriately named *Big Bill*. Prominently cut in oak in the figurehead was a likeness of the former mayor's face. Thompson announced that he intended to go on a cruise to the South Sea Islands where he would capture tree-climbing fish and bring them back to Chicago. The press greeted his announcement with jeers. But he was back in the headlines.

The launching of *Big Bill* took place at Riverview Park on Decoration Day, 1924. A huge crowd listened to the speeches. More fascinating than the customary political harangues, however, were the antics of a band of Chinese who rushed through the craft beating tom-toms and making weird noises designed to chase the devils away. On the following morning, Thompson and his crew departed on their voyage to the South Seas. Blazoning forth on a huge sign printed on the sail was Big Bill's offer to wager $25,000 that he would return from the South Seas with tree-climbing fish. Leaving Chicago from a point near the Michigan Avenue bridge, the vessel eventually reached the Mississippi River. At every river town, Thompson made speeches from the deck of the ship. Before arriving at New Orleans, however, Big Bill deserted his ship and returned to Chicago. The crew as well as the sailing yawl disappeared in thin air. For some time rumors persisted that the ship was being used to run rum out of Central American ports. Although Thompson was unable to exhibit fish that climbed trees, he had achieved his major objective, publicity — reams of it.[11]

In Thompson's future plans there was no place for the one-time medicine man, Fred Lundin. Openly breaking with him, Big Bill became closely associated with William Lorimer. Acquitted on charges growing out of the failure of his bank and accused of bribery in connection with his election to the United States Senate, Lorimer was a highly controversial public figure. Unlike most politicians, Thompson made no effort to conceal his alliance with Lorimer. Big Bill even brought Lorimer to a gathering of three hundred people at the Fish Fans' clubhouse and asked him to make a speech. This was tantamount to a public announcement by the former mayor that he had become a political partner of the discredited Lorimer. The Fish Fans' club was organized in 1922 to encourage the propagation of fish in American waters. Before long it was used primarily to propagate Big Bill's brand of politics, although the powerful Democratic leader, Anton J. Cermak, was also a member. A schooner clubhouse was opened in the North end of Belmont Harbor in Lincoln Park on March 21, 1925. Here liquor flowed freely until a sensational raid was made on the place by Federal Prohibition agents in the summer of 1925. A Federal Court order padlocked the clubhouse and Richard Mazer, proprietor of the club restaurant, was found guilty of violating the National Prohibition Act. Because the Fish Fans' club was considered to be an integral part of Big Bill Thompson's political organization, the raid by Federal officers was headline news.[12]

Thompson had a knack for keeping his name on the front pages. His actions were applauded by his friends, jeered by his enemies and deplored by serious-minded citizens who distinguished between good and bad publicity. Chicago was receiving plenty of bad publicity without any clownish performances from its former mayor. Al Capone, the new underworld ruler, was following in the footsteps of the departed John Torrio. The organization he took over was a going concern, in the full sense of that term. In Cicero, the Capone headquarters, business was booming. The Hawthorne Smoke Shop handbook operations were placed in charge of Frankie Pope, the millionaire newsboy. Pete Renovich was made overseer of the other gambling games in this establishment. It was a gold mine. From seized records the Federal government established that in the space of twenty-two months the net income to the Capone gang from the Hawthorne Smoke Shop alone was $587,721.95.[13] Another Cicero gambling establishment, the Ship, where the O'Banion-Genna feud had developed, was even more profitable. A cashbook confiscated from the Ship in 1926 showed net profits in excess of a half-million dollars a year in this place, which provided roulette, faro, craps and horse-race gambling. An employee of this establishment known as Fred Reis (alias J. C. Dunbar) was accustomed to carry as much as $300,000 in gunny sacks to the Pinkert State Bank in Cicero where the money was exchanged for cashier's checks.[14] Money was also rolling into the coffers of the Capone syndicate from illicit activities in Burnham and Stickney, as well as other suburban towns.

With Al Capone's growing opulence came a corresponding increase in his political power. The gang leader fully understood the importance of strong alliances with the right politicians. In Chicago's First Ward Capone was on friendly terms with Hinky Dink Kenna and Bathhouse John Coughlin. Since the redistricting of the city in 1923, the First Ward's sole alderman was Bathhouse John. Hinky Dink remained the ward committeeman, however, which meant that he ruled over the political affairs of this important district. Al Capone recognized Hinky Dink as a masterful organizer whose ability could be useful to his criminal empire. It is not surprising therefore, that one of Al's favorite loafing places was Kenna's cigar store on South Clark Street. There Al also transacted much business — underworld business.

Dennis "Duke" Cooney, who had been the overseer of the disreputable hotels of the First Ward for Hinky Dink since 1916, now became an integral part of the Capone organization. The gangster placed Cooney in charge of his prostitution operations. Duke Cooney brought a wealth of experience and efficient methods into the brothel business. With Capone's backing, he increased the profits from established bawdyhouses, at the same time opening new places which still further swelled the ever-increasing revenue of the gang. Placing Kenna's right-hand man, Dennis Cooney, in one of the key posts of the Capone organization was evidence of the high esteem in which Hinky Dink was held by the underworld boss. And the deference shown him by Al Capone in turn served to increase Kenna's political stature. Chicago was passing through the disgraceful period in which politicians were fawning over the gang leader and seeking his favor. Insofar as the Democratic boss George Brennan was concerned,

Kenna was then the political equal of Tony Cermak, president of the County Board since 1922 and later mayor of Chicago.[15]

Al Capone marshaled the forces of the underworld as they had seldom been marshaled anywhere before. And as the vicious criminal elements and their political counterparts became more strongly organized, government was growing more and more disorganized, until it virtually fell apart and capitulated to a ruthless and defiant underworld. During the first four months of 1926 there were twenty-nine gang killings in Chicago, bringing the total to over two hundred within four years. On April 27, 1926, Assistant State's Attorney William H. McSwiggin, who had gained a reputation for securing death-penalty verdicts, left home in the company of two friends. One of his associates was Thomas Duffy, a beer peddler and a precinct captain in McSwiggin's faction of the Republican party. The third member of the group was James Doherty, a Capone gangster who allegedly had murdered Eddie Tancl of Cicero in November 1924. About 8:30 P.M. McSwiggin and his two associates stepped out of their automobile near a saloon operated by a friend. At this moment a car roared by. Its occupants emptied their guns into the prosecutor and his two companions. McSwiggin, Duffy and Doherty were killed. This gang killing created a furor. Even Al Capone, at whom the finger of suspicion pointed, found it expedient to flee the city until public anger subsided. Lengthy official investigations were conducted but of course they resulted in utter failure. The murderers represented an organization stronger than government itself.[16]

The McSwiggin case was still fresh in the public mind when new gang violence broke out reviving the memory of Dion O'Banion's murder. At noon on September 20, 1926, eleven automobiles filled with armed gunmen, affiliated with O'Banion's former associate, Hymie Weiss, roared into Cicero. Twenty-second Street, the town's main thoroughfare, was filled with noonday shoppers and workers enjoying their lunch hour. In a restaurant next door to the Hawthorne Inn, the headquarters for Al Capone, the gang leader was having lunch. As the cars filled with Weiss gangsters neared the Inn, they reduced their speed. Suddenly from the passing cars, thousands of bullets and slugs from machine guns, pistols and shotguns went screaming into the Inn. Windows were shattered; plaster was ripped from the walls; doors were filled with bullet holes, and furniture was wrecked. When the attack started, Al Capone dropped to the restaurant floor. He was uninjured but one of his gunmen, Louis Barko, was struck in the shoulder by a bullet. Thirty-five automobiles that were parked along Twenty-second Street were raked by gun fire. One car, in which a woman was sitting with an infant, was hit thirty times. One of the bullets grazed her forehead and injured her eyes. The main business district of Cicero was thrown into a panic. A Chicago newspaper editorial blazoned, "This is War!"

Naturally, the Capone gang had no intention of allowing an armed invasion of its stronghold go unanswered. On the afternoon of October 11, 1926, Hymie Weiss and four companions stepped from their automobile near the flower shop at 738 North State Street where Dion O'Banion had been slain on November 10, 1924. As the five men were about to ascend the stairway leading to the second floor of the flower shop, bullets came screeching at them. Hymie Weiss and Patrick Murray, a beer peddler, were killed. W. W. O'Brien, a well-known criminal attorney, Benjamin Jacobs, a policeman of the bloody Twentieth Ward, and Sam Peller, the chauffeur, were riddled with bullets (but they eventually recovered).[17] Stray bullets from the assassins' guns crashed into the walls of the Holy Name Cathedral across the street. Both the chief of police and the chief of detectives accused Al Capone of responsibility for the double murder. But they did not even bother to question him. Capone offered to present himself at headquarters for interrogation but the head of the police department said that it would be merely a waste of time to talk with him. The law enforcement agencies were completely demoralized. The honest members of the police department no longer had the heart to fight back, and the balance were working hand in glove with the criminals.

Although the gangsters had no fear of the law enforcement agencies, they did have reason to fear each other. The bitter gang warfare which had been raging was proving costly to the underworld, and the time was considered propitious for a determined effort to bring an end to the gang killings. On October 21, 1926, therefore, a peace conference was held in a prominent downtown hotel within the shadows of City Hall. Maxie Eisen presided over this gathering of gunmen and plug-uglies who in the interest of self-preservation were attempting to reach an amicable agreement regarding territorial jurisdiction. Among those present were Bugs Moran, burglar, robber and ex-convict; Jack Guzik, the so-called brains of the Capone organization and a brother of Harry, the convicted pander; William R. Skidmore, Barney Bertche, Eddie Vogel, Vincent Drucci, Jack Zuta and many other prominent underworld characters. The conference allotted various sections of the city to the different warring factions insofar as beer distribution was concerned. Vince Drucci and Bugs Moran agreed to confine their illicit beer operations to the Forty-second and Forty-third Wards on the North Side, while all territory south of Madison Street was to be the domain of the Capone organization. When it came to gambling Al Capone apparently reserved the entire city for himself. Even the powerful North Side chieftains, William R. Skidmore and Barney Bertche, were told that in future they must obtain the approval of Al Capone as to all gambling and vice operations.[18] Unfortunately, "honor among thieves" actually exists only in the minds of the literati. This time it disappeared almost as soon as the peace conference ended. Contrary to the solemn terms of the truce, there were territorial infringements followed by violence, while gang killings continued as frequent as before.

The administration of William E. Dever was coming to a close. For four years Dever had labored conscientiously to bring order out of chaos. But order had not been restored. The gangsterism which still terrorized the city was the product of a criminal-political system which was now exploding in all its fury. The evils were deeply rooted. Slight headway could be made in a period of four years, particularly since the mayor had little control over patronage and none over the ward organization. And it was at the ward level that the criminal-political alliances prevailed in their most insidious aspects. Boss Brennan, with the aid of such stalwarts as Hinky Dink Kenna and Anton Cermak, ruled over the ward organization. Mayor Dever had made no friends among the criminal elements. His law enforcement policies were unpopular with some of the powerful underworld leaders who were in the habit of buying protection from policemen and ward politicians. But with Dever in the mayor's chair they could never be sure of delivery. This had been demonstrated forcefully in the Sieben Brewery raid on May 19, 1924, when leading gangsters had been arrested and turned over to the Federal government for successful prosecution. Consequently some gang overlords had concentrated their activities in the suburban towns during the Dever administration. Protection there meant protection; it could be relied upon absolutely.

In the spring mayoralty election of 1927, Mayor Dever's Republican opponent was the inimitable William Hale Thompson, fully equipped with a bag of tricks which he hoped would mesmerize the electorate. A third candidate, Dr. John Dill Robertson, was projected into the race as an independent by Thompson's former ally, Fred Lundin. The break between Lundin and Thompson had been sharp and feelings between these two cunning politicians ran high. This had been made evident when Big Bill staged his famous rat show a year earlier. Speaking before a packed audience in the Cort Theatre on April 6, 1926, Thompson appeared on the platform with a cage containing two rats. One of the rodents he addressed as Fred, after Fred Lundin, and the other as Doc to represent Dr. Robertson. In his remarks to the rat he called Fred, Big Bill explained how he had saved him from the penitentiary when Lundin and other members of the Thompson School Board had been indicted. To the rat he called Doc, the former mayor recalled how he had appointed Robertson to the post of health commissioner over the strenuous protests of almost the entire medical profession. Upon concluding his remarks to the two rodents Thompson turned to the audience and stated that originally there were additional rats in the cage to represent other followers of Lundin, but the rats Doc and Fred had devoured them. The rat show was a preview of the type of campaign that Thompson was ready to wage in 1927.

In Thompson's vigorous mayoralty campaign, he covered a wide range of issues. He stood for "America first" and for Home Rule. He was against the World Court and the "treason-tainted histories" used as textbooks in the Chicago schools during the Dever administration. Big Bill was not only running against Dever and Robertson, as in his last campaign, he was running against King George. When Dever insisted that Thompson define his position on important local problems, Big Bill dismissed the challenge with the reply that he stood for "America first." Dever complained, "How can I campaign against a brain like that?" Big Bill had Dever bewildered. He had the voters confused. But everyone had a good time as the former cowboy waged his verbal battle to save Chicago from King George and the British.

As the campaign progressed it became wilder and wilder. When it appeared that Thompson would make deep inroads in the Negro vote, Boss Brennan of the Democratic organization directed the city police under his control to make sweeping raids on gambling, liquor and vice resorts in the colored districts. Race prejudice was injected into the campaign. Boss Brennan's control of the city police department was an invaluable asset to the Democratic candidate. Thompson, however, had again made friends with Robert E. Crowe and had the influence of that important officer in his corner. When Thompson started hurling charges at his opponents no subject was considered too personal or too trivial. Even the "nasty" table manners of his former political ally, Dr. John Dill Robertson, were described. "Eggs in his whiskers, soup on his vest — you'd think the Doc got his education driving a garbage wagon," Thompson said. As to his own qualities, Thompson never resorted to modesty. He was "Big Bill the Builder," the man responsible for virtually all of Chicago's construction since the time of the Columbian Exposition. Before he came along to save the city, civic leadership was dead. Big Bill the Builder as always ran on the platform of a "wide-open town." Referring to the numerous establishments the Dever administration had closed for violating the law, Thompson promised, "When I'm elected we will not only re-open places these people have closed, but we'll open 10,000 new ones." His enemies charged that his statement was tantamount to an invitation to all the crooks in the world to come to Chicago and open illegal establishments. Big Bill pledged an end to police activity on what he termed minor infractions of the laws. His police would concentrate on the holdup men and safeblowers.

This was music to the ears of the gangsters. It constituted an assurance that the lucrative rackets upon which the underworld thrives would operate unmolested if Big Bill were elected again. Al Capone, of course, was a businessman. Thompson's platform would mean big business opportunities for his organization. The ruthless gang leader therefore contributed substantially to the Thompson campaign for mayor.[19] Some sources fixed the amount of Capone's contribution at $250,000. On election day an army of Capone gangsters patrolled the tough West Side in behalf of Thompson's candidacy.[20]

Jack Zuta, a North Side gambling boss and associate of Bugs Moran, William R. Skidmore, Barney Bertsche and Joe Aiello, contributed $50,000 to the Thompson campaign. Zuta confided in friends that Big Bill's wide-open town policies would enable him to get his $50,000 back in short order.[21] And Zuta was not mistaken. In the April 1927 election, Thompson was victorious with a vote of 512,740 to 429,668 for Dever. One election casualty was the North Side gangster Vince Drucci, admittedly a worker for the Republican candidate. He was mysteriously shot and killed by police as they were transporting him in a squad car to the Criminal Court Building for questioning. In the Forty-second Ward alone, there were two bombings and an alderman was forced to stay in hiding when thugs and gunmen at the polls became overzealous in their efforts to "preserve the American way of life." Another casualty was Big Bill's ill-fated Fish Fans' schooner clubhouse. On election night Mayor Thompson and fifteen hundred loyal followers crowded aboard the Fish Fans' ship to celebrate the victory. The load was too heavy and the schooner sank unceremoniously to the bottom of Belmont Harbor. The guests scampered ashore without loss of life but the clubhouse was never resurrected.

Big Bill Thompson's "wide-open town" was no empty campaign pledge. Politicians frequently promise church groups and ladies' clubs a program of rigid law enforcement in order to secure votes and after the election ignore such commitments. But the contrary pledges they make to the underworld are irrevocable. Thus with the return of Thompson as mayor, all bars were let down. Deluxe gambling establishments and horse race betting rooms flourished as never before.

In some sections of the city houses of prostitution ran wide-open. Beer trucks thundered through the streets unmolested.[22] Al Capone, who had been among those concentrating their activities in suburban towns during the Dever administration, returned to Chicago in full force immediately following Big Bill's election. New headquarters for the gang were set up at the Metropole Hotel, and in short order Al Capone had established himself as the most powerful political influence in Chicago. Thompson appointed Capone's close personal friend, Daniel A. Serritella, to the post of city sealer. In May 1927, Commander Francesco de Pinedo, round-the-world flyer representing Italy's Premier Benito Mussolini, landed in Chicago. Among those in the greeting party was Al Capone. Police explained that the gang leader's presence had been requested for the purpose of preventing a possible anti-Fascist demonstration.[23] The responsible authorities were not certain they could maintain order, and reliance had to be placed on the underworld leader, Al Capone — a sad commentary.

Al Capone was pleased with his growing prestige in city affairs. He and his gunmen were becoming drunk with power. Big Bill the Builder was also suffering from delusions of self-importance. Once again he was mayor of the nation's second largest city. Friendly political relations were re-established with State's Attorney Robert E. Crowe and Governor Len Small. Thompson promptly began laying plans which he hoped would place him in the White House. Armed with tons of literature, the police department quartet, scores of banners and accompanied by many of his cronies, Thompson departed in a private railway car on a 7000-mile speaking tour. He spoke on America first, farm relief, inland waterways and national flood control. He denounced the League of Nations and the World Court. Huge crowds gathered to hear Chicago's cowboy mayor speak at the Minnesota State Fair, the Live Stock Exchange in Omaha and the Denver Chamber of Commerce. His itinerary included important addresses in Kansas City, Los Angeles, Cheyenne, Wyoming and Albuquerque, New Mexico. At a San Francisco Chamber of Commerce luncheon at least 1200 leading citizens applauded Big Bill's momentous remarks on the nation's problems. A big reception was given Thompson upon his return to Chicago. A short time later, in February 1928, the mayor organized a junket to New Orleans. Three special trains were required to haul Thompson and his crowd to the Mardi Gras city. Among those who greeted Chicago's chief executive upon his arrival was Huey Long whose dictatorial regime over Louisiana was just beginning. As political demagogues, Louisiana's "King Fish" and Chicago's cowboy mayor had much in common. At a huge banquet at the Roosevelt Hotel, Huey Long spoke in glowing terms of Mayor Thompson. A Chicago Police Department octet sang a song entitled "Big Bill the Builder"; the affair was brought to a climax with the presentation of a silver scroll to Thompson which proclaimed him to be "one of the greatest living Americans." [24]

Back in Chicago, Big Bill was making headlines with his fight to remove the city's Superintendent of Schools, William McAndrew, a capable educator who had been brought to Chicago from New York by former mayor William E. Dever. It was soon evident that Thompson would not be satisfied with the mere removal of McAndrew — he wanted to force the superintendent of schools to leave Chicago in disgrace. Charges were brought against McAndrew which related principally to the use in the schools of history books which were influenced by the English — the old refrain that Thompson had used in the campaign. The prolonged trial attracted international attention. Toward the end of the proceedings, McAndrew did not even bother to attend.

Thompson's views on Americanism were widely quoted in the press. He talked glibly of Nathan Hale and George Washington. He expressed the opinion that "What was good enough for George Washington is good enough for Bill Thompson." The history books, tainted with the influence of King George, horrified him. And his one hundred per cent Americanism also included a profound sympathy for the large number of Chicago's German, Irish and Polish voters since the histories had slighted their national heroes. In Big Bill's enthusiasm to save the citizens from the evil designs of King George, he turned his attention to the public library and ordered a member of the library board to clear the shelves of all "tainted" history books. It was rumored that Big Bill the Builder intended to make a huge bonfire on the lake front with library books which did not meet his test of pure Americanism. Newspapers all over the world carried the story. London papers cabled their American correspondents to investigate the mayor's strange phobia against the English. After all, the British had helped restore the public library after the great fire of 1871 had reduced it to ashes. To the English mind, the proposed bonfire was all very mystifying.

The burlesque involving the "tainted" histories as well as Thompson's spectacular junkets to various parts of the country helped to divert attention from Chicago's major problem, crime. The power of the underworld was growing steadily. The far-flung gambling empire of the Capone organization maintained headquarters in a Loop office building located at 16 South Clark Street, with Al Capone's right-hand man and business manager Jack Guzik in charge. Jimmie Mondi, a spokesman for the gang on gambling matters, summoned the resort owners to his office and gave them the terms under which they would be permitted to continue in business. The Capone organization demanded from twenty-five to forty per cent of the earnings from each gambling establishment. Police protection would be guaranteed. Failure to agree to these terms would result in a bombing of the recalcitrant gambler's establishment or "taking him for a ride" from which there was no return. Few indeed refused to accept Jimmie Mondi's terms. On the South Side Dan Jackson, the Negro Republican committeeman was associated with Mondi. Influential politicians, some of whom occupied important posts in the Thompson administration, were allegedly part of the gambling syndicate.

Occasionally there was a rebellion of the gamblers against the existing setup. This was true during the latter part of 1927, when both gamblers and politicians turned against Mondi who was demanding the same percentage of the earnings even when politicians "fronted" for a place. Thus in December it became necessary to effect a reorganization of protected gambling, and the Capone gang suffered a temporary reverse. A deadly gambling war appeared imminent. On January 26, 1928, the homes of Charles C. Fitzmorris and Dr. William H. Reid, two powerful figures in the Thompson administration, were bombed. Fitzmorris, formerly the city's chief of police, was now the City Comptroller. The bombings were attributed to the followers of Al Capone as a protest against the reorganization of protected gambling which had recently gone into effect. A short time later bombs were hurled at the home of the secretary to the state's attorney and an undertaking establishment owned by a municipal court judge. Mayor Thompson, the members of his cabinet and the state's attorney promptly stationed armed guards around their homes. The *Chicago News* on February 23, 1928, editorially commented:

Now that leading city and county officials of this community are in a state of siege, with police details guarding their homes against assaults by bomb-throwers, the long continued farce of law enforcement which does not enforce manifestly must have the curtain rung down upon it.

The editorial inquired:

. . . if the law-enforcing agencies of this community have no moral reason for fearing the foes who strike at them so viciously why do they

not strike back with all the force of outraged virtue armed with all
the powers of orderly government? [25]

The answer to this was obvious. There was no virtue in the administration capable of being outraged. Neither was there in existence
any orderly government that could use its powers against organized
gunmen. The rulers of the city were actually the gangsters who had
become so powerful they had no hesitancy in resorting to violence
against leading officials.

Thanks to Mayor Thompson's "wide-open town," racketeering
now became the biggest business in Chicago. Legitimate enterprises
of every description, large and small, were forced to pay tribute to
gangsters for the privilege of continuing in business. Professional
bomb throwers developed a fixed rate scale for hurling their destructive missiles at establishments that hesitated in meeting the demands
of the gangsters. Morris Becker, the largest individual cleaner and
dyer in the city, had his places bombed repeatedly. His employees
were slugged and called out on strike. Finally in desperation he made
Al Capone his partner; the gang leader could assure him protection
that was not forthcoming from the police or the state's attorney. The
official law-enforcement bodies were held in utter contempt by the
lawless element. On one occasion gangsters even encircled police
headquarters. They were waiting for a rival gunman, Joe Aiello, to
leave the Detective Bureau where he was being detained for questioning in order that they might kill him. [26]

In the weeks preceding the primary of April 10, 1928, further acts
of violence focused attention on the complete lawlessness which engulfed Chicago. Diamond Joe Esposito, the Republican ward leader,
was shot and killed on March 21, 1928, as he was walking between
two bodyguards. A short time later another gangster, Big Tim
Murphy, was slain. On March 26 the homes of John A. Swanson,
who was running for state's attorney, and Senator Charles S. Deneen
were bombed. Within a period of only six months, sixty-two bombings had occurred in the city. Swanson demanded an explanation for
these bombings, particularly those of the homes of Thompson's cabinet members, Charles C. Fitzmorris and Dr. William H. Reid. Public
attention was focused on the use of bombs in the organized gambling
racket and the "inter-organization of the gambling ring with poli-

tics." The issue was clear-cut. The Chicago Crime Commission on April 6, 1928, issued a public statement "To the Voters of Cook County" which read:

The Chicago Crime Commission, believing that State's Attorney Crowe is inefficient and unworthy of his great responsibility to maintain law and order in Cook County, and that his alliances are such as to destroy public confidence in his integrity, recommends to the citizens that he be defeated for renomination.

On April 10, 1928, Judge John A. Swanson defeated Robert E. Crowe for the Republican nomination for state's attorney and in November he was elected. The primary was rife with violence and vote frauds. In the bloody Twentieth Ward ruled over by Morris Eller of the Thompson-Crowe machine there were kidnappings. Thugs and gunmen rode up and down the streets during the balloting. Watchers at the polls were strong-armed, removed from the voting places and severely beaten. After the polls were closed, hoodlums located Octavius Granady on the street and murdered him. Granady was Eller's opponent for the post of ward committeeman.[27] The gangsters were playing for high stakes, and they were playing for keeps.

Now that gambling had the blessing and the protection of City Hall politicians, police officers knew better than to enforce the gambling laws. If they performed their sworn duty with respect to such statutes they were promptly transferred to very undesirable posts or disciplined in other ways by their political bosses. In 1928, Chicago newspapers exposed huge policy operations that were flourishing among the Negro population on the South Side. The press alleged that policy racketeers and their political protectors were taking at least a million dollars a month from poor people, many of whom lived in a police district over which Deputy Commissioner of Police William F. Russell had authority. When press representatives asked Russell to explain the presence of wide-scale policy gambling in this district he said:

Mayor Thompson was elected on the "open town" platform. I assume the people knew what they wanted when they voted for him. . . . I haven't had any orders from downtown to interfere in the policy racket, and until I do get such orders you can bet I'm going to keep my hands off. . . . Look what happened over at Stanton Avenue [police district], when Captain Dennis Carroll got too efficient for his own good. He went rampaging around . . . and promptly got himself fired. Personally, I don't propose to get mixed up in any jam that will send me to the sticks. . . . If the downtown authorities want this part of the city closed up, the downtown authorities will have to issue the order. I'm certainly not going to attempt it on my own.[28]

A few months later, on August 1, 1928, William F. Russell was appointed commissioner of police and thus became head of the entire department.

When Russell received his appointment, Mayor Thompson was in hiding in the North Woods near Manitowish, Wisconsin. He was avoiding all newspaper men and only a few confidants knew where he was staying. Chicagoans had flocked to the polls in the April 1928, primary. They had registered their disapproval of Al Capone, the underworld bombings and killings which had turned Chicago into an armed camp, and the Thompson-Crowe regime which was characterized as an administration of "Pineapples and Plunder." The uprising of voters had wrecked Big Bill's political future. Shortly after the primary, a circuit court in Chicago rendered a judgment against Mayor Thompson and his associate, George F. Harding, in the amount of $2,245,604. This judgment, later set aside by the Illinois Supreme Court, grew out of a civil suit filed against the defendants for fees paid to experts in behalf of the city. Thompson was in a state of nervous collapse. It was suggested to him that he resign as mayor but this he refused to do. For almost two years the mayor took little active interest in politics, and the corporation counsel, Samuel A. Ettelson, assumed the duties of mayor.

While the Thompson Republican organization was in the process of deterioration, the Democrats were steadily growing in power. On August 8, 1928, the Democratic boss, George E. Brennan, died. His shoes were promptly filled by Anton J. Cermak, who was still President of the Cook County Board of Commissioners.

By 1928, the underworld was in the midst of one of its most prosperous eras. The political protectors of the gangsters were growing opulent and powerful. The hands of the honest police officers were tied; those of the dishonest kept grasping for more and more tainted dollars. And there were plenty to be had. Every few days reports of spectacular gang killings were flashed over the wires of the press services to all parts of the world. On September 7, 1928, a gang assassination occurred during the rush hour near State and Madison Streets, the busiest corner in the United States. Antonio Lombardo, who had been placed at the head of the Unione Siciliana by Al Capone in 1925, was shot and killed as he was walking with two bodyguards. Joseph Ferraro, one of the bodyguards, was also slain. The other, Joseph Lorlordo, escaped injury. The murderers, having completed their mission, quietly disappeared in the passing throng.[29]

But Chicago had yet to witness its most bizarre gang slaying. On February 14, 1929, St. Valentine's Day, seven of Bugs Moran's associates were awaiting the return of their leader in his headquarters, a garage at 2122 North Clark Street. Momentarily they expected Moran, Willie Marks and Ted Newberry to walk into the garage. Suddenly several men dressed in the uniforms of police officers entered the hideout. They purported to place the seven Moran hoodlums under arrest and ordered them to keep their hands up facing the wall. The commands were obeyed without strenuous objection. A brush with police officers was considered among the least of the worries of the criminal element — a temporary difficulty which could easily be fixed. The gangsters in full police regalia then raised their machine guns and mowed down their seven helpless rivals. The St. Valentine's day massacre stunned Chicagoans. It called the attention of the world to the city's lawlessness. Like virtually all Chicago gang killings it was never solved. It was known of course that Bugs Moran was an enemy of the Capone organization, but Al Capone had his usual airtight alibi. He was basking in the sun at his Palm Island estate just three miles from downtown Miami, when the assassination took place. His business manager, Jack Guzik, had been making daily long-distance telephone calls to the gang leader from the Congress Hotel in Chicago until three days before the mass slaying occurred. But for all the police ever found out, the calls may have related to the weather.[30]

Actually, officialdom did not want to delve too deeply into the affairs of the underworld. Information concerning family secrets is usually kept within the family circle if at all possible. And the ties between the gangsters and political leaders were close; they were intimate. This was amply proved in the summer of 1929, when a member of Jack Guzik's family was married. Among the guests present at the wedding were Bathhouse John Coughlin, Alderman of the First Ward, William V. Pacelli, Alderman of the "Bloody Twentieth" Ward, Captain of Police Hugh McCarthy and Ralph Capone, a brother of Al. The gang leader himself was not present. Having run afoul of an unco-operative court in Philadelphia earlier that year, he was spending a few months in an eastern jail.[31] It was evident, however, that members of the city council, high ranking officers of the police department and Al Capone's principal lieutenants were component parts of one big happy family — a family that ruled over the nation's second largest municipality for the benefit of rugged gunmen and ruthless racketeers.

The contempt in which Chicago's officials and law enforcement bodies were held by the organized criminal element had been demonstrated time and time again. Gangsters had attacked and killed an assistant state's attorney. They had bombed the homes of leading officials including those of the state's attorney, the city comptroller, a judge and a senator. And on June 9, 1930, they shot and killed a representative of the press. Alfred J. Lingle, a *Tribune* reporter, was the victim as he entered the busy Illinois Central Railroad subway at Michigan Boulevard and Randolph Street. The murder created a furor. Speculation was rife as to why "Jake" Lingle was assassinated, but investigation into his background and affiliations soon unraveled the mystery. Lingle was a gambling addict. On a newspaper reporter's salary he frequently made bets of a thousand dollars on a single horse race. He borrowed money extensively from gamblers including Jimmie Mondi. But Lingle was more than a "sucker" who made heavy donations to the gamblers. This was evident when it was disclosed that at the time he was murdered he was wearing a diamond-studded belt given him by Al Capone. This was a gift that the gang leader bestowed only upon those who were important to him. Lingle had become influential in the Capone gambling organization, particularly in Chicago's Loop area where he was somewhat of an unofficial mayor.[32] He also had his finger in the racing news service. For a long time independent news services had waged warfare against Mont Tennes and the General News Bureau. About January 1, 1930, Jake Lingle had brought the warring factions together and they agreed upon a two-year truce. There were some indications that

Lingle's activity in connection with the wire services may have been responsible for his murder.[33]

The investigation of the Lingle slaying led in many directions. His connections with gangland activities were multifarious and numerous people could have desired his death. One of the gangsters logically suspected of having instigated the killing was the North Side gambling and vice lord Jack Zuta. On July 1, 1930, Zuta was about to be released from police headquarters at 11th and State Streets where he had been questioned concerning the Lingle murder. He confided in Lieutenant George Barker of the bomb squad that he feared rival gunmen were waiting outside the police building to kill him. The police lieutenant obligingly offered to furnish the gang leader with safe transportation, so Zuta climbed into the rear seat of Lieutenant Barker's sedan, insisting on sitting in the middle. He was flanked on one side by Albert Bratz and on the other by Leona Bernstein. With Lieutenant Barker in front was Solly Vision, another associate of Zuta. Lieutenant Barker left police headquarters and drove his car north on State Street to a point just beyond Quincy Street in the Loop, when it was observed that a dark blue sedan was following. Suddenly this car speeded up and when it was alongside the policeman's automobile, one of its occupants stepped to the running board, pulled a gun from his shoulder holster and fired seven shots at Jack Zuta. Lieutenant Barker stopped his sedan and jumped into the street, which momentarily diverted the fire of two assailants who were by this time emptying their guns at the Zuta party. Jack Zuta and his three associates quickly crawled out of the policeman's automobile and disappeared in the crowd of people walking along the street. Just back of Lieutenant Barker's sedan when he stopped, was a State Street surface car which was stalled during the gun battle. One of the bullets pierced the front of the streetcar striking the motorman, Elbert Lusader, and killing him. Another bullet wounded Olaf Svenste, a night watchman, who was crossing the street on his way to the Standard Club where he worked. Following the attempted assassination of Zuta, the gunmen sped away in their car which belched forth a smoke screen and easily eluded Lieutenant Barker who started to give chase.[34]

The North Side gangster appeared to be leading a charmed life. He had been virtually trapped. Two gunmen had fired upon him several times at very close range. Nevertheless he had managed to escape. Zuta's luck was very short lived, however. Only a month later, on August 1, 1930, he was in a dance pavilion near Delafield, Wisconsin. As he walked across the dance floor to drop a nickel into the electric player piano, five gunmen quietly surrounded him, and with gangland precision fired their weapons at close range. This time Jack Zuta did not have a chance. He was killed instantly.[35]

The code of the underworld precludes a gangster from talking. But now that Jack Zuta was dead, the records and papers he left behind told an amazing story of the alliance that existed between politicians and criminals, of financial transactions between the underworld and the city rulers, of close relationships between the lawless and the law-enforcing bodies, of official corruption. For many weeks prominent politicians and police officials offered explanations concerning canceled checks which originally had been issued to them by the North Side gambler. Most of the explanations were weak and unconvincing. Judge Joseph W. Schulman of the Municipal Court received several thousand dollars from the slain gangster, between December 1921 and December 29, 1925. Schulman denied that the money came from the gambling king, although the checks were signed by Jack Zuta and were issued to and endorsed by the judge. Zuta had engaged in financial dealings with Emanuel Eller, a former judge of the Criminal Court, with George Van Lent, a former State Senator and Republican leader, with State Senator Harry W. Starr, with Louis L. Fisher, counsel for dog track interests and a former assistant state's attorney. Balance sheets reflected that a person designated as "M.K." received thousands of dollars from the profits of the Zuta syndicate. There was a strong indication that "M.K." referred to Matt Kolb, a politician-gambler known as the underworld representative of many county and city officials. The records established Zuta as one of the financial backers of the "Regular Republican Club of Cook County." The chairman of the Republican County Committee had issued to the slain gang leader a membership card in the William Hale Thompson Republican Club. And this committee was the one that named the organization candidates for the municipal, circuit and superior court judgeships. Charles E. Graydon who was the sheriff of Cook County in 1927 issued a card extending special police courtesies to Zuta, the public enemy. There were canceled checks and notes revealing that Zuta had furnished money to police officials and members of the underworld such as "Dago" Lawrence Mangano, Tony Lombardo and Hymie Levin of the Capone gang, William R. Skidmore, the political fixer, Diamond Joe Esposito and Henry Finkelstein. There was a letter from the chief of police of Evanston, Illinois, requesting a loan of four hundred dollars from Zuta. The loan had been granted.[36]

The names of prominent politicians on canceled checks, notes and other papers could not be dismissed with the customary denials accompanied by simulated indignation. While these men were busy explaining their dealings with the gang leader, Zuta's other acquaintances began to talk. His friends in Middlesboro, Kentucky, asserted that many Chicago politicians, including judges had visited the gangster there. A former county prosecutor stated that Mayor William Hale Thompson once visited Zuta in Middlesboro. To his Kentucky friends, Zuta had confided that he had raised $50,000 in the preceding Chicago mayoralty election in behalf of Thompson's campaign.[37] In Probate Court hearings in Chicago, Senator Harry W. Starr stated that in a conversation with Zuta in 1926 in the Hotel Sherman the gangster told him of an organization he was forming in behalf of Thompson's candidacy for mayor. Senator Starr informed the court that "Zuta said he expected to be a power in city politics and he was going 'hook, line, and sinker' for Thompson because Thompson would go 'hook, line and sinker' for him."[38] A woman who had been living out of wedlock with a Chicago police officer informed the state's attorney that Jack Zuta gave her $1500 to pay for the promotion of her patrolman friend to the rank of sergeant.[39] The slain gambling boss had succeeded in bringing within the orbit of his influence, public officials in every stratum of government; police officers, judges, senators, the mayor, as well as the dominant political organization of the city, were all indebted to him.

As North Side gambling and vice lord, Zuta had often found it necessary to have property available to pledge as bail in connection with court proceedings. Following his death the Probate Court initiated hearings concerning his real estate holdings. Of particular interest to the court was a check in the amount of $2500 issued by the city after the gangster's death to pay the balance due him on property that had been subjected to condemnation proceedings. Arthur X.

Elrod, who had suddenly left a job with the Corporation Counsel's office in 1929, after he was questioned about his connection with a slot-machine and punchboard company, was ordered to appear in court. Probate Judge Henry Horner issued a contempt citation for Elrod. The citation was finally dismissed when Elrod turned over to the court the deed to property valued at $20,000.[40] Several years later Elrod was to become ward committeeman of the powerful Twenty-fourth Ward of Chicago and a member of the Board of Cook County Commissioners. From his modest beginning as a bondsman for Jack Zuta, Elrod eventually became one of the most influential politicians of the city and county.

The Zuta case was featured by the press for many months. It had been front-page news from the attempted assassination of the gang leader on July 1, 1930, to his actual murder in Wisconsin a month later. It was November 15, 1930, before Arthur X. Elrod had cleared himself of contempt of court in connection with Zuta's real estate holdings. By January 1931, testimony was still being given in Probate Court regarding Zuta's connection with politicians in general and the Thompson administration in particular.

In the meantime, other incidents had occurred which further emphasized the close affiliation between the underworld and city government. When the police raided a hotel at 2138 South Wabash Avenue searching for Frank "The Enforcer" Nitti, one of Al Capone's chief lieutenants, they found confidential police instructions calling for the arrest of forty-one gunmen. Obviously someone in authority had provided the Capone organization with secret police files. Capone and his henchmen had disapproved of eight names on the list. Subsequent police instructions had accordingly omitted these names without the knowledge of the police commissioner.[41] Apparently these eight gunmen were too occupied with gangland business to leave the city while the police were ostensibly looking for them or to submit to the customary innocuous arrest.

Mayor Thompson's term of office was coming to a close. His administration was completely discredited. Even Republican leaders did not want Big Bill as their standard bearer in the 1931 mayoralty race. From 1927 through 1930 two hundred and twenty-seven gang killings had occurred in Chicago while rival criminal gangs were waging open warfare on the city streets. During that same period only two defendants were convicted for implication in a gang murder.[42]

Thompson, however, refreshed after his two years of political inactivity, was determined to seek a fourth term. He spoke glowingly of his accomplishments — of the boulevards, streets, schools and public buildings he had provided for the city. His opponents talked of crime and gang killings. At least the cowboy mayor could not be charged with having retarded the city's growth. Its population had increased by almost a million since he was elected mayor the first time in 1915. The United States Census figures for 1930 showed that 3,376,438 people resided in Chicago. This represented an increase of over 600,000 in ten years.

Thompson entered the mayoralty race with his usual vigor and scathing denunciations of his enemies. He was particularly hostile toward the *Chicago Tribune* which had been one of the bitterest foes of his administration. Big Bill had been in ill health. Perhaps that accounted for his foolish delusion that *Tribune* officials had designs on his life. The publisher of the *Tribune* learned that some of the mayor's followers had threatened to assassinate him if Big Bill met with foul play. With life then held cheaply in Chicago, the publisher bought an armored car and hired bodyguards. As Mayor Thompson raced through the city in his open car, he carried with him a sawed-off shotgun and other weapons. He was always accompanied by police guards and maintained an array of firearms in his residence.[43] Chicago could properly boast of being one of the world's greatest centers of commerce, industry, finance and communications. But the publisher of the city's largest newspaper and the mayor found it necessary to arm themselves fully to provide for their personal safety during an election campaign. Chicago resented its reputation as the crime capital of the world. But who could say that this reputation was undeserved?

CHAPTER VIII
Tammany Hall—Chicago Version

THE great depression hovered over Chicago like a huge black cloud as the 1931 mayoralty campaign gathered momentum. Business was in the doldrums. Unemployment had reached staggering heights. Men who once held substantial jobs were selling apples on street corners. Everywhere there was despair. Late in 1931, the president of the First National Bank of Chicago made a plea for economical government because, he said, "We are busted in the United States." No one could deny the need for economy in government. For years the costs of government in Chicago and Cook County had been unbearable through the extravagance, corruption and incompetence of political leaders. By 1931 the city was without credit. It lacked funds to pay the salaries of its schoolteachers, policemen and firemen. Angry citizens went on a tax strike. A contemporary observer wrote of Chicago in 1931 that "Citizens, already paying heavy taxes to racketeers, who can deliver what they promise, are refusing to pay taxes to a city government which cannot." [1] The political leadership in Chicago was bankrupt. The leadership of the underworld was in the hands of strong and ruthless gunmen.

Chicagoans looked in vain for some ray of hope in the coming city election. On the basis of past performance the prospect of another four years of William Hale Thompson in the mayor's chair was anything but encouraging. But if Big Bill's candidacy did not inspire hope, the voters were at least assured of plenty of laughs before the campaign was over. In seeking a fourth term as mayor,

Thompson knew he was entering the most difficult campaign of his career. Deserted by the leaders of his own party and running under the banner of the Republican party which was in public disfavor because of the depression, Big Bill knew that it would take more than rat shows or tree-climbing fish to swing the tide in his favor. His first obstacle was the February 1931 primary, in which his opponents were municipal court judge John H. Lyle and Alderman Arthur F. Albert. In typical Thompson fashion, Big Bill's vicious attacks on his opponents were frequently unprintable. He characterized Alderman Albert as "L'il Arthur" and referred to Lyle as "the nutty judge." He made speeches holding a long rope attached to a halter. Both of his opponents wore halters, he said. "L'il Arthur's" was attached to the Daily News Building and "the nutty judge's" to the Tribune Tower. Serious minded citizens shook their heads in disgust. But voters were amused in sufficient numbers to encourage Thompson to put on a full-scale performance at the Cort Theatre and charge admission. Big Bill's flair for showmanship had always far exceeded his capacity for statesmanship.

After a bitter campaign, Thompson won the Republican nomination. He now turned his guns on his opponent in the April election, Anton J. Cermak, boss of the Democratic machine. Big Bill was virtually without any newspaper support. He was fighting with his back to the wall but he had no intention of surrendering. And he still had some rabbits to pull out of his hat. In answer to attacks made on him by the *Tribune*, Thompson distributed a new campaign document. It featured an obituary prepared by the *Tribune* and placed in type several months earlier when it was believed that the mayor was dying. The writer of the obituary had merely followed the common principle: "Of the dead say nothing but good." During the primary campaign, the cowboy mayor had probably been the first to charge admission for a strictly political show. Now he had scored another first by publishing in campaign literature an advance obituary surreptitiously obtained from the presses of an unfriendly newspaper.

Thompson appeared to be making some headway in his fight for re-election when the state's attorney's police swooped down on the City Hall and raided the office of his City Sealer, Daniel Serritella. Records by the carload were seized and turned over to the grand jury. Indictments were promptly returned against Serritella and his chief deputy, Harry Hockstein. Serritella, a personal friend of Al Capone, and Hockstein, an associate of Frank "The Enforcer" Nitti, were charged with conspiracy growing out of money collected for Christmas baskets. Some time later both defendants were found guilty by a jury but the Appellate Court reversed the convictions, on the ground that the evidence did not establish guilt beyond a reasonable doubt. And the higher court also noted that it had become common in Chicago for politicians to "solicit more or less pointedly contributions from those who are thought to be vulnerable to such requests." The fact that "the donors may feel subjected to a kind of immoral coercion," said the court, did not make the official shakedown a crime.[2]

The raid on the city sealer's office served to highlight the presence of a personal friend of America's most notorious gang leader, Al Capone, in a key position in the city government. Chicago's long-suffering public was at last "fed up" with Big Bill and his cowboy hat. The voters were anxious to get rid of Thompson "at any price." But the price was high — much too high. On April 7, 1931, Anton J. Cermak was elected mayor of Chicago. He was the head of a political machine patterned after the infamous Tammany Hall organization of New York City. Only a few days after Cermak's election, a magazine article in *The Nation* stated:

Perhaps Big Bill Thompson was as vicious as his defamers pictured him. To the practical and unprejudiced observer it appears that Chicago has simply swapped one evil for another. . . . The people of Chicago, by electing Tony Cermak have made him the most powerful political boss in the United States today.[3]

Cermak had been tutored in the game of politics by the old master, George E. Brennan. Prior to Brennan's death in 1928, Cermak and Hinky Dinky Kenna had been two of his principal counselors and henchmen. When Brennan died, Cermak succeeded him as head of the Democratic machine. Tony Cermak had been a member of the Illinois General Assembly, where his record was largely distinguished by his vote for William Lorimer for United States Senator. Cermak had served four terms in the Chicago City Council. In 1922 he was elected president of the Cook County

Board of Commissioners and was re-elected in 1926 and 1930. In 1927 he was defeated as the Democratic candidate for the United States Senate. The Thompson machine had been a rather loosely-knit organization, built around Big Bill. It was largely a personal machine. This was not true of the machine Cermak had constructed, in which personalities counted for little. An efficient organization built around a dictatorial committeeman in each of the wards with final control and discipline vested in one boss, Anton J. Cermak, was the basis of its strength.[4] It was a machine with frightening possibilities for controlling the political life of the city for many years and decades to come. It made the most of these possibilities.

The powerful political organization which now controlled the city derived much of its strength from the lucrative gambling business, which necessarily meant strong alliance with the underworld. As a ward politician, Cermak had recognized the potentialities of the gambling business as an integral part of a political organization. Cermak was a master of detail and as mayor he continued to give his attention to gambling as a source of political power. Early in Cermak's administration there were persistent rumors that gambling was to be reorganized and new syndicates under new leadership were to replace the old. In the heart of his political stronghold on the West Side, William R. "Big Bill" Johnson had enjoyed ironclad protection for large-scale gambling activities. It was a foregone conclusion that Big Bill Johnson would rise to a place of influence in Chicago's gambling underworld. On the North Side, Ted Newberry, an associate of Bugs Moran and the slain Jack Zuta, was slated to receive important gambling concessions. On the Northwest Side, Martin Guilfoyle, who had ruled over rich gambling fields with the protection of Republican administrations, would be replaced by an underworld boss friendly to the Democratic machine. On October 1, 1931, Mayor Cermak appointed James P. Allman to the position of commissioner of police with the understanding that law-enforcement policies regarding gambling would be dictated by the political leaders. Radical changes in the city's gambling-political organization were temporarily postponed, however, until after the 1932 state and national elections.[5]

In the meantime, the Federal government had initiated action which would make the contemplated reorganization easier. In the autumn of 1931, Al Capone was placed on trial in Federal court in Chicago for evasion of income taxes. The government produced records from Capone's Cicero gambling places, the Hawthorne Smoke Shop and the Ship, which reflected an income of over a million dollars within the space of a few months. The trial was a dramatic one. Before it began Capone gunmen approached all of the prospective jurors with the view of assuring the gang leader's acquittal. To some they offered one-thousand dollar bills, to others they promised political jobs and to those who evinced no interest in either money or political preferment they threatened violence. During the trial Phil D'Andrea, Al Capone's bodyguard, had the effrontery to walk into the courtroom with a gun bulging from his clothing in a menacing manner. Federal Judge James H. Wilkerson promptly sentenced D'Andrea to six months in jail for contempt of court. The Capone gang was rudely awakened to the fact that there was a difference between the Federal court in Chicago and the city's local and state courts in which gangsters had been treated with deference for so many years. In October 1931 Al Capone was convicted.[6] Subsequently he went to Alcatraz, the Federal prison for the most dangerous convicts. George E. Q. Johnson, the United States Attorney who prosecuted Capone, became a national figure, and Johnson's assistant in the trial, Dwight H. Green, later became governor of the state of Illinois.

In 1932 Jack Guzik, the business manager of Capone's empire, was convicted in the United States District Court in Chicago for evasion of taxes on income in the amount of $1,538,155 derived from gambling establishments. He was sentenced to five years in the penitentiary at Leavenworth, Kansas and fined $17,500. Two years earlier another Capone stalwart, Frank Nitti, had been sentenced to eighteen months in a Federal penitentiary for failure to pay taxes on an income of $743,000.[7] The government's successful prosecution of Al Capone and two of his lieutenants were humiliating experiences. For many years Capone gangsters had shown utter contempt for Chicago courts and law. They had engaged in million-dollar illegal enterprises with absolute immunity. They had committed wholesale murder and extortion without fear of prosecution. Now they were going to prison for failure to share their loot with the United States Government. This was damaging to their power and prestige.

The Federal trials of Capone and his lieutenants attracted wide attention. Undoubtedly they added to the growing sentiment against national prohibition. It had become popular to blame the Eighteenth Amendment for all of the crime and official corruption flourishing in Chicago and elsewhere. Unrealistically, Al Capone was considered the product of prohibition. Beyond any question, the gang leader's wealth and power had been greatly increased as a result of the lucrative illicit liquor business which grew out of the "noble experiment." But the average citizen was inclined to overlook the fact that Capone merely took over a powerful underworld organization that had grown to menacing stature long before prohibition. Big Jim Colosimo and John Torrio, his immediate predecessors, had been strong and ruthless bosses for some time before liquor was outlawed. And Colosimo and Torrio merely followed a long line of underworld leaders who had been responsible for widespread lawlessness and violence in Chicago for many decades. Capone, like his predecessors, was the product of a deeply intrenched political system—a system based on alliances between the underworld and politicians for their mutual advantage.

As the Democratic National Convention met in the huge Chicago Stadium in June 1932, the repeal of The National Prohibition Act was a major issue. One of the foremost champions of repeal was Mayor Cermak who was in control of the Illinois delegation. Cermak's stand was to be expected. It was not based solely on the prevalent overwhelming public sentiment against prohibition. As secretary of the United Societies for many years, he had a "long record as the ruthless leader of the saloon and brewery overlords in Cook County before the Eighteenth Amendment." [8] The public was not particularly interested in the basis for Cermak's opposition to the Eighteenth Amendment. They knew prohibition had been a failure and they wanted it repealed. Before the 1932 Democratic convention, Mayor Cermak went to New York City to confer with the head of Tammany Hall, John F. Curry. The Cermak Democratic machine and Tammany Hall had much in common. Their strength stemmed from alliances with the underworld. Both organizations were corrupt and ruthless. It was only natural that the two machines should work together in perfect harmony at the national convention. They agreed upon a strategy which they hoped would result in the nomination of the "Happy Warrior," former Governor Al Smith of New York. Smith had made a distinguished record as the chief executive of the Empire State. He was popular and was known as one of the foremost opponents of the Eighteenth Amendment.

Tammany Hall was well represented in Chicago during the convention. Its most powerful leader, James J. Hines, occupied an expensive suite of rooms in one of Chicago's swanky hotels. His roommate was Frank Costello, the slot-machine king and lord of the New York underworld. Costello's associate, Lucky Luciano, a notorious pander who was later deported, was rooming in the same hotel with Albert Marinelli, a Tammany district leader. Both Costello and Luciano were friends of top-ranking members of the Capone gang and felt at home in the Windy City. In fact, in April 1932, Lucky Luciano, along with another Costello lieutenant, Meyer Lansky, had been seized by the Chicago Police Department in the company of the Capone gang leaders, Paul Ricca and Rocco Fischetti, as they were leaving the Congress Hotel. When the police could not prove that they had committed any crime, they were promptly released. Near the Costello suite of rooms in the same hotel was one occupied by former New York Sheriff Thomas M. Farley and Louis Shomberg (alias Dutch Goldberg), a gangster of tremendous wealth and power. Only a short time before the convention, Governor Franklin D. Roosevelt had removed Tom Farley as sheriff in New York and the phrase "little tin box" had become derisively associated with his name as he had attempted to explain the source of his wealth. Actually, the money that found its way into Farley's little tin box and accounted for his wealth, came in part from the lucrative rackets operated in New York by Louis "Lepke" Buchalter and Jake "Gurrah" Shapiro. "Tin box" Farley was still a man of influence in Tammany circles, however, and he was in Chicago with Frank Costello, Dutch Goldberg, Lucky Luciano and James J. Hines to lend counsel and advice in the selection of a candidate for President of the United States.[9]

Among Al Smith's most ardent supporters at the convention

was the delegation from Massachusetts. But the state's best-known Democrat, James Michael Curley, was not one of the delegates. In the belief that he had been promised the post of Secretary of the Navy if Franklin D. Roosevelt were elected President, Curley had prematurely espoused the cause of Roosevelt in Massachusetts. The Democrats of Massachusetts were furious and refused to send him to Chicago. Curley, however, possessed too much ingenuity and brass to permit this detail to keep him from active participation in the convention affairs. Coming to Chicago alone and without portfolio, he promptly conferred with F. Val Spinosa, Chairman of the Puerto Rican delegation, in the Congress Hotel. Mayor Anton J. Cermak was present. At the conclusion of the conference, Spinosa departed on a trip to Baltimore and the Puerto Rican delegation had a new acting chairman, the Honorable James Michael Curley of Boston.[10] In the back rooms and on the convention floor, Curley played an important part in the nomination of the next President of the United States. After the third ballot was taken it became evident that Al Smith could not muster the necessary votes for the nomination. On the next ballot, Mayor Cermak delivered the important Illinois delegation to Franklin D. Roosevelt, who was nominated by the convention.

Governor Roosevelt left Albany by plane to accept the nomination. He was met by Mayor Anton J. Cermak who conducted him to the Chicago Stadium. As the convention ended it was apparent that Cermak was one of the most powerful political bosses in the entire United States.[11]

But Cermak's interest in national politics was not permitted to interfere with his attention to important details in his local machine. At the very time the United States government was busily engaged in removing Al Capone and Jack Guzik from the scene of Chicago's gang warfare, the remaining underworld lords and political leaders were perfecting plans for a reorganization of the important gambling industry. During the time that Tony Cermak had been growing in political strength on the West Side, Big Bill Johnson had gradually developed into a powerful gambling-house operator. In the heart of Cermak-controlled territory, Johnson had erected a fortresslike building for his illegal operations. Johnson was by no means a neophyte in the gambling business. He had served his apprenticeship under the tutelage of Julius "Lovin' Putty" Annixter, one of the top-ranking West Side gamblers. From Annixter, Johnson had learned the "tricks of the trade." He also cemented intimate relationships with the important politicians who had served Annixter faithfully for many years.[12] He became interested in other ventures as well. The notorious William R. Skidmore was his associate in the Lawndale Kennel Club, a highly profitable dog track.[13] With Skidmore as a partner, it was obvious that Johnson would rise to importance in the gambling picture during the Cermak administration.

It was also apparent that the North Side gang chief, Ted Newberry, was in high favor with the new political regime. Newberry had been an ally of Bugs Moran in the North Side gang wars. He was a friend of Skidmore. He had shifted his allegiance from Moran to the Capone organization. And it was charged that Newberry, Danny Stanton and other Capone gunmen had murdered Jack Zuta in Wisconsin on August 1, 1930. Late in 1932 Ted Newberry was scheduled to assume the role of gambling boss of the North Side. His favored position with the new administration gave him power,[14] and it was considered a foregone conclusion that he would soon become one of the most feared gang leaders in the city. Once more he was at odds with the Capone gang. In particular, there was bitter enmity between Newberry and Frank "The Enforcer" Nitti who had become leader of the Capone forces while the boss was in Federal prison.

On December 19, 1932, Mayor Tony Cermak's special police detail headed by Detective Sergeants Harry Lang and Harry Miller conducted a spectacular raid on a Capone gang headquarters located at 221 North LaSalle Street just a stone's throw from the City Hall. Orders for the raid emanated from the mayor's office. The press was informed that the police had encountered stiff resistance from the gang leader, Frank Nitti, when an attempt was made to place him under arrest. A gun battle had occurred, and Sergeant Lang in his heroic fight with Nitti had been wounded. In the exchange of shots with Lang, Frank Nitti received bullet wounds in his neck and chest. It was believed at first that Nitti would die. Sergeant Lang had emerged from the affray as a hero; he was given an award of three hundred dollars for meritorious service. Both

Sergeants Lang and Miller received creditable mention on the police department's records.

Only a few days after Nitti had been seriously wounded by the police, Ted Newberry was the victim of a typical gang killing. On January 7, 1933, Newberry's body, riddled with shotgun slugs, was found in a ditch near Bailey Town, Porter County, Indiana. The murder was not entirely unexpected. Ugly rumors had been circulating among the underworld that the shooting of Nitti by the police "heroes" was related to Newberry's efforts to control the North Side gambling with the backing of the Cermak administration. According to gossip, Ted Newberry had offered fifteen thousand dollars for the murder of his chief rival, Frank Nitti. When Nitti did not die, preparations were made to place him on trial on charges of assault with intent to kill Police Sergeant Harry Lang.

Before Nitti could be tried, Mayor Cermak left Chicago for Miami, where a great reception was planned for President-elect Franklin D. Roosevelt on February 15, 1933. Having played an important part in the nomination of Roosevelt at the Chicago convention, it was natural that Cermak should participate in the political celebration which was to be staged in the Miami waterfront park. As Cermak approached the side of Franklin D. Roosevelt's automobile to shake hands with the President-elect, a crazed fanatic, Giuseppe Zangara, jumped out of the crowd and fired several shots at close range. Cermak, fatally wounded, slumped into the arms of Roosevelt who rushed him to a Miami hospital. Physicians and surgeons fought valiantly to save the mayor's life until March 6, 1933, when he died. The body was returned to Chicago and an elaborate funeral was held in the Chicago Stadium, the scene of Cermak's great political triumph the preceding summer. In a eulogy pronounced by the governor of the state, Cermak was credited with having redeemed the reputation of the city.

Chicago's "redeemed" reputation was in for another severe blow only a few days after the funeral. In April 1933, Frank Nitti was brought to trial in the Cook County Criminal Court for assaulting Sergeant Harry Lang with intent to kill. Police Officer Chris Callahan, a member of the squad which raided Nitti's headquarters, was called to the witness stand. He testified that when the police officers placed Nitti under arrest on December 19, 1932, the gangster was searched twice, but he was unarmed and defenseless. While Nitti was in this helpless condition, Sergeant Harry Lang shot him three times. Callahan was questioned concerning the wound Sergeant Lang had received in the fracas. His answer startled the courtroom. Officer Callahan testified, "There was only one gun fired up there. Lang must have shot himself." Sergeant Lang was then placed on the witness stand. He insisted that he shot Nitti in self-defense. The police "hero" then caused a sensation by refusing to answer any further questions on the ground that his testimony might incriminate him. The trial had badly tarnished the police hero's medals. The tables had turned completely. Nitti the defendant became Nitti the prosecuting witness, while Lang was indicted on a charge of assault with a deadly weapon. In retaliation he threatened to make disclosures that would wreck the Democratic party but apparently he was persuaded to abandon this plan of action. After nine continuances, Sergeant Lang was finally placed on trial in September 1933. Frank Nitti testified that while Police Officer Chris Callahan held him by the wrists, Lang shot him in the neck and then fired two more bullets into his chest. Callahan corroborated Nitti's story, and Sergeant Lang was found guilty of assault with a deadly weapon. He was granted a new trial, however, and the case was eventually dismissed, but before the conclusion of the weird case Harry Lang was discharged from the police department.[15]

The murder of Mayor Anton J. Cermak did not alter the complexion of city government. The same forces were in control. Cermak's body had scarcely been lowered in its grave when an emergency measure was rushed through the Illinois State legislature on March 31, 1933, which empowered the Chicago City Council to elect a mayor to complete Cermak's unexpired term of office. Although this law provided that all other Illinois cities must select an interim mayor from members of the city council, the Chicago City Council could elect anyone to fill the vacancy, whether he was a member of the council or not. The stage was set for Patrick A. Nash, Chairman of the Cook County Democratic Central Committee and a friend of Cermak's, to place a man of his choice in the mayor's chair. For many years the strength of the Democratic organization had been growing through the efforts of the triumvirate, Anton J. Cermak, Patrick A. Nash and Edward J. Kelly. Edward J. Kelly was Pat Nash's obvious choice for mayor. Kelly was not a member of the city council. On April 13, 1933, the Chicago City Council went through the formality of electing a mayor under the provisions of the new law passed only a few days before. Alderman Jacob M. Arvey of the Twenty-fourth Ward nominated Edward J. Kelly, who was promptly elected. In accepting his new job, Kelly pledged that he would follow the policies of the deceased mayor, Anton J. Cermak.[16] And no one ever questioned that he kept his solemn pledge.

With Kelly in the mayor's chair, the Cermak Democratic organization became known as the Kelly-Nash machine. It was to become one of the most ruthless political organizations in American municipal history.[17] Its roots were deep, going back at least to the period of Mike McDonald and his twenty years of misrule which began about 1873. Gambling syndicates had always been an integral part of the organization, and a change of faces in the political leadership never disturbed these close relationships with the underworld which naturally became more and more deeply entrenched.

The new mayor, Edward J. Kelly, had been chief engineer of the Sanitary District since 1920. The administration of the Sanitary District during that period was popularly known as the "Whoopee era" because of the prevalence of widespread graft and corruption which had cost the taxpayers an estimated five million dollars. The abuses were so open that an investigation was finally conducted. Three indictments were eventually returned on May 3, 1929, May 29, 1930, and June 5, 1931, implicating numerous officials. Kelly was named as a defendant in the second indictment, but the indictment against him was finally abandoned by the state's attorney and only one defendant, Frank J. Link, actually went to prison. During the trials there was a parade of over seven hundred witnesses, most of whom testified unwillingly. In the words of the presiding judge, the testimony revealed ". . . hideous corruption prevalent in a public office created by the legislature . . . to provide for the sanitation and guard the health of the community." From all walks of life witnesses admitted having received regular checks for one and one-half years although they had performed no work of any nature during that period. Legislators, members of their families and their friends were on the payroll without rendering any service for the checks they regularly received. Dummy corporations were organized for the sole purpose of dealing with the Sanitary District. Their overcharges ranged from ninety per cent to seven hundred per cent. Contractors were sometimes paid twice for the same job. A bridle path costing $1,160,000 could have been constructed for one third the amount. Although prosecution against Edward J. Kelly had been dropped, in the eyes of the public he could not escape his share of responsibility for the gross misadministration of the Sanitary District when he was chief engineer. That he awarded numerous contracts is undisputed; if any thought was given to the public interest when they were entered into, the trials failed to so indicate. In fact, Kelly had awarded eight million dollars in contracts to Patrick A. Nash's sewer contracting firm. An additional four million dollars had been expended with Dowdle Brothers, a firm owned by two of Nash's nephews.[18]

The leader of the Democratic party just before the Sanitary District scandal became front-page news throughout the nation was Anton J. Cermak. The Sanitary District was under the control of the Democrats. The graft and plunder of the Sanitary District defrauded the taxpayers of millions of dollars. The pillage of the Democratic politicians in control of this official body was comparable to the piracy of New York City's infamous Tweed Ring. In New York, William Marcy Tweed went to prison and the members of his ring were ruined politically. In Chicago, Edward J. Kelly and Cermak were to become the absolute rulers of the city and among the most influential politicians of the nation. This could only happen in Chicago.

After Kelly became mayor the Federal government began delving into his income-tax returns. Between 1919 and 1929 Kelly had received a total of $151,000 from his salary. His admitted income during the same period was $724,368 or over a half-million dollars in excess of his salary. He paid $105,000 to the Federal government in settlement of his tax claims. About the same time Pat Nash was required to pay the Federal government $175,000 for back taxes.[19] From all of these disclosures it was apparent that Kelly and Nash were ideally suited by experience and philosophy to become the rulers of Chicago.

The Kelly-Nash machine was highly efficient. Its detailed organization extended into every precinct of every ward. It was ruled
over with a discipline that was ruthless and severe. Gambling was
a business highly important to the machine. It was estimated that
graft received for the protection of gambling and vice amounted
to approximately twenty million dollars annually.[20] Mayor Kelly's
control over the police department was absolute. Police captains
agreeable to the ward committeemen were assigned to the various
police districts and took orders from the ward boss. Gambling
was permitted to flourish unless the ward committeeman needed
discipline. In this event, a police captain would be dispatched to
the district with instructions to enforce the gambling laws. The
ward boss usually made peace with the machine and gambling once
more flourished in his district.

In the First Ward, Hinky Dink Kenna and Bathhouse John
Coughlin awarded the gambling privileges to Frank Nitti, the new
ruler of the Capone syndicate. The Capone organization fully
exploited the rich gambling fields in the busy Loop area. Gambling
places were everywhere. Prominent members of the Capone gang
who were also precinct captains of the Democratic machine operated many of the most lucrative establishments in downtown Chicago. The overseer of illegal privileges in the First Ward was the
Capone lieutenant, Duke Cooney, who had risen to power under
Hinky Dink Kenna, and who ruled the district with an iron fist.
Money poured into the coffers of the ward organization. The
First Ward was always in safe hands for the Kelly-Nash machine
at election time. Neither the ward bosses nor the Capone syndicate
had any intention of losing control over this lucrative territory.[21]

In many other sections of the city, gambling was under the domination of the powerful Johnson-Skidmore combination. Big Bill
Johnson's future as a gambling boss was assured when Cermak became the chief executive of the city. His power during the Kelly-
Nash regime increased tremendously through his alliance with the
notorious William R. Skidmore. In addition to engaging in large-
scale gambling activities Skidmore at one time had been the guiding
genius of the pickpocket trust. In a saloon he operated at West Lake
and North Robey Streets in Chicago, pickpockets gathered to divide
their spoils. Shoplifters, gamblers and disorderly house proprietors

looked to Skidmore for protection. He never disappointed them. Skidmore had received his start in politics by ingratiating himself with the Democratic boss Roger Sullivan in 1902. At that time he operated a saloon across the street from the City Hall. In 1903 he became purchasing agent for the Democratic party. At the Democratic National Conventions in 1912 and 1916 Skidmore served as sergeant at arms. During the 1920's he was engaged in the lucrative business of signing bonds for criminals and then intervening in their behalf when they appeared in court. His political power gave him the run of the courtrooms. A word from Skidmore would advance any case on the docket. He had entree to the chambers of many judges.[22] Skidmore had maintained friendly relations with leaders of the Capone organization and had been allied with such important gangsters as Barney Bertsche, Jack Zuta and Bugs Moran. But none of these alliances had given him the power or the political prestige that he enjoyed as a result of his partnership with Big Bill Johnson during the Kelly-Nash regime.

Edward J. Kelly brought to the mayor's chair the outward dignity which was lacking in Big Bill Thompson. Kelly did not engage in clownish antics to attract the electorate but instead relied on the vote-getting powers of the ward organization which worked with machinelike precision. But the differences between Thompson and Kelly were largely on the surface. Their political philosophies were identical and designed to achieve the same objectives — votes and power. Thompson, cowboy hat in hand, extolled the virtues of the "wide-open town"; Kelly, with the demeanor of a department-store executive, prated about his "liberal town." Both meant exactly the same thing. During both administrations wide-open gambling flourished for the joint benefit of the gangster element and the politicians. Liquor flowed freely during the Thompson regime, notwithstanding the Volstead Act. Under Kelly, following the repeal of prohibition, the old saloons became taverns and defied every legal regulation with impunity. Under both Thompson and Kelly the police department was considered an adjunct of the political machine — a means of rewarding political friends and punishing political enemies.

When Edward J. Kelly became mayor in 1933, Chicago was celebrating its one hundredth anniversary. A Century of Progress

Exposition, which had been planned for many years, thrilled thousands of visitors from all over the world as the Columbian Exposition had done forty years earlier. Extending from Twelfth Street south to Thirty-ninth Street on the lake front, Chicago's 1933 World's Fair was a veritable magic city. Until a short time before the exposition started, the fair grounds site lay far below the surface of Lake Michigan. The grounds as well as the city reflected the ingenuity of man. The Century of Progress Exposition epitomized a new age — an age of steel, electricity, chromium, aluminum and modernistic architecture. Most of the buildings were completely without windows. Day and night they were illuminated by electricity. At night, colored illumination added to the beauty of the exteriors of the futuristic buildings. The Travel and Transport Building was a block and a half long. Inside were locomotives, multiple-motored transport planes and a cross section of an ocean liner. Building after building was a storehouse of knowledge regarding the latest developments in science, transportation and communication.[23] Although emphasis was placed on science, beauty and culture, the wants of the plain pleasure seekers were not overlooked. The "Streets of Paris," featuring Sally Rand and her fan dance, was always crowded. The same was true of the "Days of Forty-nine," "Old Mexico," the "Italian Village" and the "Ann Rutledge Tavern." Thousands of men, women and children looked down on the beauty of the fair from the "Sky Ride," one of the most spectacular features of the Exposition. The places of amusement were boundless and customers were never wanting.

Adding to the carnival atmosphere which pervaded some portions of the fair was the spirit of "wide-open Chicago" provided by members of the Capone gang who were financially interested in some of the concessions. James Mondi specialized in the operation of lucrative gambling games, including roulette. Occasionally when a patron started to leave Mondi's place with substantial winnings he was suddenly confronted with a couple of hard-looking characters who would suggest that the game be continued. The suggestion was frequently followed. Ralph Capone had an interest in a popular concession and was present each night to assist in its management. One of the well-patronized rides designed to provide thrills to the Century of Progress visitors was owned in part by

Murray "The Camel" Humphreys, another Capone gangster.

From the standpoint of the patron, the gambling games at the fair had made little progress since the frontier days of Chicago a hundred years earlier. The games in 1933 were as crooked as they were in 1833. A priest who arrived at the Exposition grounds with $170.00 was swindled out of his entire bankroll within a few minutes, playing a game which afforded the patron no chance whatsoever. However, he was more fortunate than most of the patrons of such games. His money was recovered and the operator was evicted from the grounds. Scores of similar games were in operation. Some of the concessions featuring strip-tease shows offered prosperous-looking male patrons "special" performances. A number of the girls attached to shows of this kind maintained apartments near the Exposition grounds. Men who visited the girls at their apartments were frequently jackrolled. Occasionally members of the Capone gang used strong-arm sales methods in attempting to force some of the concessions to use their brand of beer. These underworld activities were in the background and were kept to a minimum by the fair's department of Public Protection. On the whole, the Century of Progress Exposition was well managed and reflected credit on the city of Chicago. However, a sufficient amount of gambling, vice and muscling tactics existed to give it a true Chicago flavor — the flavor of a wide-open town which is secretly proud of its wickedness.

The people who thronged to Chicago in 1933 were favorably impressed with the city — with its boulevards, towering skyscrapers, beautiful lake front and spacious parks. In the holiday atmosphere of the Exposition, the depression which still engulfed the nation was largely forgotten. Chicago's financial position was particularly black. By the end of 1933 the bonded indebtedness of the city amounted to $133,000,000. There was a debt on unpaid salaries of city employees, tax anticipation warrants and current obligations which exceeded $100,000,000. The bonds of Chicago's park boards were defaulted. Banks refused to buy either tax anticipation warrants or city bonds. A suit was threatened which would have thrown the municipality into bankruptcy. Property values had deteriorated. Streets and alleys were dirty and garbage was uncollected. Blighted areas were spreading and legitimate businesses were moving out of the city.[24] These conditions did not discourage the underworld, however. Chicago still remained an ideal place for organized criminals and racketeers. Profits were high and gangsters were killing one another on the city streets to control them.

In 1933 there were thirty-five gang murders committed in Chicago, all of them unsolved. The one that created the most furor involved the machine gunning of Gus Winkler at 1:30 P.M. on October 9, 1933. His bullet-riddled body was found slumped over the doorstep leading to the Charles H. Weber Distributing Company at 1414 Roscoe Street. Weber, who was in Florida when Winkler was murdered, was a member of the Cook County Board of Commissioners and a powerful politician. He also had an interest in the "Streets of Paris" at the Century of Progress Exposition. Gus Winkler had been interested in the slot-machine business, and his headquarters on the second floor at 755 Waveland Avenue had served as a meeting place for police officers and other officials. His killing was the subject of an inquiry by a "blue ribbon" coroner's jury which heard lengthy testimony of numerous witnesses, but the murder remained unsolved. The report of the coroner's jury referred to the widespread gambling and corruption which prevailed in the city. Chicago, it found, was "honey-combed" with bookmakers.[25]

Mayor Kelly disliked the publicity that attended gang killings. They perpetuated Chicago's reputation as the crime capital of the world. Most of the gang murders were the outgrowth of warfare between vicious criminal groups over the control of gambling with its lush profits. The Kelly administration deplored the murders, but gambling was so important to the ward organization that no genuine effort was made to enforce the antigambling laws. On the contrary, there was official encouragement of the gambling business. Gangsters maintained amicable and profitable relations with the right politicians. The cost of protection was high but it was certain. Chicago, along with Hot Springs, Kansas City and St. Paul, all wide-open towns and notoriously corrupt, had become a dumping ground for the nation's major law violators.

Following the kidnapping of Charles Boettcher II in Denver, Colorado, on February 12, 1933, his abductors, Verne Sankey and Gordon Alcorn fled to Chicago, where they were apprehended by the Federal Bureau of Investigation several months later.[26] On June 17, 1933, the Union Station massacre in Kansas City, Missouri, stunned the nation. Three police officers, an agent of the FBI, and Frank Nash, a notorious escaped Federal prisoner, were mowed down by machine-gun bullets as they emerged from the Union Station. Charles "Pretty Boy" Floyd, Adam Richetti and Verne Miller manned the machine guns as they unsuccessfully attempted to liberate Frank Nash who was being returned to the United States Penitentiary at Leavenworth. Miller, who engineered the massacre, was placed in touch with Pretty Boy Floyd and Richetti by John Lazia, the gambling czar of Kansas City and a principal lieutenant of Tom Pendergast, the political boss of Missouri. Much of the investigation conducted by the Federal government in this case was centered in Chicago. Verne Miller hid out in Chicago until he escaped from a trap set by the FBI. Among Miller's friends in Chicago was Gus Winkler, the big gambler who was closely associated with important politicians.[27]

On July 1, 1933, the international swindler John "Jake the Barber" Factor was kidnapped near Chicago as he was returning home from a gambling casino. The crime was committed by Chicago's notorious Touhy gang headed by Roger Touhy.[28] While the FBI was in the midst of the Factor kidnapping investigation in Chicago, Charles F. Urschel, a wealthy oil man of Oklahoma City was kidnapped on July 22. One of the leaders of the Urschel kidnapping gang, George "Machine Gun" Kelly, and his wife headed for Chicago.[29] It was well known that every want of the professional gunman could be satisfied in Chicago — hideouts, machine guns, bulletproof vests and automobiles with smoke-screen equipment. On January 17, 1934, Edward George Bremer was kidnapped in St. Paul, Minnesota by the Karpis-Barker gang and was brought to a hiding place a few miles from Chicago. One of the instigators and alleged "brains" of the Bremer kidnapping as well as the earlier abduction of the St. Paul brewer, William Hamm, Jr., on June 5, 1933, was Fred Goetz (alias Shotgun George Ziegler). He was affiliated with the Capone syndicate. A Chicago gambler and politician, John J. "Boss" McLaughlin disposed of $57,000 of the ransom collected from the Bremer family in Chicago. Again a major portion of the investigation by the Federal Bureau of Investigation regarding the

St. Paul abductions was concentrated in Chicago, where the members of the Karpis-Barker gang received the assistance of the operators of officially protected houses of prostitution. Some of the kidnappers, notably Russell Gibson (alias Slim Gray), spent much of their time around the gambling casinos. Early in 1935 the FBI captured Arthur "Doc" Barker and Byron Bolton (alias Monte Carter), two of the Bremer kidnappers, in Chicago. Slim Gray was killed, as he tried to make his escape from a North Side apartment, by shooting it out with the Federal agents.[30]

Shortly after Bremer had been kidnapped in St. Paul, John Dillinger made his escape from the Crown Point (Indiana) County Jail. He headed straight for Chicago. For several months the members of the Dillinger gang made this friendly city their headquarters. A former city prosecutor, Louis Piquett, made arrangements to have surgery performed on John Dillinger and Homer Van Meter, to change their facial appearance and obliterate their fingerprint impressions.[31] Jack Perkins, an employee of a North Side gambling establishment, furnished members of this gang of bank robbers and murderers with bulletproof vests, machine guns and ammunition. The gaming house with which Perkins was associated enjoyed the protection of powerful ward politicians for over a decade. Dillinger, who had become one of the most widely-known criminals in American history, was shot and killed by FBI agents in Chicago on July 22, 1934. His death was headline news in virtually every newspaper in the country.

It is doubtful if any city has ever been the sanctuary for a greater number of major professional criminals than Chicago in the early and middle 1930's. Nowhere was the racketeering element more strongly protected. And the members of the underworld who controlled gambling were favored above all others. By the fall of 1934, it was estimated that 7500 protected gambling establishments were operating in Chicago. The *Chicago News* in an editorial on October 30 charged that:

. . . these joints splitting their tainted profits fifty-fifty with the politicians, are estimated to pay the tidy sum of $1,000,000 a month to the Kelly-Nash ring. . . . Not for many a year has the city been so wide open with respect to police and political protection of gambling and other forms of vice as under the Kelly-Nash regime.

Chicagoans were inclined to shrug their shoulders and exhibit but passing interest in published accounts of widespread racketeering and corruption. But they were definitely paying the bills. In 1934, the Illinois Commission on Taxation and Expenditures made public a report prepared for it by Griffenhagen and Associates, a nationally recognized firm of experts on municipal affairs. This report revealed that burglary insurance rates in Cook County were $27.50 per $1000 as compared to $12.10 in other parts of Illinois and in the entire state of Wisconsin. Apartment burglary rates were $33.00 per $1000 in Cook County while the rate of $14.85 prevailed in the other districts examined; holdup rates were in the ratio of $7.50 to $4.00. Automobile theft insurance rates were $25.40 in Chicago and parts of Cook County as compared with $8.90 in outlying sections of Cook County, the adjoining counties of Dupage and Lake, and only $3.15 in the balance of the state of Illinois. It was estimated that the annual cost of racketeering in Chicago amounted to $150,000,000.[32] Crime was profitable only for the racketeers and their protectors.

Fortified with new legislation enacted by Congress, the Federal Bureau of Investigation concentrated its efforts in Chicago. Special squads of agents were sent to the city to work exclusively on some of the major criminal gangs. These endeavors were rewarded with the apprehension of many of the nation's most desperate kidnappers, bank robbers and murderers. Crime news occupied much space on the front pages of newspapers, but the most sinister developments of the time were unnoticed. The Capone syndicate, powerful and strong in its own right, was quietly cementing alliances and close working arrangements with the most potent underworld organization on the East Coast. Frank Costello, the slot-machine king, was the most prominent member of this group. He was closely associated with the rulers of Tammany Hall and exerted a tremendous political influence in New York City.

Among Costello's chief lieutenants was the gambling boss, Joe Adonis. John Torrio had worked closely with Costello and Adonis in New York after he left Chicago. Adonis had acquired a part interest in a big Chicago brewery which had been operated by John Torrio and other members of the Capone syndicate during the prohibition era. Following the repeal of the National Prohibition Act, Capone gangsters continued to operate the brewery, reorganized to meet the new conditions. In 1933 Adonis sent his personal representative to Chicago to assist the Capone syndicate in its brewery operations. This man had worked as a bookkeeper for Adonis and Frank Erickson, another Costello lieutenant, in a Halifax, Nova Scotia hospital sweepstakes lottery in 1932. The government had seized the plates for the tickets in Long Island City and arrested some of the underlings. Perhaps it was due to the fact that Joe Adonis and Frank Erickson as well as the bookkeeper escaped implication in the lottery enterprise that the accountant was selected by Adonis to represent his interests in the Chicago brewery. He remained in Chicago about five months and held the imposing title of Consultant Director of Commercial Relations. During this period he assisted in hiring a respectable individual with important political affiliations as president of the brewery at an annual salary of $25,000. It was determined that only thirty per cent of the brewery's output could be disposed of in Illinois, so the Adonis representative engaged in a tour of other states in a sales capacity. Before he visited any prospective customer, however, Joe Adonis had previously made the initial arrangements by telephone. About January 1934, Adonis brought his trusted associate back to New York where he became a prominent figure in the liquor industry and also handled the dog-track lobby in behalf of the New York mobsters.

Members of Chicago's Capone gang, working in close harmony with New York underworld leaders, were branching out in many directions. But Chicago remained their headquarters. The political atmosphere was friendly. Protection was certain. In 1934, in a restaurant at 135 North Clark Street, across the street from the City Hall and County Building, New York gangsters held an important meeting with top-ranking members of the Capone organization. Representing the Capone gang were Paul Ricca, Frank Nitti and Louis "Little New York" Campagna. Plans were formulated at this meeting to combine the forces of the New York and Chicago gangs with the view of dominating various labor unions throughout the country. In July 1934, through the influence of Capone gangsters, George Scalise became the eastern vice-president of the Building Service Employees Union in New York. His eastern sponsor for this important job was Anthony Carfano, also known as Little Augie Pisano. Carfano was closely associated with Joe Adonis in slot-machine enterprises in Brooklyn. When the international president of the Building Service Employees Union died in April 1937, the Capone gang elevated Scalise to this vacancy. Scalise had a background which inspired the confidence of the Capone syndicate as well as its New York affiliates. In 1913 Scalise had been convicted under the White Slave Traffic Act and sentenced to serve four and one-half years in a Federal penitentiary. For many years he had worked closely in labor racketeering activities with Louis "Lepke" Buchalter and Jacob "Gurrah" Shapiro who headed the criminal organization which was aptly called Murder, Incorporated. In handling the affairs of the Building Service Employees Union, Scalise received the counsel and advice of Anthony Carfano and Lucky Luciano as well as members of Chicago's Capone gang. Prominent politicians, including judges in Chicago and New York, maintained friendly and helpful relations with the gangsters who were exploiting the workingman. But in 1940, a vigorous New York District Attorney, Thomas E. Dewey, indicted George Scalise for grand larceny. He was charged with having stolen $60,000 from the Union's treasury between May 1937 and March 31, 1940. Evidence at the trial reflected that Scalise had received over $300,000 in salary and expenses from the union. The expense items included pleasure trips to Havana with Capone mobsters. The New York trial of Scalise resulted in his conviction and a prison sentence of ten to twenty years. He also received a three-year sentence on a Federal indictment charging him with income-tax evasion. Several years later the United States government obtained a judgment of $307,947 against this racketeer for back income taxes, interest and penalties.[33]

The Capone gang found that its new affiliation with powerful New York criminals in large-scale racketeering activities, particularly those extending through many states, was highly profitable. In 1934 Frank Nitti, Little New York Campagna, Paul Ricca and Frank Rio decided on a plan of action which would enable them to take over control of the International Alliance of Theatrical, Stage Employees and Motion Picture Operators. In Chicago, Willie Bioff, a pander, labor racketeer and an employee in a Capone gambling house, had been working with George E. Browne, the business agent of Local Number 2 of the union, in extorting money from theater owners. Their profits were sufficiently high to attract the attention of Nitti, Campagna, Ricca and other Capone gangsters, who promptly declared themselves partners of Bioff and Browne and launched a program that would yield profits amounting to millions of dollars. In the development of the conspiracy the first move was to elect their representative president of the International Union. A convention of the International Union was scheduled for Louisville in June 1934. Through the assistance of Lucky Luciano and Lepke Buchalter, the New York union delegates to the convention were instructed to vote for George E. Browne for president. Lepke also promised to see Louis Kaufman, business agent of the big Newark local union, and assure his support for the Capone gang's candidate. The convention in Louisville was a mere formality. George E. Browne became the president of the powerful international union and 125,000 union members were reduced to the status of serfs of the Capone syndicate and its allies. In Chicago, Thomas E. Maloy had been at the head of the local motion picture operators union since 1920. On February 4, 1935, two men ambushed Maloy on the Outer Drive and a .45 caliber pistol and a sawed-off shotgun were emptied into his head. He was killed instantly. A week later George Browne assumed control of Maloy's union. In 1935 the Capone syndicate extorted over $100,000 from Chicago theater owners.[34]

The gang's extortion operations extended from New York City on the East Coast to Hollywood on the West. Chicago remained the headquarters for the national crime syndicate, however. This was natural. With justification, leaders of the Capone gang felt secure in Chicago. Never had a top-ranking member of the organization been committed to prison as a result of a local prosecution in Chicago. Murray "The Camel" Humphreys, an important member of the syndicate, had invaded the cleaning and dyeing industry, labor unions and the dairy business. In his racketeering activities he had kidnapped Robert Fitchie, secretary of the Milk Drivers Union and collected $50,000 ransom. Humphreys was not prosecuted locally for the kidnapping. But when he was convicted in 1934 in Federal Court for income-tax evasion the Federal government required him to pay a tax on the $50,000 ransom he had collected from the Fitchie kidnapping.[35]

The Capone syndicate was growing opulent from scores of enterprises, but gambling still remained its principal source of revenue. Never had the gambling business flourished to a greater extent than during the Kelly administration. Never had the gamblers received better protection. Never had gambling been more strongly organized. In almost every section of the city, important political leaders were closely allied with the gambling interests. The First Ward Democratic organization, still under the leadership of Hinky Dink Kenna and Bathhouse John Coughlin, continued to rely on the gamblers to control this important area politically. The vote of this ward was delivered to the Kelly-Nash machine election after election. Co-operating fully with Hinky Dink and the Kelly-Nash machine in the First Ward was State Senator Daniel A. Serritella's Republican ward organization. Senator Serritella was a lieutenant and friend of Al Capone. He was first elected to the state senate in 1930. So close was his alliance with Hinky Dink Kenna that when he was re-elected in 1934 and again in 1938, the Kelly-Nash machine significantly on each occasion obligingly withdrew the Democratic candidate, leaving Serritella unopposed. A comparable situation prevailed in the senatorial district covering the "Bloody Twentieth" Ward. Here Republican James B. Leonardo was elected to the state Senate in 1934 and 1938 when the Kelly-Nash organization withdrew his Democratic opponent.[36]

By the time the 1934 election arrived, the political rule of the Kelly-Nash organization over the city and county was absolute. Thousands of law violators from the strongly protected gambling houses, the taverns that ignored every rule of law and decency, and racketeers of every description were welded into an unbeatable vote-producing machine. The effectiveness of any political opposition had been reduced to a mere shadow. The alliance of the underworld with the Kelly-Nash political organization was highly profitable. The underworld could be expected to deliver the vote. It never failed.

On the Saturday night before the November 1934, election, Alderman James C. Moreland, the Republican candidate for assessor and an outspoken critic of the Kelly-Nash machine, was seated in the dining room of his home with his family and friends. Suddenly a shotgun blast ripped through the room. The chandelier over the alderman's head was shattered and fell to the floor. The underworld had issued a warning that it would play rough, if necessary. On election day the votes of repeaters, nonexistent persons, and floaters swelled the totals of the one-sided victory for the Kelly-Nash ticket running under the banner of "Roosevelt and Recovery." In some precincts counterfeit ballots were printed and substituted for the genuine after the polls closed. In many normally Republican precincts, the Republican election judges, clerks and watchers were hirelings of the Democratic organization. On the West Side thousands of votes were purchased at the rate of fifty cents each. The Republicans, who only four years earlier controlled the city government and held key county positions as well, were completely routed. Kelly-Nash candidates did not lose a single contest. It was estimated that over 250,000 fraudulent votes were cast in the 1934 election. All opposition to the Democratic machine was crushed. In effect, there was only one party. A few of the practical-minded Republicans decided to become Kelly-Nash Democrats.

The 1934 election was but a preview of the mayoralty contest scheduled for the spring of 1935. The Republican party found it virtually impossible to persuade a formidable candidate to oppose Mayor Kelly. And when the votes were counted following the election on April 3, Kelly was credited with 798,150 votes to 166,-571 for his Republican opponent, Emil Wetten — an unbelievable plurality of 631,579. Civic groups were outraged at the wholesale frauds committed at the polling places. The Illinois League of Women Voters sponsored a permanent registration bill in the state legislature which was intended to eliminate some of the fraud, but the power of the Kelly-Nash organization in the legislature was sufficient to defeat the bill. Chicago's Tammany machine was riding high, wide and handsome and it intended to tolerate no interference from any quarter.[37]

The opposition of the Kelly-Nash forces to the permanent registration bill was not difficult to understand. Through the reduction of vote frauds, such legislation presented a possible threat to continued success at the polls. The Chicago Democratic machine was vitally interested, however, in any law that served to increase its power. Mayor Edward J. Kelly desired a bill that would legalize handbook gambling, thus giving the politicians more autocratic power than ever over the lucrative gambling business. Through the multiplication of handbooks, which would necessarily follow their legalization, the political machine would enjoy increased patronage. And in addition to the legal license fees, the handbook operator would be required to make his regular payments to the political organization or have his license revoked on one pretext or another. Experience with tavern licenses had conclusively established that fact. The underworld in control of handbooks also favored the legalization of any kind of gambling. It would mean continuous operation and much higher profits.

Mayor Kelly had no difficulty in finding a sponsor for a bill to legalize handbooks. On Chicago's near West Side, State Representative John M. Bolton had worked diligently on behalf of the handbook gambling interests. He had arranged for the incorporation of the Handbook Employees Union and also the Handbook Operators Association. Representative Bolton was a silent partner in handbooks in the vicinity of West Madison and Paulina Streets. In 1935, he introduced a bill in the Illinois General Assembly in Springfield which would have legalized handbooks in Chicago. With the backing of Mayor Kelly, the bill was passed. Democratic Governor Henry Horner, however, vetoed the law which he characterized as a "hazardous experiment" and commented on the fact that "the members of the General Assembly living outside of Chicago permitted for that city what they would not tolerate in their own communities." Several months later, on July 9, 1936, Representative Bolton met a violent death from a shotgun blast. Police expressed the opinion that the murder was the outgrowth of efforts of the State Legislator and his brother, Joseph "Red" Bolton, to control gambling on the West Side.[38] Only a few months earlier, on December 29, 1935, another State Representative, Albert J. Prignano, had been slain in front of his home in the "Bloody Twentieth" Ward. It was alleged that the murderer of Prignano had been hired by James De Angelo, a handbook operator and politician.

Although the gambling business was booming, there was much industrial unrest in Chicago as well as in other large metropolitan centers. A wave of sit-down strikes had swept the country. Dissatisfied workers virtually took over control of huge industrial establishments, stopping all production and refusing to move out of the plants. In many places there was considerable destruction of property and violence was not uncommon. Chicago, however, had been singularly free of sit-down strikes and the Kelly administration took pride in its labor record.

But in the spring of 1937, there were rumbles of serious labor trouble brewing in the steel industry in Chicago. In particular, it appeared that strikes were imminent at the Youngstown Sheet and Tube Company and the Republic Steel Corporation. On Wednesday, May 26, 1937, a strike was called at the plant of the Republic Steel Corporation on the far South Side of Chicago. Pickets were stationed around the plant and the police department assigned a detail of officers to preserve order. The strikers and their sympathizers established headquarters in a former tavern known as Sam's Place a short distance from the plant. On Sunday afternoon, Memorial Day, a meeting was held at Sam's Place. A large crowd gathered and feeling ran high. About 3:15 P.M., from 1800 to 2300 persons started to march on the Republic Steel Corporation plant. After crossing a prairie, the strikers arrived at 116 Street and Burley Avenue where they intended to enter the Republic grounds. Anticipating this move, Chicago police officers met the strikers in force at this point and ordered them to disperse. Suddenly a shower of bricks and clubs was hurled at the police and the crowd started to surge forward. Clubs were swinging wildly on both sides. Some of the strikers were armed with short pieces of pipe and two-by-four boards. The onward movement of the strikers was brought to an abrupt halt as the air was pierced with the sharp cracking of pistol shots. Men fell with streaming wounds. Others were clubbed to the ground. Chicago was witnessing one of the bloodiest labor battles in its history. Ten pickets shot by the police during the encounter died from their wounds. Twenty-six policemen were injured and required hospital care. The Memorial Day riot became a national controversy. A United States Senate Committee headed by Senator Robert LaFollette, Jr., conducted an investigation and for weeks Chicago's bloody steel riot was front-page news.

Although strife on the labor front temporarily diverted public attention from the crime front, Chicago racketeers were far from inactive. On the South Side, the Negro population was fully exploited by the racketeers and their political friends. There powerful politicians aided in the organization of policy gambling and formed a syndicate composed of twelve Negroes and three white men to rule over policy operations. From the lowest income group in the city, the politically protected policy syndicate was reaping in the neighborhood of $280,000 a week.[39] The inhabitants of "Bronzeville" were living in squalor and poverty. But from their nickels, dimes and quarters the policy operators were maintaining huge country estates, with private swimming pools and golf courses. In 1938, the Federal government through taxation was pouring money into relief projects to help the poor unemployed, yet the children of relief workers remained underfed because so much of the relief money intended for food went to the politically protected policy operators instead. Recipients of old-age pensions poured their state aid into the coffers of the policy racketeers. Edward Jones became known as the "Policy King." By the end of 1935 he and his brothers kept their cash in twenty-five banks. Their net worth exceeded a million dollars. During his Federal trial for income-tax evasion, Jones testified that the daily income from three drawings each day at his policy wheel jumped from $2000 in 1930 to $10,000 in 1938. The ironclad protection afforded the policy operators by the Kelly-Nash political organization was highly profitable. The Policy King's daily income had increased five hundred per cent within the space of a few years. The average citizen's tax bill was also mounting — to aid the poor unemployed, whose families remained undernourished and underclothed. The policy racketeers, on the other hand, had become millionaires while their political benefactors had grown drunk with power.

The policy baron among the growing Negro population in Chicago's West Side was James Martin of 1900 West Lake Street. He was the right-hand man of the ruler himself, Pat Nash. And in Nash's own ward, the Twenty-eighth, Jim Martin was a powerful political leader. Among the more influential leaders of the South Side policy racket were the brothers Iley and Walter J. Kelly. Their relations with the Kelly-Nash machine were excellent. Aldermen, ward committeemen and other important politicians were their close friends. Walter J. Kelly had extended his operations to the highly industrialized city of Gary, Indiana, which almost adjoins Chicago along the lake front to the southeast. He had found the political climate of Gary quite healthy for his policy wheels following the Democratic victory in 1934. For almost five years he ruled policy gambling in this steel-mill city with an iron hand. He was also still associated with his brother Iley, in lucrative policy operations in Chicago. About six o'clock in the evening of January 8, 1939, Walter Kelly was sitting in an automobile parked in front of 3035 South Michigan Avenue in Chicago, when an unknown person stealthily approached the car and with deadly aim fired a shotgun at him. He was given a funeral in keeping with his standing in the community, his bronze casket costing five thousand dollars. Former Congressman Oscar De Priest was among the distinguished mourners.

At the time of his murder, Kelly was holding several thousand dollars worth of notes signed by a Gary judge.[40] The violent killing of Kelly failed to discourage the South Side policy operations. Only a few weeks later newspapers were featuring stories concerning the rich harvest that was being reaped by Edward Jones and Iley Kelly on the South Side and James Martin on the West. Big gambling establishments in "Bronzeville" posted prominent signs over their entrances which read: OPEN ALL NIGHT. It continued to be an era of prosperity for the gamblers and the Kelly-Nash machine.[41]

In the crowded downtown business district of Chicago, flourishing gambling places were operated by members of the Capone syndicate within the shadows of the City Hall. The political protection afforded Paul Ricca, Jack Guzik, Hymie Levin, Frank Nitti, Louis Campagna, Charles Fischetti, Dago Lawrence Mangano and other Capone mobsters was absolute. Their illegal places were crowded with patrons. They operated openly. Their proprietors were unafraid. The entire city and county was controlled politically by the Kelly-Nash organization. In many parts of the city and county however, the political end of gambling was bossed by the gangsters' friend, William R. Skidmore, and his associate Big Bill Johnson. Elaborate Skidmore-Johnson gambling emporiums provided every known type of game — roulette, chuck-a-luck, craps, black-jack or poker.[42]

The ruthlessness and efficiency of the political-gambling organization under the Kelly-Nash regime exceeded anything Mike McDonald had ever dreamed of a half-century earlier. And the character of city government had changed but little since the days of McDonald's rule. In the fall of 1939 the City Club issued a pamphlet which declared that Chicago was socially and politically bankrupt and all citizens were urged to co-operate in an effort to rebuild the city. An editorial in the *Chicago News* pointedly asked what the average citizen was getting from his city government. In addition to a twenty-five per cent increase in his tax bills, said the editorial, "He gets the privilege of being gypped in a crooked handbook joint. He gets aldermen sworn to support the law, conniving with gamblers and selling jobs on the police force. He gets a gangster in the State Senate. He gets machine-controlled schools and courts. He gets crime and vice and corruption."[43]

Chicago was ruled by a political machine with almost limitless power, patterned after infamous Tammany Hall. And the Chicago version was certainly no improvement over the New York variety.

CHAPTER IX
Crime Marches On

BY 1939, the Kelly-Nash machine controlled the city absolutely and except for a very few offices the entire county government as well. It also exerted tremendous influence in state and national affairs. Federal money pouring into the city for public works and relief projects gave the local Democratic organization jobs and still greater power over the political life of the community. Ruthless discipline prevailed over the ward leaders, who either obtained maximum results at the polls or were replaced with others having more ambition or ability. Hundreds of civil service jobs were filled with temporary appointments. These temporary employees worked diligently for the Kelly-Nash machine or they were dismissed. For purely political functions, police captains were allotted thousands of tickets which they were required to sell or face disciplinary action. Frequently it was possible to dispose of such tickets only to tavern keepers who were violating city and state regulations, gambling house proprietors, and others operating outside the pale of the law. Close alliances were thus cemented between the law violators and the police through the demands of the political leaders. The well-disciplined Kelly-Nash organization was invulnerable at the polls. Its word was law and few Democratic politicians with any ambition dared to challenge its edicts or incur its enmity by opposing candidates named by the machine.

In the 1939 mayoralty primary, Edward J. Kelly was again selected as the Democratic candidate. The primary was not, however, a cut and dried affair. Entering the race in opposition to Kelly on the Democratic ticket was Thomas J. Courtney, State's Attorney of Cook County and long a bitter foe of the mayor. Civic groups and the press had been levelling devastating attacks on the crime and corruption which flourished in the city. The Republican party appropriately chose Dwight H. Green, who had won recognition for his work in the successful Federal prosecution of Al Capone. His opponent on the Republican ticket was the old campaign war horse, William Hale Thompson.

During the political speeches that followed, the voters listened but were not unduly impressed. They had long been accustomed to the rantings of politicians before every primary and election. Then Thomas J. Courtney hurled a bombshell that was "too hot to handle." During a radio address Courtney pointed out that Mayor Kelly, Dwight H. Green, who had served as United States Attorney, and he himself had been public officeholders during approximately the same period of time. Courtney agreed to make public his income-tax returns covering the entire time he had been in office if Green and Kelly would make similar disclosures to the voters. Green readily agreed but when newspaper reporters called on Kelly for his reaction to the suggestion he lost his composure. Exhibiting a bad temper, he flatly refused to discuss the subject and ushered the reporters out of his office. Kelly had become a very wealthy man while he had been on the public payroll.[1] It was apparent that the Democratic state's attorney had struck the most effective blow of the campaign. Nevertheless, when the primary votes were counted, 596,856 were recorded for Kelly as compared with 314,645 for Courtney. The Republican nomination was won by Dwight H. Green.

Although Kelly had won the Democratic nomination by a substantial margin, the criticism which had been hurled at his administration during the campaign had been damaging. Following the timeworn practice of William Hale Thompson and other political leaders before him, Mayor Kelly dismissed all criticism with the charge that "bluenoses" were trying to besmirch the fair name of the city. On March 10, 1939, the mayor wrote a political letter in which he stated, "We Chicagoans have no sympathy with campaigns in which Chicago's good name is attacked." The city was then flooded with tons of Kelly literature which described Chicago before he became its savior. Said Kelly, "Chicago was flat on her back, gasping." Crime statistics were quoted to show that murderers, burglars and robbers stalked the streets. The city treasury was empty. Schools were about to be closed. There was no construction. "Labor was sullen; business frightened. Chicago's spirit drooped. The world sneered." Kelly's attack on Chicago, the city at which "the world sneered," of course referred to the place before he became its chief executive. Since that time, according to the campaign literature, Chicago had become a model, progressive, law-abiding city. A few discerning voters re-examined William Hale Thompson's campaign booklet of 1927 entitled "Big Bill, the Builder — A Chicago Epoch." They read that before Thompson became mayor, Chicago had been in a deplorable civic slump since the Columbian Exposition in 1893. There had been no major construction since the first World's Fair. "The world impression of Chicago was a city of Stock Yards, smoke, dirt, and corruption." Chicago was in the grip of an "unprecedented and appalling reign of crime." So spoke Thompson and Kelly. However, when newspapers and civic leaders said these very same things, Thompson and Kelly denounced them as defaming the reputation of the city. Yet both Thompson and Kelly attacked Chicago's reputation as a means of winning votes. It was all very confusing.

Actually there were major civic improvements in both the Thompson and Kelly administrations. But the elimination or reduction of organized crime was not one of them. The Capone gang in particular, and crime and corruption in general were major issues of the bitter election campaign that followed. On April 4, 1939, Edward J. Kelly was re-elected mayor with a plurality of 184,000 votes. This represented almost 450,000 votes less than his plurality four years earlier. His defeated opponent Dwight H. Green had waged a sufficiently impressive battle, however, to assure him of the Republican nomination for governor the following year. And for the next eight years Green presided over the state of Illinois as its thirtieth governor.

Kelly had completed almost six full years as Chicago's chief executive at the time of his re-election in 1939. Within this period, according to Democratic campaign literature, the city had paved more city streets than during the preceding twenty-five years. The Kelly administration was responsible for new boulevards, new parks and improved beaches. It was claimed that the per capita cost of government was less in Chicago than in New York or Boston. Some of the vaunted achievements, however, were subject to serious question, and Kelly's boast that his police department was unexcelled anywhere in the entire world was an outright absurdity. On the other hand there was concrete evidence of progress. On December 17, 1939, ground was officially broken for Chicago's subway system. The first installment of the system, extending from Roosevelt Road on the near South Side to Clybourn on the North, was opened five years later.

Chicago's population during the Cermak-Kelly regime, which began in 1931, was virtually at a standstill. The United States Census of 1940 showed that 3,396,808 people resided in Chicago. For fifty years, between 1880 and 1930, the city's population had increased on an average of over 57,000 each year. Between 1920 and 1930 the city had grown by 674,733. But during the period from 1930 to 1940 the increase in population amounted to only 20,370, representing a growth of approximately one half of one per cent. The percentage of increase between 1930 and 1940 was by far the smallest during any ten-year period in the entire history of the city. Undoubtedly the great depression was a major factor in the abrupt curtailment of Chicago's growth. However, during the same period U. S. Census figures showed substantial increases in population of 524,549 for New York City, 266,229 for Los Angeles and 54,790 for Detroit. Of the five largest cities of the nation, only Philadelphia made a poorer record than Chicago. Its population decreased about one per cent.

Shortly after the mayoralty campaign of 1939, Chicago was to feel the impact of world-shaking events taking place in Europe. Adolf Hitler had embarked on his campaign to conquer the world, and seven million Austrians had been annexed to the Third Reich. In the Munich settlement on September 30, 1938, the Sudetenland had been ceded to Germany to assure "peace in our time." In March 1939, the German dictator took over the balance of Czechoslovakia. These events were only a prelude to the march of the German Army on Poland, September 1, 1939, and the declaration of war on Germany by Great Britain and France, two days later. Over two years elapsed before Germany's ally, Japan, made its surprise attack on Pearl Harbor, December 7, 1941, and threw the United States into World War II.

As a result of all this, Chicago again became a great center of supply for war materials. For the first time since the depression the demand for labor was greater than the supply. Wages began to soar. Money was plentiful. Legitimate business houses prospered. And with the encouragement of Kelly's wide-open town policies, the racketeers once more had a field day. In the heart of Chicago's downtown section, the Capone syndicate frequently operated several gambling establishments within a single block. Thousands of men needed in war factories were employed as sheet writers, cashiers or lookout men in handbooks that seemed to be everywhere. While the United States was preparing to fight to preserve its very existence, the gambling racketeers with the aid of ironclad political protection were prospering as never before.

As in all Kelly's terms as mayor, the city police department was merely an arm of his political organization. Ward Committeemen determined the law enforcement policies in the various police districts. They also named the judges who administered justice in the courts. Too frequently, Municipal Court judgeships were merely plums awarded to those who displayed vote-getting abilities in their ward. Legal talent, judicial temperament and integrity were qualities given but scant consideration by many ward bosses. In fact the whole law enforcement structure was geared to provide a healthy climate for a flourishing gambling industry. Many of the arrests in gambling cases were the products of "phony" raids. It was all a big game to fool the public and protect the gamblers. The testimony of police officers in court usually made it easy for the judge to dismiss the cases on the ground that the evidence was illegally obtained and therefore inadmissible in court. The courts also applied the most technical rules of evidence in gambling cases, sometimes appearing to lean over backwards to discharge the violator.

In September 1939, a newspaper editorial took Judge Eugene J. Holland of the Municipal Court to task for "dismissing gambling cases by the score about as fast as the police bring them in. . . ." Judge Holland was particularly criticized for holding that "scratch sheets, hard sheets, and registers of bets, as kept in handbook joints, are not evidence of racetrack gambling." [2] A few weeks later, on November 8, Edward J. O'Hare, President of Sportsman's Park race track was ambushed and slain in gangland fashion. An investigation of O'Hare's murder developed facts which proved highly embarrassing to Judge Holland, particularly in view of the public criticism which had been leveled at his rulings favoring the gambling fraternity. It was revealed that Judge Holland owned stock in one of O'Hare's dog tracks, and was in partnership with a bookmaker and O'Hare in some real estate holdings. Following Holland's refusal to testify before the grand jury concerning this matter, the Chicago Bar Association instituted proceedings to suspend his license to practice law for two years, but failed. The Kelly-Nash organization, completely unabashed, promptly renamed him on its slate of judicial candidates when his term expired, thus assuring his re-election. He has continued to sit on the Municipal Court bench since that time, and as late as 1950 he was re-elected for another six years.

Associated with O'Hare in Sportsman's Park was John Patton. In his younger days, Patton had been known as the boy mayor of Burnham, a Chicago suburb famous for Capone gang vice. O'Hare had been designated by Al Capone to take charge of his dog tracks in Illinois, Florida, Massachusetts and elsewhere. He dominated the International Greyhound Association and controlled the mechanical rabbit which was used at all dog tracks. At the time of his death, O'Hare, as the Capone syndicate representative, was the undisputed czar of dog racing throughout America. His association with Al Capone, Jack Guzik, and Johnny Patton was of many years standing. In the summer of 1927, O'Hare managed the Capone-owned Hawthorne Kennel Club, also known as the Laramie Kennel Club. Both Patton and Guzik were financially interested in this establishment. The investigation determined that in this summer of 1927, five machine guns were delivered to O'Hare at the dog track, one of them by a member of the Cicero Police Department — one more incident to demonstrate that officials had always been co-operative with high-ranking Capone members. After Al Capone was committed to a Federal penitentiary, O'Hare occupied a highly important place in the management and direction of the gang's enterprises. His murder occurred only a few days before the gang leader was scheduled to be released from Federal custody. The gang slaying served to focus attention on the friendly relations O'Hare had maintained with public officials in many states, among them Massachusetts, where angry editorials appeared concerning the tactics employed in obtaining legislation favorable to the dog-track interests.[3]

With the Kelly-Nash machine so influential in national political affairs, it is not surprising that the gamblers became careless in their obligation to share their loot with the Federal government. They had good reason to believe that the immunity they enjoyed locally would follow them in any conflict they might have with the national administration. Cheating has always been a natural accompaniment of gambling, so perhaps it was inevitable that Chicago's powerful gambling bosses should engage in wholesale cheating when making their income-tax returns. William R. Skidmore was charged by a Federal grand jury on September 1, 1939, with an income-tax deficiency in the sum of $361,272.36 for the years 1933 through 1937. During those five years Skidmore's income amounted to $612,227.26. He had reported taxes totaling only $6,506.12. For the year 1934 he had not bothered to make any tax return. A second Federal indictment was returned on February 20, 1940, in which the United States Government alleged that for the year 1938 alone, Skidmore failed to pay a Federal income tax of $295,648 due on a gross income of $491,318. On March 1, 1940, Skidmore's partner, William R. Johnson, was indicted by a Federal grand jury in Chicago on charges of evading $1,389,919 income taxes for the years 1936 to 1938 inclusive. With interest and penalties the government's bill against Johnson amounted to $2,232,-497. This was on his "take" from twenty-three gambling houses which he owned and on some of the untold millions of dollars that poured into the coffers of the Skidmore-Johnson combination. To cash the thousands of checks that were honored at their gambling houses Johnson and Skidmore maintained a currency exchange.[4]

The headquarters for the payoffs for political protection was located in Skidmore's junk yard known as the Lawndale Scrap Iron and Metal Company, 2840 South Kedzie Avenue, Chicago. At appointed times gamblers and politicians from all parts of Chicago and Cook County lined up outside the junk-yard office and awaited their turn to make the required payments for the privilege of violating the law. A former investigator for the state's attorney's office acted as Skidmore's master of ceremonies. He would call out, "You're next." The gambler indicated would then enter Skidmore's office, give the address of his gambling establishment, which was duly recorded, pay the necessary protection money and depart — assured of continued immunity from police interference.

Skidmore, the gangster's friend, was well qualified to deal with the politicians. In his statement to Federal investigators, which was read at the trial, he said, "I was chief clerk and purchasing agent for the Democratic party for twenty-five years and had charge of conventions. Josephus Daniels [former Secretary of the Navy and Ambassador to Mexico] worked with me. I had charge of conventions in Baltimore, Denver and St. Louis." He boasted, "I have never worked a day in my life." In his statement Skidmore admitted his friendship with some of the most influential aldermen of the city. Several handbook operators testified that on the first of every month they paid graft to Skidmore for police protection. They named ward committeemen and precinct captains as intermediaries who approached Skidmore in their behalf. One gambler, Arthur M. Hood, testified that when he wanted to open a handbook at 1600 North Cicero Avenue, he conferred with his ward committeeman who gave him his card with the notation, "O. K. Skidmore, Arthur Hood." He presented the card to Skidmore, paid him two hundred and fifty dollars and was then ready to open up.

The friendly relations between Skidmore and the police were clearly evident from the testimony given in Federal court. When Skidmore desired to talk with one gambler he arranged to meet him in the office of Captain Herbert Burns, then Chief of the Cook County Highway Police. Another chief, Lester Laird, visited Skidmore's junk yard from four to six times a month between September 1935, and April 1939. A Chicago police captain, Thomas Harrison, borrowed ten thousand dollars from Skidmore. A powerful South Side ward committeeman admitted that he had visited the junk yard each week. He explained that he went there to get eggs for his baby. Leo Mongoven, a slot-machine gangster visited Skidmore's two hundred and sixty acre estate three miles northeast of McHenry, Illinois every Saturday. When Skidmore took the witness stand he admitted his association with police officials, gamblers and gangsters. He also admitted his friendship with members of the Bugs Moran and Jack Zuta mob over a period of twenty-five years.[5]

From the testimony introduced in Skidmore's Federal trail it was obvious that this underworld leader occupied a rank of high importance in the political life of the city during the Kelly-Nash regime. His power far exceeded that of numerous ward committeemen who were little more than his office boys in the political-gambling organization. Even influential Negro ward committeemen on the South Side found it necessary to secure protection from him for policy operations. High-ranking police officials in the city and county were in his debt.

On March 9, 1941, the jury in Skidmore's trial returned a verdict of guilty and on March 21, Skidmore was sentenced to two and one-half years in a Federal penitentiary and fined $5000.[6] But even this conviction and sentence did not immediately shear him of his power. While the case was being appealed, Skidmore continued to act as the collector. In August 1941, Chief Laird started a "crusade" against illegal handbook operations within the city limits. For the first time in over forty years the county police raided gambling establishments in Chicago. The "crusade" was of short duration, however, for on the night of August 21, a *Chicago Tribune* reporter found Chief Laird and Skidmore dining together in the International Room of the fashionable Drake Hotel. A picture was taken of the cozy twosome by a *Tribune* photographer. The flash bulb on the camera brought the meeting to a sudden end. Chief Laird jumped up from the table and hastily made a retreat through the kitchen. The following morning the picture was featured in the *Tribune*. Laird's superior, Sheriff Thomas J. O'Brien, whose law enforcement policies had won for him the appellation "Blind Tom," was embarrassed, and Laird's resignation was promptly accepted. His successor, Sergeant John J. Healy, announced that he would carry out the policies of former Chief Laird.[7] On March 20, 1942, Skidmore began serving his sentence in the Federal Prison at Terre Haute, Indiana, where he died of heart failure on February 18, 1944.

Tall, handsome Big Bill Johnson fought off his day of reckoning longer than his partner Skidmore. In October 1940, a jury in the United States District Court in Chicago found Johnson guilty of income-tax evasion, along with his co-defendants James A. Hartigan, John M. Flanagan, William P. Kelly, Jack Sommers and Stuart Solomon Brown. On October twenty-third, Johnson was sentenced to a term of five years in a Federal penitentiary for evading income taxes amounting to $1,887,846. Then began one of the longest fights in contemporary legal history to avoid paying the penalty assessed by a Federal court. With politicians in the background and lawyers and churchmen in the foreground, a vigorous campaign was waged for almost five and one-half years to prevent Big Bill Johnson from suffering the ignominy of serving a prison term. Between the date of sentence, October 23, 1940, and March 18, 1946, when prison doors finally closed on the gambling boss, the case was before Judge John P. Barnes in the U. S. District Court in Chicago five times. It was before the U. S. Circuit Court of Appeals six times and before the U. S. Supreme Court three times. Certainly no convicted defendant was ever given greater opportunities to establish his innocence. To the average layman, Federal justice as it applied to Big Bill Johnson appeared ludicrous. To the able Federal Judge, John P. Barnes, there appeared good reasons to believe that evil influences were at work to prevent justice; in October 1946, Judge Barnes demanded a Federal grand jury investigation to determine whether the lengthy delays in the case had stemmed from illegal acts on the part of Johnson's benefactors.[8] Tampering with justice is frequently difficult to prove, however, and the Federal grand jury failed to return any indictments.

Johnson had been more skillful in the handling of his public relations than his partner Skidmore. Both men had become wealthy through the corruption of officials and police officers. Johnson, however, had followed the well-established practice of almost all successful racketeers of making liberal donations to churches and charitable organizations. He thus silenced many community leaders who would ordinarily have led the fight against his illegal enterprises. In time of trouble these leaders became his friends. Donations by law violators to officials are called bribes, while donations by the same individuals to character-building institutions are usually referred to as charity. Yet the racketeer's motive in each instance is

the same — the prevention of any possible interference with his lucrative antisocial enterprises. After William R. Johnson was found
guilty in Federal court, his supporters began extolling his virtues.
They talked glibly about his charitable acts, the kindness of his heart
and his honesty. But a man is properly judged by the nature of his
voluntary associations, and Big Bill Johnson had become a millionaire
through his partnership with the gangster's friend, Billy Skidmore.
Prior to the slaying of Jack Zuta on August 1, 1930, Johnson had
been Zuta's partner in gambling houses located at 4750 Kedzie Avenue, 4822 Broadway and 3939 Milwaukee Avenue in Chicago.[9]
Johnson's dishonest tax returns had cheated the government out of
almost two million dollars, which hardly supported the contentions
of those who prated about his honesty. Perhaps it was to the credit
of Skidmore that neither he nor his supporters made any serious
attempt to hold him out as anything more than a member of the
underworld, a racketeer and a social parasite.

Chicago's officialdom was embarrassed. The trials of Johnson and
Skidmore had involved ward committeemen and prominent law-
enforcement officials. The alliance between the Kelly-Nash machine
and organized gambling had been publicly aired in court. In many
places there was a temporary disruption of the gambling business.
The Capone syndicate, however, was so strongly protected that its
lucrative Loop establishments continued without interruption. Profits were enormous. And beyond the city limits in Cook County the
gang's roulette wheels, dice tables and slot machines were yielding
monthly fortunes. Sheriff Thomas J. O'Brien, who was described in
editorials as Pat Nash's chore boy, permitted the county to run wide-
open. Numerous scandals had rocked his administration, yet when
his term of office expired, the Kelly-Nash machine rewarded O'Brien
by sending him to the nation's capital as a congressman.

The Skidmore-Johnson trials were still widely discussed when
authentic bookkeeping records of the Capone syndicate for July
1941 were located by the *Chicago Tribune* and six ledger sheets
were published. These records which related only to gambling operations *outside* the city of Chicago in Cook County, showed gross
profits of $320,966 for one month. Graft in the sum of $26,980 was
paid to officials, and after the payrolls were met and the graft paid,
the Capone bosses had remaining a net profit of $221,674 for July

1941 alone. On the basis of these figures the annual gross profits to the Capone syndicate from gambling beyond the city limits would have amounted to almost four million dollars; graft paid to officials would have totaled $323,760 and the net profits for the year would have approximated $2,660,088. And the county gambling operations were probably less profitable to the Capone leaders than those in the city itself. The records also established the existence of a dictatorship that controlled all gambling in Cook County under such practiced leaders as Frank Nitti, Jack Guzik, Murray Humphreys and Edward Vogel. Among those named in the gang's records were Vincent McErlane, a brother of the gunman Frank McErlane, and Louis Lipschultz, a brother-in-law of Jack Guzik. One item of $25,000 was believed to represent the monthly payment to Al Capone. Five thousand dollars was contributed to the syndicate's defense fund and Charles Fischetti, a cousin of Al Capone, received $3000 as a salary and expense allowance. Fischetti was then making monthly plane trips between Chicago and Miami. Large payments were recorded as having been made to certain law enforcement officials. William R. Skidmore received $2500. Nineteen payments were made in July 1941, for gambling equipment purchased from such firms as the Mills Novelty Company, H. C. Evans Company and the Bally Manufacturing Company.[10]

The Kelly-Nash machine was riding on the crest of the wave. It was openly contemptuous of large segments of the public who complained of wide-open lawlessness and corruption. The Federal trials of Skidmore and Johnson, however, had produced damaging evidence of political protection which was still fresh in the public mind when the *Tribune* published the six ledger sheets of the Capone syndicate. As usual, the Kelly-Nash leaders attempted to dismiss these disclosures lightly. They were hoping for a respite from further public embarrassment when the November 1941 Cook County grand jury launched into a new gambling inquiry. This body reported that "shocking conditions" existed in Chicago and Cook County where "protected syndicated gambling has openly and flagrantly operated for a long period of time without any real interference from the police whose duty it is to prevent this evil." The Chicago Urban League complained of increasing lawlessness in the Negro areas and warned that those in control of gambling were becoming "bolder and bolder every day." Testimony given to the December 1941 grand jury indicated that policy gamblers were taking over $7,000,000 each year from Negroes, many of whom were on the public relief rolls. A substantial portion of this huge sum was pouring into the pockets of the Capone syndicate. This was true notwithstanding the efforts of both Negro and white politicians to perpetuate a myth that the policy racket was operated and controlled exclusively by Negroes.

In January 1942, twenty-six key figures in Chicago's million-dollar policy business were indicted. Among those named as defendants were seven Negroes: Iley Kelly, Jim Knight, Julian Black, James "Big Jim" Martin and the Jones brothers, Edward, George and McKissock. Three white policy racketeers, Julius Benvenuti, Pat Manno and Pete Tremont, were also included. Tremont and Manno had received considerable publicity only a few months earlier when an investigation was launched into the affairs of Local 1248 of the Retail Clerks Union in Chicago. They were close associates of Max Caldwell (alias Max Pollock), business agent of the clerks union. Caldwell had often transported Tremont, Manno and other Capone leaders from Chicago to Miami by airplane, paying all of their expenses. As business agent of Local 1248 of the Retail Clerks Union, Caldwell had collected $910,000 from union members. When a suit was filed in 1941 for an accounting of union funds, a union representative testified that he could locate only sixty-two dollars of the huge sum collected. This case was still receiving attention when Manno and Tremont were named as defendants in the policy racket indictment.

Just before the policy case was brought to trial in June 1942, First Assistant State's Attorney Wilbert Crowley angrily declared, "City officials are not only not helping in the prosecution, but are actually out to embarrass our case in every possible way." The policy syndicate had been highly important to the Kelly-Nash machine in maintaining control over the Negro vote. It had been a source of patronage to the ward politicians. Untold numbers of people were given jobs by the syndicate at the request of ward committeemen, with the result that money rolled steadily into the cashboxes of the Democratic organization. It is not surprising that policemen and other officials, under the domination of the Kelly administration, attempted to thwart the prosecution — and were successful. Twelve defendants were found not guilty and nolle prosequi orders were entered as to the others.

The primary responsibility for the enforcement of the gambling laws in Chicago during the Kelly administration was vested in the Morals Division of the police department. After a careful study of the evidence produced before the November 1941 grand jury, this body recommended that the Morals Squad be disbanded. There was strong reason to believe that the principal function of the Squad was the protection of gambling syndicates rather than the enforcement of the law. At the insistence of the state's attorney, charges were filed before the Civil Service Commission against the commanding officer of the Morals Division, Captain Martin McCormick, and three of his subordinates, Sergeant Thomas Lee, Patrolman James Kehoe and Patrolman Fred Trauth. The four police officers were accused of neglect of duty and filing false reports.

Whenever a political machine sanctions organized gambling it is of course essential that the police officers behind whom the politicians hide must be given protection as absolute as that afforded the gamblers; otherwise, an officer who conspires with the ward committeeman and the racketeers might decide to give revealing testimony rather than suffer the ignominy of being permanently removed from the force. And it is a significant fact that in Chicago the permanent discharge of a police officer for the protection of gambling establishments has virtually never happened. In those few instances where the Civil Service Commission has ordered the officer removed from the police department, the courts have restored him to duty.

From the very inception of the charges filed against Captain Martin McCormick and the three other officers, it was apparent that the Kelly-Nash machine had no intention of disregarding its obligation to protect the four policemen. Although identical charges were filed against the four officers, only Sergeant Lee and Patrolmen Kehoe and Trauth were suspended. Captain McCormick, who was responsible for the conduct of these men, appeared to be immune. It was not until the Chicago Crime Commission publicly demanded that Captain McCormick also be suspended that this action was taken. The state's attorney presented voluminous and damaging evidence before the Civil Service Commission. It was shown that the accused officers had visited hundreds of known addresses of gambling establishments and submitted reports which indicated that the places were closed. At the time these places were found closed by members of the Morals Squad, investigators for the state's attorney's office found gambling establishments operating openly next door. Officers of the Morals Division did not bother to call at the places where gambling was actually in progress. At least their official reports did not so indicate. That these officers were able to locate gambling establishments when it served their purpose to do so, however, was clearly reflected by a "confidential special report" submitted in longhand to Captain McCormick on June 12, 1940, by Patrolmen Trauth and Russell F. Corcoran of the Morals Division, in which the officers informed Captain McCormick that they had visited eleven addresses and found gambling in operation at ten of them. No action was taken to close these illegal places. Furthermore, the Morals Division never submitted this information to the commissioner of police as required by department regulations and, according to official police reports, from four to six months elapsed before the Morals Squad even visited four of these places again. When Captain McCormick took the witness stand he claimed that he was unable to explain why he had received the special confidential report on June 12. He could offer no explanation why this report had been suppressed insofar as the official police records were concerned. He was equally in ignorance as to why he had not required any official action for several months after receiving this secret report which revealed several gambling places operating in violation of the law. Although it was common knowledge that Chicago was honeycombed with gambling places, the arrest book of Sergeant Thomas Lee's squad reported only one arrest during a five-month period in 1941.

Contrary to all proper concepts of a merit system, Joseph P. Geary, the Chairman of the Civil Service Commission which conducted the hearings involving these police officers, was one of the most powerful ward committeemen in the Kelly-Nash machine. His term of office in the Commission had expired over two years before. He was holding his office entirely at the pleasure of the mayor and was completely subservient to his wishes. A second member of the three-man commission was also a holdover appointee. His term had expired over a year earlier. In addition, he was originally appointed as the Republican (minority party) representative of the Civil Service Commission as required by law. At the time of the hearings Mayor Kelly had placed him on the Democratic ticket for a Municipal Court judgeship, leaving the Civil Service Commission without any representation from the minority party. It was quite obvious that the Commission was considered an important part of the political machine. Throughout the lengthy hearings involving Captain McCormick and his subordinates the attitude of the civil service commissioners was one of hostility toward the prosecution and leniency toward the accused officers. Material evidence which would have further supported the charges against the accused was excluded on technical grounds. From the inception of the hearings it was evident that the policemen were to be exonerated. The "whitewash" decision was conveniently handed down on Friday afternoon July 3, 1942, just as all public offices were closing for a holiday week end. The Chicago Crime Commission promptly issued a public report stating that "the Civil Service Commission, by its decision in these cases, has shown itself incompetent and has violated a public trust. There is only one remedy . . . the removal by the Mayor of the members of the present Civil Service Commission and the appointment of a new Civil Service Commission of representative citizens who will protect the interest of the public." Civic bodies were infuriated. Editorials denounced the decision. Public opinion was thoroughly aroused.

Mayor Kelly at first ignored the public outcry. But an election was approaching and it was deemed expedient to take action which would silence the mounting resentment of citizens. The mayor therefore announced the appointment of an outstanding committee to review the civil service proceedings. This committee included a judge of the State Supreme Court, a Federal judge, an appellate court judge, a former United States District Attorney and a former president of the Chicago Bar Association. While this committee was in the midst of reviewing the case, Mayor Kelly calmly approved the promotion of two of the accused officers. On December 10, 1942, the mayor's committee rendered an opinion which completely substantiated the charges made by the Chicago Crime Commission. The committee held that the civil service hearings had been conducted in a biased manner. Competent evidence which would have supported the charges filed against the officers was erroneously excluded. And based on the evidence presented to the Civil Service Commission, the four officers should have been ordered discharged from the police department. This opinion of the mayor's committee was headline news in the press. It was a moral victory but in some respects it was an empty one. Already two of the accused officers had been promoted in rank. The chairman of the Civil Service Commission was removed but he was placed on the city payroll in another capacity. The civil service commissioner who presided over most of the hearings was promoted to a judgeship.[11]

During the war years, the citizens' primary interest was naturally centered on the world-wide conflict. In the midst of the controversy over the civil service hearings, Chicago citizens became engrossed in the first treason trial in the history of the state. The defendants who were placed on trial in Federal court in Chicago in the fall of 1942 were totally lacking in the glamour that surrounds the spy in the usual novel. The principal defendant, Hans Max Haupt, was an unobtrusive German-American who had given aid and shelter to his son, Herbert Hans Haupt. The younger Haupt, a Nazi zealot, had received intensive training in the art of sabotage in Brandenburg, Germany. After landing in America for the express purpose of sabotaging the light metals industry in this country he came to Chicago where he visited his parents. He was greeted with open arms and given assistance while he was in the city. On November 24, 1942, Federal Judge William J. Campbell sentenced Hans Max Haupt to death. Two other defendants, Otto Richard Wergin and Otto Froehling who had also given aid to young Haupt, received identical sentences. An appeal of the case saved the defendants' lives, however, and at the end of another trial Hans Max Haupt received a sentence of life imprisonment and a fine of $10,000, while Wergin and Froehling were given prison terms of five years each.[12] Herbert Haupt had already been captured and executed as a Nazi spy and saboteur before his father was sentenced.

As was natural during the war, the taverns and night clubs in many sections of the city catered to boisterous crowds long after the legal closing hours. Liquor laws and regulations were violated with impunity. This was particularly true of the well-known night life district which lies north of Chicago's Loop. Long after the downtown theaters were closed and the business streets deserted, the night clubs and dives just north of the river were teeming with activity.

For many years the political affairs of the near North Side have been ruled over by William J. Connors, the powerful ward commit-teeman of the Forty-second Ward. Formerly a member of the Illinois House of Representatives, he was elected state senator from the Twenty-ninth Senatorial District for the first time in 1934. The prevalence of vice and gambling in his ward was a major issue in the 1934 campaign as well as in succeeding elections. For several years an important lieutenant in the political organization controlled by Connors was the gambler and ex-convict, Eddie Sturch, known at various times as the "dictator of North Clark Street" and "the Napoleon of the Forty-second Ward." Long before he achieved importance as a major statesman in Forty-second Ward politics, Sturch had given evidence of being a man with a forceful person-ality. As far back as October 31, 1921, Sturch and some associates entered the Benjamin Sugarman fur store in Chicago, placed guns against the body of Mrs. Ida Strumpf, the manager, and forced her to the rear of the establishment where a man by the name of August Miller happened to be waiting. The sum of $230.00 was stolen from Mrs. Strumpf; Miller was relieved of $10.00 and furs valued at $8250 were stolen from the store. After the robbery, Sturch and two ac-complices fled to St. Louis where they were arrested and returned to Chicago for trial. On February 21, 1922, Sturch was found guilty of robbery with a gun in the Cook County Criminal Court and was sentenced to the Illinois State Penitentiary. After his parole on July 24, 1928, he became influential in politics in the Forty-second Ward and prospered as a gambling-house proprietor.

Late in 1942, Eddie Sturch began "throwing his weight around" in some of the night spots on the near North Side. On September 19, 1942, the onetime "dictator of North Clark Street" entered the Diamond Cocktail Lounge, 660 North Clark Street, in an intoxicated condition. Observing a total stranger in the place, he walked over to him and brusquely announced, "I don't like your looks." He there-upon proceeded to knock the man down and while he was prostrate on the floor Sturch viciously kicked him. The victim was taken to the hospital for treatment. Disorderly conduct charges were filed against Sturch who did not even bother to appear in court when the case was scheduled to be heard, on September 21, 1942. It was claimed that the victim could not identify his assailant and the charges were dropped. Several weeks later, in the early morning hours of December 2, Sturch entered the Royal Cafe, 701 North Clark Street. Brandishing two pistols, he boldly announced that he was going to "smash up the joint." Quickly putting his words into action, he grabbed a chair which he heaved at several men who were lined up against the bar drinking. Flourishing his guns in a menacing manner, he chased various customers outside into the street. One of the patrons was a salesman from New York. He thought the situation was highly amusing. But the "Napoleon of the Forty-second Ward" did not intend to be taken lightly. And when Sturch fired with both guns, the New York salesman knew that he meant business and virtually dived out of the rear door. When three police officers arrived about 9:15 A.M. to take Sturch into custody, he was still in a bad mood. He struggled vigorously with the officers of the law and swung his fists wildly at them. A patrol wagon finally hauled him to the Thirty-fifth District police station nearby but the gambling-house operator was considered too important to be required to linger there very long. He was taken to the home of Municipal Court Judge Thomas A. Green who promptly released him on his own recognizance. This was the last official act of Judge Green, whose term of office expired on December 5, 1942. Sturch was charged with assault with a deadly weapon, malicious mischief and resisting arrest. These charges were scheduled to be heard in the Felony Branch of the Municipal Court on December 7. Again Sturch did not bother to appear in court although he was ably represented by counsel. His attorney was none other than former judge Thomas A. Green. Although Sturch had been filled with vim, vigor and fight when he staged his one-man riot only a few days before, it was now claimed that he was in need of complete rest and was confined to a hospital.

Because of the charmed life Sturch appeared to lead in the Municipal Court, the Chicago Crime Commission requested the state's attorney to present the facts in the case to the Cook County Grand Jury. On December 14, 1942, the grand jury returned an indictment charging the "dictator of North Clark Street" with malicious mischief. When Sturch was arraigned in Criminal Court on January 27, 1943, he entered a plea of not guilty. One witness testified that he had known Sturch as a "bookie" operator for about fifteen years and had leased two stores to him for gambling operations. Another witness testified that he had been a partner of Sturch in two hand-books located at 750 and 855 North Clark Street. While Sturch was forsaken by some of his gambling partners, he had friends in the police department who remained steadfast to him. In constant attendance at his trial were two policemen, Anthony Crane and his partner. These two policemen were in the courtroom solely to give comfort and assistance to Sturch and members of his family. When newspaper photographers attempted to take a picture of the defendant the officers warded them off. Officer Crane and his partner were long-time associates of the gambler and they were determined that no indignity or undue embarrassment should befall him. The jurors were not so considerate, however. They returned a verdict of guilty and on February 5, 1943, Judge Stanley H. Klarkowski sentenced Sturch to three months in the county jail and fined him $200.00 and costs. The Appellate Court on January 24, 1944, affirmed the conviction.

Policemen Anthony Crane and partner were not inexperienced in court matters. In December 1940, a private watchman confessed that he had committed a number of burglaries and named these two officers as his confederates. On January 15, 1941, the two officers were brought before Judge Thomas A. Green who dismissed the charges against them, emphasizing their unblemished records in the police department and expressing disbelief in the watchman's story. But about three years after the Sturch trial in 1943, Crane's luck ran out. Shortly before midnight on March 24, 1946, the police department received information that two men, one armed with a gun, had been seen entering the gate of the Reynolds International Pen Company, 1550 Fremont Street. Squads of police were hurriedly dispatched to the factory. Just as the squads arrived, the two robbers dashed from the factory into the arms of the police officers. One of the men seized was policeman Anthony Crane. Inside the factory the arresting officers found the janitor and a watchman bound with rope. Crane and a confederate, Frank Cunningham, had overpowered them with a gun and after binding them with rope warned them to lie on the floor and be quiet if they did not want to get shot. The storehouse locks were broken and pens valued at approximately $95,000 had been removed to the loading platform. Three days after the robbery, the Cook County Grand Jury returned two indictments against Anthony Crane and Frank Cunningham. One indictment charged them with robbery and the other, burglary. At the trial Crane was represented by one of the best-known defense attorneys in Chicago, who realized that his client had been caught red-handed. Upon his advice Crane entered a plea of guilty, and Judge Julius H. Miner sentenced the policeman friend of Eddie Sturch to a prison term of two to seven years.[13] Crane thus found it necessary to exchange the police star number which had been assigned to him for seventeen years for a number in the Illinois State Penitentiary.

The rampage of Eddie Sturch late in 1942 set in motion a series of events which served to highlight the political system which has long prevailed in many wards in Chicago. It focused attention on an ex-convict who had become a man of political influence through his vital role in the gambling industry of the ward. Police officers such as Anthony Crane owed allegiance to him. Sturch showed his utter contempt for the judiciary by refusing to appear in Municipal Court to answer charges filed against him. With some justification, he considered himself more powerful than the judges. It was evident that Anthony Crane's original appointment to the police department was a grievous mistake. But how such men became law-enforcement officers was certainly no mystery. When men like Eddie Sturch become politically influential it is inevitable that many misfits will be selected for police work. A political system which is nurtured on alliances between gamblers, politicians and law-enforcement officers naturally results in a breakdown of law and order. The counterpart of Eddie Sturch was to be found in many wards. Even in the Forty-second Ward, Sturch was only one of many gamblers who were important politically. One of the biggest handbook operators in the district was Edmund Burke, a friend of Bugs Moran. Burke's wife, a policewoman in the Chicago Police Department, is the sister of an alderman.

When Eddie Sturch received his jail sentence in the Criminal Court on February 3, 1943, another mayoralty campaign was in progress. Edward J. Kelly was as usual seeking re-election. The Sturch case was too insignificant to become an issue in the campaign, but the true implications of the case — political criminal alliances — became a major issue. The whitewash decision of Kelly's Civil Service Commission in the case involving officers of the gambling squad was fully aired in speeches of the mayor's opponents, in the press and over the radio. Charges were made that the Capone syndicate had been growing in power and wealth under the Kelly-Nash regime. The strategy of the Kelly forces was to ignore these charges and to stress Chicago's patriotism in the war effort. Then events occurred which made it necessary to discard this strategy. Spike O'Donnell, one of the city's prominent underworld characters, was shot in the back, the victim of an attempted assassination. O'Donnell claimed that he had arranged some lucrative asphalt paving contracts between the city and a contractor but had failed to receive the "commission" to which he was entitled. In an effort to collect what he considered his fair share of the profits he had administered beatings to Mayor Kelly's superintendent of streets and a paving contractor.

The Spike O'Donnell case was still fresh in the public mind when the Federal Grand Jury in New York City on March 18, 1943, returned two indictments against several leading Capone gangsters. Frank Nitti, Louis "Little New York" Campagna, Paul de Lucia (alias Paul Ricca), Phil D'Andrea, Frank Maritote, Charles Gioe, and Ralph Pierce of Chicago together with two other defendants were charged with having extorted millions of dollars from the moving-picture industry. When Frank Nitti learned that he had been indicted by the Federal Grand Jury he startled everyone by promptly committing suicide. The *Chicago Tribune* editorially pointed out:

> The gang operated nationally, but its headquarters were in Chicago and it was from citizens of Chicago that a large proportion of the money was extorted by threat and murder. Throughout all or very nearly all of the period covered by the indictments, Mr. Kelly was mayor of Chicago and as such was responsible for the maintenance of law and order in the community. The police department was Mr. Kelly's police department.

The editorial demanded that Mayor Kelly explain:

. . . if he can, how it happened that hoodlums like Nitti and O'Donnell have been allowed all these years to terrorize citizens of Chicago and rob them without effective opposition from the mayor of Chicago and the police department he commands.[14]

That the Kelly administration had taken no effective steps to weaken the Capone syndicate was an incontrovertible fact. At the very time the mayoralty campaign of 1943 was in progress, wide-open protected gambling establishments were pouring huge profits into the pockets of Capone gangsters. By this time the Capone syndicate had spread its tentacles until it was able to exact its extortionate demands from entire legitimate industries and control the fate of thousands of labor union members all over the nation.

The Republican candidate, George B. McKibbin, and the press hammered away at the menacing power of the Capone syndicate, while Kelly weakly denied the existence of any organized underworld in Chicago. Since George B. McKibbin was a man of excellent reputation and character and could not be attacked, the Kelly forces revived William Hale Thompson and campaigned against him. On Election Day, April 6, 1943, the Democratic organization functioned with its usual machinelike precision. Mayor Kelly was re-elected for another four-year term.

Times were good for the gambling business. War plants were operating to capacity. Wages were high. The Loop was riddled with gambling places, many of them operated by precinct captains of the Kelly-Nash machine. Several were in partnership with leading members of the Capone gang. Investigations by the Chicago Crime Commission in 1943 disclosed that even some of the court attachés were operating gambling places. A bailiff assigned to the Racket Court, which heard gambling cases, was himself the proprietor of a handbook. Following his duties in court which ended about noon each day he proceeded to his illegal establishment where he served as the "outside man." After a grand jury investigation in the fall of 1943, it was deemed expedient to remove him from the gambling court. He was transferred to the Boys' Court, where he could serve as a personal inspiration to youthful offenders to respect and obey the law.

Within a stone's throw of the Central Police Station, Jack Guzik's brother operated a handbook. He had been engaged in the gambling business in this same general location for almost fifteen years. Police as well as other law-enforcement officials were his friends. It was not unusual for convicted murderers to be employed in handbooks that officials referred to as "respectable places." In others, trusted employees were often close associates of some of the nation's most feared criminals. But while dangerous gunmen who were fugitives from justice received protection from gambling bosses, the police did not dare to arrest them.

Following a Chicago Crime Commission investigation, the state's attorney's police conducted a raid on September 8, 1943, on an elaborate Capone syndicate gambling house known as the Dome. The raiding officers seized gambling equipment consisting of roulette wheels, crap tables and blackjack tables, valued at several thousand dollars. These paraphernalia were placed in the custody of a lieutenant of the Cook County Highway Police with orders to hold them for evidence. Among the employees of the Dome who were arrested was James D. Larkin (alias Jens D. Larrison), who had been convicted in Federal court for doping race horses, and who seven months later was shot and killed in a tavern operated by Matt Capone, a brother of Al. On September 14, 1943, thirteen defendants were fined and a court order was entered for the destruction of the gambling equipment. Upon attempting to carry out the court order, it was discovered that someone in authority had thoughtfully returned ten roulette wheels and other valuable equipment to the gamblers.

Rocco Fischetti, Al Capone's cousin, had been night manager of the Dome, which was located in Cook County at 7448 Irving Park Road. He was also one of the proprietors of the Rock Garden Club in Cicero. On October 7, 1943, investigators for the Chicago Crime Commission were in the Rock Garden Club when a typical fake raid was conducted by the Cook County Highway Police. Just before the police arrived the patrons were requested to leave the place temporarily. They were told that it would be only a few minutes until operations would be resumed. A few minor employees were arrested for accepting bets on horse races, the entire affair was handled in a most friendly manner and within a few minutes the gambling establishment resumed full operation. The county police falsely reported that no gambling equipment was in the place when the handbook employees were arrested. At the request of the Crime Commission, the state's attorney's police raided the Rock Garden Club about two hours later. They seized blackjack tables, roulette wheels, crap tables and a bank roll of several thousand dollars.

The bold misconduct of the county police in protecting the Dome and the Rock Garden Club incensed the public. Successive Cook County grand juries, beginning with the September 1943 term, conducted one of the most vigorous and sweeping gambling investigations in local history. Numerous law-enforcement officers were indicted and removed from the public payroll. Scores of top-ranking members of the gambling syndicate were indicted. Charges were also filed before the Civil Service Commission against fourteen officers of the Chicago Police Department, nine of whom were captains. Among the hundreds of witnesses called before the grand jury were the mayor, the Cook County clerk, the commissioner of police, members of the Civil Service Commission, judges and political bosses. Overnight practically every gambling establishment in Chicago and Cook County closed, many of them permanently. In their place legitimate enterprises began to flourish.

Mayor Kelly had to bear the brunt of much of the grand jurors' fury alone. His political partner, Patrick A. Nash, who had been in ill health, died on October 6, 1943. The grand jury investigation confirmed the prevalent belief that the administration of the Chicago Police Department was based quite largely on political consideration. The county clerk, one of the most influential politicians of the Kelly machine, was questioned about political interference with the police department. Said the county clerk, "Everybody knows how promotions are made in the police department. Most captains are appointed by the Mayor on recommendations of the Ward Committeemen. Every Ward Committeeman knows that Civil Service examinations for promotions are mostly a sham — it's all handled through the Mayor." [15] Everyone familiar with conditions in the police department knew that the county clerk spoke the truth. It was only his frankness that occasioned any surprise.

While the grand jury investigation was in progress, Martin "Sonny Boy" Quirk, a well-known gangster, was slain on September 18, 1943. Quirk was allegedly involved in the killing of the Capone syndicate leader, Danny Stanton, on May 5, 1943. A gambler, James Egan, when questioned about the murder of Quirk made a confession to the state's attorney, naming John Joseph Williams, gambling lord of the Thirteenth Ward, as the "pay-off man" in the killing. The rise of Williams in the gambling business had been rapid. He had been an insignificant sheet writer in handbooks until he proved his worth as a vote producer in the Thirteenth Ward in the 1936 election. Then he suddenly became a swaggering gambling lord, boasting of his political connections. Associated with him were tough gunmen and ex-convicts. Simultaneously with his rise politically Williams had been a successful applicant in 1936 for a position in the Chicago Police Department. At the time he was publicly implicated in the Quirk murder, Williams ranked ninety-fourth on the civil service list of eligible applicants, but the publicity forced the removal of his name from the list.[16] Three policewomen, who were close relatives of Williams, found it expedient to resign following Egan's confession.

The effects of the grand jury investigations in 1943 were far-reaching. Although practically all of the numerous law enforcement officers and gamblers who were indicted won their freedom on legal technicalities, the vigorous grand jury had pierced the armor of the political leaders. The chief of the Cook County Highway Police and several of his subordinates were removed. The head of the Cicero Police Department resigned under fire. Civil service proceedings were instituted against numerous Chicago police captains and patrolmen. The politicians were uneasy. They felt it wise to send word to the gamblers that protection would be withdrawn temporarily. And since professional gamblers never attempt to operate in any locality without the assurance of official protection, there was an exodus of big gamblers from Chicago and Cook County in the latter part of 1943 and the early part of 1944. Rocco Fischetti and his manager, Gus Liebe, moved their principal operations to nearby Lake County where protection was certain. One of their establishments in Lake County was perhaps the most elaborate gambling emporium in the Middle West. Other Capone gangsters concentrated their gambling house activities elsewhere. Hundreds of handbooks and other types of gambling places throughout the city and county went out of business. This did not mean that the underworld elements had any intention of permanently abandoning the rich fields in Chicago and Cook County. On the contrary they began to form new alignments and at the same time to settle old scores. Warfare among the gambling chiefs was responsible for much violence during 1944.[17]

Scarcely had the year 1944 begun when the murder of Ben Zuckerman, gambling boss of the Twenty-fourth Ward on Chicago's West Side, caused embarrassment to some of the city's leading politicians and resulted in further turmoil among the gambling fraternity. The Twenty-fourth Ward had long been the center of large-scale gambling and the home of some of the city's most powerful political bosses. Many years earlier the ward was ruled by Moe and Ike Rosenberg. Their brother, Eddie (Itsky) Rosenberg, was arrested several times for operating handbooks but his record was never marred by a conviction. He was interested in night clubs located on Rush Street on the near North Side and on the South Side as well. One of his associates was Julius (Dolly) Weisberg, a gambler who died of a heart attack in the County Jail on May 20, 1947, while awaiting electrocution for murder. As late as 1940 Eddie Rosenberg had been sufficiently influential in political circles to be named by Governor John Stelle as his Cook County patronage dispenser.[18] Eddie Rosenberg's political influence paled into insignificance, however, when compared with that of his brother Moe, who had bossed the Twenty-fourth Ward for many years. Moe and Ike Rosenberg were credited with having started Jacob M. Arvey on his political career. Arvey was later to become the ruler of the ward and the Democratic Cook County Chairman, a position which was to make him one of the most influential politicians of the nation. It was during the regime of Moe Rosenberg that Julius "Lovin' Putty" Annixter became the aristocrat of gambling on Chicago's West Side.

By 1944, the ward committeeman of the Twenty-fourth Ward was Arthur X. Elrod, who had assumed the leadership of the ward during the absence of Jacob M. Arvey, then in the United States Army. Elrod had long been identified with politics. In 1929 he was on the public payroll as assistant office manager of the Corporation Counsel's office, which post he resigned in March of that year after the State's Attorney's office asked him to explain his connection with the Acme Sales Company which was engaged in the distribution of slot machines, punchboards and vending devices. In December 1929

the police raided Room 517 at 127 North Dearborn Street which
was reputedly the office of the Acme Sales Company, and the alleged Loop headquarters for the North Side gamblers, Jack Zuta
and Bugs Moran. A safe confiscated by the police was opened pursuant to a court order. In it were found punchboards, canceled
checks signed by Arthur X. Elrod and records which indicated
that the occupants of the office were interested in the Fairview dog
track. A few months later, Elrod again received unfavorable publicity in connection with the settlement of the estate of Jack Zuta
who was the victim of a gang murder on July 1, 1930. He cleared
himself of a contempt citation issued by the Probate Court when he
turned over a deed to some of Zuta's property.[19] By 1944 Elrod, as
ward committeeman of the Twenty-fourth Ward and the chief
deputy bailiff of the Municipal Court, had become a powerful politician. His populous ward was always in safe hands for the Kelly
machine. There was some dissatisfaction in the ward over Elrod's
political leadership but it could not be successfully challenged. However, the underworld was also dissatisfied with the gambling leadership in the ward, and it was in no mood to temporize. It was willing
to shoot and to kill.

A series of gang murders started on January 14, 1944, when Ben
Zuckerman was ambushed and slain as he was entering his home at
4042 Wilcox Street in Chicago. When his associate, Ben Glaser,
heard the news he dropped dead from a heart attack. A third partner, Louis Dann, fled to California a short time later. Gambling establishments operated by Zuckerman had been immune from any
interference by the police, and had served as hangouts and gambling
headquarters for criminals. When the October 1943 grand jury impressed upon high-ranking police officials that it would tolerate no
insincerity in their law enforcement efforts, a raid was finally conducted on Zuckerman's main establishment. Among those arrested
were eight individuals with police records, one of whom was at
that time on probation for robbery. One man was armed with a
revolver when he was seized. Another man with a prior record also
arrested was one of Zuckerman's trusted employees. Only a few days
before the raid this hoodlum appeared publicly with two judges and
a police captain at a function that was given wide attention in the
press.

It was obvious that Zuckerman and his employees had rated high
with politicians and police. One of Zuckerman's most intimate associates was the public enemy and prominent Capone gangster, Dago
Lawrence Mangano. At one time Zuckerman had a financial interest
in a well-known Capone syndicate brewery. He had maintained
cordial relations with Billy Skidmore and William R. Johnson until
they ran afoul of the income-tax laws. Along with other gamblers
and politicians he paid visits to Skidmore's headquarters, the junk
yard. This place was only a few blocks south of Zuckerman's main
gambling establishment. Just several months before Zuckerman was
killed he informed Chicago Crime Commission investigators, whose
true identity was unknown to him, that he was a Democratic precinct captain of the Twenty-fourth Ward organization, and boasted
of his political power and the absolute immunity which was attached to his illegal operations. Because of the large number of votes
he controlled Zuckerman said he was given "the gambling concession
in the ward." And in emphasizing the importance of his political influence, he pointed out that to all practical purposes the Twenty-
fourth Ward along with two others located nearby had sufficient
votes to control almost any city election.[20]

A few months after Zuckerman was slain, his associate, Dago Lawrence Mangano met his death in a hail of shotgun slugs. With
Mangano when he was killed on August 3, 1944, was Michael Pan-
tillo, a police character who was also mortally wounded. Eight
months later, on April 7, 1945, another partner of Zuckerman, Willie
Tarsch (alias Willie Kolatch), was shot and killed in the rear of a
building at 3710 West Roosevelt Road.[21] Bombs hurled by the warring gambling factions added to the turmoil into which the area had
been thrown. Businessmen who feared to voice their objections
openly complained privately that neighborhood trade was suffering.
Even influential politicians expressed the fear that conditions in the
ward were getting out of hand. The professional gamblers who
swarmed about on West Roosevelt Road were gunmen and swindlers
of the most unsavory nature. These conditions were apparently good
for politics, however. In the fall elections of 1944 Arthur X. Elrod,
the political boss of the area, won acclaim from the national leaders
of his party for the huge pluralities rolled up in the one-sided victory
gained in the Twenty-fourth Ward. In 1946 he was elected to

membership in the Cook County Board of Commissioners. He was a man of great prestige in party circles — a political leader whose photograph appeared in the press with vice presidents of the United States and other national dignitaries visiting Chicago.

Few ward organizations have been able to boast of greater importance to the political machine that has ruled Chicago for many decades than the Twenty-fourth. Few wards have produced a greater number of top-ranking politicians. Few wards have been responsible for the development of more gambling kings. The tremendous political power of the Twenty-fourth Ward organization and the prevalence of widespread commercial gambling in the area are not unrelated matters. Ben Zuckerman was not engaging in idle talk when he boasted of his political importance. Jacob M. Arvey, who was to succeed Edward J. Kelly as the most powerful politician in Chicago, referred to Zuckerman as his "very good friend." "Zucky," as he was affectionately called, had been active in behalf of Arvey's political campaigns as far back as 1923 when Arvey was a candidate for alderman.[22] The Twenty-fourth Ward organization once offered Zuckerman the position of alderman but he declined the honor. Apparently he felt that he already possessed as much political influence as would be attached to a place in the city council.

In July 1944, Chicago was host to the Democratic National Convention as it had been in 1932 and 1940. At the 1940 convention tradition was shattered when Franklin D. Roosevelt was nominated as a candidate for a third term as President of the United States. Before the convention convened in 1944, it was virtually a foregone conclusion that Roosevelt would be named again. The principal controversy centered around his running mate. Vice-President Henry Wallace had the backing of the powerful C.I.O. unions but he was in disfavor with the Southern Democrats and the city machine bosses. Wallace, an avid New Dealer and a devout worshipper of Roosevelt, took the convention by storm when he delivered his crusading speech in behalf of the New Deal. Demonstrations among the delegates supporting him gathered momentum until it appeared certain that the convention would be stampeded into renominating Wallace as its candidate for the vice-presidency. On the platform at the Chicago Stadium, Mayor Edward J. Kelly and Boss Frank Hague of Jersey City held hurried whispered conferences. The situation was obviously getting out of hand. In the face of roaring protests from the delegates, the chairman abruptly adjourned the convention. The party wheel horses went into huddles in hotel rooms to complete negotiations that would assure the selection of their candidate for vice-president. On the following day Mayor Kelly, Boss Hague, and Robert E. Hannegan of the discredited Missouri Pendergast machine had things under control. Harry S. Truman was named as the running mate of Franklin D. Roosevelt; in November, Roosevelt and Truman were elected.[23]

By April 1945, Edward J. Kelly had occupied the mayor's chair for twelve years, equalling the period that Big Bill Thompson ruled over the city. Thompson's administration was under constant fire because of the prevalence of widespread crime and for throwing the school system into the mire of partisan politics. Kelly's administration was chiefly vulnerable on exactly the same scores. The repeal of the National Prohibition Act during Kelly's first year in office had reduced the number of gang killings appreciably, and gang warfare was also diminished by agreement among the big-time gangsters themselves. Efforts had already been made by gang leaders in Chicago to define the territorial rights of one another and to end the costly gang warfare that waged incessantly. Then in 1929, Frank Costello of New York, one of America's most powerful underworld bosses, arranged for a conference with Al Capone and other gang leaders in Atlantic City. Participating in the conference was Enoch L. "Nucky" Johnson, the political boss of Atlantic City, who maintained his dictatorial rule through the control of the numbers racket. The purpose of the "get together" was to arrive at an understanding that would end the constant warfare.[24] These efforts to reduce bloodshed were not immediately effective, but they reflected a new attitude on the part of the more powerful underworld leaders — an attitude that undoubtedly played an important part in substantially decreasing the number of gang killings in the years ahead.

Thompson won international notoriety as a result of his public trial of William McAndrew, the superintendent of schools, and his battle to remove the influence of King George from text books. Mayor Kelly never indulged in such public demonstrations. He considered the public school system a part of his political organization

over which he ruled quietly but firmly. He would brook no interference from the outside. Throughout Kelly's regime, the administration of the public schools brought loud criticism from the public
and the press. Under fire, in particular, was Dr. William H. Johnson,
the superintendent of public schools. Bitter complaints by parents
and civic groups merely brought the stereotyped reply that Chicago
schools were "models" for the rest of the country. Public indignation finally reached a white heat in the summer of 1944, culminating
in formal requests to the National Education Association to investigate conditions in the Chicago schools. Among the groups that
solicited the aid of the National Education Association were the
Woman's City Club of Chicago, the Cook County League of
Women Voters, the City Club, the Chicago Citizens Schools Committee and others. At the beginning of the investigation, the co-
operation of the Chicago Board of Education was requested. The
board flatly refused its co-operation and denounced the investigation as a fishing expedition by outside groups which were trying to
discredit the Chicago schools. Said the board, "It would be more fitting if this organization devoted its energies to making some contribution to the war and defense effort instead of trying to make
this unwarranted inquiry and thereby hamper a patriotic institution
which is making a vital contribution to every phase of the war
effort."

The flag-waving tactics employed by Kelly's political school
board did not stop the investigation, however. In May 1945, the
National Education Association issued its report which was a blistering indictment of many phases of the public school administration. "Some of the personnel practices in the Chicago schools," said
the report, "are undemocratic and even fascistic in nature and they
are, or should be, of deep concern not only to the people of Chicago
but to the nation as a whole." It was established that on some occasions political interference extended to purely academic matters. In
one instance, a teacher's certificate was awarded to the daughter of
a city councilman after she had failed fifteen hours of classwork
and had been asked to withdraw from school. "The certificate was
granted to her without the knowledge of the teachers under whom
she had taken courses and as a result of political pressure from the
downtown office of the Chicago public schools." A principals' ex-

amination was described as "unprofessional, irregular, and probably illegal." Although the Illinois law prohibits any teacher or school officer from being interested in the sale, proceeds, or profits of any book used in a school with which he may be connected, Kelly's superintendent of schools "caused the adoption by the Chicago schools of more than twenty textbooks bearing his name as author or co-author." When the Chicago schools indicated an intention of changing the shorthand systems taught in the classrooms, one publishing house sent its representative to Chicago with $30,000 in cash to be used in obtaining favorable action on its system. He carried on negotiations with "one Skidmore, a notorious underworld character, with apparent prospects of success but was finally informed that 'everything is off because the other company raised the ante.'" The publishing house representatives had been accurately informed concerning the city's politicians. One more proof that until prison doors closed on him in 1942, William R. Skidmore was a man of tremendous political power.

The National Education Association report referred to an investigation started by the state's attorney in 1939 regarding the Chicago Board of Education:

This investigation was never completed but it revealed, among other things, evidence of payments of bribes to public-school officials, the awarding of contracts to relatives of public-school officials, the contribution of money to political campaign funds by firms that received school-board contracts, the rejection of low bids in certain cases, the substitution of low-grade material for first-class material specified in contracts, and the awarding of contracts to firms owned by a well-known racketeer. This report, in many places other than Chicago, would have resulted in a grand jury investigation.

The National Education Association placed much of the responsibility for Chicago's school conditions on Mayor Edward J. Kelly and it recommended that the governor or the legislature conduct an investigation of the operation and management of the Chicago schools for the preceding twelve years.

When Kelly's school board originally declined to co-operate with the National Education Association's inquiry, it gave as one reason for its action that the schools were approved by the North Central Association of Colleges, the duly constituted accrediting agency.

Before long, however, the North Central Association formally threatened to remove the Chicago schools from the accredited list. The public rose up in arms. The threatened move on the part of the North Central Association was filled with political dynamite. Kelly knew it and capitulated. His long fight to operate the school system exactly as he pleased was at an end, and he appointed an advisory board consisting of presidents of leading universities in the Chicago area. These educators severely criticized Kelly's superintendent of schools, and Dr. William H. Johnson resigned his position with its salary of $12,500 a year — to be promptly appointed by Kelly as head of the Chicago Junior College at an annual salary of $12,000.[25]

In 1931, William Hale Thompson's political career had finally been brought to an end largely through a public revolt against widespread crime and political interference in the public schools. Fifteen years later Edward J. Kelly's long political rule was tottering for exactly the same reason. Kelly prided himself upon being a practical politician, but he was not sufficiently practical to learn from past experience that even the most powerful political rule cannot defy public opinion indefinitely.

The voters of Chicago were genuinely angry over conditions in the public school system as related in the report of the National Education Association. But their fury abated somewhat as they kept their eyes glued on events of national and international significance taking place far from Chicago. On April 12, 1945, President Franklin D. Roosevelt died suddenly in Warm Springs, Georgia. The Vice-President, Harry S. Truman, consequently was thrust into the highest office of the land. Only six years earlier, in April 1939, the political career of Truman was believed ended when his principal sponsor, Boss Tom Pendergast of Kansas City, was indicted and subsequently committed to the Federal penitentiary. The new President had been awarded the vice-presidency in no small measure as a result of the efforts of Chicago's Mayor, Edward J. Kelly, Mayor Frank ("I am the law") Hague of Jersey City, and remnants of the old Pendergast machine. Kelly, together with Hague and others, could with justification claim the title of President-maker. His relations with the White House had never before been on such intimate terms. He was now assured of a place in our national political history.

* * *

Only a few days after Truman became President, Benito Mussolini, the once proud Dictator of Italy, was captured and executed on April 29, 1945, by anti-Fascist forces as he attempted to escape into Switzerland. Powerful American and English armies were closing in on Germany from the west while Russian forces were moving rapidly from the east. As the Russians fought their way into Berlin on May 1, 1945, the world received news that Adolf Hitler was dead. On May 7, 1945, the German Provisional Government headed by Admiral Karl Doenitz surrendered unconditionally. On the following day the streets of Chicago were streaming with happy people who were celebrating the end of World War II in Europe. The end of the fighting in the Pacific was also in sight. On August 6, 1945, an atomic bomb was dropped on the Japanese city of Hiroshima, leveling four square miles of factories and homes and killing over fifty thousand people. Three days later an atomic bomb shattered Nagasaki and on August 14, 1945, Japan surrendered. Again there were jubilant celebrations in Chicago and throughout the nation.

During the entire world conflict, Chicago made a noteworthy contribution to the war effort. It ranked high in the production of war materials, the sale of war bonds, salvage collection and enlistments. It was claimed that one seventh of all plasma donated to the Red Cross blood bank was provided by Chicago citizens. As early as August 13, 1941, almost four months before America's entry into the war, Chicago opened its first Servicemen's Center, located on Washington Street less than one block from the City Hall. A second Servicemen's Center was opened in the old Auditorium Hotel by the spring of 1942, and before long two others were in operation. The four Centers occupied thirty-four floors of space and provided free entertainment and food to men and women of the armed forces. Mrs. Edward J. Kelly, the charming and gracious wife of the mayor, took personal charge of the canteen which she actively supervised throughout the war. Both Mayor and Mrs. Kelly gave much of their time and effort in making the city's servicemen's centers the most outstanding in the land. Chicago gained an international reputation for its hospitality to the men and women in uniform. Over a year after World War II had ended, Lieutenant General W. R. Walker presented Mayor and Mrs. Kelly with the Award of Merit, the army's highest honor paid to civilians for distinguished service in the war.[26]

Following the close of the war, the city again was plagued with many crimes of violence. Within twenty-four hours on September 2, 1945, there were five murders in Chicago. Three of the victims were police officers. In December 1945, the police reported that thirty-one murders had been committed during that one month. Several of these crimes were sensational, attracting national attention. Frances Brown, a discharged Wave, was brutally assaulted and killed in a North Side apartment on December 10, 1945. Two days later, Lawrence A. Lange, secretary to the president of a large corporation, was murdered on the North Side following a terrific struggle with his assailant. Lange was the tenth person murdered within a period of eight days. Crime news was splashed on the front page of all the papers.

But public interest in the vicious murders of December 1945 was suddenly shoved into the background on January 7, 1946, when one of the most horrible crimes in the city's history was committed. Suzanne Degnan, a six-year-old child, was kidnapped while she was asleep in her crib. Her abductor left a note demanding $20,000 ransom, but it was soon obvious that the collection of ransom was not the motive for the kidnapping. While her father, James A. Degnan, an official of the Office of Price Administration, was making efforts to raise the money, the police found the child's severed head in a catch basin within two blocks of the Degnan home. Other dismembered parts of her body were recovered from sewers during the night. The entire city was completely aroused. Parents were terror stricken, not knowing where the fiend might decide to strike next. A police captain on the night of the murder stated, "The Chicago Police Department is on trial as never before." Everything was in confusion. Police officers and other officials milled around the room from which the child had been abducted. Articles which might have furnished fingerprint evidence were handled indiscriminately. Police officers reported the recovery of a highly important piece of evidence which might aid them in solving the case. A few hours later this "highly important" piece of evidence was discarded. It was determined that other police officers had brought it to the scene of the crime to aid them in their investigation and had left it there. It had no connection with either the murder or the crime. The crime detection laboratory of the police department was unable to make necessary examinations with the speed which the investigation demanded. Two janitors of buildings located near the Degnan home were seized by the police as suspects and severely beaten in an effort to extract confessions from them. The public was advised that the solution of the case was imminent. High officials of the Kelly administration waited anxiously at police headquarters ready to broadcast over the radio that one of the janitors had confessed and the police department had solved the case. But the janitors were innocent. They refused to confess and after their release from custody they filed lawsuits for the injuries they had suffered at the hands of the police. The cases were subsequently settled upon payment of $20,000 to one of the janitors and $5220 to the other.

Six months after the Suzanne Degnan kidnapping and murder, a traffic police officer, Abner Cunningham, who was off duty and dressed in a bathing suit, was returning to his home from the beach in the Rogers Park district. As he passed an apartment building, he heard cries for help. A youthful prowler had been observed in the building by some of the residents. Cunningham located the prowler, struck him over the head with a flower pot and knocked him unconscious. The captured prowler was William Heirens, a seventeen-year-old student at the University of Chicago. Subsequently he confessed to three murders including the vicious killing of Suzanne Degnan and the brutal slaying of the ex-Wave, Frances Brown. The third victim was also a woman, whom he had killed while committing a burglary. Heirens had committed hundreds of burglaries since he had started on his career of crime at the age of nine. His room was filled with loot. And to the chagrin of the police department, it was discovered that Heirens had previously been arrested for carrying a gun during the height of the manhunt for the slayer of Suzanne Degnan. The arresting police officers brought him in court and he was discharged when they stated that no evidence was available to connect him with any crime. The gun found on Heirens was not sent to the police laboratory for examination, and his room had not been searched. Following Heirens's last arrest his room was examined and articles stolen from a home in the immedi-

ate vicinity of the Degnan residence were recovered. His finger-
prints were then compared with those found on the ransom note
by the Federal Bureau of Investigation and identified. Heirens
entered a plea of guilty when arraigned in the Cook County Criminal Court and was sentenced to three life terms for murder.[27]

At the time Heirens was captured, the commissioner of police
admitted that the police department had failed miserably in the
Degnan case. It was obvious that the department was woefully weak
in administration and organization, in discipline and the training of
its personnel. The Chicago Crime Commission had been calling
attention to these failings for many years. Although the Degnan
case frightened the political leaders, they could think only in terms
of more policemen. Mayor Kelly announced that 1000 new policemen would be added to the force. And it was explained that these
officers were needed in such haste that it would be necessary to
by-pass civil service procedures. The ward committeemen of the
Kelly machine were requested to recommend the new officers. It
was apparent that no emergency could arise which would make it
expedient to by-pass political considerations.

During the latter part of 1945, a new gambling war started brewing which was to have tremendous political repercussions. For
several years Continental Press, with headquarters in Cleveland,
Ohio, had maintained a monopoly over the dissemination of the
racing information which is essential for the operation of illegal
handbooks. Continental Press, of which James M. Ragen was part
owner and the general manager, dispatched racing information to
distributors in various sections of the country which in turn directly
serviced the handbooks in their territories. In Chicago, the distributor
for Continental Press was the Mid-West News Service. With the
tolerant Kelly machine in political control, the Capone syndicate
handbooks as well as Ragen's wire service prospered. Until the fall
of 1945 amicable relations prevailed between Ragen and Capone
gangsters who were operating handbooks. Then, following a dis-
agreement, the Capone gang began pirating the racing information
from the Mid-West News Service and offering it to handbooks in
competition with Mid-West. Ragen was furious. In September 1945,
he had a conference with Capone syndicate leaders Jack Guzik,
Murray Humphreys, and former State Senator Daniel Serritella in

a Chicago hotel room. Humphreys suggested to Ragen that he sell the Mid-West News Service to members of the syndicate. Ragen refused. Humphreys and Guzik then magnanimously offered to cease competing with the Mid-West News Service if Ragen would give them forty per cent of his profits.[28] Ragen again declined, but he knew he was in serious trouble and needed help. He conferred with Jacob M. Arvey, Chairman of the Cook County Democratic organization, and Barnet Hodes, Corporation Counsel of the city of Chicago. With all their power, they were unable to aid him. It was obvious that he was fighting a losing battle. The Capone gang, observed Ragen, was "as strong as the United States Army."

When Ragen refused to capitulate the Capone gangsters began waging an all-out offensive. They started a rival information business called the Trans-American Publishing and News Service, Inc. Some of Ragen's trusted employees deserted him and began working for the Capone syndicate. In the early part of 1946, members of the Capone gang issued an ultimatum to many of Chicago's North Side gamblers to "get out of town." Most of them heeded the warning, but an ex-convict, Frank Covelli, affiliated with a North Side handbook, lingered on. He was shot to death on January 21, 1946. Harry "Red" Richmond, another ex-convict who was closely associated with many underworld hoodlums, operated a handbook on the near West Side at 1638 Madison Street. He was a subscriber to the Capone wire service until April 13, 1946, when he discontinued it. Two days later he became a customer of Mid-West News Service, the Chicago distributor for Ragen's Continental Press. The Capone gangsters were infuriated, and on April 18 Richmond was ambushed and slain.

Ragen pleaded with the state's attorney, the police and the Federal authorities for help. He claimed that Capone gangsters had threatened him and he feared his life was in jeopardy. A short time later, on June 24, Ragen was riding in an automobile on busy State Street. It was during the rush hour and the streets were filled with cars. As Ragen's automobile approached Pershing Road on the South Side, shotgun slugs were poured into the car, severely wounding him. His bodyguards were unable to return the fire before the assassins disappeared in a tarpaulin-covered truck in which they were riding. Ragen was rushed to the Michael Reese Hospital where he lingered until August 14, 1946, when he died.

The defiant shooting of Ragen made a mockery of Mayor Kelly's boast that he had driven the Capone gang out of the city. The public was rudely awakened to the fact that the duly-constituted authorities were still utterly helpless in coping with Chicago's strongly-organized underworld. The police and the prosecutor had been placed on notice by Ragen that Capone gangsters had threatened his life. Yet on a busy street during a rush hour, the gunmen had dared to attack him and had been permitted to leave unmolested. It was evident that Chicago's gambling business was sufficiently lucrative for gangsters to wage open warfare to control it. Mayor Kelly weakly stated, "I don't believe there is any syndicate gambling in Chicago." In the next breath he promised he would order the police department to "clamp down on all gambling." [29] Two days after the shooting of Ragen the *Chicago News* asked editorially, "How do you like it, Chicagoans?" The editorial continued:

It paints a sordid and depressing picture of what happens to a community when politicians consort with thieves and criminals; when a political machine allies itself with racketeers, when the racketeers in fact, become the real power behind local government. . . . It is a story of crooked gamblers, murderers, panders, brothel keepers, kidnapers and extortionists. All contributing to the campaign funds of the politicians whom the people thought they elected to enforce laws that would put crooks in jail.[30]

The Ragen case was never solved.

From 1925 through 1946 there were 638 gang murders committed in Chicago and Cook County. During that same period only thirteen defendants were convicted in connection with a gang killing.[31] Three powerful gamblers of the Twenty-fourth Ward were accused of the Ragen murder but witnesses repudiated statements identifying them and the prosecution was dropped. Two police officers, Lieutenant William Drury and Captain Tom Connelly, who originally secured the identifications of the three gamblers, were called before the grand jury. When they refused to sign immunity waivers and testify, charges were filed against them and after civil service hearings they were dismissed from the force. In the meantime the Capone gang's Trans-American Publishing and News Service, Inc., was expanding throughout the nation. Its representatives in most of the major cities were well-known underworld characters. There were numerous shootings. The Chicago warfare over the wire service ceased, however, with the death of Ragen.

Less than two months after James M. Ragen's death, Michael Hinky Dink Kenna, political ruler of the First Ward for almost a half century, died on October 9, 1946, in his Blackstone Hotel suite. The obituary notices correctly gave the "little fellow" credit for having made and unmade judges, chiefs of police, police inspectors, legislators and mayors.[32] As the remains of Hinky Dink lay in a funeral parlor, many of those who had benefited from his organization came to pay their last respects. The crowded undertaking rooms were visited by Jacob M. Arvey, head of the Democratic machine of Cook County, Jack Guzik, head of the Capone gang's gambling organization, Frank "Chew Tobacco" Ryan, powerful Loop gambler, Mike Potson, café operator in the ward who had made a fortune from gambling and prostitution, Fred Morelli, who had succeeded Kenna as ward committeeman and who was a product of his organization, former State Senator James M. Slattery and numerous others. And it was appropriate that these men should attend Kenna's wake and pay their respects. They owed much to Hinky Dink and his First Ward organization.

Chicago's most widely publicized citizen, Al Capone, was not able to be present at Hinky Dink's funeral, notwithstanding his affection for the "little fellow." The gang leader was suffering from an incurable disease and was confined to his luxurious Florida estate. His condition was critical. Several weeks later newspapers throughout the land carried accounts of the death of America's foremost gangster. His body was brought back to Chicago and lowered into its final resting place in Mount Olivet Cemetery on February 4, 1947.

During the heyday of Al Capone's reign over Chicago, gangster funerals were gala affairs attended by leading politicians. In contrast, the funeral ceremonies for Al Capone were quiet and unostentatious. Only intimate friends and members of the family were present. The mourners included the Chicago gambling kings Jack

Guzik, Murray "The Camel" Humphreys and "Golf Bag" Sam Hunt; the Cicero gambling lords Willie Heeney and Joe Corngold; the gambling bosses of Melrose Park, Rocco and Nick Degrazio, and Al's cousins, Charles, Rocco, and Joseph Fischetti. Tough Tony Capezio, a top-ranking member of the old Capone gang, was at the graveside bedecked in a derby hat and wearing smoked glasses. With the Cicero contingent were the wheel horses Joe Aiuppa, alias Joey O'Brien, Claude Maddox, and Robert Ansoni, proprietors of the Taylor Company, a large concern manufacturing gambling house equipment. From this factory in Cicero gambling equipment is shipped to casinos all over the nation. Charles Fischetti, who had become one of the most influential gambling lords in the entire United States, cursed and snarled at the newspaper men attending the funeral. He threatened to kill anyone who might attempt to take photographs. Even Al's younger brother, Matt Capone, hurled threats at the cameramen.[33]

Al Capone had received millions of dollars from gambling, prostitution, bootleg liquor and scores of other lucrative activities. How much of this fortune had been saved was known only by the immediate members of his family. After his death it was learned that a mortgage amounting to $35,000 had been placed on Capone's palatial Florida home. Since March 1, 1937, the mortgage had been in the name of Frank E. "Frankie" Harmon, a personal friend and political protégé of Mayor Kelly, under whose tutelage Harmon had become influential politically. His close associates included several high-ranking police officials; during the Kelly regime, Harmon frequently had a hand in formulating police department policies. In the early 1940's he was the proprietor of an illegal handbook located on the second floor at 2613 Milwaukee Avenue. In 1942 Mayor Kelly revoked the liquor licenses of three downtown cocktail lounges operated by two partners. A bottle of beer had been sold to a minor sailor in one of the places and the licenses for all three cocktail lounges were revoked. For over a year the partners were unsuccessful in their efforts to get the licenses restored. Then Frank E. Harmon obtained the necessary liquor licenses and became a part owner of the profitable business. His political prestige increased until the Democratic organization named him a ward committeeman; in 1950 he received the party endorsement for nomination to the State House of Representatives from the Twenty-fifth District, but he was defeated.[34]

Toward the end of 1946, it became evident that Mayor Kelly was losing his grip over the Cook County Democratic machine. Only two years earlier Kelly had occupied a prominent place on the Chicago Stadium platform while the Democratic National Convention was selecting candidates for the presidential election. In plain view of the thousands of people who jammed the stadium, Kelly held whispered conferences with his counterpart in American political life, Boss Frank Hague. These two powerful machine bosses had climbed to the top of the ladder in the rugged game of politics. Their influence was unquestioned. And their political sagacity was respected by the convention delegates who were convened to select the leaders of our national destiny. But such are the vicissitudes of politics that by 1946 it appeared doubtful whether Kelly could control his own local organization.

Kelly had occupied the mayor's chair for fourteen years. He wanted another term. Some of the strongest ward committeemen, however, were openly defiant. They complained that he was spending too much time in his Eagle River, Wisconsin, home. They were unable to confer with him on party matters. Actually they were reflecting a rising public resentment against the Kelly administration. In the fall elections of 1946 the Republicans exhibited unexpected strength. Many ward politicians secretly believed that any Republican candidate would emerge victorious over Kelly. And a loss of the mayor's office would naturally result in a forfeiture of patronage with a deterioration of the powerful ward organization that had controlled the city and county for so many years. The fears of the ward leaders were not ill-founded.

On December 16, 1946, Milburn P. Akers, political editor of the *Chicago Sun*, a paper then known for its strong support of the Democratic party, wrote:

What is this Chicago Democratic machine which has become so arrogant that it flouts public sentiment and frequently gets away with it? What manner of men are these machine bosses and machine followers? On what do they thrive and get rich and maintain their despotic rule? . . . How does it chance they sometimes "deliver" election day pluralities for subservient party hacks, bad in record, unappealing in personality, and void of any sense of obligation except to the machine? These questions are all easy of answer and easy of documentation.

Tracing the history of the Kelly machine back over half a century Akers said that the machine, in essence, has been a plunderbund for its fifty years of existence. ". . . Gambling, protected vice districts, and crooked franchise deals attended its birth. It was suckled on the sale of influence, it grew to maturity on political contracts." [35]

As the year 1946 was coming to a close, the "despotic rule" mentioned by Akers was being seriously threatened. The press and the public were leveling their guns at Kelly, the boss of the machine, with more telling effects than at any time since he first became mayor. Henchmen of his own party were deserting him and exhibiting open defiance of his leadership. It was apparent that Kelly's long rule was coming to an end.

CHAPTER X
Friends in the Right Places

THE position of the Kelly machine was precarious as the party leaders began making preparations for the 1947 mayoralty election. In the preceding fall election the Republicans had captured several important county offices for the first time in sixteen years. The offices of sheriff, county treasurer, probate court judge and the president of the Cook County Board of Commissioners as well as others were now in Republican hands. It is true that the Republicans in Cook County had been the beneficiaries of a national trend away from the Democratic party which had ruled over the country for such a long period of time, but their success in the fall of 1946 stemmed in large measure from a growing public resentment against the abuses of the arrogant Kelly machine. The Democratic organization had been rudely shaken from its customary self-complacency. There were also strong indications of a sincere movement to place an independent candidate of stature in the race if Edward J. Kelly should again be chosen as the Democratic candidate.

The party strategists realized that if they flouted public sentiment by running Kelly or any of the usual machine hacks the Republicans might emerge victorious. Under such circumstances the shrewd leadership of Jacob M. Arvey came to the fore. He proposed to the ward committeemen that they select Martin H. Kennelly, an outstanding businessman and civic leader of unimpeachable integrity, as the Democratic candidate for mayor. Kennelly, a bachelor, was tall, gray haired, handsome and possessed of an engaging smile. He had headed the Red Cross in Chicago and his name was well known to the voters. In politics he had been a strong backer of former State's Attorney Thomas J. Courtney and was an avowed enemy of the Kelly machine. The ward bosses had no reason to be enthusiastic over Kennelly as their mayoralty candidate, but their plight was serious and they knew it. Reluctantly, they accepted Kennelly as a candidate who could win and thereby avert ruin to the local Democratic ward organization. The Republican party simplified matters by selecting a relatively unknown and unimpressive candidate, Russell W. Root, and in the April 1947 election Kennelly won by a huge majority.

The new mayor confronted a tremendous task. The city was without adequate funds. Tax rates were high and citizens were in no mood to assume added tax burdens. Misgovernment over a period of several decades had created many difficulties that called for drastic action. The vast majority of people looked to Mayor Kennelly with hope, and were ready to follow his leadership. Kennelly had a sincere desire to restore Chicago's reputation, but it soon became apparent that he would proceed cautiously. He had no intention of discarding many of the tools which had been tried and found wanting. With few exceptions, the various department heads who had been appointed to these key positions by former Mayor Kelly were retained. This was true of the commissioner of police, who headed a department that was steeped in politics, improperly organized, unprogressive and generally unequipped to cope with the city's crime problem. Vigorous steps were taken, however, to reorganize the traffic division of the department, with the assistance of the Northwestern University Traffic Institute. Hundreds of police officers were reassigned from general police work to the traffic division, and much good resulted from this effort. But drastic measures were particularly needed to mold the department into a progressive, efficient crime-fighting body. Although these fundamental steps were not taken, the commissioner of police was given a much freer hand in the enforcement of law without regard to political considerations.

The Kelly administration had been characterized by wide-open gambling establishments throughout the city. The police appeared unable to close these illegal places. Under Mayor Kennelly, however, even with Kelly's commissioner of police, the gambling rooms disappeared almost entirely. The inveterate horse player had no difficulty in placing his bets with the corner newsboy, in a cigar store or a tavern, but this gambling was largely on a "sneak" basis. The highly lucrative establishments, fully equipped with loud-speakers, wall sheets and housing two or three hundred patrons at a time, were eliminated. It soon became evident that wide-open commercial gambling establishments cannot exist when a mayor orders the laws enforced and the police know that he means it.

In one important respect Mayor Kennelly followed the pattern instituted by his predecessors — he refused to come to grips with the organized crime problem. Echoing their amazing reasoning, he regarded the Capone gang as a myth. This attitude, of course, was assumed in the face of Federal court evidence to the contrary.

Almost two years after Kennelly became mayor, Albert Deutsch, a highly-regarded author, interviewed him and inquired about the steps he was taking to combat the Capone syndicate. The mayor replied, "I don't know about any syndicate. Isn't that man Capone supposed to be dead?"[1] Chicago's most publicized gangster could not be disposed of so easily, however. The evil influence which this underworld leader and his gang had exerted on the political and social life of the city for almost three decades was far from removed with the burial of Capone on February 4, 1947. Al Capone and his predecessors had left the city a heritage of bad government, widespread corruption, a high crime rate and an evil reputation. It was a heritage that could not be erased by an honest mayor within a few months or even years. It was also a heritage which could not be removed by denying that it existed.

About two months preceding the 1946 fall elections for sheriff and other officers, the area lying beyond the city limits within Cook County was suddenly flooded with slot machines. Many tavern keepers privately complained that against their wishes they were forced to permit the gambling syndicate to install these one-armed bandits. It was commonly understood that the Kelly machine, badly in need of campaign funds, had made a deal with the Capone organization which allowed it to operate gambling in the county in return for financial support. Such political deals with criminal groups are usually incapable of legal proof, but this time there were certain indisputable facts which clearly indicated the existence of the alleged arrangement between the syndicate and the Kelly machine. For the greater part of three years under a conscientious Democratic sheriff, relatively few slot machines were in operation in Cook

County. Yet, when the election campaign started, slot machines were everywhere. The urgent need of the Kelly political organization for campaign funds was thus fulfilled. And a few months later it became apparent that the Capone syndicate also desperately needed funds. The groundwork was being laid to secure the release of four prominent members of the gang from Federal prison. Large sums of money were required to settle Federal tax claims outstanding against the imprisoned gangsters and to retain attorneys possessing influence in the nation's capital.

On August 13, 1947, Paul Ricca, Louis "Little New York" Campagna, Phil D'Andrea and Charles "Cherry Nose" Gioe were released on parole. These underworld leaders had served only the minimum period of ten-year sentences originally imposed on them by the Federal court in New York City. Measured by any proper standards of parole procedure, the special consideration given the four Capone mobsters was completely unwarranted. The press, led by the *Chicago Tribune*, furiously demanded an investigation of the scandal. A congressional committee initiated an inquiry which lasted several months. The testimony clearly revealed the tremendous power and influence which the Capone syndicate was capable of exerting on the administration of justice. It also revealed the fact that the national government had reacted to this influence in exactly the same manner as typical ward politicians.

The four hoodlum parolees had been convicted for their part in a huge conspiracy which resulted in the extortion of over one million dollars from producers and exhibitors engaged in the motion-picture business. The funds of the union were also looted. This plot had its inception in the early 1930's, when the labor racketeer, George Browne, became associated with Willie Bioff, and the pair started to extort money from Chicago theater owners. Their activities were so lucrative that top-ranking members of the Capone gang immediately declared themselves partners in the illegal enterprise. The backing which Browne received from the Capone gangsters was also a boon to his personal ambition and he was elected president of the International Alliance of Theatrical Stage Employees and Motion Picture Operators. The syndicate now controlled the International Alliance.

In connection with the gang's extortion operations in Chicago,

Nick Circella (alias Nick Dean) was the collector. In 1938, Circella and George Browne used $65,000 which they had extorted from movie-house proprietors to open the Colony Club located on the near North Side at 744 Rush Street. The Colony Club was one of the most lavishly furnished gambling establishments in Chicago. On the first floor there were usually in progress at least a half dozen "26" dice games which were under the management of Estelle Carey, Circella's girl friend. She was later, on February 2, 1943, the victim of one of Chicago's bizarre and highly publicized gang killings. The place enjoyed police protection until wide publicity was given the robbery of two film stars, Constance Bennett and Anita Louise. Evidence was developed indicating the robbery had been planned in the Colony Club, and it was raided and closed in March 1941.[2]

The Capone syndicate found the theater business profitable. Frank Maritote (alias Frank Diamond) made demands on a burlesque theater owner to admit him as a partner in the enterprise. The theater owner feared for his life, and he acceded to Maritote's demands. Another staunch syndicate member, Phil D'Andrea, was immediately placed on the payroll of the theater although he did no work. This situation was not unusual for this gunman. He had once been carried on the public payrolls as a bailiff in the Municipal Court of Chicago and as an employee of the Board of Election Commissioners. D'Andrea was never accused of overworking on either job. But his official connection with Chicago courts and the election machinery clearly indicated the close relationship which existed between the Capone gang and officialdom. Chicago was indeed an ideal place for the gangsters' illegal operations. Through greed, however, they extended their extortionist operations to New York City and to Hollywood. Until a Federal grand jury in New York City returned an indictment against Nick Circella, George Browne and Willie Bioff on September 9, 1941, the plot had yielded the gangsters over a million dollars. Circella entered a plea of guilty on March 8, 1942, and received a sentence of eight years in a Federal penitentiary in addition to a fine of $10,000.

The Federal government was far from through with its investigation, however, and on March 18, 1943, the United States Grand Jury for the Southern District of New York returned two indictments. The first indictment charged a violation of the Federal Anti-

Racketeering Act and named as defendants Frank Nitti, Louis Campagna, Paul Ricca, Phil D'Andrea, Frank Maritote, Charles Gioe, Ralph Pierce, John Rosselli and Louis Kaufman. John Rosselli was the West Coast representative of the syndicate. Kaufman was an ex-convict labor leader from Newark, New Jersey. The second indictment charging a violation of the mail fraud statutes named the same defendants with the exception of Louis Kaufman. On the same day the indictments were returned, Frank Nitti committed suicide near his home, in Riverside, Illinois. A few months later the defendants were brought to trial in the United States District Court in New York City. Willie Bioff and George Browne gave testimony which revealed the parts played by their co-conspirators. On December 22, 1943, the jury found seven defendants guilty of the charges in the Anti-Racketeering indictment. On December 31, 1943, Louis Campagna, Paul Ricca, Phil D'Andrea, Charles Gioe, Frank Maritote and John Rosselli were each sentenced to serve ten years in a Federal penitentiary and fined $10,000. Louis Kaufman received a sentence of seven years imprisonment and a fine of $10,000. Their convictions on the anti-racketeering indictments were appealed and affirmed. After having disregarded all the rules of society with impunity for so many years the Capone gangsters at last learned that laws were intended to apply to them as well as to lesser hoodlums. Chicagoans, in particular, heaved a sigh of relief as Federal prison doors closed on these members of the most notorious criminal gang in America's history. The defendants were not brought to trial on the second indictment charging mail fraud. It was believed, however, that this outstanding indictment would act as a detainer which would prevent a premature release of the Capone gangsters from prison.

Paul Ricca, Louis Campagna and Phil D'Andrea were incarcerated in the United States Penitentiary in Atlanta, Georgia. Charles Gioe, Nick Circella and other defendants were lodged in the Federal Penitentiary in Leavenworth, Kansas. After a time, Paul Ricca and Louis Campagna became dissatisfied with the Atlanta prison and expressed a desire to be transferred to Leavenworth. The Atlanta prison officials objected because the transfer of Ricca and Campagna would violate the principles of sound prison administration. The Capone gangsters were not in the habit of having their requests denied, however, and even when behind bars they knew how to force recalcitrant officials to accede to their wishes. Through a former Missouri legislator, Edward M. "Putty Nose" Brady, the wife of Campagna retained a St. Louis attorney, Paul Dillon, to intercede on behalf of Ricca and Campagna. Dillon was a man of political influence. In 1934 he had served as the St. Louis campaign manager for President Truman when he was a candidate for the United States Senate. Boss Tom Pendergast, then in control of one of the most powerful political organizations in the nation, had personally asked Dillon to manage Truman's St. Louis campaign. Dillon had also represented Tom Pendergast's chief political lieutenant, the gangster John Lazia, when he was indicted for income-tax evasion.

On May 19, 1945, Paul Dillon called on Frank Loveland, Assistant Director of the Bureau of Prisons in Washington, D. C. Explaining that he was a former campaign manager for President Truman, he made a request that Paul Ricca and Louis Campagna be transferred from Atlanta to Leavenworth. He was aware that a similar request had been denied by the Bureau of Prisons. Loveland informed Dillon that certain Leavenworth inmates were unfriendly to Campagna and Ricca and serious trouble might result if the request were granted. The matter was not dropped, however. On July 21, 1945, the warden of the United States Penitentiary in Atlanta directed a letter to officials in the Bureau of Prisons which read in part: "From information received, it is quite evident that money is being paid to obtain the transfer of these men to Leavenworth, and I do not believe they should be transferred at this time for this reason." Notwithstanding the vigorous objections of the warden of Atlanta Penitentiary and officials of the Bureau of Prisons in Washington, D. C., Paul Ricca and Louis Campagna were transferred to Leavenworth on August 8, 1945.

Almost immediately after Ricca and Campagna arrived in the Leavenworth prison they began receiving frequent visits from Tony Accardo, regarded as the head of the Capone syndicate following Frank Nitti's suicide. With Accardo on such occasions was Chicago attorney Eugene Bernstein. Penitentiary regulations limited visits with convicts to attorneys or relatives, but Accardo overcame this obstacle by falsely representing himself to the prison officials as attorney Joseph I. Bulger of Chicago. The visits of Accardo and

Bernstein with the convicts in the Leavenworth Penitentiary were not of a social nature — Ricca and Campagna had urgent business to transact with them. By the summer of 1947 they would have served one third of their ten-year sentence — the minimum period of incarceration required before they were eligible to apply for parole. And they were intent upon securing their release at that time. As leading members of a murderous gang, they could not possibly qualify for parole upon serving the minimum period of their original sentence. That factor, however, was not troublesome to them. Their years of experience with local officials had completely convinced the gangsters that the merit of their parole applications would be unimportant. But there were two legal barriers that necessarily had to be removed before any parole applications could receive favorable consideration. In the first place, the Federal government had outstanding income-tax claims against Campagna and Ricca amounting to approximately a half-million dollars. In the second place, as long as the mail fraud indictment was outstanding against the imprisoned gangsters, they could not gain their freedom on parole.

Through the efforts of attorney Bernstein the gangsters settled their tax bills at bargain prices. Their government debt was liquidated for $126,000 plus interest. Benevolent but totally unidentified members of the Capone syndicate visited the Chicago law office of Eugene Bernstein and dumped thousands of dollars on his desk. This money represented profits to the gang from gambling, and it was to be used to pay the tax debts of Campagna and Ricca to the United States government. The action on the part of syndicate gamblers in furnishing the money clearly proved that the Capone gang was still a closely-knit underworld organization which was ruled with discipline. Honest citizens are required to work and struggle to support their families. Their taxes must be paid in full. But Campagna and Ricca, who had amassed fortunes without labor and through illegal enterprises, were permitted to discharge their debts by paying only a small percentage of the amount owed. And the favorable treatment they received at the hands of the Federal government in the tax settlement was not due to their inability to pay the full amount of the claim against them. Campagna later admitted that between 1937 and 1940 his share of the profits from the two Cicero gambling dens, the El Patio and the Austin Club, amounted to $204,152. Moreover, his actual profits were probably much higher. "Little New York" Campagna owned an eight-hundred-acre farm located near Fowler, Indiana, valued at $175,000, and another near Berrien Springs, Michigan, worth $50,000. Ricca admitted that his income from gambling establishments over a five-year period before his conviction averaged from $50,000 to $100,000 a year. From the proceeds of his illegal activities Paul Ricca had purchased a country estate of 1100 acres in Kendall County, Illinois, about twenty-five miles from Joliet. This place alone was worth about a half-million dollars. He owned an expensive home in the exclusive Chicago suburb of River Forest. Another, valued at $75,000, was located in Long Beach, Indiana, but this had burned down a few years earlier. On the very day he was released on parole, Ricca possessed $300,000 in cash. Campagna and Ricca were in fact moneyed aristocrats — aristocrats of the underworld. Their real estate holdings alone loudly refuted the time-worn adage that crime doesn't pay. It had paid big dividends to these gangsters.

Having thus settled the government tax claims against them, Campagna and Ricca began laying plans to secure the dismissal of the indictment charging them with mail fraud. This indictment could not be dismissed without the consent of the Attorney General of the United States. As products of the Chicago underworld, the Capone gangsters had long engaged the services of some of the city's most successful criminal attorneys. Now, however, they turned elsewhere to retain counsel who could assure the dismissal of the mail-fraud indictment. The attorney selected was Maury Hughes, of Dallas, Texas. For many years Hughes had been a political associate of Tom Clark, the Attorney General of the United States. Hughes testified before a congressional committee that he was retained on behalf of the gangsters by a man who used the name of Mike Rein, reputedly the owner of a string of race horses. Rein was a complete mystery man. His identity was never established, and his attorney, Hughes, seemed to know nothing about him. He could not even remember a telephone number through which Rein could be located. It was apparent, however, that the mysterious Rein was always on hand when needed. Hughes went to New York City where he talked with representatives of the United States Attorney's office. He visited Washington, D. C., where he conferred with several men in the Attorney General's office. He was assured that the mail-fraud indictment would be dismissed. It was. On the same day that Hughes was able to deliver a certified copy of the dismissal of the indictment, $14,000 in cash was paid to him for his services. He had previously received $1000 to cover his expenses.

The imprisoned gangsters had reason to be well satisfied with the strategy they had thus far employed. Their selection of counsel had proved excellent. Everything was proceeding according to schedule. Only one hurdle remained — their actual release on parole. The minimum prison term the gang leaders were required to serve before they could apply for parole was about to expire, and they intended to secure their freedom on the earliest possible date. Again they dispatched attorney Paul Dillon to Washington, D. C. On August 6, 1947, Dillon called at the Parole Department headquarters and requested paroles for Paul Ricca, Louis Campagna, Charles Gioe and Phil D'Andrea. The true character of these men had been officially described in a memorandum submitted by the Federal prosecutor to the Attorney General just the preceding year. Said this official, "The convicted defendants are notorious as successors to the underworld power of Al Capone. They are vicious criminals who would stop at nothing to achieve their ends. The investigation and prosecution were attended by murder, gun play, threatening of witnesses, perjury." Notwithstanding the known viciousness of the convicts, their release on parole suddenly became an urgent matter. Immediately following Paul Dillon's visit to the Washington Parole Department, representatives of the parole board in Chicago received telephone instructions from Washington headquarters to telegraph approval of the parole plans. Apparently there was no time to wait for the usual typewritten report. Likewise, the release of the gangsters from prison was so urgent that there was no time to make the customary investigation of the parole advisers. In some instances only a few questions were asked of the parole adviser as to his background and reputation and his answers were accepted as final. A proper investigation would have required about three weeks. On August 13, 1947, just one week after Dillon's Washington visit, Paul

Ricca, Louis Campagna, Phil D'Andrea and Charles Gioe were released on parole.

The parolees were leaders of one of the country's most vicious criminal gangs. The Federal government had been presented with an opportunity to strike a crippling blow at the power of this underworld organization. Instead, it bestowed undeserved favors upon four members of the gang. Political friends and associates of the Attorney General and the President of the United States had actively worked in their behalf as paid legal advisers. With the early release of the four gangsters on parole, the Capone syndicate again demonstrated the tremendous strength and power of the organized underworld.[3]

A congressional committee initiated an investigation of the parole scandal. Lengthy hearings were held in Chicago and Washington, and numerous witnesses were called upon to testify. It was brought out that a Republican politician, Harry Ash, while superintendent of the Division of Crime Prevention for the State of Illinois, had written letters to the Board of Pardons and Paroles in May 1947, urging the parole of the Capone mobster, Charles Gioe, and offering to serve as his parole adviser. The publicity given this incident by the press resulted in the resignation of Ash as state superintendent of crime prevention just a few days before the congressional committee hearings began. Gioe, who gave his occupation as gambler when arrested in 1943, had also once been affiliated with a so-called crime prevention project. During the New York World's Fair in 1939 and 1940, he had profited from a commercial amusement enterprise named "Crusaders Against Crime, Inc."

As a result of the evidence developed by the congressional committee, proceedings were started against three of the parolees to force their return to the Federal penitentiary. Phil D'Andrea, the one-time close friend of Bathhouse John Coughlin and Hinky Dink Kenna, was unmolested. Campagna and Gioe were finally placed behind prison bars again, but their lawyers instituted court action which freed them. Later, a Federal appellate court ordered them returned to prison. The case finally reached the United States Supreme Court late in 1950, and although the highest tribunal refused to upset the appellate court decision, new legal proceedings were instituted which enabled Campagna and Gioe to remain at large.

Through clever legal maneuvers Paul Ricca retained his freedom to enjoy the luxuries of his home in River Forest and his country estate in Kendall County. The misrepresentations made by Tony Accardo as to his name and occupation when he visited the Federal penitentiary with Eugene Bernstein resulted in action by a Chicago Federal grand jury. Both Bernstein and Accardo were later acquitted, however. After several months of uncertainty, Accardo once again assumed leadership in the infamous Capone gang without any Federal proceedings hanging over his head. And it was obvious to Accardo, Ricca and other Capone gangsters, as well as to casual observers, that the underworld organization they headed would be a strong going concern for many years to come.

The congressional committee hearings regarding the parole scandal were barely completed when the political influence of the underworld was again felt in suburban Cicero. For three decades Cicero had remained a stronghold for the Capone gang's gambling and vice operations. Throughout most of that period officials friendly to leading members of the syndicate held key positions in the village government and the wide-open policy prevailed in the most reprehensible meaning of that term. On April 19, 1948, however, John C. Stoffel, a business executive of high integrity, became the village president. He had been elected by an uprising of decent citizens who were hopeful of eliminating the conditions that had given the village its evil reputation. Stoffel promptly appointed Joseph Horejs, a patrolman, to the position of superintendent of police, with instructions to close Cicero's gambling and vice dens, many of which were flourishing in the heart of the business district. The new superintendent of police took his oath of office seriously. This, in itself, was a novel experience in Cicero. A prominent Capone syndicate collector called on Horejs and offered him $100,000 in cash if he would permit gambling places to operate. The offer was rejected. The gamblers then resorted to threats and intimidation, but neither Horejs nor Stoffel relented in their fight against the criminal elements. As a result, many of the gambling establishments operated by powerful members of the Capone syndicate were closed, and others moved outside of Cicero to unincorporated areas where the local police department could not reach them.

Stoffel's policy of strict law enforcement touched off a stormy political battle which raged for several months. And in the center of this controversy was Joseph Horejs. Since Horejs would not cooperate with the gambling chiefs, it was imperative that he be removed as the head of the police department, and a concerted drive was initiated to discredit his efforts. When this movement proved ineffective, the village board of Cicero passed an ordinance over the vigorous objection of Stoffel, which divested the village president of control over the police department. As soon as the ordinance was passed, Horejs was ousted as superintendent of police and in his place was appointed a former Cicero superintendent whose previous administration had been characterized by the tolerance of widespread gambling. This action left Stoffel with the responsibility but without the power to enforce the law. In protest, Stoffel resigned as village president, blaming in part the "corrupt influences" which he said "seem to have a strangling mortgage on our political life." [4]

After Stoffel resigned as village president, he waged a vigorous campaign to change Cicero's form of government as a means of eliminating gambling and improving law enforcement in the Chicago suburb. Actively assisting Stoffel in this campaign was Frank J. Christenson, a former assistant state's attorney and township assessor who enjoyed an excellent reputation. On December 9, 1949, Christenson was murdered outside his home in Cicero. A short time later gunmen blocked the path of an automobile driven by Stoffel but he quickly backed his car away and eluded them. The *Chicago Tribune* editorially remarked:

> The most probable explanation of the murder of Christenson was that it was committed by men paid for the job by gamblers. . . . The profits [of the gambling business] are such that the men in the business frequently murder competitors to keep a monopoly. Sometimes, as in Cicero, they grow so bold as to murder those who try to clean up gambling. That is the reason why no community can tolerate gambling and retain either self-respect or decent government.[5]

Based on a long experience, the residents of Cicero were certainly in a position to appreciate fully the soundness of these observations. Early in 1948, the gamblers of Cook County were being harassed on many fronts. In Cicero, the law-enforcement program of John C. Stoffel and his superintendent of police was driving them out of business. In Chicago, the Kennelly administration was keeping the number of gambling rooms down to a minimum. And in some of the suburban towns where gambling houses were tolerated, armed gunmen were descending on the places and stripping them of their cash. During the holdup of a gambling room in Elmwood Park, on May 2, 1948, there was some shooting and Paul Waszczyk, a patron, was killed. The incident was given much publicity, which was naturally bad for business, and it became imperative that the gamblers take prompt and drastic action against the rival gunmen who were causing them so much trouble. On May 22, 1948, George "Bulldog" Stathatos, who was commonly known as the "Barboot King" from his operation of a dice game called barbudi, was shot and killed. Only a few hours later, on May 23, assassins who had been searching for Leo "Little Sneeze" Friedman located him on Chicago's West Side. Frantically, Friedman attempted to escape, but after a chase of less than two blocks the pursuing gunmen pumped three bullets in his head and he dropped dead near the intersection of Sacramento and Jackson Boulevards. Friedman was a close associate of Stathatos and was believed by police to have been implicated in the robbery of the Elmwood Park gambling house. He was a tough hoodlum and had served seven years in Federal prison for the robbery of the St. Charles National Bank in 1936. He was also an associate of Edward P. Jones, the millionaire policy king on Chicago's South Side. Only a few days after Friedman was slain, his friend, Norton Polsky, an ex-convict and gambler, was pursued by a three-man firing squad after he left a West Side theater in the early morning hours of June 9, 1948. Just before he arrived at his home at 1865 South Springfield Avenue in Chicago, the gunmen killed him. Polsky was a former associate of two prominent gamblers of Chicago's important Twenty-fourth Ward, Harry "The Greener" Krotish, who was assassinated on December 10, 1947, and Willie Tarsch who met a violent death at the hands of rival gunmen on April 7, 1945.[6]

Murder and politics have always been closely identified with the gambling business in Chicago. At the time that gunmen were formulating definite plans for the murder of Norton Polsky, gambling-house proprietors in the Forty-fifth Ward on Chicago's North Side were giving a demonstration of their political power in that area. For some time a handbook had operated in a garage in the rear of

3025-29 North Greenview Avenue. This establishment was not equipped with sanitary facilities and every day the patrons and employees of this place created nuisances in an alley which was almost directly in the rear of a clean and respectable restaurant operated by Nona Ackley, at 3031 North Greenview Avenue. The conduct of the gambling-house patrons was offensive to civilized concepts of decency and violated health regulations. In desperation, Nona Ackley, the restaurant owner, approached two of the gambling-house employees on June 8, 1948, and pleaded with them to put a stop to the indecent conduct which was defiling the alley almost adjacent to her lunchroom. Immediately, city license, health and building inspectors descended on Miss Ackley's restaurant for the obvious purpose of harassing her. The police, who had taken no action against the illegal handbook, promptly stationed a twenty-four-hour watch on the restaurant. A precinct captain of the ward political organization telephoned Miss Ackley and told her to leave the community. Other threatening calls were received from persons who did not identify themselves. She was driven out of business. It was quite evident that the gamblers controlled the law-enforcement machinery in that section of the city and their political power was sufficient to punish a legitimate businesswoman who had the temerity to register a complaint against their illegal activities.[7]

In September 1948, the *Chicago News* in a forceful editorial urged the election of honest men to break the existing alliances between crime and government. The editorial charged that "the gambling syndicates actually control large segments of the government of Illinois at all levels. They control because they control politicians who occupy public office or those who run the party machinery." And, said the editorial, "Unless this corrupt alliance between politics and crime is broken, representative government in Illinois — or anywhere the alliance exists — will be destroyed." [8] In every section of the state the effect of powerful alliances between gambling syndicates and politicians on representative government was very apparent. In Pulaski County, located in the southern part of Illinois, there were wholesale vote frauds in the primary held on April 13, 1948. United States Attorney William W. Hart convened a special grand jury in Cairo, Illinois, to investigate charges that gamblers had used their lucrative profits to "purchase votes and influence voters." One prominent official admitted that the gamblers had "donated" regularly for the privilege of operating in Pulaski County.[9]

Adjoining Cook County on the north is Lake County where gambling rooms and slot machines have flourished for many years for the benefit of corrupt officials and hoodlums. For some time, the most elaborate gambling casino in Lake County, known as the Vernon Country Club, was operated by Rocco Fischetti. A special grand jury in January 1948 returned indictments against Fischetti, his casino manager, August D. Liebe and others. Before the investigation ended, criminal prosecution was instituted against scores of gamblers and politicians, many of whom were fined. The close relationship between powerful Lake County political figures and gangsters who enjoyed gambling concessions in the area was clearly revealed by the grand jury investigation. Yet several months later, on December 15, 1948, a Lake County gambler, Albert Cranor, entered a plea of guilty in a Federal Court in Chicago to a charge of having evaded income taxes amounting to several thousand dollars. The income on which the government's case was based came from the operation of slot machines and poker games in Lake County. Cranor's establishment, located near Waukegan, had served as a meeting place and headquarters for many prominent politicians. Following his plea of guilty he made an application for probation and several Lake County officials, including the state's attorney, the sheriff, the mayor of the county seat, Waukegan, and the chief of police of Lake Forest, wrote letters in his behalf to the Chicago Federal court praising the gambler's integrity and good character.[10]

In Peoria, scandal after scandal had rocked the community. For many years the murderous Shelton gang headed by three brothers, Carl, Bernie, and Earl, had terrorized central and southern Illinois. On one occasion the Sheltons won wide attention when they used tanks and airplanes in waging open warfare against rival gangsters. For almost eight years, prior to the reform administration of Mayor Carl O. Triebl which started in 1945, the gang leader, Carl Shelton, practically ran the city of Peoria, and his relations with county officials were most cordial. To a candidate for sheriff, he contributed $1000 for his campaign expenses and after his election he presented the new law-enforcement official with a pearl-handled revolver. In

1947, the sheriff accompanied Carl Shelton to the Kentucky Derby. The officials and the Sheltons were just one big happy family.

The gang leader's public relations with some of his gang rivals were not progressing so satisfactorily, however. On October 23, 1947, Carl Shelton was ambushed and slain near his Fairfield, Illinois, farm; his brother, Bernie, succeeded him as head of the gang's illicit activities. Bernie's rule was stormy but short-lived. On May 30, 1948, he and two associates pistol-whipped Richard Murphy, and indictments were returned in Peoria charging them with assault with intent to kill. Bernie claimed that a man who represented himself as an intermediary for the state's attorney called on him and offered to "fix" the case for $25,000, and he produced a recording of his conversation with this man to substantiate his charges. In the meantime, it was reported that the Chicago Capone syndicate was attempting to wrest control over gambling in central and southern Illinois from the Shelton gang, and a reward of $20,000 had been offered for the murder of top men in the Shelton organization. On July 26, 1948, Bernie Shelton was shot and killed in the parking lot of his Parkway Tavern on Farmington Road near Peoria. In September 1948, a Peoria county grand jury reported, "There is much evidence that too many officials are too closely associated with racketeers and gangsters . . ." In a front-page editorial in the Peoria *Journal* on September 8, 1948, it was declared, "Most Peorians don't like the reputation their city has acquired . . . Peoria is wallowing in the depths of infamy . . ." [11]

The Association of Commerce, the Council of Churches, the American Legion and other bodies in Peoria demanded a full-scale inquiry regarding charges of official corruption in that community. Theodore C. Link, an outstanding crime reporter for the *St. Louis Post-Dispatch*, had written numerous articles exposing conditions in Peoria. His articles charged that the Shelton gang had maintained alliances with some of the state officials and an employee of the office of the attorney general was named as a collector of gambling graft. Under the pressure of numerous civic bodies, Attorney General George Barrett assigned representatives of his office to conduct a grand jury investigation in Peoria in October 1948. A previous grand jury in September had praised Link for the assistance he had given its inquiry which uncovered evidence of official corruption. Yet upon conclusion of the attorney general's grand jury investigation, it was reported that no evidence of vice, gambling or official corruption could be developed. But reporter Theodore Link was indicted! He was charged with having kidnaped and intimidated Peter J. Petrakos whom he had questioned as a suspected finger man in the murder of Bernie Shelton. The indictment of the *St. Louis Post-Dispatch* reporter, however, proved to be a colossal political blunder. The Committee on Information of the American Society of Newspaper Editors, in commenting on the indictment, charged that "this would appear to be an effort by politicians to silence criticism and investigation." [12] The public was quick to show its wrath. The Illinois voters directed their ire at the Republican administration then in power, and in November 1948, they elected the Democratic candidate, Adlai Stevenson, as governor of the state. A few weeks later, the indictment against Link was dismissed on the recommendation of the Peoria prosecutor who advised the court that there was no evidence available to support a conviction.

Completely unperturbed by the results of the state election was Chicago's powerful Capone syndicate. As long as it could keep friends and associates in the right places, the Capone gang knew that its political power would continue. Some of the city's most influential ward committeemen had been friends of leading members of the gang for many years. The election of an outstanding civic leader and businessman as mayor in 1947 neither destroyed the ward organization of the old Kelly machine nor appreciably reduced its power. From wards which have long been strongholds of the Capone gang, the state receives many of its lawmakers. These legislators function as a unit to defeat and obstruct the enactment of laws which would be beneficial to the city and the state. Known as the West Side bloc, this small group of state representatives and senators frequently holds the balance of power in the legislature. During the long regime of Mayor Edward J. Kelly the votes of the West Side bloc in the Illinois General Assembly were at Kelly's command. They were frequently used against Kelly's mortal political enemy, Governor Henry Horner. Ruthless in tactics, impervious to criticism by the general public or the press and willing to resort to any means in achieving an end, the West Side bloc comprises the most feared group in the state legislature.

During two successive sessions of the Illinois General Assembly, in 1947 and 1949, five bills were introduced which were designed to improve the administration of criminal justice. Originally proposed by the Chicago Crime Commission these bills were sponsored by some of the outstanding members of the Senate and the House. They had wide support in the press and were endorsed by many civic and professional groups. All legislation is naturally controversial. Real or imaginary defects may be present in almost any law that may be proposed. One of the suggested crime bills, however, was merely intended to place the grand juries of Cook county on an equal basis with those of other counties in Illinois. In each of one hundred and one counties in Illinois, a grand jury can remain in session from sixty days in some to six months in others. In Cook County alone, prior to 1951, the grand-jury term expired at the end of thirty days and could not be extended. This limited term was frequently a serious handicap to grand-jury inquiries in Chicago relating to organized gambling, syndicated crime or official corruption. On several occasions a grand jury's term expired in the midst of an important investigation. The new grand jury impaneled often failed to grasp the full significance of the inquiry in progress and the investigation would die. The proposed bill was intended to correct this defect by permitting a grand jury to complete a particular investigation through the extension of its term for a period not to exceed a total of three months. No reasonable legislator of unassailable motives could seriously object to this proposed bill. None did.

A vicious, well-organized attack was launched against all five crime bills by the West Side bloc in both the 1947 and 1949 sessions of the legislature. In the Senate the fight was spearheaded by Roland V. Libonati, originally a Republican who turned Democrat after Mayor Kelly gained control of the city. Libonati, together with most of his colleagues in the House of Representatives fighting the crime bills, was from the old "Bloody Twentieth" Ward, once the scene of much violence and a stamping ground for important members of the old Capone mob. During the heyday of the Capone regime in Chicago, the press featured pictures of Libonati at Wrigley Field attending a baseball game in the company of Al Capone, "Machine Gun" Jack McGurn, and bodyguards. Libonati was originally elected a state representative on the Republican ticket in 1929.

The following year he was present in a room at 901 South Halsted Street in Chicago when the police raided it on November 4, 1930. Among those brought to police headquarters by the raiding officers were Paul Ricca, Ralph Pierce, Murray Humphreys, and Frank Rio, all staunch members of the Capone gang, and such political figures as Al Prignano, an alderman and state representative, Saul Tannenbaum, affiliated with the city attorney's office, and Libonati. Guns and political paraphernalia were also seized. Rushing to police headquarters to rescue Libonati and his friends were Alderman William V. Pacelli, who was then regarded as Al Capone's mouthpiece in the city council, Senator James B. Leonardo and City Sealer Dan Serritella.[13]

In 1947 there were only three votes registered against the proposed grand jury bill by members of the Senate judiciary committee. Two of the dissenting votes were cast by Roland V. Libonati and Lawrence E. Dowd. Senator Dowd was a protégé of Hinky Dink Kenna and Bathhouse John Coughlin and their First Ward organization. Dowd, a lawyer, has specialized in the defense of gamblers. In 1947 alone he represented almost five hundred defendants charged with gambling violations in Chicago. After the Senate passed the grand jury bill in 1947 it ordinarily would have been referred to the judiciary committee of the House. The West Side bloc had carefully appraised the sentiment of the members of that committee. They feared a favorable vote on the bill there would result in its referral to the members of the House with a strong possibility of enactment. It was therefore determined that neither the members of the judiciary committee nor the House as a body should have an opportunity to express the will of their constituents. Through the maneuvering of Republican Representative Peter C. Granata from Libonati's district, the bill was sidetracked; due to his obstructionist tactics a vote on the bill was prevented. Ably assisting the West Side bloc in defeating the legislation recommended by the Chicago Crime Commission was the law firm of Bieber and Brodkin. George Bieber and Michael Brodkin had long been known as the attorneys for Jack Guzik and the Capone syndicate. In 1947 an associate of this law firm represented over one thousand defendants charged with gambling violations in Chicago. The attorney for Paul Ricca also regularly appeared before legislative committee meetings in Springfield to oppose all five bills that were designed to improve the administration of criminal justice in Illinois.[14]

At the next session of the Illinois Legislature in 1949 the same forces again spearheaded the opposition to the five crime bills. Notwithstanding the vigorous fight waged by Senator Roland V. Libonati, the Senate passed three of the bills. The proposed legislation had the full support of Governor Adlai Stevenson, Mayor Martin H. Kennelly, Cook County State's Attorney John S. Boyle, the Illinois State's Attorney's Association, the Chicago Bar Association, numerous civic bodies and the Chicago press. Public sentiment, however, meant nothing to the West Side bloc which was dedicated to the defeat of the crime bills. The leadership of this group in the House was centered around James Adduci and Andrew A. Euzzino. When James Adduci was originally elected to the House of Representatives in 1934, the press stormed that Chicago had blundered into sending a pal of the Capone mobster Dago Lawrence Mangano to the legislature. Adduci's associations and background hardly recommended him for his role as a lawmaker. In 1931 he was questioned by the police in connection with the murder of Mike "de Pike" Heitler, the gambler and brothel keeper who once helped Al Capone get started in the vice business. A letter purportedly written by Heitler was found a few days after his death. In it he listed the names of those who might desire his demise. Among the names mentioned was that of the future lawmaker James Adduci. In 1933 Adduci was arrested by the police with Willie Bioff, the pander, who was later convicted with Capone gangsters in the million-dollar movie extortion plot and committed to a Federal penitentiary. Adduci's pal Dago Lawrence Mangano was one of the most important figures in Chicago's huge gambling empire. Neither Adduci's conflicts with the police nor his friends, such as Bioff and Mangano, have inspired him with a burning desire to strengthen the criminal statutes.[15]

Of equal importance with Adduci in directing the battle against the crime bills was Andrew A. Euzzino. Euzzino's political sponsor, Pete Fosco, the boss of the First Ward, is admittedly a good friend of Paul Ricca. In May 1949, when efforts were made to take the proposed grand jury bill away from the judiciary committee and place it directly before the House of Representatives, Euzzino started a filibuster. This action incensed the public. Blistering editorials denouncing the tactics of Euzzino appeared in the *Chicago News*, *Chicago Tribune* and *Sun-Times*. On May 23, 1949, the *News* warned that a compromise on the filibuster instigated by Euzzino would be tantamount to a surrender to the gangs. Said this editorial:

The filibuster against the bill to extend the life of Cook County grand juries is scheduled to get underway in the Illinois House of Representatives Tuesday. This filibuster is another brazen attempt by the powerful forces of Chicago's underworld to protect racketeers, hoodlums, organized gambling, organized crime and the gangster syndicate that has succeeded the old Capone gang.[16]

In the face of mounting public resentment and editorial lashings from the press, the West Side bloc merely redoubled its efforts to defeat the crime bills. The open fighting in the House of Representatives was largely in the hands of Adduci and Euzzino. But they received effective support from Representative Robert "Happy" Petrone, Peter C. Granata, John D'Arco and others. Petrone was a protégé of Alderman William V. Pacelli and a friend of Tony Accardo. Granata was once elected to Congress, but his opponent charged that Granata's success at the polls had been the result of bombing and violence by the Capone gang. A re-count was ordered and after it was evident that Granata had actually been defeated he was unseated in April 1932. He was subsequently elected to the state legislature. Leaving no stone unturned, the West Side bloc in the general assembly imported Joseph Porcaro from Chicago to aid in the battle. At that time Porcaro, the Republican committeeman from the Twenty-eighth Ward, was on the payroll of the county treasurer in Chicago. For several weeks he spent most of his time in Springfield. Although not a member of the legislature, he was on the floor of the house working daily with his colleagues against the proposed legislation.[17] Chicago newspapers exposed his extracurricular activities and Porcaro was dropped from the payroll of the county treasurer's office. In order to assure the defeat of the crime bills, members of the West Side bloc offered to support the pet bills of other legislators in return for votes against the legislation proposed by the Chicago Crime Commission. Many representatives were willing to deal with the Adduci-Euzzino combination. One downstate legislator, who has aspired to become a justice in the Illinois Supreme Court, was overheard talking with a member of the bloc. This would-be statesman said, "I haven't read any of the Crime Commission bills but I'll vote against every last one of them. You can depend upon it." When trading tactics failed to win the support of a legislator to the cause of the West Side bloc, he was subjected to cajoling, threats or intimidation.

The obstructionist efforts of the Adduci-Euzzino group were not limited to the Crime Commission bills. A similar fight was waged against Governor Adlai Stevenson's proposal to revise the state constitution. The governor had campaigned vigorously for a constitutional convention and he attempted to secure action by the legislature which would enable him to fulfill his pre-election pledges to the people. Members of the West Side bloc indicated they would drop their fight against the constitutional convention provided Governor Stevenson would withdraw his support from the crime bills. A similar offer was made to cease the obstructionist tactics against a revision of the constitution if the governor would support a measure to legalize gambling.[18] To the credit of the governor, both proposals were rejected and the constitutional convention met the same fate as the crime bills, all of which were defeated.

As the 1949 session of the Illinois General Assembly was drawing to a close, Milburn P. Akers, political editor of the *Chicago Sun-Times* wrote, "The current legislative session . . . has reached an all-time low-ebb." He called for co-ordinated action on the part of the decent, progressive forces of the state in order to "improve a steadily worsening situation."[19] There was a response to this call for action — but it came primarily from the forces aligned with the West Side bloc. It was known that the crime bills would be re-introduced at the next session of the legislature, and as soon as the 1949 session ended the members of the bloc and their allies began making plans for the 1950 primaries. New candidates for the legislature were approached and attempts were made to exact promises from them that they would oppose the crime bills. Representatives and senators who had actively supported the crime bills in 1949 saw the fine hand of the West Side bloc in concerted drives to prevent their re-election.

On the South Side, Democratic representative Louis G. Berman was one of the legislators marked for defeat by the West Side bloc in the April 1950 primaries. Notwithstanding efforts to intimidate him, he had actively supported the crime bills during the 1949 session of the general assembly. Opposing Berman for the Democratic nomination from the Fifth District, which includes the Fourth Ward, was a lawyer who once was the attorney for the Capone gangster, Jack Guzik. As the primary race progressed, Berman discovered that powerful gambling interests in his district as well as the Democratic Fourth Ward committeeman, Joseph Plunkett, were secretly working for his opponent. Plunkett, incidentally, was originally the product of Hinky Dink Kenna's First Ward organization. The press leveled its fire against the tactics employed on the South Side to defeat Berman. The citizens of the district were angered and Berman was victorious. Following the primary, the Democratic County Committee headed by Chairman Jacob M. Arvey took official notice of the alleged double cross of the party's regular candidate, Louis G. Berman. Chairman Arvey reported to the county committee that he had verified reports that Plunkett had actively worked for the nomination of Berman's opponent, the former attorney for Jack Guzik. In an unusual move, Plunkett was deposed as the Democratic ward committeeman of the Fourth Ward and was also removed from the payroll as the deputy county clerk.[20]

It was in the First District, however, that the forces allied with the West Side bloc gave an amazing demonstration of their political power. The struggle centered around the primary race for state senator from this district which includes the rich First Ward and extends to the south to embrace the densely populated Second Ward, which is predominantly Negro. Presiding over the political affairs of the First Ward was Ward Committeeman Pete Fosco. In the Second Ward, the ruler was Negro Congressman William L. Dawson, vice-chairman of the Democratic National Committee and the political boss of the Negroes on Chicago's teeming South Side. Several years ago Dawson was the alderman of the Second Ward and a Republican. He switched to the Democratic banner when Edward J. Kelly was mayor, and during the Kelly regime became one of the most influential politicians in Chicago.

About eighty per cent of the voters in the First District are Negroes, and with the backing of Congressman Dawson, a Negro candidate should win handily. In the April 1950 primary, Dr. Edward A. Welters, a strong Negro candidate, entered the Democratic race for state senator with the understanding that he would have the support of Dawson. Dr. Welters, a successful toilet-preparations manufacturer, was highly popular among the Negro voters. A few years earlier he had been elected to the Illinois House of Representatives as a Republican and dramatically resigned from that party on the floor of the House in 1945 as a protest against Republican opposition to an antidiscrimination bill. This action enhanced his popularity among the Negro voters of the First District, and with Congressman Dawson's support, Dr. Welters felt that his nomination was assured. He failed to take into consideration, however, the political strength of Ward Committeeman Pete Fosco and his friends; Fosco definitely had other plans. He issued an ultimatum that the coveted senate seat was to go to a virtually unknown young Italian, Fred B. Roti. In a signed statement to the Chicago Crime Commission, Dr. Welters charged that several weeks before the April 1950 primary he was visited by Congressman Dawson who offered him $10,000 to withdraw from the contest. When Welters turned down the offer, the amount was raised to $15,000. Welters still declined to withdraw and Dawson then informed him that he no longer considered himself obligated to support Welters's candidacy. Many of the Negro leaders of the First District were infuriated. Letters containing Dr. Welters's charges were sent to President Harry S. Truman, Governor Adlai Stevenson, Mayor Martin H. Kennelly and Cook County Democratic Chairman, Jacob M. Arvey. Congressman Dawson denied the allegations. But in a predominantly Negro district a strong Negro candidate was overwhelmingly defeated by an obscure Italian sales-tax investigator, Fred B. Roti, who had the support of Pete Fosco and company! [21]

In the Twenty-fifth District, the Democratic organization threw its support in the primary to Frank E. Harmon, who was seeking the nomination for state representative. Harmon held a $35,000 mortgage on the Miami Beach home of Al Capone at the time of the gang leader's death, and several years earlier, during the Kelly administration, Harmon had owned an interest in a handbook at 2613 Milwaukee Avenue in Chicago's Logan Square district. Harmon was a personal friend of former Mayor Kelly and first became influential politically during his regime.[22] In another district, the successful Republican nominee for state representative was formerly the aide to the boss of a union which was then dominated by the Capone syndicate. In district after district, vigorous campaigns were waged to secure the nomination of general assembly candidates who were either friendly with or obligated to known associates of the Capone organization.

As soon as the primary votes were counted, the eyes of the politicians turned toward the fall election. On the whole, the primary results were satisfactory to those political leaders who were allied with the gambling and racketeering interests. But they were disturbed over action that was being taken in several sections of the state. The Chicago Crime Commission, for example, made public a lengthy report on conditions in the Thirty-fifth or Chicago Avenue Police District on the near North Side. An extended investigation over a two-year period reflected that protected vice, gambling, flagrant liquor law violations and a number of perversion dens were flourishing in Chicago's well-known honky-tonk and night club area. There were charges of graft, and the activities of a police officer who was known as a collector for the district were related.

Mayor Kennelly promptly denounced the Crime Commission report and denied that the near North Side was a vice-ridden cesspool of crime and corruption. He vigorously defended the police department's fight on organized crime and was unusually incensed over the commission's conclusion that "there is no real intention in the police department or city administration to clean up prostitution, gambling, perversion and allied crime in the district." The mayor stated that instead of criticizing conditions in the Thirty-fifth Police District, which he later admitted before a grand jury were bad, the Crime Commission should praise the accomplishments of the police. In particular, he cited the outstanding police work performed in another district which had just resulted in the recovery of $500,000 worth of stolen merchandise from a notorious fence, Arthur "Fish" Johnson. The solution of this case, said the mayor, followed an entire year of careful planning and painstaking effort by the police. Ironically, only a few days later the case against Fish Johnson "blew up" in the criminal court. In two separate raids made by the police, the search warrants in each instance were faulty and the judge ruled that none of the confiscated stolen merchandise could be introduced as evidence in court against the defendant. Notwithstanding the mayor's denunciation of the Crime Commission's report, the *Chicago Sun-Times* pointed out that he "notably omitted comment on the Commission's specific charge that police and politicians are collecting . . . graft for winking at flagrant violations in the Chicago Avenue Police District." [23]

The commissioner of police when questioned by the press concerning the Crime Commission report lauded Captain Thomas Harrison, the commanding officer of the district under fire. He said that Captain Harrison had "cleaned up" more crimes of all types in the Chicago Avenue area than any other police captain in the city. When asked about the collector mentioned in the Crime Commission's report, the head of the police department replied that he had never been informed of the policeman's name and indicated he would make no effort to learn his identity. It was then brought out that a Chicago Crime Commission letter to the mayor and the commissioner of police in December 1947, had fully informed them concerning the name of the policeman and his activities as collector in the Thirty-fifth Police District. In fact, immediately following the receipt of the Crime Commission letter the collector was transferred to another police district. Early in 1948, however, Crime Commission investigators discovered that the collector was back in the Thirty-fifth District as active as ever. The official police records revealed that although he had not been reassigned to the Thirty-fifth District, he was sent back to his old stamping grounds on special detail as a result of orders emanating directly out of the office of the Commissioner of police. And during the furor raised over conditions in the Thirty-fifth Police District, two substantial out-of-town business executives visited one of the night spots in the area. When they objected to a padded check which was presented to them they were promptly surrounded by thugs and viciously assaulted. Several stitches were taken in the battered head of one of the executives while the other suffered a fractured ankle from a blow delivered with an iron bar. The case received much publicity and the license of the night spot was revoked. The police action was a trifle tardy, however. As far back as 1948, the Chicago Crime Commission had submitted to the police department a confidential report on scores of places that were flagrantly violating the law in the Thirty-fifth Police District. Among the places listed in the report was the one in which the business executives were assaulted.

A Cook County grand jury initiated an investigation into conditions in the Chicago Avenue District, and several police officers were interrogated. Much of their testimony was conflicting while some of it was downright absurd. The officers were asked to produce their income-tax returns before the grand jury but they flatly refused. Newspaper headlines and radio broadcasts featured the investigation and the business of the honky-tonks on the near North Side went into a temporary slump.

Elsewhere in the state, the racketeering elements were reeling under blows delivered by the state police. In an unusual move, Governor Stevenson directed the state police to conduct raids and confiscate gambling equipment in several localities where city and county officials were lax and corrupt. In a countermove, gamblers throughout the state of Illinois began to organize for the purpose of attempting to gain control of the House of Representatives in Springfield. This was the first step in a well-defined and adequately financed program aimed at securing the enactment of laws which would legalize gambling in Illinois. For five weeks, there was a series of daily broadcasts from several Illinois cities. These programs extolled the virtues of legalized gambling and emphasized, of course, the purported "easy revenue" which would pour into the coffers of the state from that source. Immediately following the series of broadcasts, the gamblers held two meetings on July 9 and 16, 1950, at a Springfield, Illinois club which has long been a favorite hangout of politicians. Attending these meetings were gamblers from every part of the state, and a campaign was planned which they hoped would enable the gambling interests to win control of the legislature.[24] This scheme was not a wild one without chance for success. After all, the underworld of which the gamblers were an important part, has frequently controlled government at various levels in Illinois.

As the first half of the twentieth century came to an end, thoughtful citizens somewhat shamefacedly viewed Chicago's record of political corruption, widespread crime and misgovernment. This record was largely one of civic failure — a record which was written by the social and economic parasites who had been permitted to become influential in the affairs of politics and government. But there was a much brighter picture of the city's history. This picture was one of rapid growth and development into one of the greatest centers of commerce, industry, finance and transportation in the entire world. It was a picture of towering skyscrapers, busy factories, crowded department stores, great universities, bustling railroad and airplane terminals. It was a record of achievement written by the ingenuity, industry and thrift of the substantial citizens of the community. The gamblers, vice lords and racketeers who had frequently guided the city's political destiny had contributed little, if any, to this record of accomplishment.

By 1950, Chicago's population had grown to 3,606,436, an increase of 209,628 or over six per cent during the preceding ten years. The only ten-year period in the city's history during which its population was virtually at a standstill was the one between 1930 and 1940. Some observers believed that a saturation point had been reached and the phenomenal growth which had marked every ten-year period of Chicago's existence before 1930 had ended. But with America's entry into World War II, conditions were suddenly changed. Chicago became one of the great arsenals of the nation and of the world. Thousands of persons migrated there to work in its factories. Between 1940 and 1950 the number of manufacturing plants within the city limits increased by 2453 and the number of workers employed in factories increased by 188,000. In 1939, wages paid by factories in the Chicago area amounted to $641,000,000. By 1950, this figure had soared to $2,180,000,000. According to the Association of Commerce, between 1941 and 1950 more money was invested in the Chicago industrial area, in land and plants for manufacturing purposes, than in any other industrial area in the United States.[25] No one could deny the virility of the industrial life of the nation's second-largest city. Unfortunately, Chicago's underworld could also boast of virility. Over a period of decades it had continued to grow in opulence and power. Its roots were deep and even the election of a mayor of unimpeachable character and integrity in 1947 had not seriously impaired its strength. Its influence was felt in ward politics, in the city council, in the state legislature and in the judiciary. Whenever the organized criminal element needed help it could get it. The underworld continued to keep its friends in the right places.

CHAPTER XI
Senator Kefauver Came to Town

BEFORE the summer months came to a close, both major political parties began making strong preparations for the 1950 fall election. It was soon evident that the campaign would be hard fought and bitter. This was assured when the Democratic organization named Captain Daniel A. Gilbert as its candidate for sheriff of Cook County. In recent years Democratic leader Jacob M. Arvey had enhanced his personal prestige as well as the reputation of his party by naming highly regarded candidates for key offices. He was credited with having forced the nomination of Martin H. Kennelly for mayor. It was to Arvey's credit that Adlai E. Stevenson became the Democratic governor of Illinois and Paul Douglas was elected to the United States Senate. But when Arvey announced Captain Daniel A. Gilbert as his choice for the key office of sheriff, he astounded even the members of his own party. U. S. Senator Paul Douglas was outraged and served notice that he would not actively campaign in behalf of Gilbert. Gilbert, who had amassed great wealth while a member of the Chicago Police Department and had served as chief investigator for the state's attorney's office since 1932, was a widely discussed figure. The Republican party promptly named J. Malachy Coughlan as its candidate. Several years earlier Coughlan had distinguished himself as an assistant state's attorney. While a member of the prosecutor's staff he had worked with Captain Gilbert and was an open and bitter critic of the chief investigator. It was expected that Coughlan would wage a furious campaign to defeat Gilbert.

But the worries of Cook County Democratic leaders were not solely confined to the type of campaign that might be waged against their candidate for sheriff. Their eyes were anxiously glued on the activities of a Special Committee of the United States Senate which had been appointed to investigate organized crime. Any inquiry into organized crime would naturally lead to Chicago, the home and base of operations of the Capone gang.

For many years the Chicago Crime Commission had been vigorously calling public attention to the insidious influence that syndicated crime was casting on government in many parts of the nation. Several honest mayors in widely-separated sections of the country were confronted with the organized efforts of powerful racketeering groups to drive them out of office. A number of these officials conferred with Chicago Crime Commission representatives requesting counsel and advice in fighting criminal syndicates that were attempting to control the political life of their municipalities. Many sincere officials were alarmed and public opinion was slowly mounting over the growing menace of these syndicates. Recognizing this problem, the American Municipal Association, at its annual convention held in Cleveland in December 1949, devoted considerable time to discussing methods of combatting syndicated crime. As the operating director of the Chicago Crime Commission, I addressed the closing session of the convention and it adopted resolutions which were intended to lay the groundwork for effective warfare against organized criminal groups throughout the nation. Widespread publicity was given the Cleveland convention of the American Municipal Association, which represents over 10,000 municipalities in the United States.[1]

Shortly after the Cleveland convention the Attorney General of the United States, J. Howard McGrath, announced that a conference on organized crime would be held in the nation's capital on February 15, 1950. All United States district attorneys as well as the mayors and police executives of America's principal cities were invited to attend. President Truman addressed the opening session of the conference and urged federal, state and local officials to cooperate in stamping out organized crime. The attorney general's conference lasted only one day but public interest was running high and demands for action were coming from many quarters. United States Senator Estes Kefauver from Tennessee introduced a resolution asking for an investigation of organized crime in interstate commerce.

There were several senators as well as a number of other influential politicians who had little enthusiasm for a public airing of gambling syndicates and their alliances with political organizations, and behind the scenes there was much maneuvering to sidetrack the resolution of Senator Kefauver. Then on April 6, 1950, headlines throughout the nation reported the double gang slaying of Charles Binaggio, the gambling king of Kansas City and one of the most powerful political bosses in Missouri, and his partner, Charles Gargotta, another widely-known gangster. The bullet-riddled bodies of these men were found in the First District Democratic Headquarters in Kansas City. Here was an ugly picture of the unholy alliance between crime and politics paraded before the entire American public. It was a picture that had more than passing interest in Chicago, since Binaggio was a partner in a lucrative beer distributorship with Tony Gizzo who had long been affiliated with the Capone gang. It was no longer politically expedient to ignore Senator Kefauver's resolution and a special committee was appointed to investigate organized crime in interstate commerce. Senator Kefauver was named chairman of this committee which also included Senators Herbert R. O'Conor of Maryland, Lester C. Hunt of Wyoming, Charles W. Tobey of New Hampshire and Alexander Wiley of Wisconsin. In May 1950, this committee began its investigation of organized gambling and crime in the United States and became popularly known as the Kefauver Committee.

The first hearing of the Kefauver Committee was held in Miami on May 26, 1950, and for the next several months its findings were headline news. Senator Kefauver, tall, dignified, soft-spoken and courteous, but determined and fearless, directed the activities of the committee without regard to partisan politics. He inspired public confidence as few men in political life had done before, and as never before on such a scale, he threw fear into the ranks of the gangster element and many of the political organizations as well. Numerous underworld leaders made themselves scarce, and some even departed for foreign shores. Politicians who were in the habit of exerting pressure to control official investigations found that their usual tactics failed to influence Senator Kefauver.

Toward the end of the summer of 1950, the Kefauver Committee published its first interim report which was based on its investigation in Florida. The report presented a sordid account of widespread crime, racketeering and official corruption — an account in which Chicago Capone gangsters figured prominently.[2] In August, an associate counsel of the Kefauver Committee, George S. Robinson, arrived in Chicago. Aided by the staff of the Chicago Crime Commission, which was later augmented by Committee investigators, Mr. Robinson initiated an investigation which was to lay the groundwork for hearings in Chicago at a later date. Almost as soon as Robinson launched his inquiry, there was a wholesale exodus of Capone gangsters and other underworld characters from Chicago and its environs. Charles Fischetti and Tony Accardo, who had been wearing the mantle of the deceased gang chief for many years, fled to Mexico. All prominent members of the Capone organization went into hiding. Even a state legislator who was a known associate of Capone mobsters avoided service of a subpoena for several weeks.

The presence of Mr. Robinson in the city was viewed with considerable alarm by a number of local politicians who were hopeful, however, that Chicago would be by-passed by Committee hearings until after the November election. Just as the campaign was about to begin in earnest, the Republican party was thrown into confusion when its candidate for sheriff of Cook County, J. Malachy Coughlan, died on August 25, 1950. Thus, at the last moment, the Republicans were confronted with the necessity of naming a new candidate for the key office of the campaign. John E. Babb, a lawyer and a veteran of World War II, was chosen to oppose the Democratic candidate, Captain Gilbert.

By the latter part of September, the political campaign was rapidly gaining momentum and pointing toward a whirlwind finish. But politics had to take a back seat while public interest centered mainly on the activities of the Kefauver Committee staff. Every day important witnesses were being privately interrogated and virtually tons of books and records were examined. Then within the space of a few hours on the night of September 25, 1950, two gang killings threw Chicago officials into a turmoil. A little before seven o'clock that night, William Drury, a former acting police captain, backed his Cadillac into the garage in the rear of his home at 1843 Addison Street on the North Side. With the usual precision of professional gang killing, Drury was struck in the head with four blasts from a shotgun and at least one bullet from an automatic pistol. He had no opportunity to reach for a revolver which he carried in the glove compartment of his car.

Drury's career in the Chicago police department had been both colorful and stormy. Once known as the "Watchdog of the Loop" for his numerous arrests of gangsters, he was discharged from the police force for refusing to testify before the grand jury in the investigation of the gang killing of James Ragen, the racing information wire service magnate, in 1946. Drury was an avowed enemy of Charles Fischetti, and he was scheduled to furnish information to the Kefauver Committee on September 26, the day following his murder. About three hours after the Drury assassination, Marvin J. Bas, a politician and an attorney who represented some of the near North Side night spots, was also shot and killed. Although there appeared to be no connection between the two murders, a lawyer asserted that Drury had telephoned Bas from the lawyer's office on the day of the double slaying.[3]

With public anger roused and the local election only a few weeks away, the city council met in a stormy session on October 4, 1950; a resolution was introduced asking for a Federal grand jury investigation of the twin murders. Typical of Chicago's official attitude toward organized crime was the angry statement of an alderman who insisted, "The people resent the great *publicity* given these killings. Chicago is not the crime center of the nation." This alderman and many of his colleagues were not greatly concerned over the breakdown in government which permitted the organized criminal element to commit two brazen gang killings in one night; it was the bad publicity which offended these statesmen.

The atmosphere was still charged with the excitement of murder and politics when Senator Estes Kefauver arrived in the city in October 1950, to preside over the first committee hearings held in Chicago. The murders of Drury and Bas had intensified public interest in the Senate committee's investigation. With the fall election but three weeks away, the proceedings of the Kefauver Committee gained even added significance when Captain Gilbert, the Democratic candidate for sheriff, appeared at the United States Courthouse on October 17, 1950, and was questioned in a closed executive session of the committee. Although the Senate Committee did not make public the text of Gilbert's testimony, it did reveal to the press that the Chicago police captain admitted having amassed a fortune exceeding a third of a million dollars by speculating in the stock and grain market. All local papers featured the story and editorials commented on the testimony. Actually, however, the bombshell did not explode until just a few days before the election. On November 2, 1950, the *Chicago Sun-Times,* which in years past had always supported Democratic candidates for major offices, hit the newsstands with the bold front-page headline: EXCLUSIVE! WHAT GILBERT TOLD KEFAUVER. Page after page of the newspaper was devoted to the full text of Captain Gilbert's testimony. Never before had the voters of Chicago been treated to such intimate details of a fabulous success story from the lips of a candidate for a major public office. His replies to questions from the committee explained how he, as a member of Chicago's underpaid police force, had risen to a position of wealth which gained for him the title of the "World's richest cop."

Before Gilbert became a member of the Chicago police department in 1917, he had served as secretary and treasurer of Local 725 of the Baggage and Parcel Delivery Drivers Union since 1913. His rise in the police force was phenomenal. After serving but five years as a patrolman he was promoted to the rank of sergeant; only one year later he became a lieutenant. By 1926 he had become a captain, and from 1931 until December 5, 1932, he held the rank of supervising captain. On December 5, 1932, he was assigned to the state's attorney's office as the chief investigator, a position he held continuously for eighteen years.

Gilbert's rise to affluence apparently began with his association with the powerful Democratic political boss, George Brennan, early in Gilbert's career as a police officer. As Boss Brennan's chauffeur and bodyguard, Gilbert accompanied him to a political convention in New York City in 1921. During this trip the political boss advised Gilbert to purchase Great Lakes Dredge and Dock stock. Gilbert had been speculating on the stock market since 1919 and he knew a hot tip when he heard one. The stock was selling at $18.00 a share when he made his initial purchase of 200 shares. Since he bought the stock on a ten per cent margin, his original investment amounted

to less than $400.00. With the stock soaring in price and by pur-
chasing additional shares on margin with the profits, Captain Gilbert
pyramided his investment until his holdings in Great Lakes Dredge
and Dock were worth $98,000 by September 1927. In addition to
his stock transactions he was also dealing in the grain market. When
the economic crash came in 1929, Gilbert lost much of his wealth,
but he managed to salvage $13,000 from his grain speculation and
$15,000 from his stock holdings.

Of the thousands of men who were ruined by the 1929 crash,
most of them never regained their riches. With Captain Gilbert,
the crash only retarded his accumulation of wealth for a few years.
He testified, ". . . I wound up with about $15,000 at the time of
the depression and I still had that $15,000 in 1931 and '32 and '33."
Beginning in 1933, however, he began speculating in stock again.
By October 1950, when he testified before the Kefauver Committee,
Gilbert's holdings were worth $360,000 and his admitted income for
1949 was $45,000. And the amazing part of this success story was
the negligible time and effort that he expended in building up a
fortune. The counsel for the Senate Committee was puzzled as to
when Captain Gilbert had time to perform his law enforcement
duties, since he was obviously carrying on a very active financial
business. His explanation astounded many men who had spent a
lifetime on financial LaSalle Street and had been able to eke out
but a modest living. Said Gilbert, "The telephone is all that does it."
By making a few telephone calls, which allegedly never interfered
with his vocation as a police officer, Captain Gilbert had been able
to amass a fortune.

The election campaign was nearing its end when Captain Gilbert's
testimony was made public on November 2. A major issue throughout the bitterly fought contest was gambling. Gilbert had assured
the voters that if he were elected sheriff he would drive all gambling places out of Cook County within six months. But Gilbert's
picture of himself as a crusader who would smash the gambling
interests was considerably dimmed by his testimony before the
Kefauver Committee. His income-tax returns which were examined
by the Committee reflected yearly profits from gambling. One of
his records established a wagering gain of $7310 in 1948. Gilbert
admitted that he gambled on football, baseball, prize fights and

elections, and some of his wagers amounted to thousands of dollars. In the 1936 election alone, he won about $12,000 betting on the successful Presidential candidate, Franklin D. Roosevelt. Gilbert's phenomenal success on the stock market followed his gambling ventures. He boasted to the Committee that he had won every election bet since 1921, a period of almost thirty years. When the Committee asked the candidate for sheriff where he placed his bets, he named the gambling establishment of John McDonald at 215 North LaSalle Street in Chicago. The counsel for the Senate Committee then inquired, "That is not legal betting, is it?" Gilbert answered, "No sir; it is not. Well, no, it is not legal, no." (He sounded surprised, as if he had never thought about it before.) Actually, the gambling establishment at 215 North LaSalle Street had operated in violation of the law for many years and no effective action had been taken against the place by either the police or the state's attorney's office. And here was a police captain and the chief investigator for the state's attorney admitting that he was making large profits from unlawful election wagers made with this illegal establishment. The Democratic candidate for sheriff explained, "I have been a gambler at heart." [4]

With the publication of Gilbert's testimony, the issues in the election were clear-cut. Some observers predicted that the Democratic machine would be able to roll up a sufficient majority of votes in the city of Chicago to enable Captain Gilbert to carry Cook County by a safe margin. These observers had failed to gauge the temper of the voter, however. On November 7, 1950, it was an angry throng that marched to the polls and Gilbert was overwhelmingly defeated in the city itself, the stronghold of the Democratic machine. John E. Babb, the last-minute Republican candidate, was elected by a majority of over 370,000 votes.

The citizen uprising against the Gilbert candidacy had far-reaching effects. Many Democratic voters had cast straight Republican ballots in protest. The Republicans captured a number of key county offices and won control of the important Sanitary District as well. The Democratic majority leader and President Truman's spokesman in the United States Senate, Scott W. Lucas, was defeated by his Republican opponent, Everett M. Dirksen. Bitterly disappointed, Senator Lucas blamed the Kefauver Committee hearings in Chicago for his defeat and made no effort to conceal his anger at Senator Kefauver. His ire, of course, was entirely misdirected. It was the Chicago Democratic machine that boldly placed Captain Gilbert on the ticket for sheriff — not Kefauver. And under all proper concepts of free government, the people should be entitled to learn of the true qualifications of candidates for public office *before* election — not afterward. Machine politicians so frequently get away with their utter contempt of the voter that they whimper and cry "foul" when they are held accountable.

On the day following the election, Captain Daniel A. Gilbert resigned as chief investigator of the state's attorney's office and a few days later retired from the police department. It was announced that he would head the police force at the Arlington and Washington race tracks. His brother, Maurice Gilbert, a lieutenant of the Chicago Police Department, had held the position of police chief at these two tracks since 1948. During most of that time he had been on leave from the Chicago Police Department because of "ill health" and "for reasons of business." [5]

Although the Kefauver Committee did not conduct any investigation of Chicago police officers, it did interrogate several concerning the source of their wealth. Some of the officers gave rather unconvincing explanations, but it was quite apparent that financial success was assured those who made friends with the right people. This was aptly illustrated by the testimony of Captain Thomas Harrison who commanded the Thirty-fifth, or Chicago Avenue, Police District on the near North Side.

Captain Harrison entered the Chicago Police Department on January 8, 1922. Beginning in July, 1936, he became acting captain of the Thirty-fifth District and received his promotion to captain two years later while still assigned to this area. For almost half of his service in the police department, he had commanded the Thirty-fifth District, which has long been notorious for the character of its dives and night spots. In one respect at least the career of Captain Harrison was similar to that of Gilbert. Captain Gilbert's rise to riches began with his close association with George Brennan, whom he served as chauffeur and bodyguard. Harrison, while a member of the Chicago police force, acted as an armed guard for the cash payrolls of the Nash Construction Company operated by two brothers, R. J. Nash and Patrick A. Nash, boss of the Democratic party in Chicago. Although there was no admission of large financial benefits growing out of Harrison's association with Pat Nash, it is reasonable to assume that his connection with this powerful political boss was advantageous to his career as a city policeman. In 1927, five years after he joined the police force, Harrison and his father bought a farm for $30,800 which was sold in 1946 for $60,000. In 1935, Captain Harrison purchased his home at 6030 North Forest Glen Avenue in Chicago for $18,500. Of this amount he borrowed $10,000 from William R. Skidmore. Between 1933 and 1948 Harrison purchased stock outright for which he paid about $57,000. In explaining the source of some of his wealth, Harrison admitted a profitable friendship with John J. Lynch, the well-known Chicago handbook operator and a partner of Moe L. Annenberg in the lucrative racing information wire service. Harrison explained to the Kefauver Committee that he had been a "sort of bodyguard" for Lynch between 1931 and 1937, although he stated, "I didn't work for Lynch. I was his friend. . . ." And this friendship paid big dividends. Once while Lynch was in Florida, he forwarded Harrison $2500. Later in 1937 the one-time big gambler made Harrison an outright gift of $30,000. Senator Kefauver then asked, "All the bookies all over town were right under the control of Annenberg and Lynch at that time, were they not?" Captain Harrison replied, "I suppose they were, yes." That Lynch was extremely concerned over the welfare of indigent policemen is best illustrated by Harrison's explanation of the circumstances surrounding the gift of $30,000. Said Harrison, "He gave it to me in an envelope when I had dinner with him. I will explain to you why. He asked me one night . . . 'Tom, what security have you for your wife and daughter?' I said, 'Well, only a few shares of stock, and my home that I am paying on.' . . . So a few nights later, I was having dinner with him in the Drake Hotel, and he gave me this money in an envelope. I said, 'Now, Jack, this seems like quite a bit of money. What am I supposed to do about this? Am I going to file on it?' He said, 'No; I will file on this money. This is a gift from me.'"

A number of years after he received his gift from Lynch, Captain Harrison was in difficulty over charges of laxity in the enforcement of the gambling laws. By that time Lynch was no longer connected with either gambling or wire service activities and Skidmore had been removed from the local scene by the Federal government. Gambling was rampant, however, and following a vigorous grand jury investigation charges were filed before the Civil Service Commission against Harrison and several other Chicago police officers. On June 16, 1944, Harrison and six other police captains were ordered discharged for failure to suppress gambling in their districts. The action of the Civil Service Commission was appealed to the courts and after many months of legal battling the Commission's findings were set aside and the captains were restored to duty.

It was following his restoration to duty and while he was the commanding officer of the Town Hall Police District on the North Side that Harrison received another windfall. Through Edward Hughes, an influential politician and a former Secretary of State in Illinois, Captain Harrison met William Ronan, who was engaged in the wholesale flour business. Ronan had been a member of Mayor Kelly's ill-fated Civil Service Commission that rendered the whitewash decision against four members of the police gambling squad in 1942. He resigned from the Civil Service Commission on December 12, 1942, shortly after a special committee appointed by the mayor reviewed the decision and held that the police officers should have been discharged from the force. One day in 1945, William Ronan visited Captain Harrison in the Town Hall police station. According to Harrison's testimony before the Kefauver Committee, Ronan asked him: " 'Tom, do you know anything about wheat?' I said, 'No, I don't know a thing about wheat.' He said, 'I'm going to put you in the wheat market.' . . . So one day he called me up and he says, 'You have so many bushels of wheat, and so many bushels of corn.' I didn't know. I said, 'Where do I send the money?' He said, 'You don't send no money.' So about a week or so later I got a call from him and he says, 'I sold you out.' . . . He says, 'You have $1200 to your credit.' I filed on that. You will see where I filed on the wheat." [6] From the testimony of the two police captains, Harrison and Gilbert, it was quite evident that they were well versed in how to reap the maximum benefits from the friends they had won and the people they had influenced.

The testimony of Gilbert and Harrison perhaps attracted more

attention than the disclosures made by some of Chicago's underworld leaders who were called before the committee. And the first
Chicago sessions of the Kefauver Committee had barely ended when
an event occurred which further emphasized the lucrative nature
of politics in Chicago. Edward J. Kelly, who had served as the
city's mayor for fourteen years, died on October 20, 1950, at the age
of seventy-four. Hundreds of men who owed allegiance to the
former mayor attended the funeral. Even President Truman sent
an emissary. And marching almost abreast in the long line of politicians who came to pay their respects were the former political
czar of Jersey City, Frank Hague, and State Senator William J.
Connors, the boss of Chicago's Forty-second Ward which includes
the Thirty-fifth Police District. Among those who paid homage to
the deceased mayor were many citizens who were undoubtedly
indignant over the wealth accumulated by Harrison and Gilbert as
police captains. At the time of Kelly's death, he owned homes in
Eagle River, Wisconsin, and Palm Springs, California. His executors
estimated that his estate was worth $600,000, but Mrs. Kelly insisted
that over a million dollars of the estate's assets had disappeared. She
created a furor by hiring an attorney to locate the alleged missing
fortune and to force the removal of the executors.[7] After several
months of wrangling, Mrs. Kelly appeared in Probate Court on
November 9, 1951, and accepted an amended inventory listing assets
of $686,799. Her attorney stated that she had ample grounds for
expecting a much larger estate and announced that the search for
additional assets would be continued.

In reporting on the funeral of former Mayor Kelly, *Life* Magazine, in a few words, gave a rather harsh summary of his career.
When Kelly was twelve years of age, said the article, he left school
with the admonition of his mother to "Always keep neat and never
drink out of someone else's beer can." And, concluded *Life*, "Though
he was once indicted for graft and questioned many times about
his wealth, he always kept himself financially neat. No one could
prove that Ed Kelly ever drank out of anyone else's beer can."[8]
Probably a more objective appraisal of the former mayor's career
appeared in a *Chicago Sun-Times* editorial on the morning following his death. The *Sun-Times*, which had always supported Kelly
when he campaigned for mayor, stated that "When Kelly began

his career as mayor in 1933, he was a rough and tumble schemer who had made a fortune out of political activities during the Sanitary District 'whoopee era' of 1929." And although Chicago as well as Kelly had undergone many changes "he remained a big city boss to the end." Kelly was:

. . . first of all a practical politician in every sense of the word, good and bad. . . . Kelly had the instincts of a dictator. He was confident and paternalistic. . . . He brushed aside criticism of his administration by pointing to election victories. . . . Kelly was tolerant of such areas as North Clark Street's honky-tonk town, but he personally could not tolerate open commercialized vice. . . . But Chicago was still a wide-open town with all that implies, including corruption of police and public officials by racketeers.[9]

Testimony before the Kefauver Committee amply proved that statement. The policies of Kelly and most of his predecessors had made Chicago a fertile breeding place for powerful criminal organizations. A few weeks after Kelly's death, the Kefauver Committee reported that the Accardo-Guzik-Fischetti crime syndicate in Chicago was then one of the two major underworld organizations in the nation. This was a natural and inevitable product of the policies of Kelly and most of the mayors before him.

The passing of Chicago's powerful political boss failed to divert attention from the Kefauver investigation. The public and the newspapers were demanding action by the local officials. Particularly under fire was Captain Thomas Harrison who had admitted receiving a gift of $32,500 from a gambling racketeer. "This kind of relationship," said the *Chicago News*, "clearly unfitted Captain Harrison for his position on the force. He should have quit long since. He should certainly quit now and spare the administration the bother of kicking him off the force." [10] The *Chicago Sun-Times* in a heated editorial stated:

Last May when the Chicago Crime Commission made its report that Captain Harrison's district was a vice-ridden cesspool of crime and corruption, Mayor Kennelly, in white-faced anger, defended his police department. Harrison stayed on. Shortly after that, the grand jury asked Harrison about his income. He refused to reveal it. The *Sun-Times* said he was in contempt of the community and ought to be taken before the police trial board. He wasn't. He stayed on as captain.[11]

The *Sun-Times* charged that the state's attorney had done nothing to investigate conditions in the Thirty-fifth Police District and it called for a change in attitude on the part of the mayor, a new commissioner of police and a wholesale retirement of police captains.

Even out-of-town newspapers cast a critical eye toward Chicago. The *St. Louis Post-Dispatch* recalled that "when the Kefauver Committee first went to Chicago, Mayor Martin Kennelly expressed concern for the city's good name." "Chicago mayors," said the *Post-Dispatch*, "are always worried about the city's reputation. They wince when foreigners identify the city with gangsters, and generally give the impression that this dubious renown is the result of a gigantic conspiracy of misunderstanding. Too few Chicago mayors, however, undertake to repair the city's reputation at its source." It then reviewed Captain Harrison's gifts and loans from two of the city's most notorious gamblers and pointed out that the mayor had done nothing when the Chicago Crime Commission, in May 1950, had called his attention to lax law enforcement in this police captain's district. The *Post-Dispatch* concluded that unless Kennelly "can clean up the police department . . . his excellent reputation will suffer. And Chicago's will remain what it has always been." [12]

The constant hammering of the press finally spurred the city administration into action. On October 26, 1950, Captain Harrison was given a leave of absence at his own request and was replaced by a conscientious police officer, Captain William A. Balswick. Several months later, Captain Harrison was brought before the Civil Service Commission on charges growing out of his testimony before the Kefauver Committee and he was ordered discharged from the police department. As is customary with Chicago official action in cases of this kind, very little evidence was introduced before the Civil Service Commission to show that Harrison's benefactors bore reputations as infamous gambling racketeers. Such evidence was readily available and was certainly very pertinent to the inquiry. Despite the incomplete presentation of evidence by the corporation counsel's office, the Civil Service Commission held that Harrison's acceptance of $30,000 from John J. Lynch "without disclosure thereof to the then Commissioner of Police and without his consent" was a violation of the rules and regulations of the police department and constituted adequate grounds for his dismissal. This was true, said the Civil Service Commission, "irrespective of the activities or reputation of Lynch, so that the limited evidence in the record on that score merely serves to accentuate the importance of the principle embodied in that rule." [13]

A few days after Captain Harrison was relieved of duty in the near North Side, the people of Chicago went to the polls and registered their disapproval of police captain Daniel A. Gilbert. Throughout the campaign Gilbert had pictured himself as an experienced policeman and therefore well suited for the sheriff's office. But, said the *Chicago News*, Gilbert's "record of easy tolerance [symbolized] only too clearly what has too long characterized too many officers of the law in Chicago." The insistence of Cook County Democratic Chairman, Jacob M. Arvey, on Gilbert's candidacy was characterized as "the major blunder of his career as a political manager." And the election returns carried a moral for Mayor Kennelly, too, said the *Chicago News:*

From his first day in office to the present, many of his best friends have tried to persuade him that the Chicago Police Department needed drastic reform, which can probably come only from a commander trained outside its own ranks, habits and traditions.[14]

Just one week later, on November 14, 1950, Mayor Kennelly named Timothy O'Connor as the new commissioner of police of Chicago. O'Connor was a police officer of proven ability. He was honest and conscientious and his appointment met with general approval. But, as a newspaper editorial declared, the appointment of O'Connor was not made "until after Senator Kefauver's first visit to Chicago, and after the result of that visit had been registered at the polls in November." [15]

The Kefauver Committee had made little effort to investigate the Chicago Police Department. But from a mere pinprick on the surface, enough light had filtered through on Chicago's law-enforcement setup to indicate that a thorough housecleaning was urgently needed. It was apparent that the prevalence of organized crime in Chicago was not an accident. It was inevitable.

CHAPTER XII

By Their Own Admissions

FOR years, political leaders and police executives had continued to deny the existence of organized crime in Chicago. The Capone gang was a myth, they said. At the attorney general's conference on organized crime held in Washington, D. C., on February 15, 1950, the official spokesman for the city of Chicago expressed indignation when reference was made to the Capone gang. Said this official, "I do not know that the Capone Syndicate exists. I have read about it in the newspapers. I have never received any evidence of it." [1] The various underworld leaders, their friends, lawyers, accountants and business associates who were called upon to testify before the Kefauver Committee in Chicago made every effort to preserve the myth that the Capone gang existed only in the imagination of newspapers and other defamers of the city's reputation. Most of the gangsters who appeared before the Senate Committee refused to answer pertinent questions. They were evasive and many of their statements were obviously false. But notwithstanding this conspiracy of silence and evasion, there emerged from the hearings a frightening picture of a powerful criminal organization that had flourished without interruption for over three decades. Officials might continue to deny the existence of the Capone Syndicate but the testimony of the gangsters themselves and their books, records and income-tax returns furnished incontrovertible proof of its reality.

Among the more important witnesses called by the Committee was Phil D'Andrea. He had been one of the most intimate friends of Al Capone, a traveling companion of the gang leader and one of several Capone gangsters convicted in Federal court in New York City on December 31, 1943, for extorting over a million dollars from the motion picture industry. D'Andrea boasted that Al Capone "would do anything in the world for me." When asked, "You know he had an organization that he ruled over pretty firmly, didn't he?" D'Andrea seemed surprised that anyone would even question such a well-known fact. His answer was "Of course." And many of those who were important cogs in the organization ruled over by Al Capone in the 1920's and early 1930's have continued ever since to figure prominently in Chicago's underworld. The testimony of the gangsters themselves clearly established this.

Before Al Capone went to the Federal Penitentiary on May 4, 1932, for income-tax evasion, the Lexington Hotel, just a few blocks south of the Loop, served as the gang leader's headquarters. Among those who called at the Lexington Hotel to confer with Capone were Jack Guzik, Joe Fusco, Louis "Little New York" Campagna, Paul Ricca, Phil D'Andrea, John Patton, Frank Nitti, Charles Fischetti, Alexander Louis Greenberg, Robert Larry McCullough, Tony Accardo, Murray Humphreys, and the gang leader's brothers, Ralph and John Capone. These, of course, were only a few of the associates for whom the welcome sign was always out. Other important politicians who came to the Lexington to visit with the gang chief were State Senator Daniel A. Serritella, Alderman William V. Pacelli and State Representative Albert J. Prignano. Underworld leaders from other cities, such as Tony Gizzo of Kansas City and Jack Dragna of Los Angeles, paid their respects to Al Capone in the Lexington and hobnobbed with his underlings. Gizzo was to occupy an important place in the Capone organization in Kansas City and to become one of the most powerful underworld leaders there.

Jack Guzik was one of the kingpins who strutted about the hotel and had authority to issue orders for the chief. Phil D'Andrea testified that Guzik was "one of the so-called big shots" at the Lexington — a man whom the others "looked up to." Jack Guzik was still entitled to the rank of a "big shot" underworld leader two decades later when the Kefauver Committee submitted its report in May 1951.

Friendships formed and alliances cemented in the Lexington Hotel enabled the Capone syndicate to engage in million-dollar rackets on a national scale in the years to come. The powerful New York gangsters, Frank Costello, Meyer Lansky and Lucky Luciano, became associates of Paul Ricca, an influential Capone lieutenant. On the West Coast, Ricca had such friends as Jack Dragna and John Rosselli. In the early 1930's Charles Fischetti was arrested in Los Angeles with Jack Dragna and John Rosselli as they were returning from the *Mal-Falcolm* gambling boat operated by Dragna and others just outside the three-mile limit. Many years later, John Rosselli was among those convicted in New York City for extorting millions from the moving picture industry. Jack Dragna, in turn, had become known on the West Coast as the "Capone of Los Angeles." New York gang leaders were spending considerable time in Chicago with their Capone syndicate associates. Throughout the following two decades, close working arrangements were to exist between the Costello gang in New York and the Capone syndicate in Chicago. Each organization was to continue growing in strength until the power of the two criminal syndicates virtually brought several local and state governments under their control.

The Capone gang never overlooked any opportunities for improving its organization and strengthening its grip over Chicago's underworld. Politically the syndicate became a dominant force in city elections. Its representatives sat in the city council. A personal friend of Al Capone was sent to the state senate. There were ward committeemen who were owned body and soul by the Capone gang. The Italo-American National Union, frequently called the Unione Siciliana, was utilized to advance the cause of Capone candidates for political office. Phil D'Andrea testified that from 1934 to 1941 he was president of the Unione Siciliana and was responsible for bringing his close friends, Tony Accardo, Charles Fischetti, Paul Ricca, John Capone and Nick Circella (alias Nick Dean), into this organization as members. D'Andrea, who was very influential in First Ward politics, brought before the Unione Siciliana as speakers those political candidates who apparently had the blessing of the Capone syndicate. Paul Ricca testified that he continued to pay membership dues in the Unione Siciliana until he was committed to the Federal penitentiary in December 1943. During part of the time that Ricca was active in the Unione Siciliana, Joseph Bulger, an attorney, was its president. The exploitation of the Unione Siciliana, a benevolent association, for the advancement of the Capone organization was not peculiar to Chicago. In New York, Frank Costello, Lucky Luciano and other gangsters became powerful in Unione

Siciliana activities, as did gangsters in many of the other large American municipalities.

During the 1920's and early 1930's, the Capone gang harvested millions of dollars from the manufacture, distribution and sale of liquor and beer. In an effort to satisfy Chicago's unquenchable thirst during the prohibition era from 1919 to 1933, the gang found it necessary to become stronger than ever before. And the power of the organization stemmed from ruthless discipline within the ranks of the gangsters, as well as from strong alliances with political machines and law enforcement agencies. Yet while the Capone gang found a virtual gold mine in the liquor and beer industry, it did not overlook the millions to be made from gambling and vice, always the chief props of the underworld.

From the days of Big Jim Colosimo, the group which was to become known as the Capone gang relied heavily on gambling and vice for its revenue. The Kefauver Committee asked John Patton, "Who ran the roadhouses in Burnham when you were mayor?" Patton replied, "Jim Colosimo, Ike Bloom and a fellow by the name of Reynolds." Ike Bloom was then known as the "King of the Brothels" of the levee district in Chicago's First Ward. Patton reluctantly admitted that gambling was featured in the Burnham roadhouses although he piously informed the Senate Committee that he "told them to cut it out." If this admonition were ever given, which may be seriously questioned, there is no evidence to indicate that the slot machines quit clicking or the roulette wheels stopped spinning in Colosimo's Burnham roadhouses.

The underworld mantle of Big Jim Colosimo was worn successively by John Torrio, Al Capone, Frank Nitti and Tony Accardo. For over three decades, the gambling business of the syndicate was well organized and territories were clearly defined. Virtually every top member of the Capone organization was directly connected with one or more phases of the gambling business. Many of the downtown places were handbooks which catered to the patronage of the horse race bettor. This was true of the various establishments controlled by Jack Guzik and Hymie Levin and those operated by Tony Accardo in partnership with the Russell brothers, Harry and Dave.

The handbook business is conducted on the same one-sided principles as all other professional gambling houses. The proprietor relies on a percentage system which is just as certain as a mechanically fixed slot machine. This is made possible in part by "lay-off" establishments which handle bets for handbooks. If large sums of money are wagered with a handbook on horses with long odds, the place would lose heavily if such horses should win. In order to avert this possibility, the handbook proprietor "lays off" these bets with establishments that handle only the business of bookmakers. Until the early 1940's, one of the important lay-off establishments in downtown Chicago was operated on State Street by Charles Gioe, Ralph Pierce, Harry and Dave Russell. For some time prior to his association with Pierce and the Russell brothers in this lay-off place, Charles Gioe had been in the business of printing betting tickets for handbooks. These tickets were designed to eliminate fraud on the part of the bettor. The lay-off establishment which Gioe operated with Pierce and the Russell brothers handled business amounting to a million dollars a year. Gioe testified that among the Chicago bookmakers who patronized his place were Tony Accardo, Rocco Fischetti, Frank "Chew Tobacco" Ryan, Edward M. Dobkin, Joe Grabiner and Oscar Gutter. Gioe's business branched out from Chicago to almost every section of the nation. In Kansas City, Missouri, his customer was the handbook operated by Tony Gizzo, long affiliated with the Capone gang, and the powerful Kansas City underworld boss, Charles V. Carollo. In New York City, the handbook serviced by Gioe was one in which Frank Erickson, a lieutenant of Frank Costello, had an interest.

While these and other Capone syndicate hoodlums were reaping a rich harvest from gambling in Chicago's Loop, another set of Capone mobsters were in command of gambling in Cicero. Louis "Little New York" Campagna was in partnership with Willie Heeney and Joseph Corngold, popularly known as Fifke, in two gambling places in Cicero called the Austin Club and El Patio. Campagna's testimony before the Kefauver Committee gave an insight into the lucrative nature of the racket. His original investment in 1934 was about $1500. He claimed that he knew nothing about the business which was actually handled by Corngold. Yet Campagna admitted that his share of the partnership's earnings sometimes soared to $75,000 a year. When Campagna was convicted in the moving picture extortion case in 1943, the Austin Club and El Patio continued to operate under the management of Willie Heeney and Joe Corngold.

There were, of course, numerous Capone syndicate gambling places in Cicero other than these two. Claude Maddox, also known as John "Screwy" Moore, ran a place called the Turf Club. Joseph Aiuppa operated a handbook at 4831 West Cermak Road, and from an examination of his books and records, the Kefauver Committee determined that he handled wagers amounting to $1,900,000 for the one year of 1947. Aiuppa received the necessary racing information wire service from the R and H Publishing Company of Chicago, an establishment headed by Hymie Levin.

Joe Aiuppa and Claude Maddox, both intimate associates of Tony Accardo, have not confined their activities to the retail end of the gambling business. They are also manufacturers. Taylor and Company is one of the largest manufacturers of gambling house equipment in the United States, and Aiuppa and Maddox are two of the principal partners in this firm. The present modern plant of Taylor and Company was constructed in Cicero, Illinois, a few years ago when there was a great shortage of building materials. In order to obtain the necessary governmental approval, representations were made that Taylor and Company was to be engaged in the manufacture of furniture. Instead of furniture, however, dice, roulette wheels, crap tables and other forms of gambling equipment are produced by Taylor and Company and shipped to virtually every state in the Union, including Nevada, where gambling is legal. Among the numerous customers of Taylor and Company, as reflected by its books, were Joe Corngold, the gambling house partner of Louis Campagna, the Orchid Flower Shop in Chicago operated by the wives of Campagna and Tony Capezio, and Billy's Bar run by Ralph Capone in Mercer, Wisconsin. Joseph Aiuppa, when called before the Kefauver Committee, refused to answer any questions whatever, which prompted the committee's counsel to remark, "Let the record show that the witness just sits there mute, chewing gum, saying nothing." Aiuppa's dumbness, whether real or feigned, did not prevent him from becoming a highly successful industrialist in the gambling business. The books and records of Taylor and Company show an income ranging from $200,000 to $300,000 a year. In fact, from the testimony of Campagna and the demeanor of Aiuppa and other Capone gangsters who appeared before the Kefauver Committee, it was evident that neither knowledge of the business nor general intelligence has any bearing on success in any phase of the gambling industry.

In its effort to monopolize gambling in its entirety, the Capone organization did not overlook the racing information wire service which is essential to profitable handbook operations. In the early part of the century, Mont Tennes had demonstrated that through the control of the wire service in any community, it was possible to maintain a virtual dictatorship over handbooks. On May 12, 1920, the press reported that the headquarters for racing information for the entire United States was located in the office of Tennes's General News Bureau, at 431 South Dearborn Street, Chicago. In 1950, thirty years later, the office of the general manager of Continental Press which disseminates racing information throughout the nation was located at 431 South Dearborn Street in Chicago. Conditions had changed very little during three decades. When the control of the General News Bureau eventually passed into the hands of Moe L. Annenberg, Tennes's associate, Jack Lynch, retained an interest in the business. After Annenberg named James M. Ragen as the vice-president and general manager of the General News Bureau, the team of Annenberg and Ragen proceeded to gain control of nearly every racing information service in the nation. The *Racing Form, New York Morning Telegraph, Daily Racing Record,* and scores of others were brought into the Annenberg fold. By 1939, an Annenberg holding company owned twenty-eight corporations in the United States and Canada which were engaged in various aspects of publishing, printing and distributing information to bookmakers as well as supplying forms, sheets and cards that are needed in handbook operations. Annenberg, with the aid of Ragen and the co-operation of politicians, had built up a racing information empire worth several million dollars. In a statement to the state's attorney in Chicago, Ragen admitted that as general manager of the wire services between 1933 and 1936 he had paid "$600,000 to politicians throughout the United States for political campaigns and so forth."

In Chicago, Ragen maintained cordial business relations with important members of the Capone syndicate such as Jack Guzik, Frank "The Enforcer" Nitti and Daniel A. Serritella. By 1934, relations had become strained between Jack Lynch and his associates, Ragen and Annenberg. Lynch contended that he was being cheated by his partners and eventually filed a suit in court demanding an accounting. The suit was defended on the ground that the profits which Lynch sought to share were from an illegal enterprise and since he was not coming into a court of equity with "clean hands" he was not entitled to recover. Annenberg and Ragen were determined to force Lynch out of the General News Bureau and with this end in mind they established a rival company called the Nationwide News Service. Ragen was installed as its general manager, and with the control of both companies in his hands it was obvious that the General News Bureau could not long survive. Lynch saw the handwriting on the wall and came to terms. On January 2, 1935, he accepted $750,000 from Annenberg for his interest in the General News Bureau and stepped out of the picture. Featured in the background of the maneuvering, however, was the ominous figure of Frank "The Enforcer" Nitti. Ragen, in an affidavit found after his death, stated that on the same day Lynch agreed to withdraw from the General News Bureau he met Frank Nitti in the Auditorium Hotel in Chicago and delivered to the Capone gang boss $100,000 in $100 bills. This amount, said Ragen's affidavit, was promised the syndicate if Annenberg were successful in his fight with Lynch. Just what part "The Enforcer" played in Lynch's decision to abandon the wire service was not mentioned. It can be assumed, however, that his methods were both forceful and convincing and the Capone gang benefited when Lynch was removed from the wire-service setup.

As general manager of the companies that furnished the wire service to Chicago handbooks, James M. Ragen naturally possessed first-hand information regarding their ownership and control. In a statement made to the state's attorney's office, Ragen declared that the Capone syndicate had always controlled handbook operations in the Loop. By 1939, said Ragen, every handbook in the Loop with the exception of one was owned by the Capone syndicate, and the syndicate bought the racing information service for all establishments under its control. In connection with the wire service business,

Daniel Serritella testified before the Kefauver Committee that, in 1945, Ragen told Hymie Levin to get out of the wire service business and to confine his activities to the operation of handbooks in Chicago. When Levin refused to comply with this demand, Ragen cut off the wire service. The fight then started and grew in intensity as the months passed by. On March 20, 1946, the Capone gang officially organized the Trans-American Publishing and News Service, Inc., and placed this company in direct competition with Continental Press. Patrick J. Burns, long an important figure in the racing news empire ruled by Annenberg and Ragen, left the Continental Press organization and became the president and registered agent of the new company. Ralph J. O'Hara, who had been identified with the Capone group for many years, was listed as the secretary.

The formation of a new wire service company infuriated Ragen and he promptly assumed the role of a knight in shining armor who was determined to rid the city of the evil Capone gang. His ire was particularly directed at Patrick J. Burns, who had deserted him for the rival company. Ragen suddenly remembered that his once trusted lieutenant had been a fugitive from justice since April 7, 1916, when he escaped from a bailiff in a Chicago courtroom while he was on trial for assault and robbery. Ragen demanded the apprehension of Burns and on April 29, 1946, the fugitive was lodged in the House of Correction to serve the sentence imposed thirty years before. Burns remained in this institution until he was released on August 3, 1946. Meantime, on June 24, 1946, Ragen was mortally wounded by Capone gunmen and he died seven weeks later.

The Trans-American Publishing and News Service, Inc. embarked on an ambitious program of controlling the wire service business throughout the country. The tactics of the Capone gangsters who operated the company were ruthless and blood flowed freely in many parts of the nation. In Chicago, the Trans-American wire service was distributed to the handbooks by the R and H Publishing Company owned by Hymie Levin, his brother-in-law, Phil Katz, and Ray Jones. The R and H company was more than a mere distributor for Trans-American, however. It was one of the principal financial backers of the Capone gang's wire service enterprise. Thousands upon thousands of dollars were poured into Trans-American by Hymie Levin's R and H company.

In almost every part of the nation the Capone gang's wire service representatives were dangerous underworld characters. In Nevada, the Trans-American representative was Bugsy Siegel, one of America's most infamous gangsters and long affiliated with powerful underworld leaders in New York City. Siegel's gift to Nevada was the lavishly furnished Flamingo Hotel, a gambling casino built in Las Vegas at a cost of several million dollars. Siegel was the gambling czar of Las Vegas until he was murdered in typical gangland fashion on June 20, 1947. Through terroristic methods, Siegel forced Nevada gambling houses to subscribe to Trans-American wire service. Shortly after Siegel was murdered, the police received an unsigned letter from Chicago which purported to shed light on the killing. This letter asserted that Siegel, who owned the Golden Nugget News Service in Las Vegas, had engaged in a heated argument with the Capone gangsters, Murray Humphreys and Ralph O'Hara, just a few days before the slaying. The dispute arose, said the letter, when Siegel refused to pay the Trans-American Publishing and News Service the sum of $25,000 demanded by Humphreys and O'Hara. Interest in this letter was considerably revived during the investigation of the Kefauver Committee in Nevada. Evidence produced before the Committee established that Siegel owned the handbook concession in the Golden Nugget Casino in Las Vegas. On July 26, 1946, this casino issued a check in the amount of $12,000 in favor of the Trans-American Publishing and News Service in Chicago. This check represented a loan from Siegel's gambling place in Las Vegas to the Capone gang's wire service business in Chicago. Siegel had come to the aid of the Capone syndicate which was hard pressed for cash in its nationwide racing information operations.

In Kansas City, Missouri, the Trans-American News Service was represented by Edward P. Osadchey, commonly known as Eddie Spitz, Thomas "Tano" Lacoco, Charles Gargotta, one of the most vicious gangsters in the Middle West, and Morris Klein. These men were partners in big gambling operations with Charles Binaggio, the underworld boss of Kansas City, and were closely associated with Tony Gizzo, the intimate friend of leading Capone gangsters. In 1948 they assisted Binaggio in raising huge sums of money to help elect a governor. Admittedly Binaggio wanted a chief executive of the state who would tolerate wide-open gambling. The candidate he supported was elected governor and it was conceded that the gambling boss of Kansas City had become one of the most powerful politicians in Missouri. Osadchey, Binaggio and Gargotta were part owners of the Last Chance gambling house which was the last place where Binaggio and Gargotta were seen alive before their bullet-riddled bodies were found in the First District Democratic Headquarters in Kansas City on April 6, 1950. These men were tough and ideally suited to represent the Capone gang's wire service in Missouri.

Trans-American placed distributors all over the country. In addition to Las Vegas and Kansas City, the syndicate had distributors in New Orleans, Louisiana; Columbus, Ohio; Camden, New Jersey; East St. Louis, Illinois, and Miami, Florida. The Kefauver Committee examined records which disclosed a regular flow of checks from distributors in these places to the Trans-American company in Chicago. The checks from the Miami distributor were signed by William G. "Butsy" O'Brien, a man who was to prove extremely helpful to Tony Accardo, Jack Guzik and Harry Russell long after the Trans-American wire service venture was out of existence.

The Trans-American company made deep inroads into the business of Continental Press but it was a costly enterprise. Income-tax returns filed by Trans-American listed losses of $122,958.76 in 1946 and $184,784.89 in 1947. The wire service fight was also costly in terms of blood and violence. Ragen, the head of Continental Press, and Siegel, the Capone mob's representative in Nevada, had met violent deaths in the bitter warfare. The loss of life was not important to the Capone gang, which had been dealing in murder for several decades. But the battle over the wire service was attracting attention all over the country. Some states were instituting legal action to outlaw the racing information business. Extensive publicity was bad for all phases of the syndicate's gambling activities and it was ready to make peace provided the terms were agreeable. When the shooting stopped, there was every indication that the demands of the Capone organization had been fully met.

On June 13, 1947, it was publicly announced that the Trans-American Publishing and News Service was going out of business because of insufficient funds. The actual dissolution of the company, however, did not take place until November of that year. The key men who had deserted Continental Press for the Trans-American company were promptly taken back into the Continental organization. When the wire service warfare broke out in 1945, it was loudly asserted that Dan Serritella was merely the tool of Jack Guzik and Hymie Levin in a conspiracy of the Capone gang to take over the racing information business, yet at the time Serritella appeared before the Kefauver Committee late in 1950, he testified that he was then on the payroll of the Illinois Sports News which is closely affiliated with Continental Press. In fact, Serritella stated that his pay checks were signed by George Kelly, a brother of Tom Kelly, the general manager of Continental Press. Records were also produced before the Senate Crime Committee which established that Jack Dragna of Los Angeles received $500.00 a week from the Illinois Sports News in Chicago from May 1948 until February 1950. It was also determined that the Continental Press wire service was being distributed to Chicago handbooks by the R and H Publishing Company headed by Hymie Levin, and by Mid-West News owned by John Scanlon, who the Kefauver Committee reported had "participated in the Guzik-Accardo-Russell maneuver to take over" a wire service in Florida. It was obvious that when the fight between Continental Press and the Trans-American wire service ended, the Capone gang was in a position to monopolize the lucrative handbook operations in the city of Chicago.

It was while Al Capone reigned supreme from his Lexington Hotel headquarters that he became interested in dog racing. About 1927, a dog track began operating in Cicero under the management of some of Al Capone's closest associates, including Mayor John Patton of Burnham, and Edward J. O'Hare who was to serve as Capone's representative in the dog track business in many sections of the country. This track was sometimes called the Laramie Kennel Club, and at other times the Hawthorne Kennel Club. Several years later, after dog racing was stopped, it became known as Sportsman's Park, a horse-racing establishment. When the Cicero dog track began operations, Robert Larry McCullough was living with Al Capone at the Lexington. He had left Capone's breweries to become the chief of police at the dog track. McCullough testified before the Kefauver Committee that he was originally hired by Capone about

1922 to act as "lookout" man in the illegal breweries then flourishing. McCullough's background was such that he could be trusted to protect Capone's interests. Once he served four months in the House of Correction for burglary. On another occasion he was involved in an attempted jail break after an arrest for burglary. McCullough explained this affair to the Senate Committee as follows: "Somebody gave us a saw. We were trying to saw our way out and we were caught. They gave me four months for destroying city property." McCullough was only a youngster of seventeen at the time. Several years later, in 1926, he was shot three times by rival gunmen and in the same year his name was mentioned prominently in the press in connection with the gang killing of Assistant State's Attorney William McSwiggin. McCullough's early career and intimate association with America's most notorious gangster, Al Capone, apparently equipped him to serve as the principal law enforcement officer at dog tracks and at Sportsman's Park for almost a quarter of a century.

The active management of the Cicero dog track was in the hands of John Patton and Edward J. O'Hare. In 1925, Patton had been arrested with Robert Larry McCullough and Frank "The Enforcer" Nitti, in a doctor's office across the street from the Lexington Hotel. When the dog track opened in Cicero two years later, both McCullough and Nitti were connected with its operations. From Chicago, the dog-track business expanded to other sections of the country. Edward O'Hare went to Boston and built a track near the Hub. He was a master in dealing with politicians and in Massachusetts he was successful in persuading the state legislature to enact laws which legalized dog racing. In Florida, Patton and O'Hare gained control of the Miami Beach Kennel Club and became interested in other dog tracks in the state as well. For some time Patton was a part owner of the Tropical Park dog track in Florida. Patton testified that the New York gambler, Frank Erickson, had $300,000 invested in the Tropical Park dog track and induced him to invest $50,000 in this venture. Associated with Patton and Erickson in Tropical Park were William Vincent "Big Bill" Dwyer and Owney "The Killer" Madden. This pair had formed an alliance in 1923 shortly after Madden was released from Sing Sing prison and they rose to fabulous heights as rum runners in New York City during prohibition.

When the Hawthorne or Laramie Kennel Club ran into legal

difficulties and was converted into Sportsman's Park, there was associated with O'Hare and Patton in a very minor role a man who subsequently had a phenomenal rise in the horse and dog track business. This man was William H. Johnston. Patton testified that when he first met Johnston "he was bookkeeper at the barns . . . for the horsemen." Johnston was still a relatively insignificant track employee when Edward J. O'Hare was shot on November 8, 1939. Within a few years after O'Hare's death, Johnston, with John Patton in the background, skyrocketed to the presidency of several race tracks. At the time of the Kefauver Committee investigation in 1950, Johnston was the president of four Florida dog tracks: the Miami Beach Kennel Club, Inc., the Associated Outdoor Clubs, Inc. in Tampa, the Jacksonville Kennel Club, Inc., and the Orange Park Kennel Club, Inc., also of Jacksonville. In addition he was the president of the Sportsman's Park horse race track in Cicero. John Patton admitted to the Senate Crime Committee that he was still a part owner of the Miami Beach Kennel Club and the dog track in Tampa as well. Part of Patton's stock is held in trust for him by a relative, Edward Krumrey. In fact, Patton testified that the joint interests of himself, William H. Johnston, and Johnston's brother control the Miami Beach Kennel Club.

Throughout Patton's long connection with the Miami Beach Kennel Club and Sportsman's Park, Capone's friend, Robert Larry McCullough, continued to act as the chief of police of both tracks and for several years he has also had the automobile parking concession at the two places. The auditor of both tracks was Hugo Bennett, a long time friend of Paul Ricca. According to Ricca's books and records he obtained a total of $80,000 from Bennett between May 1948 and July 31, 1950. Although Ricca contended the $80,000 represented loans from Bennett, when he was asked about the rate of interest he was paying, the gangster replied, "I don't know. I didn't pay any attention to it . . . I was tickled to get the loan, and whatever the interest was, I pay it. Those are small details that I don't pay attention to." Ricca indicated that at the end of five years he would repay the loans together with whatever interest might be demanded. In commenting on this unusual and mysterious transaction the Kefauver Committee stated that "the dog tracks . . . headed up by Patton and Johnston, through a salaried employee,

Hugo Bennett, who had no assets of his own of any substantial nature, made available to Paul Ricca $80,000, of which the committee, in its various hearings, has traced $75,000 directly to the dog tracks or people specifically concerned with the management of the dog tracks, and the other five thousand are found to be the personal funds of Bennett, an employee of Johnston and the dog track."

If mystery surrounded the $80,000 which Paul Ricca received from the Florida dog track people between 1948 and 1950, there was no enigma attending the $100,000 which was donated by the head of the four Florida dog tracks in the 1948 gubernatorial race. William H. Johnston contributed $100,000 to the campaign fund of Fuller Warren who was elected governor of Florida. John Patton informed the Kefauver Committee that he was in Florida at the time and he discussed this campaign contribution with Johnston. Patton also knew Fuller Warren socially before the election. When asked if he donated to Governor Warren's campaign fund, Patton answered, "Maybe I would have gotten into it, but I was sick in bed about that time. I had a heart attack . . . and they weren't bothering me much when I was there." Patton testified that Johnston had always been "a little nutty about Fuller Warren. He thought he was going to be the next President of the United States. . . ." Patton conceded that Johnston's large campaign contribution made him very influential politically in the state of Florida.

Almost simultaneously with the election of Fuller Warren as governor, the Capone boss Tony Accardo, together with Jack Guzik and Harry Russell, began laying plans to share in the proceeds of the lucrative S and G Gambling Syndicate of Miami Beach. The S and G Syndicate was composed of five local residents who had theretofore successfully thwarted any interference with their business by outsiders. It functioned as a highly efficient concern, furnishing wire service to numerous handbooks which were under the absolute control of the syndicate and in some instances actually financed by the S and G partners. Each bookmaker under the domination of the S and G Syndicate was required to turn over one half of his profits to the syndicate. The books of S and G for the year 1948 showed a gross income of $26,000,000 but it was estimated that this figure should have approximated $50,000,000. At any rate, it was a highly prosperous illegal venture, and Tony Accardo, Jack Guzik and Harry Russell wanted a share of the profits.

Harry Russell was well acquainted with the Florida dog track interests that had so materially helped elect Governor Warren. Both John Patton and William H. Johnston admitted knowing Russell who was a frequent visitor at the Miami Beach Kennel Club. Patton also knew Russell's long-time partner in Chicago gambling enterprises, Tony Accardo, and was intimately acquainted with Jack Guzik. In the early part of January 1949, Fuller Warren took office as governor of Florida. A few days later, on January 10, he appointed William O. "Bing" Crosby as his special investigator. Crosby was also an habitué of the Miami Beach Kennel Club and was well known to both Johnston and Patton as well as to Harry Russell. Patton testified that Crosby visited the Miami Beach Kennel Club three or four times a week.

About ten days after Crosby became the governor's special investigator, he went to Miami where he called on Sheriff James A. Sullivan. He told Sheriff Sullivan that the governor had directed him to conduct an investigation of gambling and he requested the services of a deputy sheriff to aid him in making raids. Crosby had in his possession a list of places to be raided which apparently had been furnished him by Harry Russell. It then developed that only S and G Syndicate bookmaking establishments were to be raided by the governor's special investigator. When called upon to testify before the Kefauver Committee, Crosby admitted having engaged in private conversations with Harry Russell. The Senate Crime Committee asked him, "What kind of information did he give you?" Crosby replied, "He gave me information on books and things like that." When asked if he could give any good reason why Harry Russell, big-time gambler and partner of Tony Accardo, would give him information which would enable him to raid gambling establishments, Crosby answered, "No sir, except he gave it to me." Actually, there was no mystery surrounding the sudden conversion of Harry Russell into a "stool pigeon." Only S and G Syndicate bookmaking establishments were the targets of Russell and the raiding parties, and it was not merely coincidental that the pressure on the S and G Syndicate came at the precise moment that Russell, Accardo and Guzik were attempting to acquire an interest in this enterprise. The entire affair was aptly described by the Senate Crime Committee as the "Russell muscle."

Meantime, additional troubles were heaped on the Miami Beach gambling trust from other quarters. The S and G Syndicate could not long remain a profitable venture without the wire service, and toward the end of February 1949, Continental Press suddenly cut off the flow of racing information to the Syndicate. The Miami distributor for Continental Press at that time was Butsy O'Brien. And the Kefauver Committee uncovered records which established that the S and G Syndicate's wire service was cut off by Continental Press "on the orders of O'Brien." Following this catastrophe, the S and G Syndicate attempted to secure the wire service through other bookmakers in Florida but Continental Press abruptly cut off the wire service to the entire state. The S and G Syndicate was whipped and it knew it. For two weeks it ceased operations completely and when business was resumed in March 1949, Harry Russell appeared as a full partner in the Syndicate. Although it was contended that Russell paid $20,000 for a one-sixth interest in this $26,000,000-a-year business, the Senate Committee produced records which established that the S and G Syndicate gave Tony Accardo $20,000 for his yacht, the *Clari-Jo*. And the income-tax returns filed by the partnership of Tony Accardo and Jack Guzik for the year 1949 claim a loss of $7240 which it attributed to S and G Syndicate operations. It is not surprising that as soon as Russell, Accardo and Guzik became a part of the S and G gambling syndicate, William O. Crosby, the governor's special investigator, ceased all raids on S and G bookmaking places and Continental Press promptly restored the wire service. A short time later, the S and G Syndicate paid a fee of $10,000 to John A. Rush, attorney for William H. Johnston in dog track matters, for services in drafting a bill to legalize gambling in the state.

The public disclosures of the Kefauver Committee relating to the political activity of the dog-track interests in Florida and the alleged loan of $80,000 made by Johnston's auditor, Hugo Bennett, to Paul Ricca, were embarrassing to politicians and race-track officials alike. The Senate Committee still had some unfinished business with reference to horse racing, however. In August 1951, it opened an inquiry into the Chicago Downs Association which began operating pari-

mutuel harness racing at Sportsman's Park in 1949. Shortly before
the Illinois legislature ended its session in 1949, a bill was introduced
which would permit harness racing at Sportsman's Park. Under the
state law then in effect harness racing was prohibited there. The bill
became law on July 1, 1949, and seventeen days later the first meet
was held under the auspices of the Chicago Downs Association
which had been incorporated on May 4, 1949. All of the new corporation's stock was held under a trust agreement by William H.
Johnston, president of Sportsman's Park, and Irwin S. "Sam" Wiedrick who once served a prison sentence in the state of New York for
grand larceny. Johnston and Wiedrick then distributed the stock
among their friends, relatives and politicians. Hugo Bennett was
listed as the owner of 1000 shares in the new racing enterprise, and
a number of prominent Chicago politicians such as Alderman James
Bowler of the Twenty-fifth Ward, Thomas D. Nash, Democratic
committeeman of the Nineteenth Ward, and State Senators Roland V. Libonati and Frank Ryan were recorded as stockholders.
The stock was sold for the nominal sum of ten cents a share to these
and other members of the Illinois state legislature who were active
in securing the passage of the bill during the closing days of the
general assembly. A total of nine Illinois state legislators or their
wives were revealed as stockholders in the Chicago Downs Association, and the profits to just one of these favored stockholders within
two years amounted to the tidy sum of $27,885. In fact, the legis-
lators who benefited from the stock deal could show a profit of 1650
per cent in the first two years of harness racing in Sportsman's Park.
Numerous other state legislators and politicians were also on the
payroll of the night harness racing venture at the Cicero track.

CHAPTER XIII

Eggs in Many Baskets

THE Capone syndicate could never be accused of placing all of its eggs in one basket. Led by Tony Accardo and Jack Guzik and aided by scores of underlings in the criminal world as well as friends within the realms of politics and business, the syndicate had been able to control almost every phase of the gambling industry in Chicago and many other places. Handbooks, layoff establishments, the wire service, slot machines and big casinos had all fallen under the domination of the Capone gang. It was frequently claimed, however, that the big policy racket on Chicago's South Side was reserved exclusively for Negro operators. Such assertions were often made by corrupt Negro politicians who were anxious to have policy flourish without interference from any quarter. The myth of a Negro racket operated exclusively by Negroes appealed to the strong racial feeling which prevails on the South Side. It was true, of course, that a few Negro policy kings had made a fortune from the nickels and dimes of the poverty-stricken South Side residents. Edward Jones, together with his brother George, and Theodore Roe, all Negroes, have long operated the Maine-Idaho-Ohio policy wheel and have amassed millions of dollars from the poor people living in the city's most disgraceful slum area. The policy racket is an illegitimate offspring of the lottery, originally designed to pluck the coins from the poor who could not afford to buy a lottery ticket. Policy players purchase numbers from runners or in policy stations. The operators of the game place seventy-eight pellets in a cylinder, usually called a wheel, and the winning numbers are drawn from it. Sometimes, the arduous task of actually spinning the wheel is dispensed with and the operators arbitrarily announce the winning numbers. The odds against the player frequently reach astronomical figures. In 1946,

Edward Jones was kidnaped and held for ransom in the sum of $250,000. George Jones negotiated with the kidnapers and Edward was released when $100,000 was paid to the abductors. As usual, the case was never officially solved. However, in the report of the Kefauver Committee it is stated that Jack Guzik recorded, simply as "from various sources" without explanation, a single item of income in the amount of $100,000 for the year 1946. A week after Edward Jones was released by his kidnapers, he fled to Mexico, although he continued to receive approximately $200,000 a year from his Chicago policy wheel which was managed in his absence by Theodore Roe.

The lucrative nature of Chicago's South Side policy racket was clearly reflected by the books and records of the Jones brothers' Maine-Idaho-Ohio wheel. The Kefauver Committee upon examining these records learned that in 1946, the year Edward Jones was kidnaped, the net profits of this wheel amounted to $1,120,413.87. In succeeding years the net profits were somewhat less but they still amounted to $851,978.14 in 1947, $997,564.41 in 1948 and $637,011.80 in 1949. There were relatively few legitimate business concerns in Chicago that could boast of such tremendous annual profits after all expenses had been paid. Yet, the Jones brothers were clearing almost a million dollars a year above expenses from illegal policy operations during the very period the city administration was boasting that there was no wide-open gambling in Chicago!

Naturally, the Capone mob could not be expected to overlook the easy money to be found among the policy-mad residents of the South Side, and Pat Manno, long a close associate of Capone leaders, had been exploiting the Negro passion for playing policy for twenty years. His partner throughout much of this period was Peter C. Tremont, also a friend of important Capone gangsters. The policy operations of Manno and Tremont were conducted under the high-sounding firm name of the Standard Golden Gate Company with headquarters at 6040 Cottage Grove Avenue. The books and records of this concern which were examined by the Kefauver Committee showed that in 1949 the sum of $5,150,000 was taken in by the Manno-Tremont combination; the gross income was approximately $1,000,000 and Manno and Tremont each cleared over $100,000 for the trouble involved in collecting the nickels, dimes and quarters from South Side families, many of whom were living in squalor.

Manno in turn resided with his family in a palatial residence on Lamson Drive in the exclusive North Shore suburb of Winnetka. His next-door neighbor was the president of one of Chicago's most prominent and wealthiest companies.

In 1946, Pat Manno had represented the Capone syndicate in Dallas, Texas when efforts were made to organize gambling and other rackets there for the benefit of the Chicago underworld. In the fall of that year, the Dallas police received information that a man named Paul Jones was in the city on behalf of the Chicago syndicate. His presence in Dallas was resented by local racketeers and trouble was brewing which could easily lead to a shooting, so detective Lieutenant George Butler of the Dallas Police Department was assigned to locate Jones and interrogate him. Jones gave Lieutenant Butler a vivid account of the Chicago syndicate's operations and proposed an alliance with the Dallas authorities. In particular, Jones expressed a desire to effect a working arrangement with the sheriff which he said would be worth $150,000 a year to that officer. He asked Lieutenant Butler to approach the newly-elected sheriff, Steve Guthrie, and determine if he would be willing to meet with him and talk business. Jones assured Lieutenant Butler that the Chicago syndicate would operate in Dallas only through local racketeers who would "front" for the Chicago group. During the course of the conversation he referred to Paul Labriola, a well-known Chicago gunman and the stepson of the slain Capone gangster, Dago Lawrence Mangano. Labriola, said Jones, was one of the men who would represent the syndicate in settling any differences that might arise. Other names mentioned by Jones were Jack Guzik, whom he described as one of the head men in the syndicate, and Murray Humphreys. Of the various activities in which the Chicago syndicate was engaged he discussed whiskey running from Wichita Falls into the dry state of Oklahoma, slot-machine operations, crap games, gambling houses and policy. He asserted that the Chicago Negro policy kings, the Jones brothers, had paid $200,000 ransom in a kidnaping and then fled to Mexico. He related that his organization was at that time, 1946, making every effort to take over the wire service. He spoke of big black-market transactions with Spain by way of Vera Cruz, Mexico, and of traffic in narcotics.

After his conversation with Paul Jones, Lieutenant Butler was instructed by his chief to approach sheriff Steve Guthrie and secure his co-operation in meeting with Jones. Arrangements were then made with the head of the State Department of Public Safety to send a ranger to Guthrie's residence for the purpose of recording all conversations. A photographer was also concealed on the premises to take pictures of the hoodlums who called at the Guthrie home. The first meeting at the newly-elected sheriff's home took place on November 1, 1946, when Lieutenant Butler and Sheriff Guthrie conferred with Paul Jones from eight o'clock at night until the early hours of the following morning. The conversation was recorded from an adjoining room. After this initial conference Jones left for Chicago. On November 3, 1946, he telephoned Lieutenant Butler from Chicago and stated that he would return to Dallas the following Tuesday morning with some of the "top people" in the syndicate.

On November 6, Pat Manno arrived in Dallas by airplane from Chicago and registered at the Adolphus Hotel. Early the following morning Pat Manno, Paul Jones, Jack Knapp and Lieutenant George Butler met with Steve Guthrie in the sheriff's residence where they conferred for three hours. Jack Knapp, according to Jones, was the syndicate's representative in Wisconsin and a nephew of Manno. The conversations were recorded and a photographer, concealed in the garage, snapped pictures of the party as they left. This photograph was introduced into evidence at the Chicago hearings of the Kefauver Committee and, although Pat Manno refused to answer most questions, he did identify himself in this picture. Lieutenant Butler also identified Pat Manno, Jack Knapp and Paul Jones in the photograph. He then introduced into evidence the recorded conversations of Pat Manno in Dallas on November 7, 1946. Pat Manno, unwittingly, had made a permanent record of some of the methods employed by the Capone syndicate in its large-scale activities. He stressed the importance of organization. "Once you get organized," said Manno, "you don't have to worry about money. Everything will roll in a nice quiet manner, in a businesslike way. You don't . . . have to worry about it personally. Everybody will be happy. I'm sure." Manno had then assured the Texas officials that the syndicate's actual operations in Dallas would be handled by local men. He emphasized the importance, as a matter of sound policy, in concentrating the syndicate's gambling casino activities in just one large place which should be located outside the city proper. Manno stated, "One thing I'm against, always was against, I don't like . . . five or six joints in the radius of six blocks, a joint every block. That's one thing I've always talked against. I like one big spot and that's all. Out in the country, out of the city entirely." When queried further by the Texas officials regarding casino gambling, Manno replied, ". . . these places like dice rooms or horse rooms and things like that, that's like another department I would call it. If I had a fellow sitting here with me that runs a certain game, he could give it to you in a minute. But I have my own little concession, and that's the end. . . . Policy is my business. That I could run . . . I've been at it for seventeen years."

It was evident from Manno's recorded conversations that the Capone syndicate relies heavily upon efficient organization. Like an efficient business concern, it also resorts to specialization. Manno said that his "department" was policy while other syndicate members specialized in running gambling casinos and horse rooms. Manno was actually the advance man for the syndicate in Dallas. He informed the Dallas officials that he was down there to "look the thing over" and go back to Chicago where he would "report to his people." Shortly after Manno returned to Chicago the Dallas officials made public the proposed invasion of Texas by the Chicago underworld. Paul Jones, who was still in Texas, was arrested and brought to trial on charges of bribery. He was found guilty and sentenced to serve three years in the state penitentiary. While his case was pending appeal, however, the Federal government convicted Jones for flying sixty pounds of opium over the Mexican border and he was committed to the Federal penitentiary. He was still behind Federal bars when the Senate Committee held its hearings in Chicago.

Pat Manno found that Chicago was a much safer place to conduct business in behalf of the syndicate than Dallas. He had been handling negotiations with Chicago officials for almost two decades, throughout which he had enjoyed absolute immunity. Never had his conferences with officials been betrayed, and prosecutions for bribery were unheard of. The unexpected turn of events in Texas apparently did not cause Manno to lose face with the Capone leaders, however.

Before long he was to play a major role in a typical underworld maneuver which would enable Tony Accardo and Jack Guzik to take control of a lucrative policy wheel on the South Side.

For many years, the Erie-Buffalo policy wheel owned by Julius Benvenuti and his two brothers, Caesar and Leo, had prospered in the Negro district. The Benvenutis also were in control of a paper company which specialized in the production of policy slips and was heavily patronized by many of the wheels operating in Chicago and other cities. Julius Benvenuti had always maintained cordial relations with Al Capone. In fact, the many favors he performed for Capone had made it possible for the Erie-Buffalo wheel to flourish over a period of decades without interference from the grasping hands of the syndicate. Julius Benvenuti died on January 14, 1945, and two years later on January 26, 1947, Al Capone passed away. With the deaths of these two men, the amity which had long prevailed between the Capone syndicate and the Benvenutis came to a sudden end. Covetous eyes were promptly cast in the direction of the Erie-Buffalo policy wheel, and later in 1947, the homes of both Caesar and Leo Benvenuti were bombed. But profits from the Erie-Buffalo wheel were too great for the Benvenutis to surrender without a struggle. Caesar and Leo Benvenuti each cleared approximately $105,000 from this wheel during 1947, and out of the generosity of their souls they also doled out $1500 to an underling, Sam Pardy. In 1948, however, there were sudden and drastic changes in the management of the Erie-Buffalo wheel. The income-tax returns examined by the Kefauver Committee told the story.

For many years Pat Manno's brothers, Fred, Tom and Jeff, had been junior partners of Peter Tremont and Pat Manno in the operation of the two policy wheels called the Standard Golden Gate and the Rome-Silver. In 1948, Tom Manno severed his connection with these two wheels where his income was about $40,000 a year and became associated with the Benvenuti brothers' wheel, the Erie-Buffalo. In 1948, the income of Leo and Caesar Benvenuti dropped from $105,000 each to $50,000. In contrast, the income of Tom Manno soared to $305,000. And Sam Pardy's take from the Erie-Buffalo wheel skyrocketed from $1500 in 1947 to $305,000 the following year. The significance of the change in management of the Benvenuti brothers' wheel became apparent the next year. In 1949,

Pardy and Manno each received $135,000 from the Erie-Buffalo wheel while the books and records of this business reflected that the sum of $278,000 was paid for "special services" to the partnership of Tony Accardo and Jack Guzik. The income-tax returns of these gangsters also acknowledged receipt of this money. Obviously, the Capone syndicate had taken over the Erie-Buffalo policy wheel. They could now boast of controlling three of the most lucrative policy wheels on the South Side and it was apparent that Pat Manno, through his brother, had figured prominently in this latest maneuver. It was only in Dallas, Texas, when he unexpectedly encountered some honest officials, that Pat Manno failed as a negotiator in behalf of his chiefs.

The testimony of scores of witnesses who appeared before the Senate Crime Committee and the examination of the income-tax returns of various underworld bosses told a graphic story of the power of the Capone syndicate. And the syndicate's methods as described by Pat Manno to Dallas officials were clearly verified by the official testimony and records. With Manno as head of the policy department on the South Side, money was rolling in by the truckload. Through control of the wire service Chicago's handbook industry was under the complete domination of the syndicate. And the one big gambling casino, "out in the country, out of the city entirely," exactly as described by Manno, was flourishing just a few miles north of the Loop. It was known as Ralph's Place, and Chicago Crime Commission investigators had established that Rocco Fischetti, Gus Alex, August Liebe, Eddie Vogel and other Capone hoodlums were in control of the huge crap games, roulette wheels and other forms of gambling featured. These same individuals had operated the lavishly furnished Vernon Country Club in Lake County, Illinois, until Rocco Fischetti, Gus Liebe and others were indicted by a special grand jury a few years before. Upon examination of the income-tax returns of the so-called owner of Ralph's Place, starting with the year 1944, Ralph Di Constanzo, the Kefauver Committee ascertained that he had listed Ed Vogel as the source of part of his income. For the years 1945 and 1946, he recorded his income as coming from both Ed Vogel and the Vernon Country Club. His affiliation with Ralph's Place started in 1947. The evidence linking Ralph's Place with the Capone syndicate's "slot-machine king," Eddie Vogel, was not surprising to the average citizen. But many citizens were taken aback when the Senate Committee disclosed irrefutable evidence to show that slot machines in private country clubs were owned and controlled for the benefit of the Capone gangsters. The proprietor of a nationally known country club informed the Committee that his dealings with Eddie Vogel dated back fifteen years. The Capone slot-machine boss had generously agreed to permit the club to keep sixty per cent of the proceeds from the one-armed bandits and to retain only forty per cent for himself! Then about twelve years ago, the country club proprietor decided to purchase nine slot machines outright from the Mills Novelty Company and retain all of the proceeds for the club. A few days after they were installed, a deputy sheriff called on him and explained that he was guilty of unfair trade practices — practices that would not be countenanced by either the sheriff's office or the Capone gang. The deputy sheriff indicated that unless the country club management fell in line, it would be his sad duty to confiscate the slot machines. In order to avert this catastrophe, it was suggested to the proprietor that he call a certain telephone number which the deputy sheriff furnished him. Upon calling he learned that he was talking with Eddie Vogel's headquarters. Inquiry was made of him as to the amount of money the club had paid for the slot machines. When informed that the sum of $1800 had been expended, Vogel assured him that a check would be sent him covering the club's outlay for the machines. This promise was fulfilled and Eddie Vogel's collector called at the country club every Monday. Behind locked doors, the collector and the club's comptroller removed the money from the slot machines and forty per cent of the proceeds was turned over to Vogel's representative. There were two keys to the room in which the slot machines were kept. One key was permanently in the possession of Vogel's collector and the other was retained by the club's comptroller. Whenever slot machines needed repairing, this detail was handled by Vogel's collector. And on those occasions when official action was contemplated against the one-armed bandits in private clubs, the comptroller always received a call from an official who would tell him to "close down the slots." As soon as it was safe to place the machines in operation again, a call was always received from Vogel's collector. And with the exception of one raid, the longest period the slot machines were out of operation was three hours. It was all a very cozy arrangement — an arrangement which netted the slot-machine king almost $30,000 a year and the club over $40,000.

Some Chicagoans were also surprised when the Senate Committee disclosed that much of the city's thirst was still being quenched by many of the same individuals who were prominently identified with the liquor and beer industry during prohibition. A number of Al Capone's associates and henchmen during the dry period had risen to the top of million-dollar liquor and beer enterprises while maintaining friendly relations with many of their former underworld associates. Perhaps the largest liquor distributor in Chicago and Cook County is the Gold Seal Liquors, Inc., headed by Al Capone's old friend, Joseph Charles Fusco. The Senate Committee was informed by Fusco that he owns over one fourth of the stock in the Gold Seal Liquors, Inc., which has a net worth of $2,200,000. In addition to this highly prosperous venture, Fusco is also a part owner of the Rembrandt Distributing Company, Steel City Liquor Distributing Company, Cornell Distributing Company, Bohemian Wine and Liquor Company and the Bohemian Brewing Company. Truly one of the big tycoons in Chicago's liquor industry, Fusco got his start when he was only nineteen. At that time rum running was a major industry ruled over by Al Capone. Apparently the talents of Fusco came to the attention of the gang chief early in the careers of both men. It was Capone, said Fusco, who placed him in touch with Bert Delaney, generally regarded as the superintendent of Capone's breweries. A Federal indictment returned in Chicago on June 12, 1931, charged Joe Fusco, Al Capone, Bert Delaney and scores of others with having conspired over a period of ten years to violate the United States prohibition laws. In nineteen overt acts listed in the indictment, the Federal government traced the history of the alleged conspiracy beginning with the incorporation of the World Motor Service in Chicago on January 6, 1921, by Fusco and others. It recounted the dispatching of a Western Union money order in the amount of $2000 by Fusco, on June 22, 1928, from Chicago to Al Capone in Miami, and it told of meetings between Capone, Fusco and Bert Delaney in the Lexington Hotel as late as June 12, 1930, for the purpose of carrying out the conspiracy. A few months after this indictment was returned, Al Capone, the principal defendant in the case, was convicted of income-tax evasion. The prohibition era was coming to an end and the prosecution was dropped.

Until the repeal of prohibition, Fusco's sole business for many years was bootlegging. It was during this period that he became acquainted with such leading Capone gangsters as Charles Fischetti, Louis Campagna, John Rosselli, Tony Accardo, Jack Guzik, Hymie Levin, Pat Manno, Phil D'Andrea, John Torrio and many others. These were lush days for the bootleggers but it is doubtful if they compared to the prosperity that Fusco was to enjoy in the liquor business following the repeal of prohibition. Fusco testified before the Senate Committee that about two months prior to the hearings he had placed a single order with a major distillery for liquor amounting to $4,000,000. In some instances, the Gold Seal Liquors, Inc., is the exclusive Chicago distributor for widely-demanded brands of liquor. When asked by the Kefauver Committee, "Are you the outstanding dealer in Chicago today?" Fusco replied, "In sales volume, I would say we are number one, yes sir."

Among the various distilleries for which Joe Fusco has operated as a distributor is William Whitely and Company, a British concern. Fusco testified that his original deal to handle the products of this distillery was made with Irving Haim, a personal friend and business associate of Frank Costello. In fact, in 1937 Haim negotiated for the purchase of the Whitely distillery holding company with money obtained from a New Orleans bank on notes secured by Haim, Frank Costello, Phil Kastel and William Hellis. Fusco informed the Senate Committee that his acquaintanceship with Costello's right-hand man, "Dandy" Phil Kastel, covers a period of fifteen years and on a less intimate basis he also knows Costello.

The Kefauver Committee was particularly intrigued with records of the Gold Seal Liquors which were labeled "ice sheets." Fusco explained the items on these sheets as referring to samples and breakage but the Committee did not appear convinced. When asked if it were not true that the word "ice" usually denotes graft, Fusco answered, "Yes; but if I gave a man a case of whiskey, I wouldn't give it to him for graft." He admitted that at Christmas time he habitually gives whiskey to about 250 officers of the Chicago Police Department and to a number of other public officials as well. When asked if State Representative James Adducci was one of the officials to whom he has sent cases of liquor, Fusco answered, "I may have; yes."

Everything touched by Fusco has turned to gold. His phenomenal success has even attended his horse-race gambling — an avocation that results in huge losses to most habitual gamblers. In 1949, Fusco's income from horse-race gambling amounted to $37,000. The chairman of the Senate Committee stated, "Year after year you seem to have $30,000 profit" and asked Fusco to explain how it was possible for him to win consistently. The answer filled inveterate horse-race bettors with utter amazement. He said, "You always find a lot of touts around the race track always trying to give you a winner. They may think I am a $20.00 bettor. So, if a guy comes up to you and says, 'I have a horse I think is going to win,' I will say, 'Here is $20.00, go and bet $10.00 and bet $10.00 for me.' If I like the horse, I may walk over and bet $500.00 unbeknown to him." The fraudulent character of the slimy touts who peddle their wares at race tracks is well known; yet Fusco insisted that his horse-race gambling income of $30,000 a year is based on tips given him by these spurious purveyors of inside racing information — truly a remarkable success story!

In January 1952, Chicago newspapers reported that Fusco was being forced to sell his extensive liquor company holdings to his partner, Milton Friedman, under threat of action by the Illinois Liquor Control Commission.

While Fusco's company handles the lion's share of liquor distributed in Chicago, his friend, Alex Louis Greenberg, heads one of the largest breweries in the city. Like Fusco, Greenberg was also closely associated with Al Capone and other gangsters. In fact his friend Charles Gioe, one of several Capone gangsters convicted in the moving picture extortion case, lived at Greenberg's hotel, the Seneca in Chicago, following his parole in 1947. Greenberg informed the Senate Committee that he owns 7400 shares of stock in the Seneca Hotel. As a practical matter, this gives him a working control of this valuable sixteen-story building situated in the Gold Coast area of the near North Side.

Born in Russia, Greenberg came to the United States in 1905. After living in New York City about four years, he moved to Chicago where he entered the restaurant and saloon business. Later he became a part owner and the guiding genius of the Roosevelt Finance Company. Greenberg was on intimate terms with Dion O'Banion, Maxie Eisen and Hymie Weiss, notorious prohibition gangsters. During the dry period O'Banion and Weiss were two of the principal owners of the Manhattan Brewery, and Greenberg through the Roosevelt Finance Company made substantial loans to them for their operations. O'Banion was killed in Chicago's gang warfare on November 10, 1924, and rival gunman's bullets finished Weiss on October 11, 1926. Following their deaths, Greenberg acquired their stock in the Manhattan Brewery and after the repeal of prohibition he embarked upon a reorganization program, eventually changing the name to Canadian Ace Brewing Company. As a part of this plan, Greenberg hired Arthur C. Lueder, the Republican candidate for mayor in 1923 and a former postmaster, to serve as the brewery's president. In 1940, Lueder was elected to the office of state auditor, a position he was to hold for eight years. Greenberg informed the Kefauver Committee that he contributed $20,000 to help elect his brewery president to this important state office.

Greenberg was perhaps more intimately associated with Frank "The Enforcer" Nitti than Al Capone. He testified before the Senate Committee that he had known Nitti for thirty years and when this syndicate leader committed suicide on March 19, 1943, Greenberg was holding $100,000 of Nitti's money which he turned over to the gangster's estate.

Several close friends of important Capone syndicate members have acted as distributors for Greenberg's beer. In Kansas City, Tony Gizzo obtained the agency for Canadian Ace beer, and in Chicago one of Greenberg's distributors has been Ralph Buglio, known at one time as a Capone gunman and mentioned in the press in connection with some of the city's gang killings. Buglio also buys some of his beer from Joe Fusco. Until May 9, 1950, Greenberg's beer was distributed in Des Moines, Iowa, by the Canadian Ace Beer Sales Company. This concern was a partnership which included Sylvia Zevin, a sister of Alex Louis Greenberg, Morris Greenberg, a brother, and Louis Thomas Fratto, known as Lew Farrell, a lifelong friend of Charles Gioe. Farrell had a long arrest record in Chicago before settling in the Iowa capital several years ago, where it appears that his activities have not been confined to peddling beer. The Senate Committee confronted Farrell with public accusations made against him in Des Moines that he had attempted to muscle into a local gambling casino. Records were also produced to show that Farrell has been a partner in the Sports Arcade, a Des Moines horserace gambling place. Greenberg informed the Kefauver Committee that his brother-in-law has acted as the bookkeeper for the bartenders' union which was under the domination of Frank Nitti and other Capone gangsters for many years.

The evidence produced before the Senate Crime Committee clearly established that the repeal of prohibition had not interfered with the lucrative nature of Chicago's liquor and beer industry insofar as some of Al Capone's friends are concerned. Joe Fusco admitted a personal net worth of about $800,000 while the net worth of his Gold Seal Liquors, Inc., is $2,200,000, exclusive of the other companies of which he is a part owner. Alex Louis Greenberg's Canadian Ace Brewing Company, incorporated for $200,000, does a yearly business of about $10,000,000. Both Fusco and Greenberg are certainly captains of industry!

A clear insight into the organizing abilities of the Capone gang was provided by the testimony of Eugene Bernstein. A lawyer since 1919 and an employee of the Bureau of Internal Revenue for about ten years, Bernstein resigned from the Federal service in 1923 and started a private practice specializing in tax matters. For a number of years, almost everyone in the Capone gang has retained Bernstein to prepare his income-tax return. His clients also have included, among others, the R and H Publishing Company and the Trans-American Publishing and News Service, Inc. When the Capone gang organized the Trans-American company, Bernstein recommended his brother-in-law, Morton W. Samuelson, to serve as its auditor. Bernstein, however, prepared the income-tax returns for the company and later handled the dissolution of the corporation.

The private citizen or legitimate businessman who diligently labors over his income-tax returns, only to be called down to the Bureau of Internal Revenue offices with books and records to prove the accuracy of his return or to pay a penalty for some honest mistake, is utterly amazed at the defiant attitude displayed by underworld leaders toward the Federal government. As far as can be deter-

mined, figures for income-tax purposes are pulled out of thin air by
the gangsters and forwarded to the government on a "take it or
leave it" basis. Bernstein testified that with one or two exceptions
"They wouldn't give me any information at all, except now and then
I would have some independent information and would question
them on it. They were rather reticent about that." Bernstein was
asked, "You mean they wouldn't divulge to you as their attorney?"
His answer was "No. They would give us the net amount and say
this was the amount of income." For example, Murray Humphreys's
income-tax returns prepared by Bernstein for 1947 merely recorded
miscellaneous income $27,000 and nothing else. For the year 1946,
Humphreys's return lists: "Commissions and so forth $24,000." This
return was typical of many others. During the interrogation of
Tony Accardo, it was brought out that a revenue agent, Ned Klein,
had questioned him regarding a suspicious round sum of $65,000
which appeared in one of his returns. Accardo had refused to explain the source of this money, the expenses involved in obtaining
this income or any other pertinent details. In commenting on this
incident, the chief counsel for the Senate Committee stated, "In
1948 a revenue agent attempted to find out something about the
witness' income, and then without having his constitutional rights
to plead, but simply being in the position of an ordinary citizen, he
simply refused to give the information. . . ." In disgust, Senator
Alexander Wiley remarked, "I have got to show every calf born on
my farm." And when he asked, "What ever happened in the case?"
he was advised that "The Government had to drop the case." The
leader of the Capone gang had pitted his power against the Federal
government — and won!

The true character of the Capone gang was vividly portrayed by
Bernstein's testimony regarding the settlement of the tax claims
against Paul Ricca and Louis Campagna prior to their parole in 1947.
According to Bernstein, Tony Accardo walked into his office one
day and announced that he would help him with the case. Bernstein
assumed that Joseph Bulger, one-time president of the Unione Siciliana, and an attorney who had represented Ricca in legal matters,
sent Accardo to his office. Accardo was no stranger to Bernstein
since he had prepared the gang leader's tax returns for many years.
It was only natural that Accardo as head of the Capone syndicate

should assume the leadership in arranging for a settlement of the tax cases involving two important members of his mob. This was particularly true since their incarceration resulted from a conspiracy of the entire Capone gang to extort money from the moving picture industry.

Bernstein testified that he required about $126,000 plus interest, making a total of $185,000 or $190,000, to settle the tax claims. Campagna's back tax debt was over double that of Ricca. It was apparent, however, that these claims were not considered debts of Campagna and Ricca as individuals. They were treated as obligations of the Capone organization. The committee was informed by Bernstein that several unknown men came to his office within a period of thirty to sixty days and each dumped from $10,000 to $20,000 on his desk. He believes that he personally saw six different men while others left money with his secretary in his absence. No record was kept by Bernstein as to the amount of money each man paid and he insisted that their identities were never known to him. It was never necessary for him to call anyone concerning the money. Apparently Tony Accardo directed his henchmen to deliver certain sums to Bernstein's office, and when the amount required to settle the tax claims arrived the delivery of the money automatically stopped. Since there was a vast difference between the amount of the indebtedness of Campagna and Ricca, the Kefauver Committee asked Bernstein if he divided the money left in his office into two separate funds. He answered, "No, I treated it as one fund." And it was properly considered one fund — the fund of the Capone gang as an organization.

In connection with the numerous trips made by Tony Accardo and Eugene Bernstein to Leavenworth during these negotiations, Tony Gizzo acted much in the capacity of a local branch manager for the Capone organization. Upon their arrival in Kansas City, Gizzo always met Accardo and Bernstein and either he or his representative would drive them to the penitentiary. On the day before the gangsters were to be released on parole, Bernstein went to Kansas City and Gizzo made arrangements for him to occupy the penthouse suite in the Muehlebach Hotel. When Bernstein found that he needed two additional plane tickets in order to provide adequate transportation for the paroled gangsters to Chicago, Gizzo purchased them. Bernstein testified that he never paid Gizzo for either his hotel suite or the two additional air tickets. It is a fair inference that this was all considered in the light of company expense for company business. On August 13, 1947, Bernstein was driven to Leavenworth in Gizzo's Cadillac convertible to greet Paul Ricca, Louis Campagna, Charles Gioe and Phil D'Andrea as they walked out of prison on their premature and scandalous paroles.

The Kefauver Committee thus unfolded before the public a picture of the Capone gang as a powerful and wealthy concern of frightening stature. Yet it was only a partial picture. During the investigation many of the gangsters fled and went into hiding. Others appeared before the Committee but refused to answer questions while those who testified were evasive and attempted to withhold pertinent information. But even the partial picture established the Capone gang as a criminal organization with a menacing power surpassing that of the old Camorra of Naples or the Maffia of Sicily.

The evidence clearly identified Tony Accardo as the leader of the Capone syndicate, a position he had earned while serving within the ranks of the gang since it ruled Chicago's underworld from the old Lexington Hotel over thirty years ago. In virtually all of the gang's major projects, Tony Accardo has played a principal role. It was Accardo who directed the activities which led to the parole of Ricca, Campagna, Gioe, and D'Andrea in 1947. It was Accardo, together with Jack Guzik, Murray Humphreys and Ralph O'Hara, who attempted to take over the racing information wire service on a nationwide basis. For many years Accardo with other syndicate men received large incomes from the Owl Club, a gambling casino in Calumet City, Illinois. In 1947, his share of the Owl Club's reported profits was $38,911.49, in 1948, $45,653.98 and in 1949, $32,402.12. When Harry Russell muscled into the S and G gambling syndicate in Miami, the income-tax records showed that Tony Accardo and Jack Guzik received an interest in this $26,000,000-a-year enterprise. When Pat Manno, through his brother, succeeded in taking over the Erie-Buffalo policy wheel, the income-tax returns of Accardo and Guzik reflected that this worthy pair received $268,415.08 in one year, 1949, as their share of the proceeds. Even in such matters as the distribution of juke boxes, Accardo felt entitled to a part of the profits. In 1947, he reported an income item of $2200 representing salary from the Illinois Simplex Distributing

Company, an important juke-box distributor in Chicago and Illinois. The following year, Accardo accounted for $4500 of his income totaling $110,353.98 as profits from the sale of the Illinois Simplex Distributing Company.

As head of the Capone organization, Tony Accardo is rolling in wealth — wealth obtained from manipulation, ruthlessness and terrorism — wealth made possible from a beneficent political system which has always relied heavily on the underworld for its money, votes and power. And the gang leader is determined to live in a style befitting his rank and position. Early in 1951, Accardo and his family moved into their new twenty-two room home in the exclusive Chicago suburb of River Forest. This place was built several years ago by a millionaire manufacturer at a cost of a half-million dollars and was one of the show places of River Forest. The Accardo estate, including an open-air garden on the roof of a private swimming pool, stands as a monument to prove that crime pays well in Chicago.

Accardo's number one position in the gang rests in part on luck. In the normal course of events, Frank Nitti's throne probably would have descended to Paul Ricca. But shortly after Nitti committed suicide in 1943, Ricca was committed to Federal prison, and because of the Congressional investigation which followed his scandalous parole, it was necessary for him to remain in the background of the gang's affairs. Ricca had no cause to complain, however. When he walked out of Leavenworth Penitentiary on August 13, 1947, he had cash amounting to $300,000 concealed in his home, in addition to his large real estate holdings. Ricca attributed all of his wealth to gambling, a business that yielded him $100,000 a year in profits before he was sent to prison. Money was so plentiful with Ricca that when he was confronted with his books, records and testimony, he could not account for $141,000 which had disappeared within a three-year period following his parole.

There was certainly no mystery surrounding the fantastic wealth and power of Chicago's Capone syndicate. Gangster after gangster testified before the Kefauver Committee regarding his interest and participation in city politics. Much of this activity centered in the First Ward ruled over by Hinky Dink Kenna and Bathhouse John Coughlin for so many years. Among those who became influential in the First Ward organization was Phil D'Andrea. At times D'Andrea needed aid in promoting his candidates and his intimate friend, Al Capone, helped him corral votes. It was commonly understood, said D'Andrea, that in political matters Al Capone "was able to do almost anything he wanted to do." D'Andrea also benefited directly from Al Capone's political backing. Until about 1942, he had a fleet of trucks used for city hauling and it was through Capone's political influence many years ago that this business prospered. D'Andrea testified:

> I was in the cartage business. . . . He [Capone] helped me put on a few trucks. I was doing cartage work for the city at the time. . . . Due to the fact that I had trucks working for the city it was my duty to gather votes wherever I could. Being president of the Society [Unione Siciliana], I had many meetings, many organization meetings, at which I invited the candidates to speak, financed those meetings, and so forth. The usual game of politics.

Capone was naturally interested in having his henchmen occupy positions of influence in the Chicago courts and Phil D'Andrea received an appointment as deputy bailiff in the municipal branch of the judicial system. D'Andrea's salary as an officer of the court amounted to about $300.00 a month. His income was further augmented from signing bail bonds with William R. Skidmore who became gambling king during the Kelly-Nash regime. D'Andrea's political career was no flash in the pan. He informed the Senate Committee that he remained active in First Ward organization politics until shortly before the Federal government ordered him to prison at the end of 1943.

D'Andrea was only one cog in the powerful Capone organization. Before Al Capone was committed to Federal prison he always placed his men at the voting places on election day. With Capone gunmen handling the polls, it is safe to assume that a candidate favored by the syndicate never had to worry about the outcome of the election. D'Andrea testified that the Capone gang had supported William Hale Thompson for mayor until the 1931 election when his opponent was Anton J. Cermak. "Then at the last minute," said D'Andrea, the Capone gangsters "switched over to Cermak," a move the underworld never had cause to regret.

Daniel A. Serritella, who owed much to his friend Al Capone for his political advancement, informed the Kefauver Committee that he held the important post of city sealer under Mayor Thompson from 1927 to 1931. Beginning about 1927, he was the Republican ward committeeman of the First Ward for many years and for a period of twelve years starting in 1930 he served as a State Senator in the Illinois General Assembly. Serritella, who figured prominently in the racing wire service and scratch sheet warfare that broke out in 1945, was interrogated about his association with Jack Guzik. Serritella testified, "Jack Guzik has been in the First Ward. He is the fellow that helped me politically . . . I think he is a wonderful fellow so far as I know." However, the Senate Committee did not find it necessary to rely exclusively on the testimony of Serritella for evidence of Guzik's vital interest in politics. It was furnished with a photostatic copy of a communication mailed on January 24, 1944 to Jack Guzik by one of his associates in the wire service and scratch sheet business who was vacationing in Phoenix, Arizona. The communication related to the 1944 campaign for governor of Illinois and explained why their favored candidate for this office would not be available. The situation called for prompt action and Guzik's friend expressed the hope that he could see him when he returned to Chicago the following Saturday. Hymie Levin, long associated with Guzik in Capone syndicate gambling operations, also had his finger in local politics. Serritella informed the Kefauver Committee, "When I run for Committeeman and Senator, Hymie Levin . . . went out and voted for me and had everybody vote for me. He was my friend."

With Al Capone in Federal prison, Frank Nitti directed the underworld empire. Like Capone, he became an important political figure, spending considerable time in the cigar store of Alderman Kenna on South Clark Street which served as headquarters for the First Ward organization. When Charles Gioe was questioned about his association with Nitti, he admitted knowing him for many years. Said Gioe, "I met him around the old man's cigar store . . . over on Clark Street. Alderman Kenna's place." Gioe also was interested in First Ward politics. When asked about his party affiliation, Gioe replied, "I was an opportunist. If a Republican was in power, I would ask him for favors, and if the Democrats were in

power, I would see the Democrats." Close friends of Gioe, Nitti
and Al Capone, such as Alex Louis Greenberg, have also actively
supported the campaigns of many politicians seeking important elective offices. Greenberg spent $20,000 to further the candidacy of
Arthur C. Lueder for State Auditor, $1000 to help elect Arthur X.
Elrod to the Board of Cook County Commissioners and has made
substantial campaign contributions to judges and a state senator.

Tony Accardo refused to answer practically all questions of the
Senate Crime Committee. He admitted, however, that he has aided
the cause of favored candidates by "getting votes" for them. When
asked if he has voted in any election, his answer was "No." Apparently Chicago's organized underworld is interested only in votes in
wholesale lots and Accardo is usually so busy on election day garnering votes that he is unable to find time to cast his own ballot.

In the Illinois General Assembly the West Side bloc, made up of a
number of close friends of Capone leaders, sit in the legislative halls
and vote as a unit on all matters. The leadership of this group of legislators in the House of Representatives is frequently in the hands of
James J. Adduci, a member of the state legislature for the past eighteen years. Adduci's testimony before the Kefauver Committee gave a
keen insight into the rugged game of politics as it is played in Chicago.
For almost three decades he has been on the public payroll holding various political jobs. During the regime of Mayor Thompson,
Adduci was superintendent of telephones and telegraph and for ten
years was an inspector for the Sanitary District. Born and raised
on the West Side, Adduci has had many friends identified with the
underworld. He informed the Senate Crime Committee that he has
been seized by the police eight or ten times and on one occasion
he was arrested with Willie Bioff, who was involved in the moving picture extortion case. Adduci admitted knowing the slain
gangsters Jack Zuta and Dago Lawrence Mangano. Mangano was
particularly helpful to the political aspirations of the West Side
bloc leader. Adduci testified, "On the primary and election, Lawrence used to give me a little finances to help me finance my precinct when I was precinct captain." After Adduci admitted that
Mangano operated a gambling establishment on the West Side until
he was killed in 1944, the chairman of the Senate Crime Committee

asked him, "Do you generally accept political help from gamblers and bookmakers . . . ?" His reply was, "In my precinct I would accept a little finances from any kind of a business." When asked if bookmaking establishments operate in his district, Adduci answered, "I guess you can make a bet in my district."

The district which has sent James Adduci to the state legislature for eighteen years consists of sixty-two precincts extending through three wards. Adduci testified, "I come from a very funny district. I have every element there is in the world, I guess, in my district. I have the pimp, the jack roller, the safeblower, the dope fiend . . . I come from the West Side of Chicago . . . Skid Row . . . is in the heart of my district, where all those so-called hoboes come in and congregate. . . ." It is a good district for the politician, however. Adduci explained to the Kefauver Committee how he and his friends divide the district in order to eliminate any possible hazard for the candidate. Three members of the state House of Representatives are elected from each district and in the ordinary course of events three Democrats would oppose three Republicans, a total of six candidates. But in his district, said Adduci, only ". . . two Democrats and one Republican are nominated, which is equivalent to election." Although he failed to provide any details how the West Side bloc, year after year, is able to limit the nominations to prevent any contest at the election, perhaps he felt that no explanation was necessary!

The salary of a state representative is not highly attractive but Adduci learned that for an ambitious statesman there are emoluments attached to the office not covered by the pay check. When confronted with certain items on his income-tax returns, he advised the Kefauver Committee that for the past six or eight years he has been receiving commissions from an envelope company for obtaining contracts with the state auditor's office. His commission for securing these state contracts, said Adduci, "runs around $5000 or $6000 a year." The public disclosure of this income was to prove very embarrassing to Adduci shortly after the Chicago hearings of the Kefauver Committee came to an end. The Sangamon County Grand Jury in Springfield, Illinois, indicted Adduci on February 26, 1951, for violating the state law which prohibits a legislator from being directly or indirectly interested in state contracts. When called before the grand jury, Michael R. De Tolve, president of the Central Envelope and Lithographing Company of Chicago, produced a photostatic copy of a check amounting to $5490 which was issued to Adduci on January 11, 1950, for commissions paid to him for contracts already obtained from the state auditor and for state business he was expected to secure in the immediate future. Adduci also reported income from the Windy City Sports Enterprises, a legitimate business venture in which his partner is Sam "Mooney" Giancana, an ex-convict who was once a member of the notorious "42 Gang." Commonly regarded as a right-hand man of Tony Accardo, Giancana was arrested with the gang chief in February 1945, as a suspect in a kidnaping case. Giancana has also received income from the Central Envelope and Lithographing Company but for a number of years his principal revenue has stemmed from a notorious gambling establishment known as the Wagon Wheel just northwest of the city limits. During 1947, 1948 and 1949, the Chicago Crime Commission repeatedly reported this place to the sheriff. Apparently the sheriff's office was helpless since Sam Giancana reported income of $98,258.10 as his share of the proceeds from the Wagon Wheel during those three years. It is reasonable to assume that Giancana's close association and friendship with State Representative James J. Adduci and the gang chief, Tony Accardo, may have been a factor in producing the blind spot in the sheriff's office insofar as the Wagon Wheel was concerned.

For many years, Adduci was the leader of a vigorous and frequently vicious fight against the legislation sponsored by the Chicago Crime Commission to improve the criminal laws of the state. The Kefauver Committee interrogated Adduci at considerable length concerning his opposition to this legislation. His testimony provided a sad but accurate commentary on legislative processes in the Illinois General Assembly. When asked, "Why would you be opposed to a bill that sought to extend the life of a grand jury more than one month?" Adduci answered, "I wouldn't know. I am just against them, that is all." Under further questioning, he weakly explained that his conscience would not permit him to vote for the grand jury bill but he was unable to give any reason why the proposed law should affect his conscience. In fact, when counsel for the Senate Committee stated, "You were a member of the legislature and I assume you have read the bill and understand it," Adduci, who moved heaven and earth to prevent its enactment, replied, "No; I have never read it." The Illinois statesman then finally admitted that he considered the proposed act beneficial to the proper enforcement of the law. Said Adduci, "It might be a good bill." And when counsel for the Kefauver Committee, in surprise, asked, "Nevertheless, you voted against it?" the leader of the West Side bloc gave this classic answer: "There are a lot of measures that are good measures that I vote against. I don't vote for every good piece of legislation." It was then suggested, "You aren't interested in law enforcement?" His answer was, "I certainly am." And other testimony given by Adduci left no doubt concerning the accuracy of this response. He explained to the Senate Committee that he had placed ten persons including two policemen in the sheriff's office, the principal law-enforcement agency of Cook County. This was adequate proof of his vital interest in law enforcement — the Adduci brand! [1]

The Chicago hearings of the Senate Crime Committee came to a close just before the Christmas holidays of 1950. Through the testimony of numerous underworld characters and the evidence gleaned from their books, records and income-tax returns, the Committee concluded that the Capone organization is one of the two major crime syndicates in the nation, with its operations extending from Chicago to Kansas City, Dallas, Miami, Las Vegas, and the West Coast. The evidence was incontrovertible and although the Committee had exposed to public light only a partial picture of organized crime in Chicago, the citizens were thoroughly outraged. Throughout the hearings, which lasted only a few days, many politicians were squirming. Heaving a sigh of relief as the Kefauver Committee and its staff left the city, they firmly expected to be doing business again at the old stand within a few days. They hoped the people would soon forget the Senate Committee's revelations. Voters' memories are unbelievably short and, with an aldermanic race and a mayoralty election to be held within a few weeks, political leaders were most anxious to help the electorate forget. Taking the usual political line, the commissioner of police assured the newspapers that no syndicated organized crime existed in Chicago. But the press, which had followed the senate inquiry closely, was far from willing to accept this official statement at face value. In a scathing editorial, the *Chicago News* called attention to the evidence uncovered by the Kefauver Committee and concluded that the Capone syndicate "is swindling the public out of more money than ever before. It is strengthening its political power in the state legislature and in the City Council." The syndicate, said the editorial, "must be fought by every law enforcement agency. It cannot be fought by pretending it doesn't exist." [2]

Efforts of the West Side bloc to become further entrenched in the city council were concentrated in the First Ward consisting of the Loop area and the near South Side and the Twenty-eighth Ward on the West Side. In the aldermanic election scheduled for February 27, 1951, John D'Arco, who had been a loyal member of the bloc in the state legislature, was running for a place in the city council from the First Ward. D'Arco was not a lawyer and the West Side bloc had found it expedient for him to resign from the legislature in favor of a member of the legal profession who would automatically become a member of the House judiciary committee. A bitter fight was expected on bills sponsored by the Chicago Crime Commission and, if they were defeated in the judiciary committee, a vote on them by the House of Representatives could be eliminated. In the Twenty-eighth Ward, Alderman George D. Kells, long one of the most influential Democratic politicians in the state, had been threatened by elements close to the Capone gang and feared to run for re-election to the city council. In a series of vigorous editorials the *Chicago Tribune* attempted to rally the citizens for a fight against this threat to decent government. Said one editorial:

Capone is dead, and his brothers are bums, but he lives as a cancer in Chicago politics. We have the 'West side' bloc, the 'Italian' bloc, composed of six or seven members whom the gangsters have put in the legislature. . . . They vote Capone. They belong to the mob. . . . Now the mob is branching out. It wants to get a similar Capone bloc in the city council. . . . These adroit criminals demand, and get, political patronage. . . . Given their bloc in the city council, they will be running the town through minority control.[3]

The *Tribune* urged the chairmen of the Democratic and Republican central committees to combine forces in every ward where a "Caponeite" was running for alderman and defeat him, to bring pressure on officeholders to cut off patronage from the gang, and to continue this limited form of coalition until the gang leaders are politically liquidated. These sound suggestions were promptly ignored by the Republican and Democratic party leaders. Understandably, they have never had any stomach for fighting either the Capone gangsters or their political satellites.

While the press was unsuccessfully attempting to spur the political leaders and the citizenry into action against the hoodlum element, the West Side bloc was perfecting its strategy, which was designed to eliminate any opposition to its candidates in the First and Twenty-eighth wards. On January 23, 1951, in a typical maneuver, Daniel A. Serritella announced his candidacy for alderman from the First Ward, ostensibly to oppose the West Side bloc candidate, John D'Arco, who was running under the Democratic banner. Serritella handed the press a long eulogy on himself in which he was described as a "born leader, a man with flashing eyes, a pleasant personality and . . . one who is able to instill in others the confidence he has in himself." He was credited with possessing "an uncommon ability of persuasion." [4] With his long close personal friendship with Al Capone, Jack Guzik and Hymie Levin, no one questioned his "ability of persuasion." As was expected, however, Serritella withdrew from the race before the election was held on February 27, and the West Side bloc candidate, John D'Arco, became the new councilman from the First Ward.

In the Twenty-eighth Ward, once the headquarters of Boss Pat Nash of the Kelly-Nash machine, the maneuvering was considerably less subtle. For many years, George D. Kells, the protégé of Nash, had controlled the politics of the ward in the dual capacity of alderman and ward committeeman. One of Kells's principal lieutenants in corralling the ward vote year after year was Big Jim Martin, the policy king of the West Side. Apparently Martin refused to switch his allegiance from Kells to the hoodlums who were attempting to take over control of the ward and on November 15, 1950, he was shot and seriously wounded. This was language the policy king could clearly understand and following his recovery he fled the city for California. A few weeks later, Kells announced that he would not seek re-election to the city council from the ward he had represented for so many years. With his wife he left on an extended motor trip to Florida, explaining that Mrs. Kells was in ill health. But Mrs. Kells's ill health, said a *Tribune* editorial:

. . . arises principally from telephone calls from agents of the Capone mob, telling her that her husband would be killed if he did run. The gangsters proved that they were not fooling by shooting Big Jim Martin, the policy gambler who was Kells' leader in the Negro section of the ward. Martin has been run out of town, the home of the alderman's secretary has been bombed.

Fearing gang vengeance, Kells's precinct captains were shifting to the opposition. These conditions, the *Tribune* editorial stated, are:

. . . a reproach to Mayor Kennelly . . . Alderman Kells is one of the Mayor's leaders in the council. He was until recently state chairman of the Democratic party. He is Kennelly's man, and Kennelly can't protect him from the hoodlums. . . . The Chicago police are Kennelly's police. . . . Maybe the gangsters own too many of the captains. If that is the situation it is time the people of Chicago found out who is really running the town, the Mayor or the gangsters.[5]

With Kells driven out of the picture, the West Side bloc was in a position to take control of the Twenty-eighth Ward with ease. Running as an independent candidate was Patrick Petrone, a cousin of Robert "Happy" Petrone, powerful Twenty-sixth Ward politician and a member of the West Side bloc. The Republican committeeman of the Twenty-eighth Ward, Joseph Porcaro, named Cornelius Mahoney as his candidate for alderman while the Democrats selected Roy Friello. Porcaro, a close political associate of the Petrones, had been removed from the payroll of the Cook County treasurer's office in 1949 when the press revealed that he was spending most of his time in Springfield aiding the West Side bloc in its fight against the Chicago Crime Commission bills. As expected, early in February 1951, both Democratic and Republican candidates, Roy Friello and Cornelius Mahoney, suddenly announced they were withdrawing from the aldermanic race. All opposition had thus vanished in thin air and the election of Patrick Petrone as the new city councilman from the Twenty-eighth Ward became a mere formality. A few weeks later, the victory of the West Side bloc was complete. George D. Kells resigned as the Democratic Ward committeeman of the Twenty-eighth Ward and, again without opposition, Patrick Petrone was named to that post. Porcaro, the Republican Ward committeeman, could be expected to work in close harmony with Petrone, thus keeping all politics of the ward, both Republican and Democratic, safely in the hands of the West Side bloc.[6]

The aldermanic contest in February was but a preview of the mayoralty election scheduled for April 3, 1951. Martin H. Kennelly who was seeking a second term as mayor was opposed by the Republican candidate, Robert L. Hunter. Both candidates were men of high personal integrity and reputation. Kennelly campaigned on his record and undoubtedly relied heavily on his great personal popularity as well as the solid backing of the powerful Democratic machine. Perhaps the outstanding accomplishment of Kennelly's first administration was the removal of cheap partisan politics from the Chicago school system. He had appointed a good school board, composed largely of civic-minded citizens of excellent reputation, and had sought the advice of a screening committee of outstanding civic leaders to aid him in selecting an unusually well qualified superintendent of schools. These moves paid big political dividends and ended the burning school issue which had plagued the Kelly administration. In the city Civil Service Commission, Kennelly had appointed as chairman a lawyer of fine ability and unimpeachable integrity. On the other hand, progress in improving Chicago's law enforcement machinery had been much slower than expected. The primary emphasis of Kennelly's administration had been placed on traffic control and, although there had been some criticism because of the large number of police officers assigned exclusively to the traffic division, the new policy was defended on the ground that life and property in the city streets were being made safer. While wide-open gambling and vice had been materially reduced, few steps had been taken to conduct a badly-needed housecleaning within the ranks of the police department. Underworld lords who had used Chicago as their base of operations for thirty years were still reaping rich harvests from illegal activities of the not so wide-open type within the city, and no effective action had been taken against them. Kennelly's police department had shown no inclination to wage a relentless warfare against gang leaders and it was only following the revelations of the Kefauver Committee a few months before election

that a new commissioner of police was appointed. In the campaign
waged by the Republican candidate, Robert L. Hunter, Kennelly
was attacked as a "do-nothing" mayor. However, Hunter failed to
receive vigorous support from any major newspaper and there
was little interest in the election on April 3, 1951, as reflected by unusually light voting. Kennelly was re-elected with a plurality over
his opponent of 152,545 votes as compared with the plurality of
275,000 which he obtained four years earlier.

The election returns were interpreted by the *Daily News* as a vote
of confidence expressed by the electorate in Kennelly personally,
who it was stated is "one of the kindest and most courteous of men,
he is personally known to many thousands of voters, and warmly
regarded by nearly all who know him. . . ."[7] The splendid personal
qualities of Chicago's mayor could not be questioned. But as the
New York Times pointed out:

A notable and depressing fact about Chicago's Mayoralty election was
that it brought out a smaller proportion of the registered vote than any
previous election of comparable importance within memory. . . . The
amazing apathy among the electorate of the nation's second largest city
makes one wonder if the apparent revival of nationwide interest in
municipal affairs, sparked by the Senate's crime investigation, was genuine
and can be lasting. . . . No matter how uninteresting or uninspiring the
campaign, there is certainly a distressing unconcern about local government — which is, after all, the wellspring of democracy — in a city in
which 37 per cent of those eligible do not even bother to go to the polls.[8]

In discussing the apathy of the Chicago electorate the *Times* overlooked one important factor. Interest in the Senate Crime Committee's findings was genuine. Voters were shocked at the mass of evidence which had been made public regarding Chicago's underworld
organization. But many of them were bitterly disappointed over the
failure of Mayor Kennelly to exert the leadership necessary to end
the reign of the Capone organization. Instead, he was still repeating
the refrain of Thompson and Kelly that no organized crime exists
in Chicago. On the other hand, the Republican candidate in his campaign had failed completely to demonstrate his capacity for leadership in solving the city's crime problem. In fact, he had refused to
take a firm public stand against the elements in his own party that
were definitely allied with the gangsters. Many voters who wished

to register their disgust over the absence of leadership in both parties, insofar as combating organized crime was concerned, stayed away from the polls.

The public indignation over the Kefauver Committee findings was bearing fruit on many fronts. In Springfield, the Illinois General Assembly was in session. For many years a number of legislators had been in the habit of making deals with the West Side bloc and voting against all bills designed to improve law enforcement. But now the public temper was such that it became politically inexpedient to line up with the West Side bloc in opposition to all measures sponsored by the Chicago Crime Commission. The bill which would permit the extension of the Cook County Grand Jury beyond a period of thirty days was one which could not logically be opposed on any ground, and many legislators who had voted against it in previous sessions now found it met with their approval. A bill was therefore passed by both the House of Representatives and the Senate, which made it possible to keep a Cook County Grand Jury in session for three months when required in the interests of justice. This law became effective July 1, 1951, and that same month it became necessary to continue the deliberations of a grand jury beyond the thirty-day period to complete an important investigation it had started.

In Chicago, there was renewed activity on the part of all law-enforcement officials. Action was taken against some of the big Capone syndicate gambling establishments in the county. The state's attorney launched a full-scale inquiry into the million-dollar policy racket on the South and West Sides and a number of the policy kings were indicted. However, this did not deter the Capone gang from making further efforts to take over the rich policy wheels operated on the South Side by Theodore Roe for the Jones Brothers. On the night of June 18, 1951, Theodore Roe, a millionaire racketeer, reported that his car was curbed by three gangsters on South Parkway. These men attempted to kidnap him and when he resisted, a furious gun battle took place. According to Roe, he shot and killed Leonard Caifano during the melee. Before reporting the shooting to the police, however, he threw away his gun and it was never found. The police scoffed at his story and a few days later the press flatly asserted that a Chicago police officer who was acting as the policy racketeer's bodyguard actually fired the fatal shot. Sam "Mooney"

Giancana was sought as one of Caifano's accomplices in the kidnap attempt.[9]

The renewed vigor of Chicago officials was heartening to many citizens. Whether it would continue after public indignation had subsided was a matter of conjecture. There was no question, however, about the city's future as one of the world's greatest centers of commerce, industry and transportation. Between 1940 and 1950, the expansion of the Chicago area in plants and equipment amounting to $2,300,000,000 exceeded that of New York and every other city of the nation. The Chicago area could boast of 12,300 manufacturing plants which employed 1,008,000 workers and produced annually goods valued at $12,000,000,000, representing seven and one half per cent of the total manufactured output of the nation. In the production of machinery and fabricated metal products, Chicago leads all cities in the country. In 1950, the city's 11,879 wholesale firms made sales amounting to over $15,000,000,000 which was seven and seven tenths per cent of the nation's wholesale business. As a transportation center, Chicago has no peer. Nineteen trunk line railroads and fifteen shuttle systems handle eleven per cent of the total freight car loadings in the United States. More than one passenger train arrives and departs every minute while airplane arrivals and departures average 642 a day. In 1950, Chicago's lake traffic of 52,800,000 tons was the highest in its entire history and 13,000,000 tons were shipped over the Great Lakes-Gulf of Mexico waterways. The *New Orleans Port Record* in June 1951, concluded that "Chicago is in an enviable position to continue the leadership pace for a long time to come."[10] About the same time this report was receiving nods of approval from the Chicago business world, the Senate Crime Committee made public its findings and conclusions. Said this report:

> Chicago, by virtue of its size and its location as a center of communications, transportation, and distribution of goods, has been and remains a focal point for the activities of organized criminals in the United States. . . . Because of the history of the city, its physical location and its great size, the job of law enforcement in Chicago remains a tremendous responsibility and challenge to the law-enforcement agencies and to the citizens of Chicago and its surrounding areas."[11]

CHAPTER XIV
Barbarian Rulers and the Citizen

A FAMOUS Anglican prelate, William Ralph Inge, once observed that while "Ancient civilizations were destroyed by imported barbarians, we breed our own." Chicago's Capone gang possessed the ideals and frequently employed the methods of ancient barbaric tribes. But the political system upon which the Capone gang has thrived for several decades is not peculiar to Chicago. On the contrary, it has prevailed over long periods of time in most of our large municipalities. About twenty years ago, the famous Wickersham Commission pointed out that:

In the main the funds which really make successful campaigns possible, come from the owners and habitués of vice, gambling and bootlegging resorts. . . .[1] Nearly all of the large cities suffer from an alliance between politicians and criminals . . . Los Angeles was controlled by a few gamblers for a number of years. San Francisco suffered similarly some years ago, and at one period in its history was so completely dominated by the gamblers that three prominent gamblers who were in control of the politics of the city and who quarreled about the appointment of the police chief settled the quarrel by shaking dice to determine who would name the chief for the first two years, who for the second two years, and who for the third.

In Detroit several years ago, when the professional gambling places were closed, the gamblers were so strong politically that they forced the removal of the commissioner of police. This was true notwithstanding the fact that he was recognized as one of the strongest and most able police executives in America.[2]

In Florida, the head of four dog tracks contributed $100,000 to help elect Fuller Warren governor of the state in 1948. In certain parts of Florida, such as Broward County, the gamblers have controlled local politics for many years. Jake Lansky, affiliated with Frank Costello and Joe Adonis, has been a tower of political strength in that area.

In Louisiana, some of the parishes are controlled politically by the underworld. One Louisiana official blandly told the Senate Crime Committee that he did not know that prostitution was against the law. In the middle 1930's the late Huey P. Long, then dictator of Louisiana, made an alliance with Frank Costello, who promptly flooded the state with slot machines and brought in Dandy Phil Kastel, a convicted swindler, to look after his illegal interests. Kastel, Costello and Meyer Lansky, all New York gangsters, entered into a partnership with Carlos Marcello, one of the most sinister underworld leaders in the New Orleans area. This group opened the lavishly furnished gambling casino called the Beverly Club outside of New Orleans, and for many years their influence has been felt in local and state politics. Sheriffs and city marshals in various Louisiana areas have been elected with the aid of the vice and gambling interests and have become personally wealthy.

In virtually every section of the country the underworld has become part and parcel of political organizations that rule over cities and sometimes states. During the many years that Boss Tom Pendergast reigned over Kansas City and large portions of Missouri as well, one of his principal lieutenants was the gangster John Lazia. This ex-convict was the gambling boss of Kansas City, but earlier in his career he had engaged in a gun battle with police after staging a holdup and had served a term in the Missouri State Penitentiary for highway robbery. Yet it was this same Lazia who was to become a dominant figure in determining the policies of the Kansas City Police Department. At his specific request, sixty ex-convicts were placed on the payroll of this law-enforcement agency. By 1934, one out of every ten men in the Kansas City Police Department had a criminal record.[3] This Midwestern city became the headquarters and meeting place for criminal gangs from every part of the country. Kidnapings attracted nationwide attention. Known robbers and murderers roamed the streets unmolested by the police. Elections were accompanied by kidnapings, sluggings and murders. Ghost votes swelled the majorities rolled up by the Pendergast machine. On July 10, 1934, John Lazia fell in a hail of gangsters' bullets. He was buried in a grand style befitting his political importance. Two of the pall-bearers at his funeral were Charles Gargotta and Charles Binaggio. Immediately following Lazia's death, the leadership of the Kansas City underworld was taken over by Charles V. Carollo, and Kansas City remained one of the most crime-ridden and corrupt cities in the nation. In a charge to a United States grand jury in 1939, Federal Judge Albert L. Reeves stated, "Kansas City is a seething cal-dron of crime, licensed and protected." Regarding Carollo, the judge quoted from an official report which stated: "I never saw any one individual, in all the years I have been connected with the United States government, who seemingly had so much power." [4]

On March 29, 1939, Federal prison doors closed on Tom Pender-gast, then one of the country's most powerful political bosses. A be-lated wave of civic indignation swept over the city and many re-forms in municipal government followed. But the underworld was far from dead. Quietly in the background, the gamblers, vice mon-gers and narcotic peddlers were building strength and waiting for the moment when they could again become an important factor in city politics. During this period of watchful waiting the leadership of the underworld was gradually taken over by Charles Binaggio. Among his top lieutenants were the gunman Charles Gargotta and Tony Gizzo, a close associate of Capone gangsters. By 1948, Binag-gio had become one of the most powerful political bosses in Missouri and during this rise to political eminence, he was surrounded by some of the most vicious criminals in the Middle West. When the governor of Missouri initiated action designed to cripple the gam-bling business, Binaggio determined to place a man of his choosing in the state capital. One of the aspirants for the Missouri govern-ship in 1948 was Roy McKittrick, a former state senator and attorney general of Missouri for twelve years. Binaggio urged McKittrick to stay out of the race for governor since he wanted to place Forrest Smith in the executive mansion. Binaggio told McKittrick that he "just had to have a governor" and eventually McKittrick was offered $50,000 to withdraw his candidacy. McKittrick informed the Ke-fauver Committee that he knew the gambling king could elect any-one governor because he held the political "balance of power" in the state. Said McKittrick, "He had a lot of friends and supporters in St. Louis, and he was the controlling factor in Kansas City. He had good alliances at St. Joe. He was very active. He was well supplied with money to operate with." When the Senate Committee expressed surprise that one man, "even through gambling outlets, could be such a political figure," the former attorney general replied, "Senator, he had several committeemen in St. Louis who were friendly to him, very friendly to him, and the sheriff of St. Louis was very friendly." McKittrick explained that there were over five hundred Democratic leaders in the state who would follow Binaggio in any political decision he might make.

Needless to say, Forrest Smith was elected governor of Missouri in 1948 and Binaggio was firmly established as a man of great influence in the affairs of government. His power lasted until April 6, 1950, when the bullet-riddled bodies of Binaggio and his partner, Charles Gargotta, were found in the First District Democratic Headquarters in Kansas City. At the time of Binaggio's murder, there were officeholders at almost every level of city and state government who owed their positions to this gambling czar.[5]

Almost everywhere the underworld has become an integral part of the political machinery. In some places this situation has prevailed with little interruption for over a century. In New York City during the early 1850's, Fernando Wood built an invincible political organization which relied in no small measure on the active support of the criminal elements. On election day, November 4, 1854, when Wood was a candidate for mayor, the *New York Times* characterized him as totally unfit for office and declared it would be a disgrace to the city if he was elected. Wood relied upon the vote-getting abilities of such underworld lieutenants as Isaiah Rynders, the political protector of the notorious Five Points gang, and John Morrissey, an ex-convict, rough and tumble fighter, bartender, and gambling house proprietor. With such formidable support, Wood served three terms as mayor of New York City and then went to Congress where he helped guide the nation's destinies for almost twenty years.

John Morrissey, one of the nation's widely known gambling kings, played a prominent part in New York City politics for many years. When William Marcy Tweed succeeded Wood as the boss of New York City, Morrissey was one of several underworld leaders who materially aided the Tweed Ring in establishing its grip over the political life there. Frauds totaling millions of dollars were perpetrated by the Tweed Ring on the people of New York before Boss Tweed was arrested. While in custody Tweed made a prepared statement to the Board of Aldermen explaining Morrissey's importance to his political organization. Tweed told the aldermen that he had known John Morrissey for twenty-four years and was aware that Morrissey had been named in several indictments which included charges of burglary, assault with intent to kill and assault with a dangerous weapon. He mentioned the jail sentences which had been imposed against Morrissey and the nine months he had served in the Albany prison. As to Morrissey's career Tweed said:

He has been a professional prize-fighter and public-gambler — a proprietor and owner of the worst places in the City of New York, the resort of thieves and persons of the lowest character. Perhaps one of the worst faults which can fairly be attributed to me, is having been the means of keeping his gambling houses protected from the police. As an organizer of repeaters he had no superior, and at the time when the ring was in power, such capacity was always fully recognized.[6]

Morrissey was important to the corrupt Tweed machine because he could be depended upon to deliver the votes necessary to keep the Ring in power. From Morrissey's time until the present, there has been a steady succession of gambling and vice lords who have exerted tremendous power in New York City politics. In recent years Frank Costello has been a man before whom men with political ambitions have found it necessary to bow and scrape. Costello's intimate associates have included most of the nation's most prominent gangsters. Yet notwithstanding his close relationship with murderers, narcotics peddlers, overlords of prostitution and gambling kings, Costello has been responsible for placing men in office at almost every level of government. Even judges have pledged their "undying loyalty" to this underworld chief. In March 1951, almost thirty million American citizens observed former Mayor William O'Dwyer on television as he testified before the United States Senate Crime Investigating Committee in New York City. They heard him admit that he had paid a visit to Frank Costello's apartment in 1942. Present with Costello and O'Dwyer in the cozy surroundings of the gangster's home were former Congressman Michael Kennedy, then the leader of Tammany Hall, Bert Stand, secretary of Tammany, Anthony P. Savarese, a judge, and Irving Sherman, a mutual friend of Costello and O'Dwyer. Bert Stand testified that he had been invited to Costello's apartment for a cocktail party and during the course of the conversation the 1941 election campaign was discussed. Three years later, O'Dwyer, a former Kings County District Attorney, was to become the mayor of America's largest city, a position he held until 1950 when he resigned in the midst of a grand jury investigation of police corruption in New York City. He was promptly appointed ambassador to Mexico. From irrefutable evidence produced at the New York hearings, the Senate Crime Committee concluded:

There can be no question that Frank Costello has exercised a major influence upon the New York County Democratic organization, Tammany Hall, because of his personal friendships and working relationships with its officers, and with Democratic district leaders even today in ten of the sixteen Manhattan districts. Costello also had relationships with some Republican political leaders.

The committee then commented on former Mayor O'Dwyer's intimate personal friendship with men who were also close associates of Frank Costello and Joe Adonis. It is not surprising that while O'Dwyer was mayor he "appointed friends of both Costello and Adonis to high public office." The committee pointed out that:

During Mr. O'Dwyer's term of office as district attorney of Kings County, between 1940 and 1942, and his occupancy of the mayoralty from 1946 to 1950, neither he nor his appointees took any effective action against the top echelons of the gambling, narcotics, water-front, murder, or bookmaking rackets. In fact, his actions impeded promising investigations of such rackets. His defense of public officials who were derelict in their duties, and his actions in investigations of corruption, and his failure to follow up concrete evidence of organized crime, particularly in the case of Murder, Inc., and the water front, have contributed to the growth of organized crime, racketeering, and gangsterism in New York City.[7]

There is no mystery surrounding the menacing political power of America's underworld — a power which enables criminal groups to elevate men of their choosing to governorships, to the mayor's chair in some of our largest cities, to city councils, to the legislative chambers where they influence the laws of the state and to the judiciary which passes on the guilt or innocence of those charged with a crime. It is a power which in many places has made it possible for law violators to control the law enforcers and to formulate law-enforcement policies. The Capone gang of Chicago, the Costello-Adonis syndicate of New York City and the Charles Binaggio organization of Kansas City are natural products of a political system that has become commonplace in almost every large city in America and many rural areas as well. Andrew D. White once stated, "With few exceptions, the city governments of the United States are the worst in Christendom — the most expensive, the most inefficient and the most corrupt." This situation has been due in part to the influence of the underworld on politics. The underworld as an important source of political power has frequently been completely ignored or greatly minimized by students of government and politics. But the practical men who control the party machinery and name the slates of candidates for public office fully understand the importance of the gambling, vice and liquor interests as a means of political strength. From these sources, the very backbone of the underworld, they obtain regular financial support to maintain their political organization on a year-round basis, and, at election time, huge campaign funds not readily available elsewhere. Of equal importance, the racketeering element can be depended upon to recruit an army of campaign workers to deliver the vote at the polls. The underworld, in return, is in a position to exercise influence on the selection of candidates, to have its friends placed in appointive offices including important posts in the field of law enforcement, and to exert pressure on the policies of the administration it has materially helped elect.

It is commonly believed that underworld organizations develop and grow to power only because corrupt officials are elected to major city offices. The solution, it is claimed, lies solely in the election of honest public officials to places of authority in municipal government. Both the premise and the solution are only partially true, however, and they fail to strike at one of the vital phases of the organized crime problem. Naturally, personal honesty is an essential qualification for men who manage the affairs of the city. But per-

sonal integrity alone on the part of mayors and other key city officials will not eliminate organized crime. In fact, unless honesty is
accompanied by great independence and courageous leadership, it
will scarcely make a dent on organized crime as it exists in Chicago,
New York, and elsewhere.

The power of the underworld stems from the fact that the racketeering elements have become an integral part of the political machinery which places men, *both honest and dishonest*, in public
office. Substantially honest and well-intentioned men who aspire
to political office usually find it expedient to accept the support of
strong ward organizations even though they are aware that such political units rely heavily on the gambling and vice interests for
money and votes. It is extremely rare, in fact, for candidates to re-
pudiate the leaders of even the most corrupt ward organizations of
their party. Not infrequently, wards in which the underworld is the
most deeply entrenched are those that deliver the largest pluralities
at the polls — at times, the outcome of city elections hinges on these
very wards. Following election, mayors and other high officials, notwithstanding their original good intentions, usually find it inexpedient to ignore completely the wishes of these ward leaders in matters affecting law-enforcement policies or personnel. Resorting to the
usual process of rationalization, they find logical reasons why vigorous law-enforcement programs are not applicable in these particular wards. In the normal course of events police captains who are
friendly or at least acceptable to these ward leaders are assigned to
their districts. Those who might disregard a ward leader's wishes
and vigorously wipe out gambling and vice are seldom placed in
command of precinct stations within his jurisdiction. To assign
unfriendly police personnel or initiate vigorous law-enforcement
programs in districts in which the underworld has been flourishing
would of course result in the alienation of future political support
from the leaders of these wards. The mayor may further rationalize
that the aid of these ward leaders is vital to the success of important
city programs other than those relating to the elimination of crime
and rackets. He also may begin to think of the next election when
the backing of powerful ward organizations may be essential to his
continued success at the polls. Consequently, except on very rare
occasions, the underworld is not seriously injured or its organization

appreciably disrupted even during administrations headed by men who are personally honest. The same situation prevails with reference to the administration of virtually all important offices including those of the sheriff, the prosecutor and the courts.

In some of Chicago's most powerful wards many of the taverns are owned and operated by individuals closely allied with the underworld. A large number of these places are hangouts for criminals and racketeers of every description, and in many instances the tavern serves as a focal point for the operation of vice rings. But this situation is by no means new. As far back as 1911, the Vice Commission of Chicago reported that "to all intents and purposes . . . many saloons are actually houses of prostitution with inmates." [8]

At the present time many taverns work hand in hand with the oldest profession, and gambling violations in taverns are commonplace in many sections. In fact, throughout America virtually all laws designed to control the liquor traffic have been systematically violated since colonial times. Tavern owners and night-spot proprietors are therefore particularly anxious to remain in the good graces of their ward committeeman, who possesses such great power over law enforcement in his district. A word of disapproval from the ward committeeman may prevent the issuance of a liquor license in the first place, and once the license is issued it can be revoked on one or more of the countless regulations which govern tavern operations. At best, the liquor business is a precarious one that readily lends itself to political shakedown. Even taverns operated on a legitimate basis by reputable persons find it expedient to become a part of the political system. It is much cheaper to contribute to the ward organization than run the risk of constant harassment from officials for real or alleged violations of the liquor license laws.

In addition to contributing money to the ward organization, the tavern owner can be relied upon to deliver the vote at the polls. During a municipal election in Cicero a few years ago, there came to public light the determined efforts of the tavern keepers to retain a friendly administration. The president of the Tavern Service Guild wrote letters to all liquor licensees in Cicero, urging the tavern keepers, many of whom were closely allied with Capone gangsters, to pledge the use of their automobiles to bring voters to the polls in order to assure the re-election of the village president. If he were defeated, warned the letter, their licenses might be revoked for selling liquor to minors, gambling or failing to abide by the closing hours. The letter reminded the tavern owners that if the administration changed they would have no assurance of enjoying the same extralegal rights and privileges that had attended their business operations in the past.[9]

In almost every large American city the saloonkeeper has been an important part of his ward organization. "In fact, the liquor interests and the political machine have been almost identical in many cities." [10] In some states even the legislature has fallen under the domination of the liquor and brewing interests. In California, for example, the brewing industry is represented by one of the nation's most fabulous lobbyists, Arthur H. Samish. The United States Senate Crime Committee in 1951 reported that during the past six years he had a fund totaling one million dollars at his disposal. Samish, admittedly a friend of such underworld bosses as Joe Adonis of New York and Dandy Phil Kastel of New Orleans, once boasted: "I am the governor of the legislature. To hell with the Governor of the State." [11]

During the past century, the saloon and liquor interests have been highly influential in municipal politics.[12] Throughout Chicago's history some of the leading ward committeemen have been saloonkeepers. Even Anton J. Cermak owed much of his early strength to the backing of the saloonkeepers, brewers and distillers. Although the majority of persons connected with the various phases of the liquor and brewing industry are reputable businessmen, the underworld and its allies have always been closely identified with the distribution and sale of beer and liquor. At the present time, some of the nation's most formidable gangsters hold exclusive franchises for leading brands of whiskey and beer in many of our principal cities.[13]

It is the gambling business however, above all others, that is peculiarly adapted to the requirements of corrupt machine politics. Existing solely to prey upon emotional weaknesses which defy all forces of logic and common sense, and operating on a percentage basis which assures huge profits, the gambling business has always appealed to the criminal classes. In recent years, the entire nation was shocked when it was revealed that professional gamblers had bribed youthful college athletes in order to fix basketball games. Generally overlooked was the fact that activities of this nature are part of the gambling business. It deals only in certainties – the certainty of large profits for the gambling-house proprietor and the certainty of loss for the patron. The gambling business always has been and always will be under the control of the underworld.

Until Federal prosecution broke up the Skidmore-Johnson combination during the Kelly administration, the control of gambling in Chicago was centralized. Many of the ward committeemen found it necessary to make the final arrangements for gambling in their districts with William R. Skidmore, the gambling boss. But with the Federal conviction of Skidmore and his partner, William R. Johnson, there was a decentralization of the gambling control setup. Again the decision of the ward committeeman became final regarding gambling in his locality.

In some communities there are many people who condone or tolerate the presence of gambling places. Under such happy circumstances, the ward leader can afford protection without fear of political repercussions from an aroused electorate. In this respect, gambling differs from prostitution. In some wards, of course, vice flourishes with official protection, but in the average locality prostitution is offensive to the moral sense of too many people to be permitted on a wide scale. The saloonkeeper who is dealing in a legitimate commodity, governed by the economic rules of competition, has only limited profits which he may share with his ward organization in the form of political contributions or payoffs. The gambling business, which thrives on the emotional weaknesses and superstitions of its patrons, is naturally very lucrative. It can afford to pay handsomely for protection. Thus to a greater extent than almost any other type of business, legitimate or illegal, the gambling racket necessarily lends itself as an excellent source of political funds on a year round basis. In addition to adequate financing, the strength of a ward organization rests largely on patronage. The number of jobs which the average ward leader may have at his disposal for rewarding faithful party workers is limited. It also frequently happens that some of the most vigorous and effective workers in a ward are those with criminal backgrounds. It would be politically inexpedient to recompense their efforts with jobs ordinarily requiring substantial

qualities of respectability — a scandal might arouse public indignation which could easily prove embarrassing in subsequent political
campaigns. But the gambling business serves as an ideal outlet for
patronage of this type. Gambling establishments need doormen,
cashiers, bouncers, dealers, or croupiers. Handbook and policy station employee requirements are numerous. The strata of society from
which their employees come are unimportant, and a criminal record
is no handicap. A ward leader who makes it possible for gambling
establishments to operate with impunity in his district obviously is in
a position to insist that these places afford employment to many
people of his selection. In some corrupt wards, the number of gambling house jobs at the disposal of the ward committeeman may reach
several hundred. The power from this added patronage has made
some ward leaders the most influential political figures in an entire
city.

It is indisputable that the underworld has derived tremendous political and economic power from the gambling business. Frequently
the evils arising from commercialized gambling have been attributed
to the laws which declare it illegal, but such explanations fall into the
commonplace error of attempting to oversimplify a difficult social
question. They fail to take into consideration the inherently illegitimate character of the business — a business totally parasitic in nature
which exists solely to prey upon human weaknesses. Legalization
does not alter either the character of the business or its highly profitable nature. On the contrary, legalization only makes it far more
profitable. This accounts for the migration of many of America's
racketeers to Nevada where they can operate million-dollar gambling casinos under the protection of the state law. And some of
Nevada's most influential political leaders are themselves engaged
in the gambling business. William J. Moore, a member of the Nevada
State Tax Commission which supervises gambling licenses, testified
before the Senate Crime Committee that he is one of several partners
who own the Last Frontier gambling casino. Moore informed the
committee that his share of the income from this establishment in
1949 was "somewhere between $75,000 and $84,000." The lieutenant
governor of the state, Clifford Jones, also admitted receiving a large
annual income from his interest in three gambling places. It was in
one of these, the Golden Nugget Casino in Las Vegas, that Bugsy

Siegel owned the handbook concession before he was slain in 1947. Siegel had once made the boast, "We don't run for public office, we own the politicians." The licensing system in Nevada, said the Senate Crime Committee, "has not resulted in excluding the undesirables from the State but has merely served to give their activities a seeming cloak of respectability." And under such circumstances, "There is no weapon which can be used to keep the gamblers and their money out of politics." The Senate Committee concluded that "as a case history of legalized gambling, Nevada speaks eloquently in the negative." [14] And the evils which attend legalized gambling in Nevada are similar to those that developed from earlier experiments with state lotteries and other forms of licensed gambling. History clearly reflects that legalized gambling in America has never eliminated any abuses. Instead it has greatly increased economic, social and political evils.[15]

The ward committeemen and other politicians who make up our ruling political class — the slate makers and string pullers — are for the most part political opportunists. This is true because municipal politics, particularly at the ward level, does not easily attract men of both integrity and ability. Such men find the professional or business world a much better place in which to develop their talents. Political jobs rarely provide salaries which will attract able men of high character. Likewise, there is little honor attached to the position of ward committeeman or most of the other elective or appointive offices. Hence, there is little or no inducement for able men to seek such offices other than the opportunity offered to render public service. And as James Bryce pointed out, "To rely on public duty as the main motive power in politics is to assume a commonwealth of angels. Men such as we know them, must have some other inducement." [16]

But for the man who is not troubled by an oversensitive conscience, many political offices with meager salaries are highly attractive. The unofficial emoluments of public office can be extremely lucrative. In Chicago, men have spent thousands of dollars to become elected ward committeeman, a position which carries with it no salary whatever and confers little, if any, honor. The job is one of great political power, however, and when used to exploit government it becomes a source of wealth, as the fortunes of many Chicago political leaders have fully attested. The prospect of illicit profits, said Bryce, "renders a political career distinctly more attractive to an unscrupulous man." [17] The first requisite, however, is to remain in power, an objective which can be attained through the financial support and campaign workers made available by the gambling, vice and liquor interests. And although it is a disgusting and revolting spectacle, it is not surprising that we find men who have ambitions to become mayor or aspire to the judiciary on bended knee before notorious gangsters such as Frank Costello or Joe Adonis. We have governors who preside over state governments because they have met with the approval of underworld leaders like Charles Binaggio. We have Capone gangs who are able to control important city wards for generations and place their friends in many key offices of city and state government.

It should be a disturbing fact to all decent citizens that in most large cities the racketeering element has developed into a major political power — a power without any responsibility to the electorate and actually beholden only to the enemies of the community. There can be little question regarding the menace presented by organized crime when it is realized that frequently the actual political rulers of cities and states are underworld bosses who possess the instincts, traditions and methods of barbarians.

To break the grip which the underworld has fixed on municipal politics is a vital American problem. During the past several decades the influence of a relatively few cities on national politics has been steadily growing. Huge pluralities rolled up in as few as thirteen of our largest municipalities have been sufficient to decide most national elections.[18] In several of these cities the political influence of the underworld has been the strongest. Many congressmen and senators sent to Washington to guide our national affairs are the products of local machines that are closely allied with the racketeering element. A few of our statesmen selected to represent this nation in its relations with foreign countries owe their rise to political eminence to the power of the underworld. The breakdown in political morality which has been in evidence everywhere is a matter of grave concern to many of our leaders. But how could it be otherwise when so many officeholders owe their positions to an immoral underworld?

If it were possible to eliminate the underworld as an essential source of power to local machines, both city and national government would be strengthened. But there is no single device or mechanism of government which can accomplish this end. Under our form of government there is no substitute for eternal vigilance on the part of the citizens along with an active interest and participation in political affairs. To most people that is a totally unsatisfactory answer. It is trite and meaningless. Yet it is nevertheless true. There is no gadget or scheme that can relieve the citizen of his responsibility. The average citizen complains with justification, however, that city government is too large, too complex, and too impersonal for him to exercise vigilance or to make his voice heard. He cannot become intensely interested in elections since the long list of candidates appearing on the ballot are hand picked by party organizations and are generally unknown to him. He feels it is impossible to accurately appraise the merits of rival candidates. And anyway, he reasons, his vote will be offset by scores of others that are cast by professional party workers who are bought and sold like an ordinary commodity. Usually the disinterest of such citizens is attributed to public apathy but actually much of it comes from a feeling of helplessness which engulfs the average voter when he attempts to consider governmental and political affairs.

It must be admitted that free government is far more difficult than any other form. As is true of all precious articles, it can be preserved only through great individual effort. The price is high. But some of the obstacles presented by the bigness and complexity of the city can be overcome if the individual citizen keeps in mind the true nature of his municipality. A city is not just a city — it is a collection of communities. There are of course areas in which it is virtually impossible to arouse any community spirit or interest. In general, however, the most effective approach to big city government is at the community level. Almost all citizens have a good knowledge of conditions prevailing in the neighborhood in which they reside. They usually know whether their community is infested with gambling establishments, vice dens, narcotics peddlers, or taverns and night spots which mock the law and serve as breeding places for crime and delinquency. If any of these conditions exist the citizen can rest assured that the underworld has a foothold in his neighborhood. He can also fix the responsibility. His neighborhood will never become a stamping ground for the underworld unless his ward committeeman, alderman and police captain either are in league with the criminal elements or are totally incompetent to represent the district.

There are at least two vital reasons why every citizen should insist upon the elimination of all racketeering activities in his community. In the first place, once a neighborhood tolerates gambling, vice or disorderly taverns, property values begin to deteriorate. The presence of racketeering is thus costly to the legitimate property owner when measured in plain dollars and cents. In the second place, such conditions present a threat to the security of families residing in the locality. Vice, gambling and bad taverns exist only through official protection, which invariably extends far beyond that afforded the handbook proprietor and the brothel owner. Murderers, robbers and burglars who are allied with the gambling or vice lords also become untouchables insofar as the police are concerned, and it is a well-known fact that criminals and racketeers of all types are attracted to gambling houses and vice centers. Raymond B. Fosdick, an authority on police matters, once stated, "Just as yellow fever was successfully attacked by draining the swamps and morasses where it bred, so the attack on crime is, in part, at least, a matter of eliminating its breeding places." The old "red-light" districts, Fosdick observed:

. . . let loose upon the community an army of pick-pockets, shop-lifters, and petty robbers, of both sexes, who found retreat and stimulation in the protected district. . . . Similarly, gambling and pool-selling places, and the various rendezvous where narcotics are illegally obtained, are breeding grounds of crime to which the conscientious police executive will give careful attention.[19]

In the annual report of the New York Police Department for 1918, Commissioner of Police Richard Enright warned that gambling houses:

. . . are invariably the headquarters of the most dangerous criminals, as the vast majority of society's enemies appear to have a passion for games of hazard, a reflection of their precarious existences, perhaps. Besides, many of the keepers of such resorts are ex-convicts and if not, then they are apt to be surrounded by such men and women and are not at all averse to financing the criminal projects of their hangers-on and the vicious parasites who flock to every gambling house to which access can be had. . . . The suppression of these establishments . . . is preventive police work of the highest quality.[20]

The security of his family and his economic welfare are perhaps the most vital concerns of the average citizen. The powerful motive of self-interest should therefore cause citizens to band together for the purpose of attempting to eliminate bad conditions. In many instances, the prevailing citizen inertia results from an absence of leadership and a failure to understand how efforts may be directed to improve conditions. But the residents of any locality should bear in mind that to the average politician they represent a valuable commodity — votes. When gambling, prostitution or bad tavern conditions exist in a neighborhood, the citizens should present a solid front and through able spokesmen proceed to the offices of the ward committeeman and alderman where they should demand a neighborhood housecleaning. The responsibility should be placed squarely on the shoulders of these political leaders who are definitely in a position to alleviate underworld racketeering in their district. They should be made to understand that if they refuse to take action, the respectable citizens of the locality will hold them accountable at the next election. This is a language they will not fail to understand provided the citizens' group is well organized and under capable leadership. If conditions are not promptly improved, the community organization should exert its utmost efforts to defeat the ward committeeman and alderman at the first opportunity.

Simultaneously with appeals to the ward leaders, a demand should be made of the police captain to enforce the laws in his district and if he fails to do so, the mayor should be requested to remove him. With constant pressure applied on these responsible leaders by the respectable citizens, the power of the underworld can be broken. Unfortunately, in the past, virtually all of the pressure on ward leaders and police captains has originated with the racketeering elements or their spokesmen. The substantial citizens have a tendency to complain privately but they fail to exert pressure where it counts.

If it were possible to obtain vigorous community action throughout the city it is obvious that the political power of the underworld would be destroyed. As a practical matter, however, it is equally apparent that community action is impossible in many localities. Even in good communities effective leadership is frequently lacking and too many citizens are fearful of either political or underworld retribution. And the very nature of some areas — usually those in which the underworld is most deeply entrenched — makes group action highly improbable. The near North Side of Chicago, for example, has been aptly pointed out as an area of "extreme personal and social disorganization" where there exists a "total indifference to community issues and interests." The problem of crime and vice lies "almost completely outside the realm of political action. . . . The vote is organized from 'higher up' outside the community." [21]

The mobility of the population of the near North Side and similar districts adds to the social disorganization and makes community action impossible. There are few protests from the residents of North Clark Street against the vice and corruption that have characterized this area for so many years and there are numerous localities in the city where comparable conditions prevail. It is fundamentally true that "The areas where the need for community organization is most apparent are areas in which the very nature of city life makes community organization impossible." [22]

Notwithstanding the presence of such localities, it is nevertheless true that Chicago abounds in districts in which many citizens are vitally concerned with prevailing conditions. With proper leadership, this interest is capable of being transformed into political action which can deal devastating blows to the system which relies so heavily on the underworld for political support. As late as the 1950 fall election for sheriff, there was ample proof that when the issues are clear-cut, the people of Chicago are capable of expressing their wrath at the polls in such force that even one of the nation's most powerful machines can be overwhelmingly defeated.

The underworld has become a powerful factor in municipal politics everywhere because of the strong motive of self-interest which impels it to contribute money and manpower to political organizations. From purely a selfish standpoint, it is intent upon keeping in power an administration, on either a ward or a city-wide basis, which will enable it to reap rich harvests from gambling, prostitution, narcotics or similar lucrative activities. The decent people, on the other hand, usually do not feel a self-interest motive strong enough to impel them to devote appreciable time, effort and money in behalf of good government. The average citizen, like the politician, must have inducements other than that of rendering public service if he is to be spurred into action for the good of his community or city. Good government is an abstract principle to which most citizens subscribe, but too few have a strong feeling that political-criminal alliances adversely affect their personal welfare. They may deplore the immoral nature of such alliances but it must be admitted that to the average citizen moral issues are seldom as vital as those affecting his personal welfare. This was clearly evident from the riots in Cicero in the summer of 1951. For over thirty years, the home owners and other residents of Cicero had tolerated the presence of the infamous Capone gang. There was little genuine public indignation over commonplace alliances between officials and gangsters. At least, the public was never aroused to an extent where officials found it necessary to rid the village of Capone gunmen. Then in the summer of 1951, a young Negro family moved into Cicero. The moral as well as the legal right of Negroes to live in the village could not be questioned. Immediately, however, the people of Cicero rose up in arms. The building in which the Negro family was living was virtually wrecked, and the family had to flee for safety. Violence reached such heights that it became necessary for the governor of the state to dispatch troops to restore order. Whether the uprising resulted from a fear of a decline in property values or from just plain race prejudice is not known. Both factors probably played a part in this disgraceful episode. Almost everywhere, a threat to property values or economic security will stir people to action far more quickly than indignation over official immorality.

Citizens are properly urged to become morally indignant over alliances between politicians and the underworld. Spasmodically, a wave of moral indignation results in the overthrow of a venal political regime. But experience clearly indicates that moral indignation usually must be accompanied by a strong feeling of self-interest if citizen action is to be sustained and effective. It is the business interests of America, perhaps more than any other single group, that should feel this strong self-interest. They have a great economic stake in furnishing leadership that will destroy the power of the underworld. Scores of legitimate businesses and industries have fallen under the domination of infamous gang leaders. Belatedly, businessmen are learning that criminals who have been permitted to operate lucrative rackets have invested their profits in oil wells, finance companies, transportation systems, the iron and steel industry, communication companies, hotels, office buildings, textile and garment factories, food concerns, automobile distributorships and virtually every other type of business enterprise. More belatedly, leaders in business and industry are learning further that they cannot possibly hope to compete with the gangster element on an equal basis. Almost without exception, when members of criminal gangs became engaged in the fields of legitimate business they resort to jungle methods of competition — the application of brute strength, terrorism and violence. Through cheating on state and Federal taxes they are frequently in a position to undersell legitimate competitors and still enjoy huge profits. If underselling fails to win customers, there always remain the persuasive methods of threatened gun play, bombing or the destruction of merchandise purchased from rival concerns. The underworld always engages in monopolistic practices. Territories are divided and any infringement means certain violence. Whether the business of the gangster is legitimate or illegitimate, he follows only one code — the code of the underworld. Businessmen have not completely lacked interest in the crime problem, however.

Over thirty years ago, the Chicago Association of Commerce, alarmed over unrestrained lawlessness then prevailing in the city, decided that businessmen should assume the leadership in attempting to reduce crime and official corruption. A committee of business leaders was appointed to study the situation and make recommendations. As a result, there was formed a civic organization called the Chicago Crime Commission with a membership of outstanding citizens chosen largely from the business and professional field. Its purpose was to exercise constant vigilance over the police agencies, prosecutors and courts with a view to improving their standards and holding them responsible for the full performance of their sworn duties. Employing a full-time staff in order to obtain accurate facts regarding crime conditions and the conduct of law-enforcement officials, the Crime Commission makes known its findings to the public. A number of citizens' organizations, patterned after the Chicago Crime Commission, have been formed in other cities, several of them, like the Chicago Commission, organized by local chambers of commerce. The Kefauver Senate Committee, favorably impressed with the work of these commissions, recommended the formation of similar citizens' crime commissions in each large community in the nation. The Senate Committee blamed the prevalent public apathy in many cities to a lack of knowledge and, in particular, to the absence of "leadership to do something about malodorous crime conditions." The function of a local crime commission, observed the Senate Committee, is to furnish the necessary leadership and to expose pitilessly the alliances that exist between the racketeers, corrupt law-enforcement officials, and political organizations.[23] Under our form of government, exposure is the first vital step in holding public officials responsible. Exposure alone, however, will not automatically result in improved conditions. These will only come about when the decent people are organized to transform public indignation into political action.

It must be conceded, however, that even with a well-organized and alert citizenry it is not easy to hold all officials responsible. A number of suggested reforms for better municipal government have consequently attempted to reduce the number of elective offices, thus fixing responsibility on fewer officials. Many decades ago, Seth Low, a former mayor of Brooklyn and president of Columbia College, aptly observed that "greatly to multiply important elective officers is not to increase popular control, but to lessen it." [24] In the field of law enforcement, the most frequent suggestion is to remove it completely from political influence. The same idea has been expressed with reference to the office of prosecutor and the judiciary. Unfortunately such suggestions are much more easily made than placed into effect. The responsibility for the administration of the police, the prosecutor's office and the courts must be fixed somewhere, and ultimately the responsible person is almost invariably a political officeholder.

In a report of the American Bar Association Commission on Organized Crime, a recommendation was made that "local prosecutors should be appointed by the Governor instead of elected as heretofore. . . . Appointment by the Governor," said the report, "will concentrate responsibility for designating able prosecutors. The public will know to whom to look, if there are serious deficiencies in the administration of the prosecutor's office. . . ."[25] It was also suggested that local prosecutors should be directly answerable to a state department of justice which would have general supervision of law enforcement throughout the state. Placing much of the responsibility for the growth of organized crime "at the door of the ineffective functioning of the prosecutor's office," the report recognized the fact that in the larger metropolitan offices, "the assistants of the prosecutor . . . are in reality named by the local ward bosses and district leaders who comprise the political machine."[26] The same statement would apply equally to judges and court attachés including bailiffs and clerks. This situation assumes serious proportions when ward leaders who are closely allied with the underworld have a strong voice in naming prosecuting and judicial officials. It may be seriously questioned, however, whether the appointment of the prosecutor and his staff by the governor would remove the influence of local ward bosses. As a practical matter, except on rare occasions, the appointments would probably continue to be dictated by the same ward politicians.

When the United States government was originally formed, it was the generally accepted principle that judges should be appointed for good behavior and thus remain completely removed from the arena of partisan politics. This was the plan adopted by the Federal government and it has been adhered to since that time. Before long, however, the various states introduced the system of electing judges for fixed terms, thus compelling them to campaign for re-election at frequent intervals. Alexis de Tocqueville, who published his celebrated treatise on America in 1835, predicted:

. . . these innovations will sooner or later be attended with fatal consequences; and that it will be found out at some future period that by thus lessening the independence of the judiciary they have attacked not only the judicial power, but the democratic republic itself.[27]

Even Tocqueville, however, perhaps never dreamed that eventually judges in Chicago, New York City and other municipalities would be deeply obligated to corrupt ward organizations with under-world backing; that judges would curry the favor of the Big Jim Colosimos, the Al Capones and their satellites, or pledge their "undying loyalty" to such gangsters as Frank Costello for their place on the bench. In Chicago, it is in the Municipal Court that political influence is frequently seen at its worst. This is true not-withstanding the presence of many able men who have long served in this branch of the judiciary. During election time, some of the municipal court judges brazenly decorate their courtrooms with campaign posters urging their re-election while their bailiffs hand out cards to the friends and relatives of defendants asking for their vote at the polls. Some of the judges have frankly admitted that a place on the Municipal Court bench is frequently a consola-tion prize for garnering votes for the machine. The late Fiorello H. LaGuardia, who distinguished himself as the mayor of New York for twelve years, spoke of the "damaging and demoralizing influence of the political machine" on the judicial system in his state. He pre-dicted that "once the courts are taken out of politics, the machine will be greatly weakened." [28]

The elective system for judges has in many respects borne out Tocqueville's dire predictions. The average voter is not in a posi-tion to obtain information on which he may base an accurate ap-praisal of candidates for judicial office. Judicial slates are made up largely by the ward bosses and elections are usually determined solely on partisan issues having nothing to do with a man's fitness to sit on the bench. A former judge of the Supreme Court of Missouri, Fred L. Williams, once said, "I was elected in 1916 be-cause Woodrow Wilson kept us out of war. I was defeated in 1920 because Woodrow Wilson did not keep us out of war. In both of the elections not more than five per cent of the voters knew I was on the ticket."

Various plans have been advanced to remove the judiciary from the realm of partisan politics. A number of the proposals place the selection of judicial candidates in the hands of a nominating com-mission consisting of both lawyers and laymen and presided over by the chief justice of the state supreme court. Most of the plans vest the actual appointive power in the governor though some sug-gest that this duty should be exercised by the chief justice of the state supreme court. A few of the proposals give the appointing power to the nominating commission itself. The Chicago Bar Association has recommended the appointment of municipal court judges by the mayor. All of the reforms accept the principle that "once a good judge has been put on the bench, he ought to be able to keep his seat indefinitely until death, retirement or resignation." At the same time it should be possible to remove "worthless, incompetent, and dishonest" judges. Keeping these objectives in mind and retaining the elective principle, it has been suggested that upon the expiration of a judge's fixed term of office, his name should be submitted to the voters only on the question as to whether he should or should not be retained on the bench.[29] The possibilities of adopting a new method of selecting judges in Illinois in the near future are not particularly promising; however, some states, notably Missouri, already have in effect a plan which does appear to have raised judicial standards. Briefly, under the Missouri plan the governor makes a judicial appointment from a list of three names presented to him by a Selection Commission composed of both lawyers and laymen. After a judge is appointed he serves a minimum of twelve months and at the next general election the people vote solely on whether he shall or shall not be retained in office. But no plan, states Associate Justice Laurance M. Hyde of the Missouri Supreme Court, is foolproof nor will it "operate automatically to select good judges. Like all institutions of democracy, it will require eternal vigilance to prevent its perversion and to make it work properly." [30]

It is not only in the matter of improving the judiciary that local bar associations have a genuine public duty to perform. Within the ranks of the bar are attorneys who unethically counsel and advise gangsters on methods of evading the law. Some of them are so closely identified with the day-by-day operations of criminal gangs that they are actually part of them. This fact became clearly evident from the revelations of the Kefauver Committee and prompted the American Bar Association Commission on Organized Crime to report that "many specific instances have come to the attention of the Senate Committee where members of the bar have co-operated with notorious gangsters quite outside of the obligations they owe their clients." After commenting on the aid given members of the Capone gang by a Chicago lawyer, the report stated:

There were other instances and cases where it was clear that unethical practices were being followed by lawyers and tax accountants in advising their clients on how they could avoid prosecution. It is well known also that certain members of the bar frequently facilitate the activities of criminal gangs.

The report urged local and state bar associations to conduct forthright campaigns "to eliminate lawyers who go outside their proper duties to co-operate with criminals or assist them in their unlawful schemes. . . ." [31] Judging from past experience, these recommendations will probably be ignored. There has been very little inclination on the part of bar associations to rid their ranks of lawyers who unethically aid and abet the illegal operations of powerful gangsters.

Of the various official bodies which need strengthening, the police department ranks first in importance. When controlled by a corrupt political organization, the police department is an ideal agency for rewarding political friends and punishing enemies. Machine rule in American municipalities has been possible only through control of the police. A leading authority on police in this country, Bruce Smith, has stated that few American police departments "have escaped the direct influence of political patronage, all live within its shadow, and some are tarred from head to heels with political corruption and criminal participation." [32]

Throughout Chicago's history its police department has been steeped in politics. Realistically, the department probably can never be completely removed from political influence. Perhaps the only practical objective is to place it under a *good* political influence — an influence exerted by the citizens.

Among the improvements urgently needed is a sound recruiting program that will assure the appointment of only high-caliber officers who will not be subjected to pressure from the political associates of the underworld interests. A program of this nature necessarily includes a thorough independent character investigation of all applicants for police positions. New recruits must be adequately trained and in-service training programs should be devised to improve the capabilities of men already on the force. But the most glaring weakness in the Chicago Police Department is the absence of proper discipline — a weakness that is not attributable solely to faulty police administration. The ever-present political influence on the department itself, on the Civil Service Commission and on the courts makes sound personnel management virtually impossible. In recent years, during Mayor Martin H. Kennelly's regime, there has been a great improvement in police administration. The Civil Service Commission has been headed by a man of outstanding legal ability and unquestioned integrity. But even under the best of conditions, it is highly questionable whether sound personnel management in the police department can ever be achieved under the present concept of civil service. While the original purpose of civil service was to improve the efficiency of the public service, its principal contributions in the field of law enforcement have been the maintenance of negative controls. Although vastly superior to the old spoils system which once governed police agencies, it has not assured the appointment of well-qualified personnel or the promotion of those who are deserving. During most of the period that the Civil Service Commission has governed Chicago's police personnel, it has been politically controlled, enabling politicians to place unqualified men, some of them the associates of racketeers, on the force. And once an applicant is appointed to the police department, civil service regulations, particularly as interpreted by the courts, make it almost impossible to effect his removal. Under present conditions the maintenance of proper discipline is hopeless. Yet, "A sound discipline," observes Bruce Smith, "will probably contribute more to the solution of our municipal police problems than any other single recourse now available." [33]

Another pressing need of the police department in Chicago, as in most other cities, is an efficient intelligence unit. Criminals organize and become powerful through a constant effort to engage uninterruptedly in lucrative activities. On the whole, police efforts to combat the gangster element have been unplanned, spasmodic and totally ineffective. There has been little, if any, co-ordination of information. The activities, backgrounds, and associates of well-known underworld leaders are usually recorded only in the minds of individual police officers. Efforts to develop such data are seldom made except in connection with the investigation of a specific offense, and police files frequently contain only stereotyped records of arrests relating to members of the underworld. Obviously, organized crime presents a problem totally unlike the individual offense of burglary, robbery or rape. It can be effectively suppressed only through intelligence work of a high order.

The function of an intelligence unit in the police department is to keep a constant check on the activities of underworld characters through confidential investigations, surveillances and the maintenance of a proper liaison with official and other sources of information, locally as well as in other cities. The intelligence unit should be adequately manned with able investigators of unquestioned integrity. These men will develop accurate data regarding all principal racketeers and their associates living in the metropolitan area. They will uncover alliances between the underworld and those occupying positions of trust in political life, in business or the professions. In particular, improper relations between the underworld and venal police officers will come to light and enable the head of the department to cause their removal or, if this is impossible, to assign them to tasks that will not jeopardize the efforts of honest police personnel. All data obtained will be co-ordinated and maintained in a manner that will make it readily available to the head of the police department. Through such effective intelligence work, the department will be able to anticipate the plans and future activities of the racketeering element. Men assigned to the intelligence unit ordinarily should not be engaged in making arrests. Their primary function is to gather secretly the information that is essential if the police expect to wage effective warfare against organized crime.[34]

In considering various proposals for improvement of the judiciary, the prosecutor's office and the police, it is important to observe that none of them are substitutes for a vigilant public that is willing to accept the responsibilities of good citizenship. Systems do not function in a vacuum, they are operated by men. Honest, able officials without any direct or indirect obligation to the racketeering element can overcome a bad system. But no system, regardless of its theoretical perfection, will provide good government when it is operated by men who owe their positions to the direct or indirect political influence of the underworld.

It is trite to say that people receive the type of government they demand and for which they are willing to labor. Nevertheless it is true. To say that the criminal-political system which has disgraced Chicago during the greater part of the past century is identical with those prevailing in most other large municipalities is likewise true. But it is also begging the question. In a speech made by former President Herbert Hoover in August 1951, he warned that the greatest danger to this government is:

> . . . not from invasion by foreign armies. Our dangers are that we may commit suicide from within by complaisance with evil. Or by public tolerance of scandalous behavior. Or by cynical acceptance of dishonor. These evils have defeated nations many times in human history.

In a similar vein, Arnold J. Toynbee, one of the great historians of the modern era, observed, "There is no doubt that it is a moral challenge rather than a physical challenge that confronts our own society today." [35]

Will the challenge be accepted? Few will deny that the tremendous political power now vested in the underworld is one of the perplexing problems facing most large municipalities in America. It cannot be solved through new laws or new systems. The remedy lies primarily with the people themselves.

Notes

CHAPTER I

1. Lloyd Lewis and Henry Justin Smith, *Chicago, the History of Its Reputation* (New York: Harcourt, Brace & Co., 1929), pp. 7, 8, 22, 28.
2. *Ibid.*, pp. 30, 33, 34; Charles Edward Merriman, *Chicago, a More Intimate View of the Urban Politics* (New York: Macmillan Co., 1929), pp. 17, 18; Herbert Asbury, *Gem of the Prairie* (An Informal History of the Chicago Underworld) (New York: Alfred A. Knopf, 1940), p. 36.
3. A. T. Andreas, *History of Chicago* (3 vols.; Chicago: A. T. Andreas, 1884, 1885, 1886), I, 421, 422.
4. *Ibid.*, I, 202–203.
5. M. L. Ahern, *The Political History of Chicago* (Covering the Period from 1837 to 1887) (1st. ed.; Chicago: Donohue & Henneberry, 1886), pp. 23, 87.
6. J. W. Norris, *General Directory and Business Advertiser of the City of Chicago for the Year 1844; Together with a Historical Sketch and Statistical Account to the Present Time* (Chicago: Ellis & Fergus, 1844).
7. *Ibid.*
8. Joseph Kirkland and John Moses, *History of Chicago, Illinois* (Chicago and New York: Munsell & Co., 1895), I, 113.
9. Andreas, *op. cit.*, I, 464, 465.
10. John J. Flinn, *History of the Chicago Police* (Chicago: Chicago Police Book Fund, 1887), p. 57.
11. Andreas, *op. cit.*, I, 152.
12. John Philip Quinn, *Fools of Fortune* (Chicago: G. L. Howe & Co., 1890), p. 389.
13. Andreas, *op. cit.*, I, 248, 262, 263; Kirkland and Moses, *op. cit.*, pp. 119–121; Ahern, *op. cit.*, p. 87.
14. John S. Wright, *Chicago: Past, Present, Future* (2d. ed.; Chicago Board of Trade, 1870), p. 24.
15. Kirkland and Moses, *op. cit.*, p. 119.

16. Andreas, *op. cit.*, I, 595.

17. *Ibid.*, I, 155.

CHAPTER II

1. Ernest Poole, *Giants Gone — Men Who Made Chicago* (New York: Whittlesey House, 1943), p. 61.

2. Andreas, *op. cit.*, I, 197; *see also* p. 192; Lewis and Smith, *op. cit.*, pp. 56, 60.

3. Wright, *op. cit.*, p. 75.

4. Andreas, *op. cit.*, I, 159.

5. *Ibid.*, p. 157.

6. Ahern, *op. cit.*, pp. 27–29; Andreas, *op. cit.*, I, 609–611.

7. Mayor Levi D. Boone's version of the riots appeared in the *Chicago Times*, August 5, 1877; Andreas, *op. cit.*, pp. 614–616; *see also* pp. 453, 454.

8. Flinn, *op. cit.*, pp. 71, 72; Andreas, *op. cit.*, I, 203.

9. Kirkland and Moses, *op. cit.*, pp. 125, 126; Andreas, *op. cit.*, I, 193.

10. Flinn, *op. cit.*, p. 80; Andreas, *op. cit.*, I, 159.

11. Quinn, *op. cit.*, pp. 389, 390, 391.

12. Kirkland and Moses, *op. cit.*, pp. 128, 129; Andreas, *op. cit.*, I, 159.

13. Wright, *op. cit.*, p. 17.

14. Flinn, *op. cit.*, pp. 83, 84, 87.

CHAPTER III

1. Kirkland and Moses, *op. cit.*, pp. 134, 135; Wright, *op. cit.*, p. 75.

2. Paul M. Angle (ed.), *The Lincoln Reader* (New Brunswick: Rutgers University Press, 1947), pp. 265–273.

3. Flinn, *op. cit.*, pp. 88, 89, 93, 94, 95, 96; Kirkland and Moses, *op. cit.*, p. 136.

4. Frederick Francis Cook, *Bygone Days in Chicago* (Recollections of the "Garden City" of the Sixties) (Chicago: A. C. McClurg & Co., 1910), p. 11.

5. Flinn, *op. cit.*, pp. 103, 104, 105.

6. Quinn, *op. cit.*, pp. 394, 395.

7. *Ibid.*, pp. 396, 397.

8. *Ibid.*, p. 398; Flinn, *op. cit.*, pp. 103, 104, 105; Cook, *op. cit.*, pp. 138, 139; Lewis and Smith, *op. cit.*, pp. 98, 100, 101.

9. *Ibid.*, p. 97; Cook, *op. cit.*, pp. 135, 136, 137.

10. Flinn, *op. cit.*, pp. 105, 106.

11. Cook, *op. cit.*, pp. 43, 44.

12. *Ibid.*, pp. 150, 153.

13. Dixon Wecter, *When Johnny Comes Marching Home* (Boston: Houghton Mifflin Co., 1944), p. 150.
14. Cook, *op. cit.*, pp. 141, 142, 143.
15. Andreas, *op. cit.*, II, 614, 615.
16. Cook, *op. cit.*, pp. 143–149.
17. Kirkland and Moses, *op. cit.*, pp. 141, 142, 145.
18. Wright, *op. cit.*, p. 109.

CHAPTER IV

1. Andreas, *op. cit.*, II, 51, 701–780; Kirkland and Moses, *op. cit.*, pp. 204–208.
2. *Ibid.*, p. 216.
3. *Ibid.*, p. 236.
4. Flinn, *op. cit.*, pp. 136–141.
5. Quinn, *op. cit.*, p. 401; Kirkland and Moses, *op. cit.*, p. 236.
6. *Ibid.*, p. 219.
7. Andreas, *op. cit.*, III, 860.
8. Kirkland and Moses, *op. cit.*, pp. 219–221.
9. Louis Adamic, *Dynamite, the Story of Class Violence in America* (New York: Viking Press, 1934), p. 44; *see also* pp. 33–35.
10. Flinn, *op. cit.*, pp. 153–201.
11. Andreas, *op. cit.*, III, 865.
12. *Chicago News*, August 9, 1907; Quinn, *op. cit.*, pp. 401–403; Alfred Prowitt, "Dora McDonald's Trial," *Chicago News*, March 18, 1944; Lloyd Wendt and Herman Kogan, *Lords of the Levee* (Indianapolis: Bobbs-Merrill Co., 1943), p. 27.
13. Poole, *op. cit.*, pp. 161, 164, 167; Lewis and Smith, *op. cit.*, pp. 158, 159.
14. Wendt and Kogan, *op. cit.*, pp. 27, 28.
15. Andreas, *op. cit.*, III, 868, 869.
16. *Ibid.*, p. 869.
17. Kirkland and Moses, *op. cit.*, p. 232.
18. *Ibid.*, pp. 232, 233.
19. Andreas, *op. cit.*, III, 870.
20. Adamic, *op. cit.*, pp. 59–86; Flinn, *op. cit.*, pp. 223–323.
21. Kirkland and Moses, *op. cit.*, p. 234.
22. *Ibid.*, p. 236.
23. Quinn, *op. cit.*, pp. 404, 405.
24. Poole, *op. cit.*, p. 167.
25. *Handbook of the World's Columbian Exposition* (Chicago: Rand, McNally & Co., 1893); Harry Thurston Peck, *Twenty Years of the*

Republic, 1885–1905 (New York: Dodd, Mead & Co., 1932), pp. 350–352.

26. Kirkland and Moses, *op. cit.,* pp. 246, 247.
27. Lewis and Smith, *op. cit.,* pp. 177, 178; Wendt and Kogan, *op. cit.,* pp. 65, 67.
28. Kirkland and Moses, *op. cit.,* p. 254.
29. Wendt and Kogan, *op. cit.,* p. 71.
30. *Ibid.,* pp. 28, 29, 146.
31. *Ibid.,* pp. 76–80.
32. *Ibid.,* pp. 78, 79.
33. *Chicago News,* October 9, 1946.
34. Peck, *op. cit.,* p. 350; For description of the Exposition itself see *Handbook of the World's Columbian Exposition, loc. cit.*
35. Lewis and Smith, *op. cit.,* p. 214.
36. William T. Stead, *If Christ Came to Chicago!* (Chicago: Laird & Lee, 1894).
37. Adamic, *op. cit.,* pp. 108–123; Lewis and Smith, *op. cit.,* pp. 220–226.
38. Lewis and Smith, *op. cit.,* pp. 236, 237; Poole, *op. cit.,* pp. 165, 166.

CHAPTER V

1. Lewis and Smith, *op. cit.,* pp. 243, 244.
2. *Ibid.,* pp. 240–242.
3. Charles H. Hermann, *Recollections of Life and Doings in Chicago,* [*From the Haymarket Riot to the End of World War I*] (Chicago: Normandie House, 1945), pp. 153–154.
4. Hoyt King, *Citizen Cole of Chicago* (Chicago: Horder's, Inc., 1931), pp. 46, 47; Wendt and Kogan, *op. cit.,* pp. 69, 146.
5. *Chicago News,* October 9, 1946.
6. Hermann, *op. cit.,* pp. 52–55, 155.
7. Carter H. Harrison, *Stormy Years* (The Autobiography of Carter H. Harrison) (Indianapolis: Bobbs-Merrill Co., 1935), pp. 80–84. On p. 75 Harrison states: "Beyond the peradventure of a doubt, my first nomination was due to the determination of two men . . . Robert E. Burke and Joseph S. Martin."
8. Hermann, *op. cit.,* pp. 92–96.
9. Harrison, *op. cit.,* pp. 92–120.
10. M. R. Werner, *Tammany Hall* (New York: Doubleday, Doran & Co., 1928), pp. 452–456; *see also* pp. 356, 442–445.
11. Harrison, op. cit., pp. 129–133.
12. Franklin Matthews, " 'Wide-Open' Chicago," *Harper's Weekly,* January 22, 1898.

13. Wendt and Kogan, *op. cit.*, pp. 201, 202.

14. Harrison, *op. cit.*, p. 85.

15. *Ibid.*, p. 79.

16. *Ibid.*, pp. 78, 79.

17. Lewis and Smith, *op. cit.*, p. 304.

18. *Ibid.*, pp. 230, 231, 265–267.

19. *Ibid.*, pp. 250–251.

20. King, *op. cit.*, p. 122; *see also* pp. 119–121.

21. Harrison, *op. cit.*, p. 227.

22. Willis J. Abbot, "The Harrison Dynasty in Chicago," *Munsey's Magazine*, September 1903, pp. 809–815.

23. Lewis and Smith, *op. cit.*, pp. 298–303.

24. Harrison, *op. cit.*, p. 256.

25. Hermann, *op. cit.*, pp. 39, 40; Lewis and Smith, *op. cit.*, pp. 353–362.

26. *Ibid.*, pp. 165–169.

27. *The Illinois Crime Survey*, Part III ("Organized Crime in Chicago," John Landesco, [Illinois Association for Criminal Justice in co-operation with Chicago Crime Commission, 1929]), Ch. XIX, "The Rule of the Underworld — Tennes as a Vice Chief," pp. 868–873; *see also* John T. Flynn, "Smart Money," *Colliers*, Jan. 20, 1940.

28. *Chicago News*, August 9, 1907; Alfred Prowitt, "Dora McDonald's Trial," *Chicago News*, March 18, 1944.

29. "A Memory of Old Chicago," editorial, *Chicago News*, August 8, 1907.

30. *The Illinois Crime Survey*, *op. cit.*, pp. 871–874.

31. *The Social Evil in Chicago* (A Study of Existing Conditions as Recommended by the Vice Commission of Chicago in a report to the Mayor and City Council) (Chicago: Gunthorp-Warren Printing Co., 1911), p. 1.

32. *Ibid.*, pp. 2, 3, 4.

33. *Ibid.*, pp. 5, 6, 7, 8.

34. Harrison, *op. cit.*, p. 294.

35. *The Illinois Crime Survey*, pp. 879–882.

36. *Ibid.*, pp. 884–887.

37. *The Social Evil in Chicago*, *op. cit.*, p. 113.

38. *Ibid.*, p. 34.

39. *Ibid.*, pp. 72, 73.

40. *Ibid.*, p. 74.

41. *Ibid.*, p. 152.

42. *Ibid.*, p. 78.

43. *Ibid.*, p. 74.

44. *Ibid.*, pp. 108, 119, 120, 121, 130.
45. *Ibid.*, p. 79.
46. Charles Washburn, *Come Into My Parlor* (A Biography of the Aristocratic Everleigh Sisters of Chicago) (New York: Knickerbocker Publishing Co., 1934).
47. *The Illinois Crime Survey, op. cit.*, pp. 848–851.

CHAPTER VI

1. Lewis and Smith, *op. cit.*, pp. 370–377; Harrison, *op. cit.*, pp. 346–348.
2. William H. Stuart, *The Twenty Incredible Years* (Chicago: M. A. Donohue & Co., 1935), pp. 7–10 gives an account of the early history of William Hale Thompson.
3. Charles H. Hermann, *op. cit.*, pp. 254–257.
4. Fletcher Dobyns, *The Underworld of American Politics* (New York: Fletcher Dobyns, 1932), pp. 184, 185.
5. *The Illinois Crime Survey, op. cit.*, pp. 890, 891.
6. *Ibid.*, pp. 891, 892.
7. *Ibid.*, pp. 892–898.
8. Stuart, *op. cit.*, pp. 35–43, 58, 59.
9. St. Clair Drake and Horace R. Cayton, *Black Metropolis* (A Study of Negro Life in a Northern City) (New York: Harcourt, Brace & Co., 1945), pp. 65–73.
10. Fred D. Pasley, *Al Capone* (The Biography of a Self-Made Man) (New York: Garden City Publishing Co., 1930), pp. 13, 14; "The Murder of Colosimo — How Torrio Framed Him," *Illinois Policeman* and *Police Journal* (Chicago), March-April, 1947.
11. Herbert Asbury, *The Gangs of New York* (An Informal History of the Underworld) (New York: Alfred A. Knopf, 1927, 1928), p. 355; Elmer L. Irey (as told to William J. Slocum), *The Tax Dodgers* (New York: Greenberg, 1948), p. 155. The year 1910 is fixed as the time Colosimo brought Torrio to Chicago. Torrio was allegedly a nephew of Colosimo.
12. *Illinois Policeman* and *Police Journal*, *loc. cit.*
13. Irey, *op. cit.*, p. 156.
14. *The Illinois Crime Survey, op. cit.*, p. 909.
15. Pasley, *op. cit.*, pp. 18, 19, 24.
16. *The Illinois Crime Survey, op. cit.*, p. 899.
17. Lewis and Smith, *op. cit.*, p. 437.
18. Stuart, *op. cit.*, pp. 91, 92, 94–105.
19. *Ibid.*, pp. 158–161.

20. This law was approved June 19, 1923; *see Illinois Revised Statutes* 1949, Ch. 127, Sec. 177.
21. Stuart, *op. cit.*, pp. 147–151.
22. *Ibid.*, pp. 135–140.
23. *The Illinois Crime Survey, op. cit.*, pp. 948–953, 1034.
24. Stuart, *op. cit.*, 141–143.
25. *The Illinois Crime Survey, op. cit.*, pp. 960–968.
26. M. L. McKinley (Chief Justice, Criminal Court of Cook County 1922–1923), "Crime and the Civic Cancer — Graft," *Chicago News* reprints, No. 6, 11–14.

CHAPTER VII

1. Dobyns, *op. cit.*, pp. 53, 54.
2. *The Illinois Crime Survey, op. cit.*, pp. 900, 910.
3. *Ibid.*, p. 912.
4. *Ibid.*, pp. 913, 1011.
5. *Ibid.*, p. 1012.
6. "O'Banion Wanted $15,000; Genna Gave Him Death," *Illinois Policeman* and *Police Journal*, May-June 1947; Lewis and Smith, *op. cit.*, pp. 438, 439, 440, 448, 449; *The Illinois Crime Survey, op. cit.*, p. 916.
7. *The Illinois Crime Survey, op. cit.*, p. 927.
8. *Chicago Tribune*, April 7, 1925; Irey, *op. cit.*, pp. 154–165; *The Illinois Crime Survey, op. cit.*, pp. 913–919.
9. Stuart, *op. cit.*, pp. 192, 193.
10. *Ibid.*, pp. 225, 226.
11. *Ibid.*, pp. 206–208.
12. *Ibid.*, pp. 203, 204, 235–243.
13. Elmer L. Irey and William J. Slocum, "Twilight of a Gangster," *Coronet*, November 1947, p. 72.
14. Frank J. Wilson (Chief, Secret Service retired), as told to Howard Whitman "Undercover Man — He Trapped Capone," *Collier's*, April 26, 1947.
15. Wendt and Kogan, *op. cit.*, pp. 344, 345.
16. Lewis and Smith, *op. cit.*, pp. 451–453.
17. *The Illinois Crime Survey, op. cit.*, p. 928.
18. *Ibid.*, pp. 928, 929. Pasley, *op. cit.*, pp. 140–144.
19. *The Illinois Crime Survey, op. cit.*, p. 902; Stuart, *op. cit.*, pp. 268, 269 on Rat show in 1926; pp. 288–320 on mayoralty campaign of 1927.
20. Stuart, *op. cit.*, p. 317.
21. *Chicago News*, August 27, 1930.

22. Lewis and Smith, *op. cit.*, p. 469.
23. Pasley, *op. cit.*, p. 82.
24. Stuart, *op. cit.*, pp. 336–338, 353–355.
25. *The Illinois Crime Survey*, *op. cit.*, pp. 902, 903, 904.
26. Lewis and Smith, *op. cit.*, pp. 470, 471; Pasley, *op. cit.*, pp. 170, 171, 205, 206.
27. *The Illinois Crime Survey*, *op. cit.*, pp. 954, 955, 956; Lewis and Smith, *op. cit.*, pp. 477–481.
28. *Chicago News*, March 15, 1928.
29. Pasley, *op. cit.*, pp. 230, 231, 232.
30. *Ibid.*, pp. 252–256.
31. *Ibid.*, p. 71.
32. *Ibid.*, pp. 265–300.
33. *Chicago News*, July 11, 1930.
34. *Chicago Tribune*, July 2, 1930.
35. *Chicago Post*, August 2, 1930.
36. *Chicago Tribune*, August 17, 1930; *Chicago Times*, August 18, 1930; *Chicago American*, August 22, 1930.
37. *Chicago News*, August 27, 1930.
38. *Ibid.*, January 17, 1931.
39. *Chicago Times*, January 17, 1931.
40. *Chicago Times*, October 25, 1930; *Chicago Examiner*, September 30, 1930; *Ibid.*, October 26, 1930; *Chicago Post*, November 15, 1930; *Chicago Times*, November 15, 1930.
41. *Chicago News*, September 27, 1930.
42. *Criminal Justice*, Journal of the Chicago Crime Commission, May 1947, No. 74, p. 40.
43. Stuart, *op. cit.*, p. 456.

CHAPTER VIII

1. John McConaughy, *From Cain to Capone* (Racketeering Down the Ages) (New York: Coward-McCann, 1931), p. 148.
2. Stuart, *op. cit.*, pp. 457–460, 464–470.
3. Mauritz A. Hallgren, "Chicago Goes Tammany," *The Nation*, April 22, 1931, p. 446.
4. *Ibid.*, pp. 446, 447.
5. Stuart, *op. cit.*, pp. 501–503.
6. Wilson, *loc. cit.*
7. *Chicago News*, September 10, 1947.
8. *Better Government Association Report*, 1931; *see* Dobyns, *op. cit.*, p. 172.

9. Craig Thompson and Allen Raymond, *Gang Rule in New York* (The Story of a Lawless Era) (New York: Dial Press, 1940), pp. 244, 366, 367.

10. Joseph F. Dinneen, *The Purple Shamrock* (The Hon. James Michael Curley of Boston) (New York: W. W. Norton & Co., 1949), pp. 187–191.

11. Dobyns, *op. cit., see* Introduction, pp. viii, ix.

12. *Chicago Times*, March 1, 1940.

13. *Chicago Tribune*, August 18, 1939.

14. Stuart, *op. cit.*, p. 502.

15. *Chicago American*, January 7, 1933; *Chicago Tribune*, April 7, 1933, April 8, 1933, September 12, 27, 28 (1933), December 30, 1933; *Chicago News*, September 27, 1933; December 29, 1933.

16. *Chicago Tribune*, April 14, 1933.

17. Robert S. Allen (ed.), *Our Fair City* (New York: Vanguard Press, 1947), pp. 169, 173, 175, 176.

18. *Ibid.*, page 176.

19. Charles W. Van Devander, *The Big Bosses* (New York: Howell-Soskin, 1944), p. 265.

20. Allen, *op. cit.*, p. 177.

21. Wendt and Kogan, *op. cit.*, pp. 352, 353.

22. *Chicago News*, August 1, 1923.

23. Glenn A. Bishop and Paul T. Gilbert, *Chicago's Progress* (A Review of the World's Fair City) (Chicago: Bishop Publishing Co., 1933), pp. 9–19.

24. *Chicago's Report to the People, 1933–1946* (Chicago: City of Chicago, March 1947), pp. 1, 2.

25. Ernest W. Burgess, "An Open Letter to Governor Horner," June 24, 1935.

26. Melvin Purvis, *American Agent* (New York: Garden City Publishing Co., 1936), pp. 117–123.

27. *Ibid.*, p. 39; Courtney Ryley Cooper, *Ten Thousand Public Enemies* (Boston: Little, Brown & Co., 1935), pp. 247, 248, 263–269.

28. Purvis, *op. cit.*, pp. 70–97.

29. *Ibid.*, pp. 123–129.

30. *Ibid.*, pp. 144–169.

31. *Ibid.*, pp. 201–220, 262–288.

32. Stuart, *op. cit.*, p. 535.

33. Malcolm Johnson, *Crime on the Labor Front* (New York: McGraw-Hill, 1950), pp. 34–54; Thompson and Raymond, *op. cit.*, p. 355; *Chicago Tribune*, October 11, 1947.

34. Johnson, *op. cit.*, pp. 14–33; James Bartlow Martin, "Who Killed Estelle Carey?" *Harpers*, June 1944.

35. *Chicago News*, September 10, 1947.

36. *Chicago Tribune*, October 12, 1938.

37. Stuart, *op. cit.*, pp. 363, 551–557.

38. *Chicago Tribune*, July 10, 1936.

39. Lewis A. H. Caldwell, "Chicago Policy Racket" (Master's thesis, Northwestern University, June 1940).

40. Raymond Grow, "De King is Daid!" *American Mercury*, October 1939.

41. *Chicago News*, June 14, 1939.

42. John T. Flynn, "Too Much Fun," *Collier's*, October 7, 1939.

43. "Old Wine in New Bottles," editorial, *Chicago News*, September 20, 1939.

CHAPTER IX

1. "Kelly in Angry Mood Rejects Any Showdown on Income," *Chicago News*, February 16, 1939.

2. "Questions for Judge Holland," editorial, *Chicago News*, September 9, 1939.

3. Dan Parker, "Massachusetts Goes to the Dogs," *The Saturday Evening Post*, January 6, 1940; "Crime's Bid for Power — Racket Ruled Dog Racing Born in Legislative Deal," editorial, *Boston Evening Transcript*, December 30, 1939; "Capone Bared as Purchaser of Five Weapons," *Chicago News*, April 30, 1929.

4. *Chicago News*, September 1, 1939; *Chicago Tribune*, March 1, 1940; John T. Flynn, "These Our Rulers," *Collier's*, July 13, 1940.

5. *Chicago Tribune*, February 27, 1941; *Chicago News*, February 26, 1941; *Ibid.*, February 28, 1941; *Ibid.*, March 3, 4, 5, 1941.

6. *Chicago Tribune*, March 9, 1941; *Chicago News*, March 21, 1941.

7. *Chicago Tribune*, August 22, 1941; *Chicago News*, March 28, 1941; *Chicago Sun*, March 21, 1942.

8. *Chicago Sun-Times*, March 31, 1948.

9. *Chicago Tribune*, August 25, 1930.

10. *Ibid.*, October 25, 26, 27, 28, 29, 1941.

11. Virgil W. Peterson, "First Things First," *Criminal Justice*, March 1943, pp. 6, 7; Virgil W. Peterson, Operating Director, Chicago Crime Commission, statement to committee appointed by the mayor to review the civil service hearings in the case of Captain Martin E. McCormick *et al.*, October 15, 1942.

12. *Chicago Tribune,* November 25, 1942; *Chicago Sun,* January 26, 1946; *Chicago Tribune,* August 28, 1946.

13. "Ethics, Politics, and Crime," *Criminal Justice,* January 1944, pp. 3, 4; Official records of the Clerk, Criminal Court of Cook County, reflect that on March 27, 1946 two indictments bearing numbers 46–719 and 46–720 were returned against Anthony Crane, Lawrence Bradi and Frank Cunningham. On September 19, 1946, the three defendants entered pleas of guilty to both indictments, one of which charged robbery and the other burglary. Sentences were imposed the same date.

14. "The Alliance of Nitti and Politics," editorial, *Chicago Tribune,* March 22, 1943.

15. Virgil W. Peterson, "Chicago's Crime Problem," *Journal of Criminal Law and Criminology* (Northwestern University Press, May-June, 1944), pp. 3–15.

16. *Ibid.*

17. Among the acts of violence growing out of gambling warfare during the period were the following: On March 2, 1944, the body of Sam Gervase was found in the rear of 609 Division Street. On March 11, 1944, the body of James De Angelo was found stuffed in the luggage compartment of his automobile which was parked in front of 1526 North LaSalle Street. Gervase and De Angelo were associates of Thomas Neglia who had been killed in a barber shop at 1608 Sedgewick Street on December 6, 1943. On March 13, 1944, John Joseph Williams was ambushed and riddled with shotgun slugs. Williams recovered. On April 7, 1944, J. Livert Kelly alias St. Louis Kelly, a Negro gambler and labor racketeer, was shot and killed during a political brawl. On April 13, 1944, Jack Guzik, Capone gambling overlord, was kidnapped. He was released the next day. On April 18, 1944, James D. Larkin (alias Jens D. Larrison), an employee in a Rocco Fischetti gambling establishment, was shot and killed in a tavern at 4839 Ogden Avenue operated by Matt Capone. Larkin had been convicted in Federal Court, Chicago, in 1940 for doping race horses and ruled off the tracks for life by the Illinois State Racing Commission. On November 1, 1944, Robert Bock, a brother-in-law of the slain Capone gangster Danny Stanton, was ambushed and shot in front of his home at 7558 Kingston Avenue. Bock recovered. On December 28, 1944, Joseph Mundo, a handbook operator and the nephew of State Representative James Adduci, was found shot to death in his automobile at 14th Street and Wolcott Avenue. On December 29, 1944, Paul Kare, gambling czar of the Greek colony, was shot and critically wounded.

18. *Chicago Tribune*, July 18, 1947.
19. *Chicago News*, March 13, 1929; *Chicago Tribune*, March 14, 1929; *Chicago News*, December 30, 1929; *Chicago Post*, November 15, 1930; Lester Velie, "The Capone Gang Muscles into Big-Time Politics," *Collier's*, September 30, 1950, p. 62.
20. Peterson, *loc. cit.*
21. Peterson, *Gambling — Should It Be Legalized?* (Springfield, Ill.: Charles C. Thomas, 1951), pp. 40, 45, 46.
22. *Investigation As to the Manner in Which the United States Board of Parole Is Operating and As to Whether There Is a Necessity for a Change in Either the Procedure or Basic Law.* Hearings Before a Subcommittee on Expenditures in the Executive Department. House of Representatives. 80th Cong. 2d sess. (Washington, D. C.: Government Printing Office, 1948), p. 412.
23. William M. Reddig, *Tom's Town* (Kansas City and the Pendergast Legend) (Philadelphia: J. B. Lippincott Co., 1947), pp. 380–384.
24. Herbert Asbury, "America's No. 1 Mystery Man," *Collier's*, April 19, 1947, p. 34; Regarding a reduction of gang killings by the gangsters themselves, in 1950 a leading American gangster confided in a Federal official, "We don't handle things like we used to." He said that the gang operated on a "businesslike" basis without unnecessary killings. He intimated that it was only in case of a "double cross" that murder was resorted to. Gangsters know that murder arouses public interest and demands for official action. This forces the underworld to temporarily cease operations and reduces profits.
25. Report of an Investigation. *Certain Personnel Practices in the Chicago Public Schools*, (Washington, D. C.: National Commission for the Defense of Democracy Through Education of the National Education Association of the United States, May 1945), pp. 5–66; Allen, *op. cit.*, p. 183.
26. *Chicago's Report to the People* . . . , *op. cit.*, pp. 33–40.
27. Jack McPhaul, "Lesson for Chicago, Night of Horror Recalled," *Chicago Sun-Times*, January 7, 1951; Virgil W. Peterson, "Appraisal of Chicago's Law Enforcement," *Criminal Justice*, May 1946, pp. 3–7.
28. Jack Guzik, in a statement to the state's attorney, claimed that Hymie Levin, an important member of the Capone syndicate, operated the wire service for Ragen following Ragen's conviction in Federal Court in 1940. Ragen was placed on probation and was ordered by the court to stay out of the racing information business. Guzik claimed that large sums of money were lost by Hymie Levin during the period he operated the wire service for Ragen. It was indicated that

the demand for forty per cent of the profits was based on this indebtedness to the Capone syndicate; *see Chicago Tribune,* September 10, 1947.

29. *Chicago Sun,* June 27, 1946.

30. *Chicago News,* editorial, June 26, 1946.

31. *Criminal Justice,* No. 74, May 1947, p. 40.

32. *Chicago News,* October 9, 1946.

33. *Chicago Sun,* February 5, 1947; regarding the Taylor Co., *see Chicago Sun,* March 26, 1947.

34. *Ibid.,* January 31, 1947; *Chicago Sun-Times,* January 21, March 15, 1950.

35. Milburn P. Akers, "The Machine: Born, Bred in Corruption," *Chicago Sun,* December 16, 1946.

CHAPTER X

1. Albert Deutsch, "Chicago Pollyanna," *New York Post-Home News,* February 18, 1949.

2. John Bartlow Martin, "Who Killed Estelle Carey?" *Harper's,* June 1944, pp. 48–60.

3. *Investigation As to the Manner in Which the United States Board of Parole Is Operating and As to Whether There Is a Necessity for a Change in Either the Procedure or Basic Law.* Hearings before a Subcommittee on Expenditures in the Executive Departments. House of Representatives. 80th Cong. 2d sess. (Washington, D. C.: Government Printing Office, 1948), pp. 1–938. This volume contains a transcript of the testimony given before the Congressional Subcommittee and is the source of most of the information concerning the parole scandals. *See also:* "The Parolees' Local Angle Is Neglected," editorial, *Chicago Sun,* October 4, 1947; "National Crime and National Politics," editorial, *Chicago Tribune,* October 1, 1947; Articles in *Chicago Tribune,* September 29, October 1, 1947; *Chicago Sun-Times,* February 11, 1948; *Chicago News,* February 18, 1948; *Chicago Tribune,* January 13, 1948; *Chicago News,* February 9, 1948; *Chicago Tribune,* October 7, 1947; October 11, 1947; October 13, 1947; February 12, 1948; July 24, 1948; August 19, 1948; November 14, 1949; "The Capone Paroles," editorial, *Chicago Tribune,* November 14, 1949.

4. *Chicago Tribune,* September 17, 1948.

5. "The Cicero Murder," editorial, *Chicago Tribune,* December 18, 1949.

6. *Chicago News,* May 24, 1948; *Chicago Sun-Times,* May 25, 1948; *Chicago Sun,* December 11, 1947; *Chicago Tribune,* June 10, 1948.

7. *Chicago Tribune,* July 12, 1948; *Chicago News,* July 13, 1948.

8. "Back the Honest," editorial, *Chicago News,* September 20, 1948.

9. *St. Louis Post-Dispatch,* April 4, 1949.

10. *Chicago Tribune,* February 16, 1949.

11. Elise Morrow, "Peoria," *The Saturday Evening Post,* February 12, 1949; *St. Louis Post-Dispatch,* August 8, 1948 and October 24, 1948; *Chicago Tribune,* September 4, 1948; John Bartlow Martin, *Butcher's Dozen and Other Murders* (New York: Harper & Bros., 1950), Chap. 5, "The Shelton Boys," pp. 101–152.

12. *Chicago News,* October 27, 1948.

13. *Chicago Tribune,* September 6, 1948; *Ibid.,* May 31, 1949.

14. Virgil W. Peterson, "Nation-Wide Implications of Organized Crime," *Criminal Justice,* September, 1948, pp. 7, 8.

15. Walter C. Reckless, *Vice in Chicago* (Chicago: University of Chicago Press, 1933), p. 81; *Chicago Tribune,* May 31, 1949.

16. "Time to Fight Crime Is Now — Compromise on Filibuster Would Surrender to Gangs," editorial, *Chicago News,* May 23, 1949; "For Another Capone," editorial, *Chicago Sun-Times,* May 18, 1949; "Crime Leader of Illinois," editorial, *Chicago Tribune,* May 19, 1949; "Critical Moment at Springfield," editorial, *St. Louis Post-Dispatch,* May 17, 1949.

17. *Chicago Tribune,* May 31, 1949.

18. Robert S. Allen (ed.), *Our Sovereign State* (New York: Vanguard Press, 1949); *see* Introduction, pp. xx–xxi.

19. Milburn P. Akers, "Legislature at All-Time Low," *Chicago Sun-Times,* June 21, 1949.

20. *Chicago Tribune,* April 14, 1950.

21. Madison West, "Behind the Front Page — Protest Dawson Activities," *Chicago News,* March 31, 1950; Velie, *op. cit.,* pp. 18, 63.

22. *Chicago Sun-Times,* January 21, 1950 and March 15, 1950.

23. *Ibid.,* May 10, 1950.

24. Harry M. Beardsley, "Map Drive to Legalize Gambling," *Chicago News,* July 22, 1950.

25. "The City Is Not Slipping — Chicago's Growth Warrants Full Confidence for Future," editorial, *Chicago News,* November 29, 1950; "'Chicago Still Growing,' Says Industrial Chief," article, *Chicago Sun-Times,* November 29, 1950.

CHAPTER XI

1. Walter W. Ruch, "Crime War Urged by Unity of Cities," *New York Times*, December 3, 1949; "War on Syndicated Crime Urged of A.M.A.," *The American City* (New York City), January 1950; Virgil W. Peterson, "Barbarians in Our Cities," *Criminal Justice*, January 1950, No. 77, pp. 20–23; Virgil W. Peterson, "Nation-Wide Implications of Organized Crime," *Criminal Justice*, September 1948, pp. 4–8; Virgil W. Peterson, "The Myth of the Wide-Open Town," *Criminal Justice*, September 1948, pp. 20–24.

2. *Interim Report on Investigations in Florida and Preliminary General Conclusions; Interim Report of the Special Committee to Investigate Organized Crime in Inter-State Commerce.* 81st Cong., 2d sess. Pursuant to S. Res. 202 Senate Report No. 2370 (Washington, D. C.: Government Printing Office, 1950), pp. 1–18.

3. *Chicago Tribune*, September 26, 1950.

4. *Investigation of Organized Crime in Interstate Commerce.* Hearings Before Special Committee to Investigate Organized Crime in Interstate Commerce. Senate. 81st Cong., 2d sess.; 82d Cong., 1st sess. Pursuant to S. Res. 202 (Washington, D. C.: Government Printing Office), Part 5, Illinois, pp. 570–592.

5. "Dan's Brother Chief," news item, *Chicago News*, November 3, 1950. Also lists names of a number of Chicago police officers who were then on payrolls of various race tracks.

6. *Investigation of Organized Crime in Interstate Commerce, op. cit.*, pp. 622–636.

7. "Ex-Mayor 'Ed' Kelly Leaves Estate Valued at $600,000," *Chicago News*, December 12, 1950; "Kelly Estate Row Heads for Court," *Ibid.*, May 14, 1951; "Fortune Left in Vault Gone — Mrs. Kelly," *Chicago Herald-American*, May 14, 1951; "End Kelly Fight; Estate $686,799," *Chicago News*, November 9, 1951.

8. "Funeral of a Boss," (Politicians and Flowers Pile Up to Honor Chicago's Edward J. Kelly), *Life*, November 6, 1950.

9. "Edward J. Kelly," editorial, *Chicago Sun-Times*, October 21, 1950.

10. "Captain's Income," editorial, *Chicago News*, October 19, 1950.

11. "Honky-Tony Cleanup — at Last!" editorial, *Chicago Sun-Times*, October 29, 1950; "Memo From F. D. R. to Capt. Gilbert," editorial, *Chicago Sun-Times*, October 19, 1950.

12. "How to Guard a City's Name," editorial, *St. Louis Post-Dispatch*, October 22, 1950.

13. *Case No. J 28014, before the Civil Service Commission of the City of Chicago* (In the Matter of Charges against Thomas Harrison, Captain, Department of Police of the City of Chicago, Respondent), March 6, 1951.
14. "Babb's Victory," editorial, *Chicago News,* November 8, 1950.
15. "Mob Money," editorial, *Ibid.,* December 22, 1950.

CHAPTER XII

1. *Transmission of Gambling Information.* Hearings Before Senate Subcommittee on Interstate and Foreign Commerce. 81st. Cong., 2d. sess. On S. 3358. A bill to Prohibit Transmission of Certain Gambling Information in Interstate and Foreign Commerce by Communications Facilities (Washington, D. C.: Government Printing Office, 1950), p. 31; Source for material in this chapter is testimony before the Kefauver Committee, *see* note 1., Ch. XIII.

CHAPTER XIII

1. The data which appears in this book following note I, Ch. XII, through this note is based on a careful analysis of the Senate Crime Committee testimony given by the gangsters themselves, their associates and counsel together with evidence presented to the Kefauver Committee in the form of income-tax returns, books and records of members of Chicago's underworld. Since the hearings lasted but a few days and relatively few gangsters were examined by the Committee, the power, wealth and insidious influence of the Capone gang are far greater than portrayed by this testimony. This is particularly true since those who testified attempted to evade answering pertinent questions. Some of their answers were obviously false. It was also evident that their income-tax returns were incomplete in many instances and there is good ground for believing some of them are also false. Nevertheless, this partial picture reveals the Capone gang as a criminal organization with staggering power and wealth and possessing political alliances and strength which threaten the future welfare of free government. This is particularly true since conditions similar to those in Chicago have prevailed in most of the large municipalities in America. The testimony analyzed is found in the following volumes:

Investigation of Organized Crime in Interstate Commerce, op. cit., Part 5, pp. 1–1417; *Interim Report on Investigations in Florida, op.*

cit., pp. 1–18; *Second Interim Report of the Special Committee to Investigate Organized Crime in Interstate Commerce.* 81st Cong., 82d Cong., 1st sess. Pursuant to S. Res. 202. Senate Report No. 141 (Washington, D. C.: Government Printing Office, 1951), pp. 1–35; *Third Interim Report of the Special Committee to Investigate Organized Crime in Interstate Commerce.* 81st Cong., 82d Cong., 1st sess. Pursuant to S. Res. 202. Senate Report No. 307 (Washington, D. C.: Government Printing Office, 1951), pp. 1–195.

Testimony of pertinent individuals was also examined in the following:

Investigation of Organized Crime in Interstate Commerce, op. cit., Part I and IA, Florida; *Ibid.*, Part 4 and 4A, Missouri; *Ibid.*, Part 10, Nevada-California.

2. "Not a Myth," editorial, *Chicago News*, March 2, 1951.
3. "The Capone Camorra," editorial, *Chicago Tribune*, December 20, 1950; "The Hoodlum Terror in Chicago Politics," editorial, *Ibid.*, December 30, 1950.
4. "Serritella's in a Draft—Files for Alderman," article, *Chicago News*, January 23, 1951.
5. "A Reproach to Mayor Kennelly," editorial, *Chicago Tribune*, January 23, 1951.
6. "Probes Started in 28th Ward Gang Activities, Ald. Kells, Wife Leave on 'Extended Trip,'" *Chicago Tribune*, December 30, 1950; "GOP Cool to Coalition to Replace Ald. Kells," *Chicago News*, January 3, 1951; "Kells' Man Out, Petrone Has One To Go In 28th," *Chicago Sun-Times*, February 7, 1951; "Opponents Clear Path For Petrone," *Chicago Herald-American*, February 7, 1951; "Petrone Replaces Kells as 28th Ward Leader," *Chicago Sun-Times*, June 21, 1951; John Dreiske, column, "Petrone's Rush Act Resented," *Ibid.*, June 24, 1951.
7. "It's Kennelly," editorial, *Chicago News*, April 4, 1951.
8. "Chicago Elects A Mayor," editorial, *New York Times*, April 5, 1951.
9. *Chicago Tribune*, June 19, 1951; *Chicago News*, June 19, 1951; *Chicago Tribune*, June 20, 21, 1951; "Find Roe 'Kidnaper' Slain by Policeman," *Chicago Sun-Times*, June 21, 1951.
10. "Is Chicago Slipping? The Figures Say 'No,'" *Chicago News*, June 5, 1951.
11. *Third Interim Report* . . . , *op. cit.*, p. 50.

CHAPTER XIV

1. *Report on Police* (National Commission on Law Observance and Enforcement), (Washington, D. C.: Government Printing Office, June 26, 1931), No. 14, p. 46.
2. *Ibid.*, p. 45.
3. Maurice M. Milligan, *The Inside Story of the Pendergast Machine by the Man Who Smashed It* (New York: Charles Scribner's Sons, 1948), pp. 18, 19.
4. Reddig, *op. cit.*, pp. 317, 318.
5. *Investigation of Organized Crime In Interstate Commerce*, *op. cit.*, Part 4, Missouri, pp. 39–81, 193–203, 204–226, 286–311; *Ibid.*, Part 4-A, Missouri (1951), pp. 35–66, 372–408.
6. Werner, *op. cit.*, p. 256.
7. *Third Interim Report . . . , op. cit.*, pp. 143, 144.
8. *The Social Evil in Chicago, op. cit.*, p. 130.
9. *Chicago Tribune*, April 3, 1948.
10. Edwin H. Sutherland, *Principles of Criminology* (Philadelphia: J. B. Lippincott Co., 1934), p. 191.
11. *Third Interim Report . . . , op. cit.*, pp. 104, 105.
12. James Bryce, *The American Commonwealth* (3d ed.; New York: Macmillan Co., 1898), II, 126. " 'In not a few of our cities the liquor-saloon keepers have combined to "run politics" so as to gain control and secure a municipal management friendly to them. This is in part the explanation of the great uprising of the Prohibition party.' " On p. 114, Bryce refers to the political power of the liquor dealers in New York. Said Bryce, "Of the 1007 primaries and conventions of all parties held in New York City preparatory to the elections of 1884, 633 took place in liquor saloons."
13. *Third Interim Report . . . , op. cit.*, pp. 172–175.
14. *Ibid.*, pp. 90–94; *Investigation of Organized Crime in Interstate Commerce, op. cit.*, Part 10, Nevada-California (1951), pp. 1–34, 37–41.
15. Peterson, *Gambling, Should It Be Legalized? op. cit.*, pp. 48–92, provides a history of legalized gambling in the U. S.
16. Bryce, *op. cit.*, II, 59.
17. *Ibid.*, p. 60.
18. Graham Hutton, *Midwest at Noon* (Chicago: University of Chicago Press, 1946), p. 296.
Bryce, *op. cit.*, II, 349. "This tendency to acquiescence and submission, this sense of the insignificance of individual effort, this belief that the

affairs of men are swayed by large forces whose movement may be
studied but cannot be turned, I have ventured to call the Fatalism of
the Multitude."

19. Raymond B. Fosdick, *American Police Systems* (New York: Century
Co., 1920), p. 357.

20. *Ibid.*, pp. 358, 359. Angelo Patri, "Children Should Be Protected
Against Gambling Habit," *Chicago News*, November 6, 1945.

21. Harvey Warren Zorbaugh, *The Gold Coast and the Slum* (A Socio-
logical Study of Chicago's Near North Side) (Chicago: University of
Chicago Press, 1929), p. 193.

22. *Ibid.*, p. 268.

23. *Third Interim Report . . . , op. cit.*, p. 30; Herbert R. O'Conor
(Former Chairman, Senate Crime Investigating Committee), "Watch-
dogs Against Crime," *This Week* magazine, September 30, 1951, p. 16.
Senator O'Conor stated, "If there is a citizens' crime commission in
your town, support it by volunteering your time, money or effort —
or at least by adding your voice to those of other indignant citizens.
If no such committee exists, help your Chamber of Commerce or
some other civic group to form one. As the number of watchdog
committees grows, the vicious elements in our population will find it
harder and harder to operate. Focusing the spotlight of public opinion
is the surest way to lick organized crime." Bryce, *op. cit.*, II, 328;
R. M. MacIver, *The Web of Government* (New York: Macmillan
Co., 1947), p. 265.

24. Bryce, *op. cit.*, I, p. 644.

25. *Report of the American Bar Association Commission on Organized
Crime to the American Bar Association* (New York: Grosby Press,
September 1, 1951), p. 29.

26. *Ibid.*, pp. 27, 28.

27. Alexis de Tocqueville, *Democracy in America* (The Henry Reeve
text as revised by Francis Bowen now further corrected and edited
with Introduction, Editorial Notes and Bibliographies by Phillips
Bradley) (New York: Alfred A. Knopf, 1945), I, 279.

28. Fiorello H. LaGuardia, "Bosses are Bunk" (Reply to Ed Flynn),
The Atlantic Monthly, July 1947, pp. 23, 24.

29. Glenn R. Winters, "Concensus of Judicial Selection Proposals,"
Journal of the American Judicature Society (Ann Arbor; December
1944), pp. 107–110.

30. Laurance M. Hyde, "Judges: Their Selection and Tenure," *New
York University Law Quarterly Review*, July 1947, XXII, No. 3,
pp. 389–400.

31. *Report of the American Bar Association Commission on Organized Crime* . . . , *op. cit.*, pp. 62, 63.

32. Bruce Smith, *Police Systems in the United States* (New York: Harper & Bros., 1949), pp. 2, 3.

33. *Ibid.*, p. 157; *see also* pp. 333-337.

34. O. W. Wilson, *Police Administration* (New York: McGraw-Hill, 1950), pp. 67, 68.

35. Arnold J. Toynbee, *A Study of History* (Abridgement of Vols. I-VI by D. C. Somervell) (New York and London: Oxford University Press, 1947), p. 206.

Appendix

Appendix

Officials Principally Responsible for Law Enforcement in Chicago
1833–1951

(See pages 375–378 for explanation of symbols and additional data)

Year	(A) Mayor	Head of Police Dept.	(L) State's Attorney (Cook County, Ill.)	Sheriff (Cook County, Ill.)
1833			Thomas Ford	Stephen Forbes
1834			Thomas Ford	Silas W. Sherman
1835		O. Morrison (Constable)	James Grant	Silas W. Sherman
1836		O. Morrison (Constable)	James Grant	*Silas W. Sherman
1837	William B. Ogden (D)	John Shrigley (High Constable)	Alonzo Huntington	Silas W. Sherman
1838	Buckner S. Morris (W)	John Shrigley (High Constable)	Alonzo Huntington	Isaac R. Gavin
1839	Benjamin W. Raymond (W)	(H) Samuel J. Lowe (High Constable)	Alonzo Huntington	Isaac R. Gavin
1840	Alexander Loyd (D)	(H) Samuel J. Lowe (High Constable)	Alonzo Huntington	Ashbel Steele
1841	Francis C. Sherman (D)	(H) Samuel J. Lowe (High Constable)	James M. Strode	Ashbel Steele
1842	Benjamin W. Raymond (D)	Orson Smith (City Marshal)	James M. Strode	Samuel J. Lowe
1843	Augustus Garrett (D)	Orson Smith (City Marshal)	James Curtiss	Samuel J. Lowe
1844	(B) Alson S. Sherman (D)	Orson Smith (City Marshal)	James Curtiss	*Samuel J. Lowe
1845	Augustus Garrett (D)	Phillip Dean (City Marshal)	Patrick Ballingall	Samuel J. Lowe
1846	John P. Chapin (W)	Phillip Dean (City Marshal)	Patrick Ballingall	Isaac Cook
1847	James Curtiss (D)	Phillip Dean (City Marshal)	Patrick Ballingall	Isaac Cook
1848	James H. Woodworth (D)	Ambrose Burnham (City Marshal)	A. B. Platt	*Isaac Cook
1849	*James H. Woodworth (D)	Ambrose Burnham (City Marshal)	Daniel McIlroy	Isaac Cook
1850	James Curtiss (D)	James Howe (City Marshal)	Daniel McIlroy	William L. Church
1851	Walter S. Gurnee (D)	James Howe (City Marshal)	Daniel McIlroy	William L. Church

1852	*Walter S. Gurnee (D)	James Howe (City Marshal)	*Daniel McIlroy	Cyrus P. Bradley
1853	Charles M. Gray (D)	James Howe (City Marshal)	Daniel McIlroy	Cyrus P. Bradley
1854	Isaac L. Milliken (D)	Darius Knights (City Marshal)	Daniel McIlroy	James Andrews
1855	Dr. Levi D. Boone (K–N)	(I) Cyrus P. Bradley	Daniel McIlroy	James Andrews
1856	Thomas Dyer (D)	James M. Donnelly (City Marshal)	Carlos S. Haven	John L. Wilson
1857	John Wentworth (R–F)	James M. Donnelly (City Marshal)	Carlos S. Haven	John L. Wilson
1858	John C. Haines (R)	Jacob Rehm (City Marshal)	Carlos S. Haven	John Gray
1859	*John C. Haines (R)	Jacob Rehm (City Marshal)	Carlos S. Haven	John Gray
1860	John Wentworth (R)	Iver Lawson (City Marshal)	*(M) Carlos S. Haven	Anthony C. Hesing
1861	Julian S. Rumsey (R)	(J) Cyrus P. Bradley	(M) Carlos S. Haven	Anthony C. Hesing
1862	Francis C. Sherman (D)	(J) Cyrus P. Bradley	Joseph Knox	David L. Hammond
1863	*Francis C. Sherman (D)	(J) Cyrus P. Bradley	Joseph Knox	David L. Hammond
1864	*Francis C. Sherman (D)	William Turtle	Charles H. Reed	John A. Nelson
1865	John B. Rice (R)	William Turtle	Charles H. Reed	John A. Nelson
1866	John B. Rice (R)	Jacob Rehm	Charles H. Reed	John L. Beveridge
1867	*John B. Rice (R)	Jacob Rehm	Charles H. Reed	John L. Beveridge
1868	John B. Rice (R)	Jacob Rehm	*Charles H. Reed	Gustav Fischer
1869	Roswell B. Mason	Jacob Rehm	Charles H. Reed	Gustav Fischer
1870	Roswell B. Mason	Jacob Rehm	Charles H. Reed	Henry L. Cleaves
1871	(C) Joseph Medill	W. W. Kennedy	Charles H. Reed	Henry L. Cleaves
1872	(C) Joseph Medill	Elmer Washburn	*Charles H. Reed	Timothy M. Bradley
1873	Harvey D. Colvin (D)	Jacob Rehm	Charles H. Reed	Timothy M. Bradley
1874	Harvey D. Colvin (D)	Jacob Rehm	Charles H. Reed	Francis Agnew
1875	(E) Harvey D. Colvin (D)	Michael C. Hickey	Charles H. Reed	Francis Agnew
1876	Monroe Heath (R)	Michael C. Hickey	Luther L. Mills	Charles Kern
1877	*Monroe Heath (R)	Michael C. Hickey	Luther L. Mills	Charles Kern
1878	Monroe Heath (R)	Valrous A. Seavey	Luther L. Mills	John Hoffman
1879	Carter H. Harrison (D)	Simon O'Donnell	Luther L. Mills	John Hoffman
1880	Carter H. Harrison (D)	William J. McGarigle	*Luther L. Mills	Orrin L. Mann
1881	*Carter H. Harrison (D)	William J. McGarigle	Luther L. Mills	Orrin L. Mann

Year	(A) Mayor	Head of Police Dept.	(L) State's Attorney (Cook County, Ill.)	Sheriff (Cook County, Ill.)
1882	Carter H. Harrison (D)	Austin J. Doyle	Luther L. Mills	(N) Seth F. Hanchett
1883	*Carter H. Harrison (D)	Austin J. Doyle	Luther L. Mills	(N) Seth F. Hanchett
1884	Carter H. Harrison (D)	Austin J. Doyle	Julius Grinnell	(N) Seth F. Hanchett
1885	*Carter H. Harrison (D)	Frederick Ebersold	Julius Grinnell	(N) Seth F. Hanchett
1886	Carter H. Harrison (D)	Frederick Ebersold	Julius Grinnell	Canute R. Matson
1887	John A. Roche (R)	Frederick Ebersold	Julius Grinnell	Canute R. Matson
1888	John A. Roche (R)	George W. Hubbard	Joel M. Longenecker	Canute R. Matson
1889	Dewitt C. Cregier (D)	George W. Hubbard	Joel M. Longenecker	Canute R. Matson
1890	Dewitt C. Cregier (D)	Frederick H. Marsh	Joel M. Longenecker	James H. Gilbert
1891	Hempstead Washburne (R)	Robert W. McClaughry	Joel M. Longenecker	James H. Gilbert
1892	Hempstead Washburne (R)	Robert W. McClaughry	Jacob J. Kern (D)	James H. Gilbert
1893	(F) Carter H. Harrison (D)	Michael Brennan	Jacob J. Kern (D)	James H. Gilbert
1894	John P. Hopkins (D)	Michael Brennan	Jacob J. Kern (D)	James Pease (R)
1895	George B. Swift (R)	John J. Badenoch	Jacob J. Kern (D)	James Pease (R)
1896	George B. Swift (R)	John J. Badenoch	Charles S. Deneen (R)	James Pease (R)
1897	Carter H. Harrison, Jr. (D)	Joseph Kipley	Charles S. Deneen (R)	James Pease (R)
1898	Carter H. Harrison, Jr. (D)	Joseph Kipley	Charles S. Deneen (R)	Ernest J. Magerstadt (R)
1899	*Carter H. Harrison, Jr. (D)	Joseph Kipley	Charles S. Deneen (R)	Ernest J. Magerstadt (R)
1900	Carter H. Harrison, Jr. (D)	Joseph Kipley	*Charles S. Deneen (R)	Ernest J. Magerstadt (R)
1901	*Carter H. Harrison, Jr. (D)	Francis O'Neil	Charles S. Deneen (R)	Ernest J. Magerstadt (R)
1902	Carter H. Harrison, Jr. (D)	Francis O'Neil	Charles S. Deneen (R)	Thomas E. Barrett (D)
1903	*Carter H. Harrison, Jr. (D)	Francis O'Neil	Charles S. Deneen (R)	Thomas E. Barrett (D)
1904	Carter H. Harrison, Jr. (D)	John M. Collins	John J. Healy (R)	Thomas E. Barrett (D)
1905	Edward F. Dunne (D)	John M. Collins	John J. Healy (R)	Thomas E. Barrett (D)
1906	Edward F. Dunne (D)	John M. Collins	John J. Healy (R)	(O) James Pease (R) 3–29–06 to 11–6–06 Christopher Strassheim (R)

Year	Mayor	Chief of Police	State's Attorney	Coroner
1907	Fred Busse (R)	George M. Shippy	John J. Healy (R)	Christopher Strassheim (R)
1908	Fred Busse (R)	George M. Shippy	John E. W. Wayman (R)	Christopher Strassheim (R)
1909	Fred Busse (R)	Leroy T. Stewart	John E. W. Wayman (R)	Christopher Strassheim (R)
1910	Fred Busse (R)	Leroy T. Stewart	John E. W. Wayman (R)	Michael Zimmer (D)
1911	Carter H. Harrison, Jr. (D)	John McWeeny	John E. W. Wayman (R)	Michael Zimmer (D)
1912	Carter H. Harrison, Jr. (D)	John McWeeny	Maclay Hoyne (D)	Michael Zimmer (D)
1913	Carter H. Harrison, Jr. (D)	James Gleason	Maclay Hoyne (D)	Michael Zimmer (D)
1914	Carter H. Harrison, Jr. (D)	James Gleason	Maclay Hoyne (D)	John E. Traeger (D)
1915	William Hale Thompson (R)	Charles C. Healey	Maclay Hoyne (D)	John E. Traeger (D)
1916	William Hale Thompson (R)	Charles C. Healey	*Maclay Hoyne (D)	John E. Traeger (D)
1917	William Hale Thompson (R)	Hermann F. Schuettler	Maclay Hoyne (D)	John E. Traeger (D)
1918	William Hale Thompson (R)	John J. Garrity	Maclay Hoyne (D)	Charles W. Peters (R)
1919	*William Hale Thompson (R)	John J. Garrity	Maclay Hoyne (D)	Charles W. Peters (R)
1920	William Hale Thompson (R)	Charles C. Fitzmorris	Robert E. Crowe (R)	Charles W. Peters (R)
1921	William Hale Thompson (R)	Charles C. Fitzmorris	Robert E. Crowe (R)	Charles W. Peters (R)
1922	William Hale Thompson (R)	Charles C. Fitzmorris	Robert E. Crowe (R)	Peter M. Hoffman (R)
1923	William E. Dever (D)	Morgan A. Collins	Robert E. Crowe (R)	Peter M. Hoffman (R)
1924	William E. Dever (D)	Morgan A. Collins	*Robert E. Crowe (R)	Peter M. Hoffman (R)
1925	William E. Dever (D)	Morgan A. Collins	Robert E. Crowe (R)	Peter M. Hoffman (R)
1926	William E. Dever (D)	Morgan A. Collins	Robert E. Crowe (R)	(P) P. J. Carr (D) elected — died before taking office.
1927	William Hale Thompson (R)	(K) Michael Hughes	Robert E. Crowe (R)	Charles Graydon (R)
1928	William Hale Thompson (R)	William F. Russell	John A. Swanson (R)	Charles Graydon (R)
1929	William Hale Thompson (R)	William F. Russell	John A. Swanson (R)	John E. Traeger (D)
1930	William Hale Thompson (R)	John H. Alcock (acting)	John A. Swanson (R)	John E. Traeger (D)
1931	Anton J. Cermak (D)	James P. Allman	John A. Swanson (R)	William D. Meyering (D)
1932	Anton J. Cermak (D)	James P. Allman	Thomas J. Courtney (D)	William D. Meyering (D)
1933	(G) Edward J. Kelly (D)	James P. Allman	Thomas J. Courtney (D)	William D. Meyering (D)
1934	(G) Edward J. Kelly (D)	James P. Allman	Thomas J. Courtney (D)	John Toman (D)

Year	(A) Mayor	Head of Police Dept.	(L) State's Attorney (Cook County, Ill.)	Sheriff (Cook County, Ill.)
1935	*Edward J. Kelly (D)	James P. Allman	Thomas J. Courtney (D)	John Toman (D)
1936	Edward J. Kelly (D)	James P. Allman	*Thomas J. Courtney (D)	John Toman (D)
1937	Edward J. Kelly (D)	James P. Allman	Thomas J. Courtney (D)	John Toman (D)
1938	Edward J. Kelly (D)	James P. Allman	Thomas J. Courtney (D)	Thomas O'Brien (D)
1939	*Edward J. Kelly (D)	James P. Allman	Thomas J. Courtney (D)	Thomas O'Brien (D)
1940	Edward J. Kelly (D)	James P. Allman	*Thomas J. Courtney (D)	Thomas O'Brien (D)
1941	Edward J. Kelly (D)	James P. Allman	Thomas J. Courtney (D)	Thomas O'Brien (D)
1942	Edward J. Kelly (D)	James P. Allman	Thomas J. Courtney (D)	Peter B. Carey (D)
1943	*Edward J. Kelly (D)	James P. Allman	Thomas J. Courtney (D)	(Q) Michael F. Mulcahy (D)
1944	Edward J. Kelly (D)	James P. Allman	William J. Tuohy (D)	(Q) Michael F. Mulcahy (D)
1945	Edward J. Kelly (D)	James P. Allman	William J. Tuohy (D)	(Q) Michael F. Mulcahy (D)
1946	Edward J. Kelly (D)	John C. Prendergast	William J. Tuohy (D)	Elmer Michael Walsh (R)
1947	Martin H. Kennelly (D)	John C. Prendergast	William J. Tuohy (D)	Elmer Michael Walsh (R)
1948	Martin H. Kennelly (D)	John C. Prendergast	John S. Boyle (D)	Elmer Michael Walsh (R)
1949	Martin H. Kennelly (D)	John C. Prendergast	John S. Boyle (D)	Elmer Michael Walsh (R)
1950	Martin H. Kennelly (D)	Timothy J. O'Connor	John S. Boyle (D)	John E. Babb (R)
1951	*Martin H. Kennelly (D)	Timothy J. O'Connor	John S. Boyle (D)	John E. Babb (R)

Population Figures

Chicago: 1833–1950

Year	Population	Year	Population
1833	200	1854	65,872
1835	3,265	1855	80,023
1837	4,179	1856	86,000
1840	4,470	1860	109,420
1843	7,580	1870	298,977
1844	10,864	1880	503,185
1845	12,088	1890	1,099,850
1846	14,169		
1847	16,859	1900	1,698,575
1848	20,023	1910	2,185,283
1849	23,047	1920	2,701,705
1850	29,963	1930	3,376,438
1852	38,734	1940	3,396,808
1853	60,662	1950	3,606,436

Notes for Appendix

Note: An official's name appears opposite the year in which he was elected or appointed regardless of the month of the appointment or election and even though his predecessor may have occupied the office for most of the year.

Symbols following an official's name relate to party designation:

D – Democrat	KN – Know-Nothing
W – Whig	RF – Republican Fusionist
R – Republican	

Symbols preceding an official's name explained below:

(*)   Indicates that the official was re-elected in that particular year for another successive term in office.

(A)   Mayoralty terms were for one year until 1863. Francis C. Sherman was first mayor to hold office for a two-year term, 1863–1865. Two-year terms prevailed until 1907 when Fred Busse was elected for a four-year term. Since 1907 mayors have been elected for four years.

(B)   In 1844, Augustus Garrett was originally declared elected. His election was invalid because one of the judges had never been naturalized. At the second election Alson S. Sherman was successful.

(C)   In 1873 Mayor Joseph Medill went to Europe and during his absence Lester Legrand Bond acted as mayor.

(E)   A new city charter in 1875 changed the time of city elections from November to April, causing utter confusion. After a dispute it was decided to hold the next mayoralty election in April 1876, when Thomas Hoyne was overwhelmingly elected mayor. Colvin, the holdover mayor, challenged the legality of the election and until a special election was held in July 1876, Chicago had two mayors, Hoyne and Colvin. Monroe Heath was elected in July of that year and was re-elected for a two-year term in April 1877.

(F)   Carter H. Harrison was assassinated October 28, 1893; John P. Hopkins was selected to fill out his unexpired term at a special election.

(G)   Anton J. Cermak was shot in Miami, February 15, 1933, and died March 6. Alderman Frank J. Corr served as mayor until the city council selected Edward J. Kelly on April 13, 1933, under an emergency law passed by the state legislature on March 31, 1933.

(H)   Samuel J. Lowe, who headed law enforcement in Chicago from 1839 to 1842, was known as the high constable, chief of the city watch and city marshal.

(I)   In 1855, Mayor Levi D. Boone reorganized the police department. Darius Knights continued to serve as city marshal but the real head of the police department was Cyrus P. Bradley, a former sheriff.

(J) Cyrus P. Bradley became Chicago's first chief of police in 1861. The head of the police department continued to be known as chief of police until 1927.

(K) Beginning in 1927, the head of the police department became known as the commissioner of police. Chicago's first commissioner of police was Michael Hughes.

(L) Under a legislative act approved February 17, 1827, a prosecuting attorney was appointed for a circuit by the governor and approved by the legislature. In 1829, two years before the organization of Cook County, Illinois, Thomas Ford commenced to act as prosecuting attorney and continued to serve until 1835. Some of the early records are incomplete and even contradictory. However, the following information was secured through Margaret C. Norton, Archivist, Illinois State Library, Springfield, Illinois, in a letter to the governor's office dated January 14, 1952, and is based on an examination of Public Laws, Senate and House Journals, Executive Records, and Revised Statutes governing this early period. Prior to 1837 Cook County was in the Sixth Judicial Circuit. In 1837 it was placed in the Seventh Judicial Circuit and Alonzo Huntington was commissioned as the circuit attorney (i.e. prosecuting attorney) for that circuit on March 4, 1937 for the first time. He was again commissioned on February 25, 1839 and appears to have served until Edward G. Ryan was commissioned as circuit attorney on February 26, 1841. Ryan resigned on December 29, 1841 and on the same day James M. Strode was commissioned. Strode appears to have served until James Curtiss was commissioned on January 21, 1843. In 1845 "Cook County Court" was established which was to have concurrent jurisdiction with the circuit court and the prosecuting attorney was also to be elected by the House of Representatives. On February 24, 1845, Patrick Ballingall was commissioned prosecuting attorney for Cook County under these new provisions and received a second commission on January 6, 1847. During this same period William A. Boardman was commissioned to represent the Seventh Judicial Circuit on February 24, 1845 and was again commissioned on December 21, 1846. As the attorney for the Seventh Judicial Circuit he probably had concurrent jurisdiction with Patrick Ballingall. The constitution of 1848 provided that a state's attorney could be elected for a four-year term, although the general assembly was authorized to provide for a county attorney in his stead.

(M)   Carlos S. Haven, who was re-elected as state's attorney in 1860, died in 1862.

(N)   The term of office for sheriff was two years until 1882 when the term became four years. Seth F. Hanchett, elected in 1882, was the first sheriff to serve a four-year term.

(O)   Thomas E. Barrett died March 29, 1906, and the county board appointed James Pease to serve as sheriff until his successor, Christopher Strassheim, was elected in November 1906.

(P)   P. J. Carr, who was elected sheriff in 1926, died before taking office. Charles Graydon was appointed by the county board on December 27, 1926, to fill the vacancy and served until John E. Traeger became the sheriff in November 1928, for the balance of the term.

(Q)   Michael F. Mulcahy was appointed sheriff on December 20, 1943, to fill the unexpired term of Peter B. Carey, who died in office.

Acknowledgments

DURING the several years this book has been in preparation I have received assistance and encouragement from so many persons that it is possible to mention only a few. My thanks are due to Senator Estes Kefauver, who graciously contributed the Introduction. Professor Fred E. Inbau, Northwestern University Law School, read the entire manuscript and offered valuable suggestions. Particularly helpful in every stage of the book's development was my associate in the Chicago Crime Commission, Nat Cosnow. Other Crime Commission associates who aided me materially by finding various documents relating to Chicago were Walter Devereux, Frederick Pretzie, Jr., Daniel I. McCain and Albert W. Wright. For searching through numerous files and records of the Chicago Crime Commission, my gratitude to Patrice Anderson, Elsie Bezemek and Virginia Bobinski. From the time of the original outline until the final manuscript was completed, the typing was handled in a most conscientious and painstaking manner by Jo Sbarboro. Also I sincerely appreciate the efficient secretarial aid received from Grace Dawe Riddlesworth. And deep gratitude also to my wife, who undoubtedly sacrificed more than anyone else in the preparation of this book.

V. W. P.

Index